VOICES
FROM THE
GREAT BLACK
BASEBALL
LEAGUES

VOICES
FROM THE
GREAT BLACK BASEBALL LEAGUES

REVISED EDITION

John Holway

WITH A FOREWORD BY
Frank Ceresi

Dover Publications, Inc.
Mineola, New York

Bibliographical Note

This Dover edition, first published in 2010, is an unabridged, slightly emended republication of the 1992 revised edition of the work published by Da Capo Press, Inc., New York. The book was originially published by the author in New York in 1975. Frank Ceresi has provided a new Foreword to the Dover edition.

Library of Congress Cataloging-in-Publication Data

Holway, John
    Voices from the great Black baseball leagues/John Holway; foreword by Frank Ceresi.
        Rev. ed., Dover ed.
        p. cm.
    Includes index.
    ISBN-13: 978-0-486-47541-7
    ISBN-10: 0-486-47541-7
    1. African American Baseball players—Biography. 2. Negro leagues—History. I. Title.

GV865.A1H615 2010
796.3570922—dc22
[B]

2009041620

Manufactured in the United States by Courier Corporation
47541701
www.doverpublications.com

To my fellow authors,
the blackball stars

I wish to thank Ric Roberts and Merl Kleinknecht of the American Society for Baseball Research for their enthusiastic help. Mr. Roberts, a long-time sportswriter for the Pittsburgh *Courier*, provided incomparable insight into the lives and times of the black ball stars. Mr. Kleinknecht, like myself a recent explorer in this uncharted landscape, compiled the lifetime playing records of these and many other veterans of those days. Cliff Kachline, historian at the National Baseball Library at Cooperstown, assiduously collected biographical data on all the players and began the impressive job of adding exhibits of the old Negro leagues to the museum at the Hall of Fame. I also wish to thank my fellow author, Ocania Chalk, for generously sharing his photographs with me.

History is a myth agreed upon.
—NAPOLEON

CONTENTS

	Foreword to the Dover Edition	xiii
	Preface to the 1992 Edition	xvii
	Introduction: The Invisible Men	xix
1.	The Major League Nobody Knows	1
2.	Bill Drake	22
3.	David Malarcher	39
4.	Crush Holloway	59
5.	Webster McDonald	70
6.	Newt Allen	90
7.	Cool Papa Bell	107
8.	Ted Page	141
9.	Ted "Double Duty" Radcliffe	169
10.	Bill Foster	189
11.	Larry Brown	205
12.	Willie Wells	218
13.	William "Sug" Cornelius	234
14.	Buck Leonard	250
15.	Hilton Smith	280
16.	James "Joe" Greene	299
17.	Mrs. Effa Manley	315
18.	Tom "Pee Wee" Butts	327
19.	Othello Renfroe	339
	"Sunset Before Dawn"	353
	Appendix	355
	Index	393

FOREWORD TO THE DOVER EDITION

It was a couple of decades ago that I began to develop an interest in, and later a passion for, the circuit that today we call simply "the Negro Leagues." My journey into that slice of Americana blossomed slowly, in fits and starts, when I learned some fascinating tidbits from various sources over the span of several years. Being a typical baby boomer baseball fan, by the time I was in my mid teens I was vaguely acquainted with the names of legendary black players like Satchel Paige and Josh Gibson. But my knowledge of black baseball stars who did not play in the major leagues pretty much ended with those two. And information about Satch and Josh was, in my world, sketchy at best.

I knew Paige was supposed to have been quite a pitcher and a colorful character to boot. It seemed that any discussion about him revolved around his "real age." In fact, my college dorm room wall even featured a yellowed copy of Paige's six "rules of life," my favorite being rule number four, which I totally ignored at the time, but which read: "Go very lightly on the social vices such as carrying on in society, the social ramble ain't restful." Anyway, Paige's counterpart was the fearsome looking but smiling Josh Gibson. He was much more mysterious. I knew that someone had dubbed him "the black Babe Ruth," and I also learned that during the war years Gibson had played at Griffith Stadium right in my hometown of Washington D.C. Somewhere I picked up that he played for a ball club that I—a typical kid who knew every major league statistic before I knew how to balance a checkbook—had never heard of before, a team called the Homestead Grays.

Huh? What league were they in?

But Paige plied his trade on the mound and Josh's big bat graced the Gray's lineup long before Jackie Robinson cracked the color barrier in 1947. And, just as important, long before television came into each of our living rooms (that box brought the game to my generation). Also, critically, the Topps baseball cards of my youth featured exactly zero cards of Paige as a Negro Leaguer or of Gibson. Nor, in fact, did the cards show any member of any team from the so-called "Negro Leagues" (those Topps cards were, after all, my generation's currency).

So how was I supposed to know that Paige threw far more no hitters in his professional career than Walter Johnson, Bob Feller and Sandy Koufax combined? Or that Gibson's Grays, featuring top flight players across the board, won eight Championships over the span of nine years while playing in my hometown and were perhaps the greatest team of professional ballplayers ever assembled?

I would not learn those interesting morsels for another couple of decades.

In 1966, during his own Hall of Fame induction speech, Ted Williams, my favorite player then and now, told me (and anyone else willing to listen) that there were countless men who had toiled in rural ball fields all along America's blue highways. Those men were, however, not white or Hispanic, those men were black. It was the Williams speech that first struck a chord with me, as his words hinted that something in the museum honoring our National Pastime was not quite right, or fair. Ted's words precisely: "Baseball gives every American boy a chance to excel . . . I hope someday Satchel Paige and Josh Gibson will be voted into the Hall of Fame as symbols of the great Negro Players who are not here only because they weren't given the chance."

What? There were others? You mean that Paige and Gibson actually had teammates?

So as I began life in the real world (translation: after college), I knew that something just did not add up in "my" baseball world, something was missing. What did Williams mean? Was Paige more than just a clever "ageless" man with funny retorts about life and baseball? What about this Josh Gibson, a man who had played championship ball a few miles from the United States Capitol in the very same ballpark where my woeful Washington Senators languished in last place, or close to it, year after year after year? Who were these guys who were prevented from playing in the majors simply because of the pigment of their skin? There was no mention of them either on my gum cards or in Cooperstown's hallowed halls.

Nor were there any books on the shelf that talked of these guys. What gives?

That is when John Holway, a man who I consider a national treasure, stepped into the breach. To help answer those questions for my generation and for all those to come, he embarked upon a task that was not easy. I have since learned from John, who today is a close friend of mine, that his interest in black baseball was piqued right in my own backyard. This was in 1945 when, as a teenager, he saw Satchel's Kansas City Monarch's play against Gibson and the Grays at Griffith Stadium. John tucked this childhood memory away until years later when, as an accomplished sports historian who had written the very first books in English on Japanese baseball and on sumo wrestling, he began to comb the sports pages of arcane newspapers stashed at the Library of Congress for coverage and statistics related to those who had played in that "other" league, the Negro Leagues.

Like so many others who share a passion for history and baseball, you might say that John's curiosity got the best of him. An occasional free night or weekend at the Library turned into months and months of archiving and research. Months then turned into years. John was, after all, exploring uncharted waters. And there were not too many who had the same passion or, at the very least, the same doggedness and determination, to go forward. However, John had heard that there was at least one fellow whose interest mirrored his own. In 1970 that fellow historian, scribe and friend, Robert Peterson, had published his own extraordinary book, *Only the Ball Was White*. That was important. It only added to John's thirst for knowledge. So he forged ahead.

John learned that African Americans had been playing "America's Game" for as long as whites, but that mainstream newspapers rarely, if ever, actually reported upon and covered the black ballplayers and their teams. This might have been an impediment for some, but for John it was an opportunity. Why not hear, John thought, about the game from the player's themselves? Certainly some must be alive and perhaps they would be willing to share their stories. So John took it upon himself, at his own expense, to travel across the country to interview many of the very ballplayers who had plied their trade in the years before Robinson's historic debut in 1947. Over the span of several years, John interviewed well over a hundred Negro Leaguers, preserving from each their own unique and colorful stories.

Let John tell us what happened. "One of the first men I was referred to was (Buck) Leonard in Rocky Mount, North Carolina. I grabbed a tape recorder and my two sons and drove down there. Buck referred me to "Cool Papa" Bell in St. Louis and Hilton Smith in Kansas City . . . from there the trial fanned out." And the stories, ripe for the telling, kept coming. Soon words and recollections, reminiscences and memories, were tumbling out of the mouths of a proud group of men. Over time John would come to realize that it was precisely these stories that gave the Negro Leagues the color and substance that continues to give life to the players and their joys and struggles.

Eventually, by piecing together bits and pieces of information culled from his copious research notes and interviews, John published a series of six books dedicated exclusively to the Negro Leagues. And, God willing, there are more to come! He has also written a fantastic screenplay, *Kick Mule,* which is ripe for the right filmmaker. What you are holding in your hands is the very first book of the series, the influential and classic *Voices from the Great Black Baseball Leagues.* Thirty-five years ago, this wonderful book introduced us all to the exploits on and off the diamond of great baseball players, many of who were virtually unknown at the time. Today their ranks include no less than five Hall of Famers—"Cool Papa" Bell, Buck Leonard, Bill Foster, Willie Wells and Effa Manley, the only woman so honored. If you have never read the book, I envy you, for you are about to enjoy a rare treat. For those of you (like me) who did read it many years ago, I invite you to once again savor the stories of the greats who played our National Pastime the way it was supposed to be played, simply for the love of it.

Frank Ceresi

Frank is an attorney who has enjoyed baseball his entire life. He has written numerous articles about the history of the National Pastime (see www.fcassociates.com) and has co-authored *Images of America: Baseball in Washington D.C.* (Arcadia Publishing 2002) and *Baseball Americana: Treasures at the Library of Congress* (Harper Collins, 2009). He is currently working on a book about Bob Feller and another on baseball in Cuba. Ceresi has known John Holway, one of his writing heroes, for over a decade.

PREFACE TO THE 1992 EDITION

Once an uncharted moonscape, the landscape of Negro League baseball is now much better mapped.

Little Willie Wells was considered a slap hitter. But now we have proof that he's the Roger Maris of the Negro Leagues. No Negro Leaguer hit more home runs than his 27 in 1929.

Bill Foster's lifetime records may be found in the Macmillan Encyclopedia, 1990 edition, along with the statistics on most of the men found in this book, thanks to the labor of love of many researchers who devoted thousands of hours to searching the newspaper record and compiling the data.

The scholarship will go on—more box scores will be found, and the numbers updated or corrected.

Of the 18 persons herein who told their tales into my tape recorder, 16 have passed on. But the stories they left behind will go on. They have enriched the history of baseball—and our country—by recalling to life the heroes and the days now gone. Through them we can dial up on some celestial VCR the games and the lives of yesteryear.

And now, with this new edition, a younger generation of fans can read them and enjoy meeting the men who made the history.

–JOHN B HOLWAY
Alexandria, VA
October 1991

PUBLISHER'S NOTE:

Since *Voices from the Great Black Baseball Leagues* was originally published in 1975, hundreds of statistics covering the careers of the men in this book have been uncovered. These statistics may be found in an appendix beginning on page 355.

Introduction: The Invisible Men

*As I look back on my career—and it was wonderful
to me, and I'm thankful that I was given the chance
to play baseball; it's about the only thing I could do
—and I've thought many a time, what would have
happened to me if I hadn't had a chance to play
baseball? A chill goes up my back when I think I
might have been denied this if I had been black.*

> —TED WILLIAMS, accepting a
> brotherhood award at How-
> ard University, 1971

The first time I saw Josh Gibson was on a humid Tuesday night
in May of 1945 in the old, green-painted, ad-studded but inti-
mate confines of Washington's Griffith Stadium. I was fourteen
then. The park was a long ride by bus from my home in Alexandria to Washington, where we changed from the segregated
Virginia bus—whites in front, blacks in back—and boarded the
integrated Washington trolley. The stadium, long since fallen
under the wrecker's ball, seemed a long ride from downtown
then. Today the site is deep inside "the inner city."

Gibson was wearing the pin-stripe uniform of the old Homestead Grays, who were then working on their eighth of nine
straight pennants in the Negro National League. Their bitter
rivals, the Kansas City Monarchs of the Negro American
League, were in town for an interleague game, and the great
Satchel Paige himself would pitch the first two innings, as he
generally did, to draw a crowd.

And it was a crowd. The white paper, the Washington *Post*,

had devoted two paragraphs to the game, more than its usual ration of news about the Grays, since, after all, Paige was in town. But the park was swarming with black fans, and every now and then a pink face or two, out to watch these two greatest players in black baseball, Josh Gibson and Satchel Paige, renew their long-standing warfare.

I remember crowding against the railing beside the Monarchs' dugout with a swarm of scorecard-waving kids to watch Satchel warm up, his big windmill windup reminiscent of Joe E. Brown in *Elmer the Great*. Across the field Gibson, warming up his own pitcher, looked round-faced and cheery, a beardless black Santa throwing his head back and chuckling at a dozen things that had touched his funny bone.

Josh didn't hit any home runs that night. And that's all I remember about the game, frankly. I'm not even sure what the score was, although I think the Monarchs won. The only other player I knew by name was the Grays' hard-hitting first base-man, Buck Leonard, sometimes dubbed "the black Lou Gehrig." The rest of the names were a blank to me.

Did Cool Papa Bell roam center field for the Grays? Did he steal a base that night? Did Hilton Smith come in to relieve Satchel and sew the game up as he had done for so many years? Did the veteran Newt Allen cavort at second base for the Mon-archs?

Later these men became friends of mine. But that night I looked right at them and didn't even see them. Their names meant noth-ing to me. Like most fans of that day, I considered them semi-pro's, maybe AA minor leaguers at best. Otherwise, why would they get so little attention in the papers?

Six months later a Monarch rookie, Jackie Robinson, was signed by the Dodgers, the Monarchs were in town again, and I returned to see them in a Sunday doubleheader. I remember Buck Leonard hitting a fly ball high against the right field wall, close to the spot I had seen Charlie Keller of the New York Yankees reach just a few days earlier. Too bad, I thought idly, that Leonard and Keller couldn't play on the same field so we could really compare.

Then I forgot about the subject, until some twenty-five years later, when I happened to read Satchel Paige's book, *Maybe I'll Pitch Forever*. Perhaps the story of the long dead Josh Gibson would be just as fascinating, I mused. I began calling people in the Washington area who might have known Gibson. One of the first men I was referred to was Leonard, living in Rocky Mount, North Carolina. I grabbed my tape recorder and two sons and drove down there. Buck referred me to Cool Papa Bell in St. Louis and Hilton Smith in Kansas City, so on my vacation I took the boys out West for more recorded talks. From there the trail fanned out.

For what I had stumbled on by accident was a virtually unexplored continent. The world of black baseball history was not a mere footnote to baseball history—it was fully *half* of baseball history!

And maybe—the thought was stunning—the bigger half.

Soon I was collecting interviews the way other people collect stamps. I traveled to Harlem, to Newark, to Philadelphia and Baltimore. When my article on Gibson came out in the Washington *Post*, I got a surprise call from an old teammate of his right in my home town of Manassas, Virginia. I journeyed to Chicago, to Pittsburgh and York, Pennsylvania, to Atlanta, Jacksonville, Birmingham, Memphis, and Houston. I flew to Los Angeles, where I found a large fraternity of ex-players.

In terms of time, the journey took me through five decades, from players who had begun their careers in 1914 or before, to men who were still playing baseball in the fifties. They ranged in age from forty-five to over eighty.

Sociologically, I traveled from the worst, most soul-destroying ghettos, where former players ushered me into tenements swarming with roaches, to beautifully landscaped split-levels in the suburbs. (Most of the veterans, I'm happy to say, live comfortably, if modestly, in neat-well-kept neighborhoods.) I interviewed players in dingy Harlem bars, in posh downtown hotels, in hermits' cabins in the woods, and on the lovely lawn overlooking Glimmerglass Lake at Cooperstown.

Day by day, month by month, miles of stories wound onto my tape reels. In all, I interviewed more than seventy veterans of the old "blackball days." Some of them have since died. Seeing a new obit in the *Sporting News* hurts keenly. But in a sense these men have not died. Their voices and their memories are as vibrant on my tapes as when I first met them.

The tape recorder has revolutionized historical writing. Here is history come alive. The language is direct. Sentences are declarative and short. Adjectives are few. Similes abound. Humor is droll. The language is gentlemanly, in contrast to much modern-day sports reporting. No expletives were deleted, because few if any were used. Many of the stories are confirmed—more drily, to be sure—in the microfilm files of old Negro newspapers (and in some white papers) in the Library of Congress, where I also spent days upon days searching out the record. But the men themselves conjure up the past with a liveliness that no journalist could duplicate. When Ted Williams read Buck Leonard's interview in the Washington *Star*, he told Buck, "I knew that was a ballplayer talking, I knew it wasn't a writer."

What a pity I didn't start just five years earlier. I could have met, and preserved the priceless memories of, such legendary old-timers as John Henry 'Pop' Lloyd, Raleigh 'Biz' Mackey, Mule Suttles, Jud Wilson, Bullet Joe Rogan, Dick Lundy, and many more whose deaths had only recently stilled their tongues.

In 1970 I made a pilgrimage to Cooperstown, some twenty-four years after my first, boyhood visit. But it all seemed different this time. After strolling through the plaques of the gods—Babe Ruth, Ty Cobb, Walter Johnson—I climbed to the second floor office of Ken Smith, the curator. I told him I could no longer look at the Hall of Fame as I had as a boy because, I said bluntly, "You have only half a Hall of Fame here. It won't be complete until the great black players before Jackie Robinson are admitted."

I'm afraid I shocked him. It shocks all devout believers to be told that a fundamental article of faith is built on error. But I had learned what Smith, a long-time New York sportswriter, had not: The blacks were playing probably the most exciting—yes, and very possibly the best—baseball seen in America before 1947. Certainly they beat barnstorming white big leaguers more often than they lost. Between 1886 and 1948 I have uncovered newspaper box scores of 445 games between them. The blacks won 269, lost 172, and tied 4!

From Smith's office I strolled around the corner to the National Baseball Library, filled with row upon row of books on baseball history, and asked historian Clifford Kachline to see what material he had on black baseball. He led me to a bank of filing cabinets, opened a drawer marked "N" and pulled out one thin manila folder marked "Negro." Inside were half a dozen random newspaper paragraphs and my own article on Josh Gibson. That was all, except for a scorecard of the old Indianapolis Clowns (Hank Aaron's first team) illustrated with various comic costumes and poses.

In America's national baseball library, half the history of baseball was missing!

Even the much heralded *Encyclopedia of Baseball*, with over 2,000 pages and 100,000 lines, devoted not a single line to the hundreds of black men who were playing—and beating—the best of the white big leaguers. Men like Rube Foster, Oscar Charleston, Pop Lloyd, Smoky Joe Williams, Cool Papa Bell, and all the rest are simply not there.

Slowly this has changed. Kachline compiled a voluminous biographical file of Negro Leaguers. The Hall of Fame has admitted 11 Negro Leaguers—although many more still remain outside. It has given a corner of the museum to exhibits of the history of black baseball. The Society of American Baseball Research has a lively committee on the Negro Leagues, which is tracking down more interviews and new stats. The Macmillan Encyclopedia, the "complete and official record" of major league baseball, now includes lifetime stats on leading Negro Leaguers. Many books have now been written on the subject, including three more of my own, plus several TV documentaries. And Cooperstown welcomed several dozen black old-timers to a huge reunion in the summer of 1991, although it is still slow to admit them to the pantheon.

The fan who wants to know the full story of baseball in America must go beyond the voluminous but conventional histories and explore the rich and exciting story of black baseball. Fans both black and white, young and old, will gasp, as I did, at their first glance at this as yet largely uncharted moonscape. Yet, like Tranquility Base, it has been there all the time, just waiting to be discovered.

Of course the black vets got no pensions for their long service to the game. A few are still in baseball as scouts, but most were forced to start new careers after their playing days were over and have at last earned comfortable, if modest, retirement.

All are confident that they could have been big-league stars. "You just *knew* you were better than the major leaguers," says peppery little Jake Stephens, shortstop on the old Philadelphia Hilldales—"you just *knew* it. Why, Chick Galloway of the Athletics didn't have anywhere near the range I had at shortstop. He couldn't carry my glove."

Should the black stars have raised black fists and demanded integration? Would such a tactic have worked? Probably not—not given the world of thirty to forty years ago, not with the stern and unbending Kenesaw Mountain Landis in the baseball commissioner's chair. Instead of speeding integration, they might have set it back by decades. So they bit their lips and waited, and when the door was finally opened, they stepped back like Moses on Pisgah and watched the rookie, Jackie Robinson, walk through, while they remained outside, cheering him on.

Robinson, Roy Campanella, Larry Doby, Willie Mays, Hank Aaron—these and many more learned their baseball from the black stars of the past who had been their coaches. When they reached the majors, they were better prepared than most white rookies who had come up through the minors.

None of the black old-timers show any bitterness, however. But they all would agree with ex-catcher Joe Greene's quiet statement:

"I still say we did a lot for the game, even if nobody knows about us. They say Jackie Robinson paved the way. He didn't pave the way. We did."

VOICES
FROM THE
GREAT BLACK
BASEBALL
LEAGUES

Chapter 1

THE MAJOR LEAGUE NOBODY KNOWS

> *We had eleven out of the top twelve hitters in the National League last year [1969] and four out of the top five in the American. Hell, we've always had players of that caliber, only we never got any recognition.*
>
> —BILL YANCEY, shortstop
> New York Black Yankees

IN THE BEGINNING, 1872–99

In 1920 the Paris Academy of Sciences reported that mosaics from the ruins of a Carthaginian nobleman's home depicted an early baseball game of 2,000 years ago. Whether or not baseball was actually born in Africa (Russia, Mexico, Britain, France, and the American Indians also claim it), it has been played by Afro-Americans for a century or more.

Back in 1872 Bud Fowler, a Negro, broke the color line and became the first man of his race to play in organized ball. Other blacks followed, and in 1884 two brothers from Ohio, Welday and Moses Fleetwood Walker, briefly crashed the major leagues with Toledo of the old American Association.

The first organized Negro team we know of was formed in 1885 in Babylon, Long Island, by waiters of Babylon's Argyle

1

Hotel. They talked gibberish on the field, hoping to pass themselves off as Cubans, and played the best white semipro teams in the area. Most of the Babylon players later turned professional as the Cuban Giants, the first great black team in history. By 1886 they were strong enough to beat the Cincinnati Red Stockings of the National League. A year later they almost beat the champion Detroit Tigers, losing 6–4 in the ninth on an error.

Would the majors open their doors to them? That hope was dashed one April morning in 1887 in Newark, New Jersey. The Chicago White Stockings were scheduled to play Newark of the Eastern League, whose pitching star, thirty-five-game winner George Stovey, was a light-skinned Negro from Canada. Chicago captain Adrian "Cap" Anson, the greatest player of his day, stomped off the field rather than face Stovey. His walk set a pattern that would last for exactly sixty years. One by one the blacks were eased out of organized baseball. The long blackball decades had begun.

THE NEW CENTURY, 1900–1909

In 1902 the great John "Muggsy" McGraw tried to sign a black second baseman for his Baltimore Orioles, who were then in the American League. The man was Charley Grant, whom McGraw tried to pass off as an Indian, "Chief Tokahoma." The masquerade worked fine until the Orioles reached Chicago for an exhibition, and every black in town turned out to present Tokahoma with an alligator handbag and cheer "our boy Charley Grant" on every ground ball he fielded. White Sox manager Charles Comiskey quickly became suspicious, and it was back to the reservation for Charley.

The "reservation" was the Cuban X-Giants, then based in Philadelphia, and probably the best black team in the country. The X-Giants' main rivals were the Philadelphia Giants, managed by the first great black organizer, mustachioed Sol White. In 1903, just one month before the Pittsburgh Pirates and Boston Red Sox played the first modern white World Series, the X-Giants and White's Phillies had played the century's first black World Series, won by the X-Giants two games to one.

The next year White enticed Foster to jump to the Phils, who trounced the X-Giants in a September rematch and remained king of the black baseball roost for the next few years. In 1906 the Phillies won 108 and lost only 31, and their white owner, sportswriter Walter Schlichter, sent a letter to the New York papers challenging the winner of the white World Series to meet his club "and thus decide who can play baseball the best, the white or the black American." Unfortunately, the White Sox, who defeated the Cubs that year, didn't take him up on it.

In 1907 Foster led a walkout from Schlichter's team to the Leland Giants of Chicago. He challenged the Cubs to a three-game series in 1909, and though the Cubs won all three, the games were close. The Cubs' great Mordecai Brown won a squeaker 1–0, and Foster lost a disputed contest when the winning run scored after Rube thought time had been called.

The Lelands voyaged to Cuba, where they found a well-developed baseball establishment only a decade after the end of Spanish rule—as touring white big-league clubs were also finding out. In 1908 the Cincinnati Reds had visited the island for eleven games. The Cubans won seven of them, including a one-hit shutout by young José Mendez. The next year the American League champion Detroit Tigers made the trip, minus Ty Cobb and Sam Crawford but with the rest of the club intact. They could only win four and lose eight—one of their losses a no-hitter by Eusaquio Pedroso. Even the *Reach Guide* conceded that the tour had been "disastrous." An all-star club featuring pitchers Addie Joss, Mordecai Brown, Nap Rucker, and Howie Camnitz followed the Tigers and did little better, splitting the four games they played.

The Tigers returned for revenge in 1910, this time with Cobb and Crawford. They won seven and lost four, though Cobb was thrown out every time he tried to steal and three American blacks all outhit him—John Henry Lloyd, Grant Johnson, and Bruce Petway. Ty stomped off the field vowing never to play blacks again. The world champion Philadelphia A's were next, and their performance was enough to bring a blush to Connie Mack's cheek. In six games the only victory they could salvage was 2–1 over Pedroso.

In 1911 the Philadelphia Phils tried their luck, winning five and losing four. Then the world champion New York Giants arrived to win nine and lose three, though Pedroso and Mendez combined to whip the great Christy Mathewson 7–4. Thus after four years and sixty-five games on the island, the big leaguers had won thirty-two, lost thirty-two, and tied one.

RAGTIME BALL, 1910–19

Meanwhile, New York was developing into the capital of black baseball in the East. In Harlem the Lincoln Giants, transplanted from Lincoln, Nebraska, boasted two of the best pitchers in black ball history, Cyclone Joe Williams and Cannonball Dick Redding. Williams, since voted the greatest black pitcher of all time, hooked up in many a memorable duel with the best white pitchers of his day, including Grover Alexander, Walter Johnson, and Rube Marquard, and beat all three of them.

Just out of Howard University, Lincolns' shortstop Frank "Strangler" Forbes—who would go on to play with the New York Rens basketball team—played in many of those battles. "That's where we made our money," he says. "I was only getting $115 a month in the regular season. But in October, aw hell, we would clean up in October. They didn't allow Negroes in the league, but we were very attractive to them in October. Hell, we would practically get more games in October than we could play. I'll tell you how good we were: We would win 60 percent of our games against the big leaguers. We played the Giants. The Yankees were nothing—we used to call them the Highlanders—hell, they were no competition. We played against the Braves when they had Dick Rudolph, Bill James, Rabbit Maranville. Yeah, we beat 'em—we beat everybody. In 1915 we beat the Phils three out of four ball games. Alexander started three times against us, never got by the fourth inning. Sure."

Out West several new clubs had been founded: the Indianapolis

ABC's, the St. Louis Giants, and the All Nations, a multiracial team out of Kansas City. And in Chicago Foster had broken with Leland to form his own club, the Chicago American Giants, and challenged the Cubs and White Sox in a head-to-head attendance war. On one Sunday when all three teams were playing at once, the Cubs drew 6,500, the Sox 9,000, and Foster's American Giants 11,000.

What about a contest on the field as well as at the box office? Booker T. Washington's paper, the New York *Age*, clamored for a four-way series among the Giants, Yankees, Lincolns, and Royals for the championship of New York. At least one white paper, the St. Louis *Post-Dispatch*, took up the cry. "There is some doubt," it wrote, "if baseball, after all, is the great American game. We play it, to be sure, but the colored people play it so much better that the time is apparently coming when it shall be known as the great African game. . . . It requires some courage to predict that colored baseball, like colored pugilism, is to supersede the white brand, but someone has to think ahead and indicate whither we drift, and we therefore go on record as having said that it will."

The Giants and Yankees, however, replied only with silence.

But their players continued to meet the blacks in October and split some tidy gate receipts. On one of those autumn afternoons in 1917 Smoky Joe Williams faced the National League champion New York Giants with their entire World Series lineup intact and set them down on a no-hitter with twenty strikeouts! (He lost 1–0 on an error.)

JAZZ DAYS, 1920–29

After World War I the black players returned from their segregated regiments to their segregated teams. In 1920 the "Black Sox" scandal erupted, and several members of the Chicago White Sox were thrown out of baseball for throwing the 1919 World Series. It created a flurry of hope that the big leagues might try to woo the disillusioned fans back by signing some of the most exciting stars of the black leagues. Of course nothing ever came of it.

Ironically, black baseball was on the threshold of its finest decade.

Rube Foster had called a meeting of several western club owners in Kansas City in February 1920 and proposed a revolutionary idea, a Negro National League. It would cut down on the mutual raiding, he argued, and would replace the hand-to-mouth scheduling with something more dependable, thus assuring the players a regular payday. And so the first black league was born. It included the American Giants, Indianapolis ABC's, St. Louis Giants, Detroit Stars, and Kansas City Monarchs—the old All Nations team but now all black. Casey Stengel himself had discovered most of the Monarchs playing on the all-black 25th Infantry team on the old Indian outpost of Fort Huachuca, Arizona.

At last a professional black player could enjoy a measure of security. Without Rube Foster's historic achievement, it is fair to say, black baseball might not have survived for another quarter century, and the nation might never have heard of Jackie Robinson, who at the time of Foster's meeting was a baby not yet one year old.

Foster's American Giants were a team of "racehorses" built around speed and bunting. Their specialty: the hit-and-run bunt. The runner broke for second, the batter bunted down the third base line, drawing the third baseman off the bag, and a really speedy runner could make third on the play. If the third baseman was foolish enough to throw to first, some runners could even continue flying around third and score on the play! They ran away with the pennant the first three years.

Meanwhile, the East began signing some of the best stars away from the West. Pop Lloyd, the great shortstop, and Biz Mackey, who later taught Roy Campanella how to catch, made the jump. So did Oscar Charleston, regarded by most authorities as the greatest black player of all time. Now Ed Bolden of the Philadelphia Hilldales was ready to propose an Eastern Colored League, including the Hilldales, Atlantic City Bacharachs, Baltimore Black Sox, New York Lincoln Giants, Brooklyn Royals, and the Harrisburg Giants. The league was formed in 1923, and Bolden's Hilldales won the first pennant. But the enraged Foster would hear nothing of a World Series.

So instead, Bolden had to content himself with playing white big leaguers that autumn. In seven games against them, Hilldale won six. Out West the American Giants played the Detroit Tigers (still minus Cobb, who was sticking to his vow) and divided them neatly—one win, one loss, one tie. The Detroit Stars, however, did better against the St. Louis Browns, sweeping three games straight.

That was the last time a big-league club could play the blacks while wearing its own uniform. The new commissioner, the hard-bitten Carolinian Kenesaw Mountain Landis, perhaps embarrassed by the scores, issued orders against it. Henceforth, the big leaguers would have to call themselves "all-stars" if they wanted to barnstorm.

The Hilldales repeated as Eastern champs in 1924, and at last Foster was ready to make peace. The Kansas City Monarchs had won the pennant in his own league, and Foster magnanimously went to Philadelphia to open the first modern black World Series, meeting Bolden at home plate with a symbolic handshake. It was a spectacular series, going ten games, including one tie, before the Monarchs finally won it. But it was a disappointment at the gate. Only 45,000 fans turned out to see the ten games at one dollar apiece. One valuable Saturday date had to be missed because the Kansas City stadium was hosting a high school football game.

In 1926 tragedy struck in Chicago. Foster suffered a severe mental breakdown and had to be rushed to the state insane asylum.

Down South the Birmingham Black Barons, a team of coal miners, joined the Negro National League in 1927, with their skinny rookie named Leroy "Satchel" Paige. In post-season barnstorming that year, the maverick Homestead Grays, who were not in the league, won three straight from the big leaguers; two of them were shutouts by Joe Williams. The Baltimore Black Sox won five straight from their big-league opponents.

In 1929 Baltimore's Laymon Yokely beat the big leaguers three more times, giving the blacks a final record for the decade of seventy-four victories and forty-one defeats against major league competition. A week earlier the stock market had crashed. Black baseball didn't know it yet, but it would be a long, cold decade ahead.

THE BLUES, 1930–39

Nineteen-thirty was a watershed year for black baseball. Rube Foster died in December, raving about one more World Series win. His death closed an era. Just eight months earlier, a new era had been born when J. L. Wilkinson, the white owner of the Monarchs, threw a switch to begin the first modern night game in baseball history, beating Des Moines of the white Western League by a scant few days. Soon afterward he took his lights to Pittsburgh for the first night game there, and a young Samson, nineteen-year-old Josh Gibson, walked into the spotlight and began bashing eye-popping homers over every fence he saw.

There were no black leagues that year; the Depression had killed them. Salaries were suspended and players passed the hat, dividing the receipts among themselves after expenses had been paid. Many of the oldest and proudest clubs were forced to go under.

Nineteen thirty-two was an Olympic year, and in the games at Los Angeles blacks like Eddie Tolan, Ralph Metcalfe, Ed Gordon, and Cornelius Johnson brought home gold medals. In pro football Joe Lillard, a black, signed with the Chicago Cardinals.

Baseball, its attendance badly hurt by the hard times, desperately needed an attraction to bring the fans back. Could Satchel Paige or Josh Gibson do the trick? Sportswriter Westbrook Pegler declared in print that he couldn't understand why Negroes weren't playing in the majors. In Washington, old Clark Griffith watched Mule Suttles and Rap Dixon blast some long pokes in Griffith Stadium, agreed that they looked pretty darn good, but merely counseled them to continue to play a high caliber ball. He didn't suggest that they play for the Senators. Pegler would just have to wait for his answer.

The highlight of 1933—one of the biggest events in all black ball history—was the first East-West, or all-star, game, a showcase for the best black talent and the financial savior of the black teams. Often in the years to come the only profit some teams would make would be their share of the receipts of that one game, which drew 40,000 to 50,000 people to Chicago's Comiskey Park. The classic may also have been the wedge that finally opened the big leagues to blacks. When the white owners saw all those black fans rushing the turnstiles, integration began to look more attractive.

Gus Greenlee of Pittsburgh gets credit for reviving the Negro National League that same year. It included clubs in both the East and the West, from Baltimore to Chicago.

It was a hand-to-mouth life for the players. Gone were the private Pullman cars of Rube Foster's day. Now the players bounced across the countryside in buses, napping overnight, then tumbling out to play two and three games a day before wearily getting back into the bus for another long overnight haul. The winter leagues in Cuba and Florida had folded, but some lucky players could still earn money in the off-season playing in California. For the rest it meant finding a job somewhere to pay the bills until April came around again.

The white big leaguers were only a little better off. A young fellow named Bill Veeck watched attendance plummet in the majors and warned that baseball would have to do something drastic or go under. There were dozens of black stars waiting and eager to give attendance a boost. Apparently, however, the crisis hadn't gotten that drastic yet.

In 1936 Jesse Owens made history in the Berlin Olympics, reopening the perennial speculation about blacks in the big leagues.

The next spring Paige, Gibson, Cool Papa Bell, and many other stars heeded Dominican dictator Trujillo's well-financed call for a championship team. When they got back, Greenlee was so mad, he suspended the lot of them. Paige ambled out to North Dakota, following his rainbow; Bell headed toward Mexico; and Gibson landed back in the delighted arms of his former owner, Cum Posey of the Homestead Grays. Josh and Buck Leonard teamed in a formidable one-two home run punch that would bring the Grays nine straight pennants.

The 1937 season opened auspiciously in February. Bill Terry took the defending National League champion New York Giants to Havana and could win only one out of six against the well-conditioned Cubans, who of course had been playing all winter. Muttered Terry after the sixth game: "This thing has long ceased to be a joke."

In August 1938 sportswriter Jimmy Powers of the New York *Daily News* permitted himself a little fantasy in print as the National League season moved into the stretch with the Giants in a hard fight for the pennant. There are seven black players, he said, who could practically insure a flag for them. With Ray Brown and Barney Brown supporting Carl Hubbell on the mound, and with Josh Gibson joining Harry Danning behind the plate, plus Buck Leonard, Pat Patterson, and Ray Dandridge in the infield, and Sammy Bankhead between Mel Ott and Joe Moore in the outfield, the Giants could win in a walk— or so Powers dreamed.

More pragmatic, National League president Ford Frick said the league hasn't used Negroes because the public "has not been educated to the point where they will accept them." He cited the problem of traveling in the South, but declared that "baseball is biding its time and waiting for the social change, which is inevitable." Times, he said, "are changing."

But the change seemed slow. Yankee outfielder Jake Powell blurted out in a radio interview that he was a policeman in the off-season and "enjoyed cracking niggers' heads." Yankee owner Ed Barrow apologized profusely, and Judge Landis suspended the outfielder for ten days. Oddly, Powell had often barnstormed with blacks, who said they thought he was a fine fellow.

The blacks brought the decade to a close in the autumn of 1939 by splitting four games with the big-league all-stars. It was their finest decade yet. In 167 games against the white major leaguers from 1930 to 1939 the blacks had won 112, lost 52 and tied 3.

Yet the bars of segregation seemed rigidly in place. Bill Terry for one predicted that "Negroes will never get into the big leagues." He may have been merely stating a belief rather than a prejudice. But American League president Will Harridge disagreed. He took one look at the 40,000 fans at the East-West game that August and said he believed the bars would be down in five years or less.

SWINGTIME AT LAST, 1940–48

The new decade saw a rush of black players south of the border to Jorge Pasquel's Mexican League. Josh Gibson was one of those jumping, but the Grays won without him, their fourth straight flag.

The biggest news the following year was probably Satchel Paige's comeback from arm trouble. Kansas City's Wilkinson had given him a chance when nobody else would, and Satch helped lead the Monarchs to their second straight flag, and to a four-straight sweep of the Grays in the first World Series since 1927.

In the summer of '42 Satchel Paige and his Kansas City Monarch sidekick Hilton Smith set down a big-league all-star squad and caused a crisis. Playing in Chicago's Wrigley Field, the Monarchs defeated Dizzy Dean, Cecil Travis, Zeke Bonura, and others on only three hits, winning 3–1 before 30,000 fans. Across town only 19,000 had seen the White Sox and Browns in a doubleheader that same day. Why not, the Communist New York *Daily Worker* asked Judge Landis, open organized baseball's doors to blacks? It quoted Dodger manager Leo Durocher as saying he'd leap at the chance to hire one if he could. "Hell," Leo said, "I've seen a million good ones."

Landis promptly called Durocher into his office for a conference, and when Leo emerged he said he'd been misquoted. Landis also had a statement to read: "There is no rule, formal or informal," he said, "no understanding, subterranean or otherwise" against black ballplayers in the majors.

"One hundred percent hypocrisy!" snorted Brooklyn owner Larry McPhail, although Larry added the warning that signing black stars would destroy the Negro leagues.

Dr. J. B. Martin, president of the new Negro American (Western) League, declared that he for one wouldn't oppose the signing of black stars; it would be a big boost to black baseball, he said.

With the war taking more and more white stars, rumors persisted that the Pittsburgh Pirates would try out Gibson and Leonard. Pirate boss Bill Benswanger declared that "colored men are American citizens with American rights. I know there are many problems connected with the question, but after all, somebody has to make the first move." Finally, however, he denied the whole thing, although of course, he added, it is the Pirates' policy to give a job to any qualified man.

In Philadelphia there was talk of a Phils' tryout for home-town star Roy Campanella. Phils' owner Gerry Nugent quashed the rumors, saying that was strictly up to the manager and reminding the reporters modestly that "I'm just the owner." ("All I ask," Campy commented, "is a break.")

The irrepressible Bill Veeck listened to the debate with keen interest. He hatched a plan to buy the Phils, stock them with black stars, and waltz to the National League pennant. Unfortunately, Landis got word of the scheme and killed it. "I realize now," Veeck grins, "that it was a mistake to tell him."

Out in Chicago the White Sox' Jimmy Dykes actually did summon up courage to hold a tryout for pitcher Nate Moreland and a college football whiz named Jackie Robinson. Robinson reported with a charley horse. Whistled Jimmy: "I'd hate to see him on two good legs!" Jackie, he reported, "is worth $50,000 of anybody's money. He stole everything but my infielders' gloves." But Robinson and Moreland didn't get the jobs. "Personally I'd welcome them," Dykes shrugged, "and I believe every one of the other managers would do likewise."

Moreland was bitter. "I can play in Mexico," he said, "but I have to fight for America where I can't play."

Why did the racial bar, so firmly in place for over half a century, resist attempts to lower it? Organized ball seemed to blame it on the fans. Said National League president Ford Frick: "We have always been interested in Negro players but have not used them because of the public."

"There's no law against Negroes playing with white teams,"

baseball's "bible," the *Sporting News*, editorialized, but leaders on both sides "know their crowd psychology" and will not risk an explosion. Joe Louis and Jesse Owens, it said, are "different." "Clear-minded men of both races have realized the tragic possibilities and have stayed clear of such complications, because they realize it is for the benefit of each and also of the game."

Looking back today, Ric Roberts, then a sportswriter on the Pittsburgh *Courier*, sighs: "I thought somebody would come along and pull us aboard the train, as Toscanini did for Marian Anderson in 1934. He said, 'once in a thousand years' a voice like that. But we just didn't have a Branch Rickey back then."

The draft took many top black players as well as whites. Ironically, the war also brought a belated prosperity to the black leagues. Wartime crowds boosted black baseball into a two-million-dollar-a-year business. At an estimated $40,000 Satchel Paige was not only the highest paid black player in America but the highest paid of any color, black or white. In the spring of '45 the Red Sox took a look at Robinson, Sam Jethroe of Cleveland, and Marvin Williams of Philadelphia. Coach Hugh Duffy watched them line hits off the fence, shook their hands, and promised to get in touch if the Red Sox ever needed them. He never did. It looked like the same old runaround.

Judge Landis was still as immovable as ever. "Paul Robeson had made a speech to Landis and to all the owners," Ric Roberts says. "The theme was 'Have a Heart.' But at the end of all that, Mr. Landis affirmed his stand. The last thing he told Wendell Smith of the Pittsburgh *Courier* was: 'There is nothing further to discuss.' He died with those words on his lips."

In New York Mayor Fiorello La Guardia set up a committee on equal employment opportunity. Larry McPhail, then owner of the Yankees, bluntly told the committee: No colored players will play on the Yankees. The campaign is being pushed by "groups of political and social-minded drum beaters," he charged. All this Jim Crow propaganda, he said, is just "talking through their hats." Few if any blacks could qualify for the big leagues "A major-league player must have something besides natural ability," McPhail said. He must possess the technique, the coordination, the competitive attitude, and the discipline usually acquired only after years of training in the smaller leagues." McPhail may have been really thinking of the $100,000 a year the Yankees took in in rent and concessions from black teams that used Yankee Stadium plus Yankee farm clubs' parks in Newark, Kansas City, and Norfolk, Virginia. But he said that signing blacks would contribute little or nothing to solving the basic problem, would be disadvantageous to the black players and fans alike, and would restrict rather than broaden opportunities for black players. McPhail favored a limited number of blacks entering the majors, perhaps a few each year, "after they show their ability and character."

McPhail didn't realize it, but things were already changing—and changing fast.

In April 1945, just after President Roosevelt's sudden death, the major leagues announced the name of their new commissioner. He would be a Southerner, Kentucky Senator A. B. "Happy" Chandler. "We went right down to see him the morning the story broke," Roberts says. "Chandler came out immediately, shaking our hands and said, 'I'm for the Four Freedoms. If a black boy can make it on Okinawa and Guadalcanal, hell, he can make it in baseball.' And he told us, 'Once I tell you something, brother, I never change. You can count on me.'" I always thought that was a pretty stout thing for a Southerner to say.

"The *Courier* headlined that! Rickey couldn't have made a move but for that. The moment Rickey read that in the *Courier*, he began to move. And Chandler paid for it. Mr. Griffith was outraged. He was outraged! They never forgave Mr. Chandler for that. The first time he stubbed his toe, he was a goner. And it broke his heart. Mr. Chandler has never been the same. None of those people could have done a doggone thing if they hadn't gotten a green light from the commissioner. And he never got credit for it. I think he's long overdue for what he deserves."

That winter the electrifying news was finally out: Rickey and the Dodgers had signed Robinson. The Sol Whites and Charley Grants, the Rube Fosters and the Josh Gibsons had come at last to the end of the long dark trail. The door had been opened, but it would not be they who would step inside.

As the 1946 season opened, most eyes were on Montreal, where Robinson was making history in the Dodger farm system, not in the Negro leagues. "We couldn't even draw flies," Buck Leonard shrugs.

It's too bad, because with the returning veterans the black clubs were playing some of the best baseball ever. The World Series that fall between Kansas City and Newark opened in New York's Polo Grounds, well-attended by scouts from several teams. Newark, with Monte Irvin and Larry Doby in the infield, won it in seven games.

In October Bob Feller put together a truly outstanding all-star squad to tour against Satchel Paige: Mickey Vernon, Phil Rizzuto, Ken Keltner, Charley Keller, Jeff Heath, Johnny Sain, Bob Lemon, Dutch Leonard, and Spud Chandler. In thirteen games from coast to coast they played on almost even terms. In the end the Fellers won seven and lost six and, best of all, made more money than the Cardinals would make winning the World Series against Boston.

Nineteen forty-seven, Robinson's first year with the Dodgers, opened on a note of tragedy. Josh Gibson died suddenly at the age of thirty-five, a broken, frustrated man, just too old to make the majors after so long a wait. Many other veterans eager to sign, lied about their ages, some successfully, others in vain. Younger ones were signed up quickly—Campanella, Don Newcombe, Doby, Hank Thompson. Older ones, those already forty, knew there was no hope, but these men—Cool Papa Bell, Mule Suttles, George Scales, Willie Wells and many others—gave everything they had to helping the youngsters coming up.

The rush to raid the black leagues accelerated: their old fans deserted them, and their newspapers ignored them. One by one the black clubs folded.

In October 1948 Satchel Paige got together one more club of youngsters to barnstorm against his world champion Cleveland Indian mates, Bob Lemon and Gene Bearden, plus Murray Dickson, Al Zarilla, Roy Partee, and others. To bolster the youngsters' morale, he added forty-five-year-old Cool Papa Bell to the squad to play a few innings and lend his experience. In the final game, with Dickson on the mound, Bell walked and Paige laid down a neat sacrifice that pulled the third baseman off the bag, a classic example of the hit-and-run bunt that Rube Foster had perfected almost half a century earlier. Bell was almost to second when ball hit bat and almost on third when the third baseman picked the ball up. When the startled catcher, Partee, ran down the line to cover third, Bell brushed right past him and raced across the wide-open plate. He had scored from first on a bunt!

Rube Foster's ghost must have looked down and smiled. It was to be the last play in the history of the black ball days. A chapter of Americana had closed—forever.

THE CHAMPIONS

Gradually, scholars are filling in the blanks of black baseball history. Contrary to belief, quite a few statistics are already available from black newspapers of the day, and the Society of American Baseball Research is steadily at work reconstructing those that are not available now.

Before 1920, when no leagues were operating, championships were informal and based on challenges, or often on disputed claims. Sol White's history of black baseball, published in 1906, is the source for much of the early history. Black newspapers fill in many of the later details. No eastern league existed from 1928 through 1932, but in 1930 the Grays defeated the Lincolns in a challenge series. Of course white papers ran little or nothing on the Negro leagues. Maddeningly, the black press was inconsistent in its coverage, which ranged from thorough to exasperating. Especially during the Depression, when presumably budgets were cut, black coverage of black baseball was too often amateurish.

I am indebted to the late John Coates for uncovering the batting statistics of 1921, and to Paul Doherty, who pored through hundreds of box scores to help reconstruct the 1926 statistics. (More often than not, box scores did not contain at-bats, doubles, triples, home runs or pitching statistics. At-bats thus had to be estimated.) Ric Roberts has supplied his own personal statistics on Josh Gibson, whom he covered for many years when Josh played with the Pittsburgh-based Grays. Although other players' averages for some of those years are not yet known, Gibson's are so astronomical that it is presumed no one else could have topped him.

The statistics are based on league games only. The majority of black games were nonleague against both black and white opponents, up to 180 total games a year.

NEGRO CHAMPIONS

Year	West	East
1887		NY Gorhams (Cuban Giants)
1888		Cuban Giants
1889		NY Gorhams (Cuban Giants)
1890		
1891		Big Gorhams
1894	Chicago Unions	Cuban Giants
1897		Cuban X-Giants (Gorhams)
1898		
1899	Columbia Giants (Union Giants)	*Cuban X-Giants*
1900	Union Giants/Columbia Giants	Cuban X-Giants/Genuine Cuban Giants
1901		
1902		Cuban X-Giants/Genuine Cuban Giants
1903	Algona (Iowa) Brownies (Union Giants)	Cuban X-Giants/Philadelphia Giants
1904		Cuban X-Giants (Philadelphia Giants)
1905		Philadelphia Giants
1906		Philadelphia Giants
1907		Philadelphia Giants
1908		
1909	St. Paul Gophers (Leland Giants)	
1910		
1911	Chicago Leland Giants	
1912		
1913	American Giants	NY Lincoln Giants
1914	*American Giants*	Brooklyn Royal Giants
1915	American Giants	NY Lincoln Giants
1916	Indianapolis ABC, American Giants	Brooklyn Royal Giants
1917	*American Giants*	Lincoln Stars
1918		
1919		
1920	American Giants	Bacharach Giants

East-West winner, if any, is in italics.
Playoff loser is in parentheses.
A slash indicates a disputed championship.

NEGRO LEAGUE PENNANT & WINNERS

Year	West	East
1921	Chicago	Bacharachs, Philadelphia Hilldale
1922	Chicago	
1923	Kansas City	Hilldale
1924	*Kansas City*	Hilldale
1925	Kansas City (St. Louis)	*Hilldale*
1926	*Chicago* (Kansas City)	Bacharachs
1927	*Chicago* (Birmingham)	Bacharachs
1928	St. Louis (Chicago)	—
1929	Kansas City	Baltimore
1930	St. Louis (Detroit)	Homestead Grays (Lincoln Giants)
1931	St. Louis	—
1932	Chicago (Nashville)	—
1933[1]	Chicago (Pittsburgh)	
1934[1]	Philadelphia (Chicago)	
1935[1]	Pittsburgh (Cubans)	
1936[1]	Pittsburgh/Washington	
1937	Kansas City (Chicago)	Homestead Grays
1938	Memphis/Atlanta[2]	Homestead Grays
1939	Kansas City (St. Louis)	Baltimore (Grays)[3]
1940	Kansas City	Homestead Grays
1941	Kansas City	Homestead Grays (Cubans)
1942	*Kansas City*	Homestead Grays
1943	Birmingham (Chicago)	*Homestead Grays*
1944	Birmingham	*Homestead Grays*
1945	*Cleveland*	Homestead Grays
1946	Kansas City	*Newark*
1947	Cleveland	*Cubans* (Newark)
1948	Birmingham (Kansas City)	*Homestead Grays* (Baltimore)
1949	Chicago (Kansas City)	*Baltimore*
1950	Kansas City	Indianapolis

World Series winner, if any, in italics.
Loser of Play-off, if any, is in parentheses.

[1] Only a single National League operated 1933–36.
[2] No play-offs were held 1936 and 1938; divided season produced two champions.
[3] Homestead finished first in 1939 but lost play-off to third-place Baltimore.

YEARLY LEADERS

WEST

Year	Batting		Home Runs	
1920	Cristobal Torriente	.411	Edgar Wesley	11
1921	Charles Blackwell	.448	Oscar Charleston	15
1922	Oscar Johnson	.389	Charleston, Joe Rogan	16
1923	Cristobal Torriente	.412	Oscar Johnson	18
1924	Dobie Moore	.463	D Moore, T Stearnes	10
1925	Edgar Wesley	.416	Wesley, Stearnes	18
1926	Mule Suttles	.418	Mule Suttles	27*
1927	Red Parnell	.426	Willie Wells	23
1928	Pythias Russ	.405	Turkey Stearnes	24
1929	Clarence Smith	.390	Willie Wells	27*
1930	Willie Wells	.404	Willie Wells	14
1931	Turkey Stearnes	.350	Turkey Stearnes	8
1932		Single league		
1933		Single league		
1934		Single league		
1035		Single league		
1936		Single league		
1937	Willard Brown	.371	Willard Brown	8
1938	Willard Brown	.356	Willard Brown	8
1939	Turkey Stearnes	.350	Stearnes, Ted Strong	2
1940	Buck O'Neil	.345	Turkey Stearnes	5
1941	Joe Greene	.443	Willard Brown	2
1942	Barney Serrell	.357	Willard Brown	6
1943	Lester Lockett	.408	Willard Brown	6
1944	Sam Jethroe	.353	Alec Radcliff	5
1945	Sam Jethroe	.393	Alec Radcliff	7
1946	Buck O'Neil	.350	Willard Brown	13
1947	John Ritchey	.381	Bob Boyd	4
1948	Artie Wilson	.402	Willard Brown	18

* Record

	Victories		Total Run Average	
1920	Bill Gatewood	15- 4	Dave Brown	2.36
1921	Bill Drake	20-10	Dave Brown	2.47
1922	George Myers	17- 2	Jim Jeffries	2.84
1923	Andy Cooper	15- 8	Bill Foster	3.11
1924	Bullet Joe Rogan	16- 5	Luis Padrone	2.83
1925	Bullet Joe Rogan	15- 2	Bullet Joe Rogan	2.17
1926	William Bell	16- 3	Bill Foster	1.98
1927	Bill Foster	21- 3	William Bell	2.27
1928	Ted Trent	21- 3	Willie Powell	2.94
1929	John Williams	19- 7	Yellowhorse Morris	2.79
1930	Eggie Hensley	17- 6	Double Duty Radcliffe	2.80
1931	Webster McDonald	8- 2	No data	
1932			Single league	
1933			Single league	
1934			Single league	
1935			Single league	
1936			Single league	
1937	Hilton Smith	10- 0	Ted Trent	2.08
1938	Hilton Smith	9- 1	Hilton Smith	3.01
1939	Hilton Smith	8- 2	Hilton Smith	2.06
1940	Jack Matchett	5- 0	Jack Matchett	1.27
1941	Smith, Satchel Paige	6- 0	Satchel Paige	2.08
1942	Hilton Smith	8- 3	Booker McDaniel	1.60
1943	Booker McDaniel	8- 1	Booker McDaniel	2.58
1944	Gentry Jessup	14- 9	George Jefferson	1.99@
1945	Gentry Jessup	15-10	Willie Jefferson	1.57@
1946	Satchel Paige	9- 1	No data	
1947	Jim LaMarque	12- 2	No data	
1948	LaMarque, Newberry	14- 5	No data	

@ ERA

EAST

Year	Batting Average		Home Runs	
1920	Dick Lundy	.344	Dick Lundy	2
1921	Dick Lundy	.363	Louis Santop	6
1922	Pop Lloyd	.387	Highpockets Hudspeth	3
1923	Biz Mackey	.433	Charlie Mason	5
1924	Pop Lloyd	.433	Lundy, Oscar Charleston	14
1925	Oscar Charleston	.445	Oscar Charleston	20
1926	Highpockets Hudspeth	.365	Biz Mackey	10
1927	Chino Smith	.482	Oscar Charleston	11
1928	Pop Lloyd	.565*	Pop Lloyd	11
1929	Chino Smith	.454	Chino Smith	20
1930	John Beckwith	.480	John Beckwith	19
1931	Oscar Charleston	.396	John Beckwith	9
1932	Vic Harris	.363	Josh Gibson	7
1933	Oscar Charleston	.372	Oscar Charleston	10
1934	Ray Dandridge	.436	Josh Gibson	12
1935	Turkey Stearnes	.430	Josh Gibson	13
1936	Lazaro Salazar	.367	Josh Gibson	11
1937	Wild Bill Wright	.410	Mule Suttles	12
1938	Ray Dandridge	.404	Mule Suttles	9
1939	Ed Stone	.503	Josh Gibson	16
1940	Buck Leonard	.383	Buck Leonard	8
1941	Monte Irvin	.380	Buck Leonard	6
1942	Willie Wells	.351	Josh Gibson	11
1943	Josh Gibson	.521	Josh Gibson	14
1944	Jimmy Austin	.390	Josh Gibson	8
1945	Josh Gibson	.398	Josh Gibson	9
1946	Cool Papa Bell	.429	Josh Gibson	8
1947	Larry Doby	.414	Doby, Monte Irvin	14
1948	Buck Leonard	.395	No data	

PITCHING

EAST

Year	Victories		Total Run Average	
1918	Joe Williams	7- 1	No data	
1919	Joe Williams	8- 2	No data	
1920	Dick Redding	6- 3	Dick Redding	3.33
1921	Dick Redding	17-12	Dick Redding	3.59
1922	Nip Winters	4- 3	Nip Winters	6.58
1923	Rats Henderson	8- 6	Nip Winters	2.44
1924	Nip Winters	19- 5	Nip Winters	2.84
1925	Nip Winters	21-10	Nip Winters	3.40
1926	Nip Winters	15- 5	No data	
1927	Rats Henderson	19- 7	No data	
1928	Rats Henderson	8- 4	No data	
1929	Conie Rector	20- 2	Laymon Yokely	1.90
1930	Bill Holland	12- 1	Joe Williams	2.64
1931	Webster McDonald	8- 2	No data	
1932	Satchel Paige	14- 8	Satchel Paige	3.79
1933	Bill Foster	8- 4	Bill Foster	3.64
1934	Slim Jones	22- 3	Slim Jones	1.69*
1935	Leroy Matlock	18- 0	Leroy Matlock	2.22
1936	Satchel Paige	7- 2	Bill Byrd	2.96
1937	Terris McDuffie	7- 3	Webster McDonald	2.28
1938	Terris McDuffie	11- 3	Ray Brown	0.75
1939	Leon Day	12- 4	Leon Day	3.75
1940	Ray Brown	24- 4*	Ray Brown	2.09
1941	Ray Brown	11- 6	Bill Byrd	3.52
1942	Ray Brown	12- 4	Ray Brown	2.83
1943	Johnny Wright	15- 3	Johnny Wright	1.93
1944	Bill Ricks	10- 4	No data	
1945	Roy Welmaker	12- 4	No data	
1946	Wilmer Fields	13- 3	Leon Day	2.55
1947	Max Manning	15- 6	No data	
1948	Bill Byrd	11- 6	No data	

PUERTO RICO BATTING CHAMPIONS

Year	Player	Team	AB	H	BA
1938–39	Perucho Cepeda	Guayama	170	62	.365
1939–40	Perucho Cepeda	Guayama	210	81	.386
1940–41	Roy Partlow	San Juan	122	54	.443
1940–41	Joshua Gibson	Santurce	123	59	.480
1942–43	Francisco Coímbre	Ponce	144	39	.342
1943–44	Esteban Vargas	Santurce	134	48	.358
1944–45	Francisco Coímbre	Ponce	106	45	.425
1945–46	Fernando Díaz Pedroso	Ponce	95	35	.368
1946–47	Willard Brown	Santurce	254	99	.390
1947–48	Willard Brown	Santurce	115	52	.452
1948–49	Luke Easter	Mayagüez	249	100	.402
1949–50	Willard Brown	Santurce	331	117	.354
1950–51	George Crowe	Caguas	285	107	.375
1951–52	Bill Boyd	Ponce	305	114	.374
1952–53	George Freese	Mayagüez	185	61	.330
1953–54	Luis A. Márquez	Mayagüez	282	94	.333
1954–55	Willie Mays	Santurce	172	68	.395
1955–56	Victor Pellot	Caguas	243	87	.358
1956–57	Roberto Clemente	Caguas	225	89	.396
1957–58	Bill Harrell	Santurce	201	66	.317
1958–59	Orlando Cepeda	Santurce	207	75	.362
1959–60	Orlando Cepeda	Santurce	145	51	.352
1960–61	Elmo Plaskett	Ponce	204	69	.328
1961–62	Miguel de la Hoz	San Juan	243	86	.354
1962–63	Joe Gaines	San Juan	219	77	.352
1963–64	Tony Oliva	Arecibo	208	76	.365
1964–65	Lou Johnson	Santurce	235	81	.345
1965–66	Jim Northrup	Mayagüez	241	85	.353
1966–67	Tony Pérez	Santurce	261	87	.333
1967–68	Tony Taylor	San Juan	196	67	.342
1968–69	Félix Millán	Caguas	227	72	.317
1969–70	Félix Millán	Caguas	229	79	.345

CUBAN BATTING CHAMPIONS

Year	Player	AB	H	BA
1923–24	Oliver Marcelle	105	39	.371
1924–25	Valintin Dreke	48	19	.396
1925–26	Jud Wilson	139	56	.403
1926–27	Pablo Mesa	115	47	.409
1927–28	Jud Wilson	118	52	.441
1928–29	Bejerano, Abernathy	19	8	.421
1929–30	Alejandro Oms	143	57	.385

Chapter 2

BILL DRAKE

Big Bill Drake, otherwise known as "Plunk," had a good curve ball and good control, the old-timers say, "but when he put that uniform on, he was mean."

"He liked to throw at people," agrees George Sweatt, his teammate on the early Kansas City Monarchs. "He'd throw three balls—one at your foot, one at your head, one behind you. Then he'd pitch. You didn't know what he was going to do, he was so crazy."

Drake himself laughingly admits that his reputation for throwing at hitters was well-deserved. "I guess I was just too chesty," he says, grinning. "I was a little like Jackie Robinson."

Drake had a right to be chesty. In 1921 he pitched against the St. Louis Cardinals and came within an ace of beating them, losing 5–4 on an error in the eleventh inning. The next year, against the Kansas City Blues of the American Association, he won easily, 6–2, and smashed a home run in his own cause. In the regular season that year Bill won 20 and lost 10, one of only six men to win 20 games in the short Negro League season.

"Big Plunk," smiles Sweatt, shaking his head. "That ol' Plunk was something. He and Lemuel Hawkins were the craziest guys. When we'd go to a different town, they'd just walk through the halls all night, fooling around. That's all they *did*!"

"Big Bill liked to laugh. He'd laugh at anything. He was comical. He'd be sitting on the bench, you'd tell a story and he'd just fall out laughing. He'd stop the ball games lots of times he was laughing so loud.

"One time we were playing a World Series game in Philadelphia, and stopped by Baltimore to play an exhibition game. Big Bill wasn't pitching that day, he was sitting on the bench. Now he and Hawkins were good buddies. Hawkins went to steal second, and when he went to slide, the catcher threw the ball and hit him right side of the head. It bounced about fifteen feet in the air, and Big Bill was sitting on the bench, and he laughed: 'Ha ha ha!' Hawkins started toward the bench after him and Big Bill cut out. I laughed. I never will forget that! They were good buddies, but Hawkins was going to get him.

"And now somebody told me he's a professional gambler. Well, I knew he wasn't going to go to *work!*"

Cool Papa Bell introduced me to Bill Drake in 1969. He was still in bed after a night of cards, propped up on pillows. He flashed a constant grin as he regaled us with tales of how it was to be a black player in 1914 and after.

Bill Drake Speaks . . .*

I'll tell you something—I don't imagine you've been told this —but you know Satchel Paige had what he called a "hesitation pitch." Do you know who taught Satchel to throw the hesitation pitch? You're talking to him, man, you're talking to him.

I met Satchel the first year he came out, 1926. He was with Chattanooga and I was with Memphis He had just come out of reformatory school, about seventeen or eighteen years old. I used

* Parts of this interview are courtesy of the Oral History Program of the University of Missouri.

to call it a "delayed" pitch—stride and then throw. Satchel called it a "hesitation" pitch. Whether Satchel copied it from me or some other fellow, I don't know. I wouldn't say definitely that he learned it from me, but if he didn't, he learned it from someone who learned it from me. I don't remember anyone who was doing it before me, and I started pitching in 1914. There aren't many ballplayers living today that are much older than I am that played back there fifty-odd years ago.

I kind of had a bad name for knocking men down. If you got a toehold on me, down you went. That was my plate up there, don't crowd me. One time we played in Fort Worth. Old Bib Haines, a first baseman there, he'd say, "Go on, you old ballplayers on the Kansas City Monarchs." I turned his cap bill around with a pitch. He nearly died! Next time he came up, you could drive a team of horses between him and home plate.

In 1922 when the Kansas City Monarchs went down to Montgomery, Alabama, to train, they had a one-armed pinch hitter, Lefty Maddox. Made me so damn mad I blew the bat out of his hand.

I was managing a ball club in Tulsa once, and they had a kid down there, a doggone good pitcher, and I pitched against him. The ladies all brought their pillows to watch this big man from Kansas City. So this boy was pitching and he got a little too close to the plate, and I hit him. Hell, at nine o'clock that night he didn't know whether he was in Tulsa or where he was. He was walking around looking up like that. I didn't try to hit the boy. Of course, after I hit him, I won my ball game, but I never just deliberately tried to hit him. I'd get a man loose, now. But I didn't try to just hurt somebody.

But you've got to be careful who you hit. I found that out real early. I was pitching down in Oklahoma one day. There was this big old boy, going up to the Cubs. He hit a home run off me I never will forget. When he sat down on the bench, it looked to me like he said, "Well, I sure hit that one off that shine." Well, the next time he came up to bat, I stuck my thumb up like this, you know, for a curve ball. Next pitch, same thing: stuck my thumb up and threw him a curve. The third time I stuck my thumb up again, but I threw him a fast ball instead. Didn't

Bill Drake, Kansas City Monarchs, back row center

break, see? Hit him right in the side. But that was the end of that. I didn't go back there again. The crowd didn't like that at all. So you got to watch out who you hit.

I remember one year I was with Kansas City, and Bob Meusel and Babe Ruth were putting on an exhibition of long-distance hitting and throwing. It rained all that morning and I'll bet there were two inches of mud on the infield, but we played anyway. Ruth was up four times and he hit four down through the infield that knocked up dust, let me tell you. Knocked up *dust*! They hit just that hard. But I didn't do what I would have liked to do. I used to like to kind of brush them back a little bit. But you couldn't brush one of those superstars like that. It would have been suicide. Cocked up like that—he never would have cocked up on me, I'd have laid one in there. But how could you afford to hit a ballplayer like Ruth? You don't hit a ballplayer like that.

Ruth was a regular fellow though. He used to chew tobacco. I'd say, "Ruth, give me a chew." He'd pull out a plug, give me a bite, he'd take a bite, put it back in his pocket.

And I used to cut the balls, I used to sail them. Here's one of our old balls. See how that's rough there? I'd put the sandpaper down on my belt, and when you hitch your pants up like this, you cut it, see. And when you throw it, you can make it break four ways: up or down, in or out. You hold the cut side up and throw it sidearm, she goes down. You have to throw it overhand for it to go in and out.

We were out on the Coast one year playing the White Kings— Ping Bodie, Buzz Arlett and some other big leaguers. They had a boy out there, Bill Pertica, a sandpaper man who used to pitch for the Cardinals. Well, our team got to squawking, and our pitcher, Rube Currie, said to Lonnie Goodwin, our manager: "Why don't you put in old Drake? He can throw a cut ball." So I went on in, and that stopped all that. I was sailing it right in on 'em. They didn't want no more of that cutting the ball. They told Pertica, "Forget about it, get off it." It was okay as long as Pertica was throwing it, but when I started throwing it, that was a different story.

There's no ball club I played against twice that I didn't beat at least one game, and that includes the big leagues. I threw a couple of no-hitters in my time. I threw one against an awful strong ball club in Sioux Falls, South Dakota, and another against a ball club in North Dakota. That's where I used to play baseball, with a white ball club. More money. See, back in those days the merchants of the town would take up about $7–8,000 and hire a battery, a pitcher and a catcher. All the rest would be local talent.

I started out playing in 1900 and 14. I'll tell you how I got started in baseball. I was born in 1895 in Sedalia, Missouri. Used to be an old feller there in my home town would get us kids up on the prairie—wasn't nothing but prairie back then—used to throw fly balls up to us. And then we had a preacher there who organized a baseball team. Well, I couldn't make the team—I could not make that team, I wasn't good enough to be on that team. Yet of all those boys, only one ever left there and made good, and that was myself.

Here's a picture of the old Tennessee Rats. That's the first team I played with, 1914, in a little town, Holden, Missouri. We had a baseball team and a minstrel show. We played a game in the afternoon and put on a minstrel show in the evening, and traveled around. My salary was $12.50 a week. I played a whole season and my salary was $144.

The next year I hit Brinswade, North Dakota. They asked me how would I like to stay there and play ball. I had one suit of clothes and it was in the manager's trunk—Old Man Brown, the fellow who owned the ball club. I didn't have a trunk, but we had a wardrobe trunk for the team. I said, "Where we going tomorrow?"

He said, "Cheyenne, North Dakota."

"Give me my suit," I said. "Shucks, I'm going to get me one of those Indian girls." That's the only way I had of getting my suit back. After I got my suit I said, "Well, I ain't going no further."

He got mad. "It's a good thing you didn't tell me, or I never would have given you that suit."

So I stayed in Brinswade. We used to ride around going to different towns. We never had any trouble. On the road my roommate was a white boy. And the owner used to run interference for me. If there was any trouble, he would block it. And all the kids used to follow us around. You couldn't hardly get in the park with all those kids hanging around. One would carry your glove, one would carry your shoes, one had your uniform roll. It used to take me ten minutes just to get all my paraphernalia together for the game. And the manager had one of those long sheep-lined black coats. He used to put that on me, say, "I don't want you to catch cold." Shoot, I lived like a king in that town—lived *like a king*. Brinswade, North Dakota.

And you talking about lights. They say the Kansas City Monarchs were the first team with lights, but they weren't. The Nebraska Indians were first, in 1913. Guy Greene had the Indians out of Lincoln, Nebraska. They were a regular Indian team and traveled and played in chautauquas and things like that. They used to pull the outfield in a little and put a white wall around the outfield. They'd hang gas lights with a flat round base around the outfield. They played with a larger ball than regular. I didn't play against them, but I heard about them. At that time I was scared of Indians, I had never seen them except in a circus.

Then the All Nations team came through and I jumped to them

and had a ball. At that time the headquarters was out of Des Moines, Iowa, the Hopkins Brothers sporting goods store. J. L. Wilkinson, a white man, and another man name of J. E. Gall had the club. We had four or five different nationalities and we had a private car that we traveled on. Here's a picture: John Donaldson, Pancho Snider, this boy was from Hawaii, this is a Jap over here, this is Sam Coley. Coley caught for All Nations. He used to throw a curve ball to second base. His fingers were all gnarled, and when he threw the ball it would just curve like that. José Mendez was shortstop. Here's me: "Plunk" Drake. That's what I was known as. I don't know where I got that name. Like this boy named Sue, I guess, I don't know why they called me that. This girl, "Carrie Nation," was with the All Nations then too, played second base. Oh no, she couldn't play much, she was just a novelty, a drawing card.

Now that was the ball club! That's all the men we had on it: ten men—two pitchers. You had to pitch; you had to win in those days. I was the right-hander. John Donaldson was the left-hander. I don't guess you've heard of him.

All Nations used to go out to North Dakota and around, and I've seen Wilkinson get 90 percent of the gate receipts. I used to make him so doggone mad. He'd say, "They tell me that fellow is a pretty good hitter."

I said, "If he's any good, what's he doing out here?"

He said, "You don't know anything about it."

I said, "I know that if he's a good hitter he wouldn't be out here. He's a white boy. I've *got* to be out here, there's nowhere else I can go. But if he's that good, he'd be in the big leagues. What's he doing out here?" I had to stay there. I couldn't go anywhere but out there.

In 1916 I came here to St. Louis to play with the St. Louis Giants. At that time the Giants were playing in Finley Park, the old Federal League park, at Grand and Laclede. See, the Federal League only ran two years, '14 and part of '15. Charles Mills owned the Giants then. He was a saloon keeper, but he had a white fellow in the background named Ed Brock, an automobile salesman. His brother was Johnny Brock, used to play for the Cardinals. He's the one got us into that park.

Jimmy Lyons was with the Giants then. And I'd feel awful bad if I failed to mention Sam Bennett: outfield, a great hitter, good arm—in later years he started catching. And the Giants had one of the greatest shortstops back in those days, a boy named Dick Wallace. They used to compare him with Bobby Wallace of the Browns. And we had a good second baseman in Bunny Downs, a short little guy. You've heard of him?

Now that was the ball club we had in '16, when I first came here.

It was rough when I came up, awful rough. They used to file their spikes. They'd cut your throat if you got in the way. And those old ballplayers, they wouldn't help you. They couldn't afford to because they'd be pushing themselves out of a job. See, we only had twelve men on a team. If a young ballplayer said, "I play first base," why the first baseman would say, "I play first base on this club, how you going to play first base?"

In those days the old-time ballplayers had what you call a uniform roll. So I walked in the clubhouse and unrolled my stuff. I had a pair of real good shoes, and they said, "Look at him, he's got the tools. He must be pretty good." I impressed them, see?

My best pitch, I might say, was the curve ball. I loved to throw it on three-and-two. I didn't believe in throwing a man a fast ball. I called that a "Johnny Pick" ball—they'd be waiting for it. You don't find many boys could hit a curve ball on three-and-two, and you didn't have many pitchers with nerve enough to throw it. My biggest success was control.

Bill Gatewood was manager, he was my tutor. Did you ever hear of Bill Gatewood? Tremendous pitcher. At the ball park he'd make you throw at things. Just like a shooting gallery: you got to aim, you got to pick a target. If you want to throw at a man's knees, you aim at his knees. You want to throw around his shoulders, you aim at his shoulders. It requires practice, just practice. I got so I could wake up in the morning and throw in a quart cup. You had to have control to pitch back in those days.

I guess every series we played, I opened the series and then came back the next two or three days and did relief work. No, it's not tough on your arm. You take a man that throws sidearm or three-quarters and follows through, it's no wear and tear on your arm. A curve ball is. That snap is what throws your arm out. I pitched seventeen or eighteen years, and see how straight my arm is? You see some of those old boys carry their arm crooked. I followed through.

I was getting $100 a month. Back then that was tops. But that was a fortune when you consider prices. The best room in town only cost $2.50. A T-bone steak was a quarter—biscuits a nickel extra. And if you wanted to eat soul food, why that was even less.

We had some strong ball clubs back in those days. You take around Chicago we had the Logan Squares, the Pirates, any number of teams. Those white boys who didn't make the big leagues or got a little too old, they played on those ball clubs. And they had some good ball clubs. Back in '16 they had a ball club called the Henry Grays. They had this boy Hod Eller, pitched a no-hit game for Cincinnati. I played a lot of ball games against Hod Eller. We used to do a whole lot of barnstorming.

Oooh, please don't ask me about 1921! That was the greatest year of my life. That's the year I played the Cardinals, the premier year of my life. We played the St. Louis Cardinals eight ball games in '20 and '21, and they beat us five of the eight. They had Jacques Fournier at first base. They had the whole team except Rogers Hornsby. Hornsby wouldn't play us. He was very frank about it. He just came right out and said, "I won't play with any Negroes." But the others, they all came out—Jess Haines, Doc Lavan, Austin McHenry, Verne Clemens, all the other regulars. They had the whole team except Hornsby.

We played the Cardinals in Sportsmen's Park. At that time Negroes had to sit in the pavilion in right field and in the bleachers. Negroes didn't go in the grandstand. I remember Jesse Haines shut us out 6–0, and Freddie Schupp shut us out 5–0. Then Carter beat me 4–3 in twelve innings.

In '22 C. I. Taylor had formed the Continental League, and he had offered me a nice salary to pitch for them. In the meantime he died, and his brother Ben was going to take care of things.

Well, Wilkinson had the Monarchs by then, and I'd also been out to Kansas City a couple of times that winter to talk to him, unbeknownst to people here in St. Louis—he was way too sneaky for these people. Anyway, I joined Kansas City. They traded Branch Russell and Dempsey Miller for me. Rube Foster in Chicago like to died. He said, "They got the best pitching staff in the league, now they've grabbed another good pitcher."

At that time the Monarchs were what you might call the Yankees of Negro baseball. They were organized in 1920, and in '21 Wilkinson got Bullet Rogan, Dobie Moore, Lemuel Hawkins, Heavy Johnson, and a boy name of Bob Fagan. They all came out of the Army. They were playing in Fort Huachuca, Arizona, and Casey Stengel was out there and discovered those boys.

I know you heard of the great Rogan Well, down deep in my heart, I don't believe Rogan ever saw the day he could pitch as much baseball as I could pitch. You know what made Rogan such a great pitcher? Now you know your best ballplayers in the big leagues were Yankees, because they got more publicity. You know that is a fact. Rube Foster was owner of our league, and he wouldn't let you beat Rogan. Played the bunting game on him all the time—they wouldn't slug him. Now Rogan I would consider a little better fielding pitcher than myself, but they would bunt him and slug me, wouldn't bunt me. They never would let anyone beat him. That kept him as a drawing card. That was Rube's smart idea. We used to go to Chicago back

Bill Drake, St. Louis Giants, 1916, back row second from left

in them days and draw 7, 8, 10,000 people, which was a nice crowd at the time.

When I was with Kansas City with Rogan, they couldn't feature the two of us. Rogan's disposition was different from mine. There was a picture show at 18th and Lydia. They used to advertise the ball games, and they'd put a ballplayer's picture on the screen. "Well, don't put that fellow Drake's picture on there," they said, "he'll want a raise." I'd talk a whole lot. I *wanted* something. I told them, "The hell with you, I'll go back and fish. I don't have to play no damn baseball." I sometimes think I was a little too impetuous.

I have some very fond memories. I recall we used to barnstorm. We'd go out in the small towns in Iowa, and we would take our tents and put them up and we would sleep in those tents. And we'd go to those restaurants and eat during the day, and in the evening we'd go fish. We had just a dandy good time.

When we'd leave Kansas City to go to Chicago or someplace, we always had a tourist coach so we could sleep. Wilkinson had a special car that we traveled around in, and a cook. We ate and slept right on the car. And we stopped at the best Negro hotels and we ate in the best Negro restaurants.

A ballplayer is like a contented cow. A contented cow gives good milk, see? And you got to keep your ballplayers satisfied. If you underpay a man, he's not satisfied. He's not going to give his best. You couldn't put all those other teams on the same par with the Monarchs, 'cause I remember later I played with a ball club in Nashville, Tennessee, and they didn't allow as much expense money as the Monarchs. Frankly speaking, the Monarchs lived awfully good.

In 1922 we played six games against the Kansas City Blues of the American Association, and beat them five of the six.* When we played a team like the Blues we were off salary. We played what you called "cold" playing: you get a certain percentage of the gate receipts, which would run maybe a hundred or so dollars. That was a wonderful feeling for the Blues to play the Monarchs. It was just something exciting, and the crowds were won-

---

* Drake won his game 6–2 on a six-hitter. He hit a home run to help his own cause.

derful. And when we played the Blues or those teams, we got a lot of recognition from the fellows. We talked with those boys. They'd come right over and chat with you and tell you what a good ballplayer you were. I've had lots of white ballplayers say to me, "It's a shame you're black," meaning if I was white, I'd be playing up there too. But everybody was up in arms about us playing the Blues when we beat them. A fellow by the name of Hickey was president of the American Association, and he wouldn't sanction any more games. We never played them again.

We had a lot of great ballplayers. But to tell you the truth, you just can't hardly compare a man with Satchel Paige. I only saw one man I believe was anyways as fast as Satchel, and that's Feller. And I'll tell you a boy threw an awful hard ball, Steel Arm Tyler from Memphis. He threw a big ball. Now Satchel threw a little ball, a little fast ball, like an aspirin tablet.

You should have seen Cool Papa Bell. He joined St. Louis after I left. I used to get a little shaky myself when he got on first base. I knew he was going to steal. I don't know where Bell got his speed from—I don't know *where* he got that speed from. He'd just be standing there like that, and then he'd be gone. A lot of fellows got to lean off. He'd stand up straight, like nothing was going to happen, and was off just like a streak of lightning. I don't guess Bell had any kind of weakness. He had a good arm, could run, could throw and could hit.

There were a lot of good ballplayers, but when you have an outstanding one, he just shines above those others. Now you take Hornsby. They've had 10,000 second basemen, but how many Hornsbys have you had? They've had 10,000 center fielders, but how many excel Cool Papa Bell? When a man stands out in his position, he just stands out, there's nothing you can do about it. Cool Papa Bell is due in the Hall of Fame.*

They had some Cuban ballplayers back then: Hooks Jimenez, Pelayo Chacon—a little fellow, real short; his son used to play for Cincinnati. In fact, just name a Cuban that came over here and wasn't a good ballplayer. Just name one. I don't know of any. Of course, some of them never played on prominent ball clubs.

---

* Bell was elected to Cooperstown in 1974.

Red Parnell played in the South most of the time. If he'd played out East, why, he'd have gotten a lot of publicity. He could hit. And I can tell you when a man can hit.

I'll tell you this much: a newspaper makes a ballplayer. What about the Mets? Look at Seaver. We got a boy here that's just as doggone good a pitcher, Bob Gibson, but he doesn't get the publicity that that boy gets. But why should the white papers have told about us? They weren't interested. In the late years we always had a scorekeeper, and they would send that box score to the press, and they would publish it in the morning paper. I've had some nice write-ups from white papers. I remember in Sioux Falls, South Dakota, I pitched a no-hit game there, got an awful nice write-up. But as far as having a press agent or something like that, no, we didn't have anything like that. We didn't keep any averages. There's no record of the Negro ballplayers unless you kept it yourself. We used to kid each other. Somebody would say, "Look at him, he's carrying his batting average on his cuff."

I have seen the time when if you would say the Negro is as good a ballplayer as the white, the majority of people just didn't believe it. But those old ballplayers I'm telling you about, they didn't have any shortcomings. They could do anything: they could think, they could hit, they could run, they could throw. You just couldn't say who was the best hitter. Too many of those boys could hit. You can't say the Negro is not as good a ballplayer as the white. Just look at the records. See who's leading in the big-ten hitters today, see who your leading base stealers are.

We played more semipro baseball and they played professional baseball. And their umpires were schooled; I've played ball when they called a man out of the stands to umpire. It was complicated back in those days. Everywhere we went to play ball they had a different baseball. We used a Leacock ball here, you go to Chicago they used the Wilson ball, go to Kansas City they had a Schmeltzer ball. All of them were sporting goods houses. Some of the balls were larger, some smaller, and no telling how good some of those boys would have been if they had had the regular ball like they do in the big leagues. And those boys were kind of tricky back in those days. If a ball club came to town that was a good-hitting ball club, they'd take a dozen balls and lay them on fifty pounds of ice and let them stay there overnight. You could hardly hit that ball out of the infield.

And all those boys used to cheat back in those days. For instance, I used to put my heel on the front of the rubber instead of putting my toe on the back. That gave me an extra foot. Instead of 60' 6", I was pitching at 59' 6". I'd cheat that much.

If you didn't have brains back in my day, you couldn't get by. We had what we called "the old angle play." When a man is stealing third base, a left-handed hitter can see the play. If the third baseman comes in to field the ball, the hitter lets it go; if he stays back to take the throw, you bunt it. We played smart baseball back in them days.

In 1924 the Monarchs played the Philadelphia Hilldales in the first Negro World Series. I never will forget. They got the bases loaded and put me in to pitch. Everybody used to cheat then. I had what they called a "half balk." There ain't no such thing as a "half balk" in baseball. It's either a balk or it's not a balk. I'd get on the mound and just bend my left knee a little, like I was going to throw home, then wheel and throw to first. Sure it's a balk, but I used to pick off a whole lot of runners that way. Anyway, the first base umpire said to me, "You have to do away with that move." I says, "Good God Almighty, something I've been doing for thirty years, they're going to take it away from me." The other umpire, Buck Freeman, says, "Hell, he's been playing like that all season." So they let me keep it.

We used to have a lot of fun, used to go out in California in the winter and play ball. For a lot of the players the first thing you're going to do is get yourself a chick for the winter. Back in those days you couldn't get a ballplayer to work in the winter. You wanted to find someone to take care of you. And that's what you needed, because you sure weren't making enough in the summer.

I wouldn't go to Florida. I heard so many funny things about the South, I didn't care to go down there. And I was afraid to go to Cuba. I had a pretty bad habit of throwing at players, and that was one thing they didn't tolerate in Cuba. If you hit a ball-player over there, they'd put you in jail. I was afraid to go down there, because I had cracked two or three of them in the States, and I think they were laying for me to go to Cuba, but I never would go.

But they had some good ball clubs out in California. One good club was the White Kings, nothing but big leaguers—Bob and Irish Meusel. I tell you who got his start out there umpiring— Beans Reardon. He used to umpire all our ball games. Harry Geisel, Barr, Majerkurth, they were all out there in '24 and '25.

Rube Marquard won nineteen straight ball games one year, and he was pitching against us. You know he had kind of a funny neck, and he twitched it like that and throwed to first base. When he threw to first, one of the boys struck at the ball!

I left the Monarchs in 1926, went to Indianapolis and then Detroit and then the Nashville Elite Giants. I played with Donn Clendenon's daddy, Nish Williams. He was a catcher with Nashville, and just like Clendenon, he was a good hitter.

Bingo DeMoss was a pretty good man. He managed the Indianapolis ABC's, and I was over there working for him. We had been out all night long, got in about six o'clock that morning. But I knew it was all right, 'cause I was out with the manager all night. So one o'clock came along, time for the ball game, I'll be doggone, that son of a bitch tossed the ball to me, said, "You're going."

"What!"

Well, we were playing the Cubans. They scored four runs off me first inning. I met him at the coach's box coming in from the pitcher's mound. He said, "Nine innings, win or lose." After that I never let DeMoss know nothing about me. He went his way and I went mine. That taught me not to fool with the boss.

Did I ever tell you what happened to me in Memphis? We went down there to play the Dixie Series. The owners split 65 percent and the players split 35 percent. So the money's got to run up in the thousands for you to make any money. When they got to the ball park the players went on strike. I am the spokesman. So I went on in to see Bubber Lewis, the owner of the Memphis ball club. I said, "Bubber, the players are dissatisfied." So he came on out to the clubhouse, said, "What about you, Hall?"

"I'm all right."

"What about you, Bill?"

"Okay with me."

He said, "Well, it looks like everyone's satisfied except you, Mr. Drake." That's the last time I ever fronted for somebody else. You look out for yourself and I'll look out for myself.

When I had the ball club in Tulsa, a boy wrote me a letter and asked me for a job. He came to the hotel one morning and said "My name is MacIntosh." I said, "Well, we work out at ten o'clock this morning." So we went out to the park and I gave him a uniform and said, "Go on out there in left field and I'll hit you some." He said, "Where's left field? I've never been in this park before."

I left baseball in '31. You know, I never traveled by bus. Kansas City had always traveled with a tourist car, a Pullman car. When buses came in, I was leaving baseball. We used to play poker on those long train rides. I was as good a poker player as I was a ballplayer. All the players used to play poker then, not for big money—they weren't making big money in those days.

After I got out of baseball, I managed a basketball team. This fellow, a bootlegger, had the money, and I gave him the idea. He bought us uniforms and an automobile, and we just jumped in that car and lit out for the South. We played colleges around Atlanta, Morehouse, Tuskegee.

I've never been out to the new park in St. Louis, I don't have time. I used to get a pass to Sportsman's Park, but since I got old, my balance is a little bad, I can't protect myself in a crowd, I can't walk up a flight of steps without something to hold on to, so I avoid crowds.

These young ballplayers, they got it easy. You know, we went to Kansas City to play in '65. I used to dress in that same clubhouse. They'd enlarged it, and you know what those ballplayers had in there? They had free access to all the soda, milk, beer and everything. There are two rubbing tables in there, just everything. And the manager has his own office in the clubhouse. We never had anything like that. If a man can't play ball now, I don't know what's wrong with him. Two or three trainers, and they still can't stay in there and pitch nine innings. And they're getting all the breaks in the world.

I was out there for a reunion, an old-timers' game. A park full of people. They say Charlie Finley's no good, but I admire him. I've never seen anybody else do that. Bell and I went up, we stopped at the best hotel in town and had a lot of fun. Finley paid all our expenses. I told them, "I got to have more expense money." They said: "Oh, that Drake. He hasn't changed a bit!"

Bill "Plunk" Drake

*Brown's Tennessee Rats, 1914. Bill Drake is
fourth from the left in the back row.*

*Bill Drake is far right in photo from 1916 in Brinsmade,
North Dakota*

Dave Malarcher

Andrew "Rube" Foster

Crush Holloway

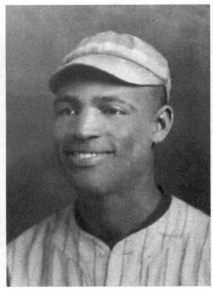

Crush Holloway

Chapter 3

DAVID MALARCHER

Scholarly, soft-spoken David Malarcher has been too long overlooked as one of the giants of black baseball. He was perhaps the finest third baseman of his day just before and after World War I—and he went on to write a record as manager that rivaled if not surpassed that of his illustrious mentor, Rube Foster. His players adored him, and even today, when old-timers gather to trade stories, Malarcher is deferred to as the dean of them all.

"He was a good man, a very good man," says out-fielder George Sweatt, who, like Malarcher, was college educated in an era when many ballplayers bordered on illiteracy. "He was more the quiet type. What I liked about him, he was a gentleman at all times. Dave didn't carouse around like the rest of the ballplayers."

"He was a very intelligent man," agrees pitcher Webster McDonald. "Used to make us go to church Sunday mornings, wherever we were. A very fine man."

Malarcher's career resembled that of his white contemporary, Bucky Harris, the good-field, no-hit, boy wonder manager who won pennants for the old Washington Senators, 1925-26.

Malarcher was even more successful as a manager. In his nine years at the head of the American Giants, he led them to the play-offs six times; to the league championship four times; and to the black world championship twice, the only years the black World Series were held while he was manager—1926 and 1927.

"Best manager I ever saw? Malarcher!" declares Alex Radcliff, who played under him in Chicago. "Because he was an intelligent man. And understanding. If you made a great catch or a great hit, he would come up and shake your hand, congratulate you, make you feel good. He was in the ballplayers' corner. He didn't let the owners of the team abuse the ballplayers. If he thought you needed a raise, he'd ask for you. Incidentally, I think that's why he quit managing. Because we wanted a raise—the ballplayers. He said to me, 'I'm giving it up because I don't like riding the buses all night.' But I couldn't see that. I think he did it because of us.

"He won so many one-run ball games with inside baseball. He said he got it from 'Rube Foster's School.' I asked him one day, I said, 'To what do you attribute your success as a manager?' And he said: 'I went to Rube Foster's School.'"

When I met Malarcher in his neat brick home in Chicago in 1970, he was well over seventy-five, yet as trim as he had been in his playing days. He could still touch his toes without bending his knees. We talked in his study, surrounded by books ranging from Emerson and Shakespeare to Zen Buddhism. With sparkling eyes and a velvet voice, he recalled a unique American life and revealed why his players almost venerated him.

David Malarcher Speaks . . .

I had the two greatest teachers, Rube Foster and C. I. Taylor, the two greatest men ever to manage. I learned from C.I. how to put a ball club in condition. And I learned from Rube how to put them in condition and then how to direct them, which makes me know that Rube was the greater of the two. Rube was a master, he was a master. After I became manager I used to win so many ball games the fans would say to me, "You're a greater manager than Rube." You know what I said? "I'm just doing what the master taught me."

I never shall forget the first time I saw Rube Foster. His team, the American Giants, came down to New Orleans in 1915 to play against the Eagles, the semipro team I played with. I never saw such a well-equipped ball club in my life! I was astounded. Every day they came out in a different set of beautiful uniforms, all kinds of bats and balls, all the best kinds of equipment.

I was born in Whitehall, Louisiana, October 18, 1894. That's a long time ago, a long, long time ago. I was born right under the Mississippi River levee, about fifty-seven miles from New Orleans and thirty to thirty-five miles from Baton Rouge, right on the river road, as we call it, Route 61.

This is my scrapbook. I got it in France in World War I. A kind French family gave it to me. I call it "A Treasury of the Beautiful." This is my mother; these are my sisters. I had seven sisters and three brothers. I was the youngest. My mother educated all of her children to some degree. They all got some education.

My mother was born in slavery. She was just a girl in the Civil War, and after that she told us she worked in the homes of the rich plantation owners. She never worked in the fields. She told me she learned to read and write from the white children she nursed. It gave her a fine background. She became a midwife and delivered many white babies up and down the river. I believe there are grown-ups down there now that might have been delivered by my mother.

My father worked at this big plantation, Charboné. They were very kind white people. Most of them were French people, Catholics. My father was the leading worker there. He worked digging ditches, planting the sugarcane and harvesting it. As little boys, my brother and I took food to him on the weekends. And when he got paid he'd take us to the big white general store and set us up on the counter, and nothing was said about it.

My family attended a church that my grandmother was one of the founders of. One of my nephews is minister there now. And we were in church every Sunday, of course. My family came under the influence of these educated ministers, so my family has always striven for education.

When I was about five or six years old my mother and father bought another home at Union, Louisiana, up the road on the Mississippi, right on the levee, to be near the country school. My sister Cathy had gone down to New Orleans to a school and came back and opened a private school right in my own house. That was the first school I attended.

It was a pleasant life. Oh yes, it was very, very pleasant. I played baseball, tops, marbles, ran in the woods, looked for rattlesnakes, swam in the Mississippi—all of the kids just lived in the river. We had a ball. It was a wonderful life.

The first baseball team I played on was down in the country, called the Baby T's. I'm sure we were very young, because that was prior to 1907. I was a catcher in those times. We played all around in the country there. And there were other boys' teams, maybe down the road, up the road. We used to go across the Mississippi to play against the small boys' team. Just a lot of baseball. My oldest brother played on the men's team, and my brother just older than I played on the big boys' team, and I was on the little boys' team. So we played baseball all our lives.

They had some fine players. There was a team in New Orleans called the Eclipse, which was a men's team, and there was another men's team at Donaldsonville, Louisiana, called the Joneses. They played all up and down Louisiana, all up and down the river. And at my home there was a team called the Pelicans; my oldest brother played on the Pelicans. There was another team at a plantation just about ten miles up the road called the Black Rappers. And there was another team called the Blue Rappers.

Dave Malarcher

All these white boys had baseball teams too, and they knew us
very well because my mother worked in their homes. Of course
we didn't socialize with the whites, but there was never any
trouble that put fear into us like certain places in Mississippi
where white people were mean to Negroes. That made a difference, it made a difference in your life. I remember once after I
was grown I made a trip down to see my mother in the country.
One of these white boys about my age knew about me up here
in Chicago playing baseball, and when he saw me on the road
he ran to me to shake my hand. All of a sudden it occurred to
him, the difference between us, and he just stood there and

smiled and laughed, he was so glad to see me.

When you come up among kind white people, where you didn't have all these problems, you don't feel any different. I never think of myself as colored. I mean, I'm in business here in Chicago, I'm a real estate broker, and when I go down to the Chicago Title and Trust Company, they accept you as a good broker. I have never had the feeling that Negroes have—that people *think* Negroes have. It never bothered me, not a bit, not in my life!

Now I have felt as free all of my life as I feel now. And I've never worried about it like people think most Negroes worry about the problem. I went to good schools, had white teachers from the North. That is where they say Negro schools were founded—by whites in the North, from the churches, you know. Methodist churches, Congregational churches, churches that came down there right after the Civil War. They founded these associations to work for the education of the Negro. And they founded New Orleans University and Strait College and Talladega and all of the other great Negro schools. They were white, and of course they had problems with the white people, because they were sort of ostracized. But because we associated with them, we had no feeling of being inferior. They treated us as equals.

I went to New Orleans University in 1907. I was in grade school then. For a number of summers I'd come home and work in the rice fields with the other boys. And I was so strong that when I went to New Orleans the city boys didn't have a chance against me in athletics. It was because of that country upbringing.

In New Orleans I worked for a rich white family. I worked in the mornings and afternoons cleaning the yard, a yardman as we called it. I was living on the place, had all the food I could eat, and in the summer they'd give me clothes. Most boys who went to college in those days lived right out in the rich neighborhood, with the rich white people. I was making $2.50 a week, but with food and clothing and a place to stay, and doctors' bills if necessary, that kept me in school.

Strait College and New Orleans University were founded about 1869, one by the Methodist Church and one by the Congregational Church. They operated all through those years, for seventy years, and then they merged to form Dillard University.

That's where I met my wife. These are all pictures of my wife down through the years. Here's her family. You can see they were proud, well-educated people. She had a beautiful voice, she could have been an opera singer. Gorgeous voice. Everybody that heard her would tell you this. She was a great church worker, taught Sunday school and taught in the public school. Here's a picture of her quartet group. They traveled in the summer for Strait University all through the North.

Of course I played ball at school, from 1913 to 1916. Here's a book with the history of New Orleans University. It says, "Between 1913 and 1916 the baseball team lost not a single game." That's right. "The success was due to two stars, David Malarcher and Robert Williams, who acted as coaches." It says my nickname was Gentleman Dave: "Malarcher went directly from the campus into professional baseball in Indianapolis."

C. I. Taylor's Indianapolis ABC's had been to Cuba during the winter of 1915 and '16, and they barnstormed back through New Orleans and played against my city team, the Eagles. Their second baseman, Bingo DeMoss, had left, and the ABC's needed a second baseman. They saw me play and offered me a job. When C.I. offered me $50 a month, that was a lot of money. I could give my mother half and still get along. So I went with him that summer, and went to school in the winter.

When I first came to Indianapolis, we played in the old (white) Federal League park. The Federal League had disbanded, as you know. It was a big park, a good playing field and a good big grandstand. Later on they tore that down and we played in the American Association team's park, Wylie Field. We played a lot of games there.

I made three plays in my career when the fans came out and carried me around on their shoulders. One was in Detroit, one was in Chicago and one was in California. The game in Detroit was my first year, 1916. I was playing outfield. If you ever go to Detroit, if you look in the Detroit *Free Press* in 1916, you will probably find it in the record. We were barnstorming against the American Giants, and we played in Detroit in Navin Field, the

Tigers' park. Bruce Petway was the guy that hit the ball, one of those long drives, a hard, long, high fly. I guess I nearly ran a mile. I finally reached up and caught it with one hand, my left hand, over my right shoulder. We played sixteen innings 1–1 and it was called on account of darkness. We had white umpires, and they made quite a few mistakes, we thought. We didn't argue with them, but after the game they came in and said, "Definitely, fellows, we made some mistakes, but we have never seen this kind of baseball before." The next morning the newspaper came out and said that if the National and American leagues could play this kind of baseball that we saw today, they would have to enlarge their seating capacity. That is in the record.

Now I kept that clipping for a long time. Maybe about eight or ten years ago I gave it to a friend, a reporter. He was going to make use of it, because one time we played in an old-timers' game at Cubs Park. The Old-Timers' Association took us all in. When they took Negroes in the major leagues, they took us in the Old-Timers' Association. So they invited us out as a group, and this particular year we played an old-timers' game. They wanted to write us up, you know, publicize the game, and the reporter came out to ask me about my records. I told him about this day, and he said, "You know, that's significant, what that paper said. You know what it meant? That reporter back there was telling the American and National leagues then that they should put Negroes in the major leagues." "If the American and National leagues could play this kind of ball, they would have to enlarge their seating capacity." But nothing, of course, was done. The white fans missed all that. They missed it.

Another of the three plays during my career when the fans came out and carried me around on their shoulders was in Chicago. We were playing the Kansas City Monarchs, and I think they had the bases loaded in the ninth inning with Big T. J. Young up, a good hitter, a catcher. He hit a line drive—wheee— over my head, breaking to my right. I had to jump and reach over and get it. That was the end of the ball game, and the people came out of the grandstands and got me and carried me around. It was a thrill. Many people say, in cases like that, "Well, it was an accident." But it wasn't an accident. You see, I had to be thinking, I had to be fast and I had to know what I was doing. I had to go up and I had not only to put my hand up, I had to reach over my head. I was thinking, it wasn't an accident.

The third great catch I made, I was playing shortstop in California, one of those games against the major leaguers. We had been sent for to come out and boost the Los Angeles White Sox, a colored team, to play against those big leaguers. Well, the ball was hit over second base, and I had to go way back and around, circle the ball and toss it back this way, underhanded and backwards to second base, and it was a double play.

Well, in 1917 and 1918 they were calling me the best third baseman in the world. Another time I raised a lot of cain was when we were playing the Cubans in 1918 in Kokomo. This was a twilight game at Kokomo, and you know there are very few colored people in Kokomo. Just masses of white people out there, and they loved the ABC's. C.I. loved to win in Kokomo; that was his territory. We were playing the Cuban Stars, and it was getting late in the afternoon. They had us one run behind in the ninth, and it was getting dark. I came to bat in the ninth inning and tripled. Rodriguez was the Cubans' catcher, kind of a proud fellow, a big tall fellow—a good catcher. Anyway, I was on third, the pitcher pitched, and I didn't even give Rodriguez time to throw it back. When he lobbed the ball back, I went home. Safe. On the first throw back to the pitcher—he didn't have any idea that I was going home. I took the chance, because the next guy might fly out, then we would lose the ball game. C.I. was so happy, he ran out and grabbed me and kissed me. He gave me five dollars right there on the field—five dollars was a lot of money in those days

I was drafted in 1918. I was in college then, playing baseball in the summer, but I didn't try to get out of it: I went to war. Here's an interesting picture; this is when we were drafted in Indianapolis. They took seven of us together. It broke up the team, really. We went in August to the war.

I was in the 309th Pioneers. Here is a picture taken Christmas Day in 1918 in St. Luce, France. See, my outfit didn't get to the front lines. We landed in France around September or October in 1918, when the war was almost over. It just happened that we were out walking on Armistice Day and of course everybody, every Frenchman, welcomed us, and we went in and met this family. They were fine people, and here's a picture that they made with me. This is one of the girls and this is the other daughter. And here's a picture when they invited a couple of us soldiers up for luncheon. We had it right out in the back yard, a beautiful rose garden—lovely country, you know. This little drawing was done by one of the girls.

After the war I played ball in the AEF League—the American Expeditionary Forces—and I traveled all through the AEF. I was very fortunate, I had a lot of nice experiences.

Do you know where I was when I got my first letter from Rube Foster? I was in France. I had been C.I.'s third baseman. The papers were saying I was the greatest at third base. They knew I was—C.I. knew I was, Rube knew I was. I'm in my bunk in St. Luce, France, and they bring me a letter from Rube Foster, back in the United States, telling me he wanted me to play with him when I got back.

When I got out of the Army, times were rough. The Army gave me $60 and nothing else. That was standard. They sent me back to Indianapolis, where I had left from, and I had $60—not enough to even buy civilian clothes. So I went to C.I. and said, "Well, here I am back home. I want to go and see my mother and my girl friend. I've been away a long time from the folks down South, and I need $75." Well, C.I. kind of hesitated a little bit. I guess C.I. had had a little difficulty with some of the ballplayers, letting them have a little money. They probably didn't show up afterwards, didn't appreciate it, so he said, "Naturally, when you put out money like that in the winter time, you just don't know what will be the result. . . ."

So the next morning I just took the train and came on to Chicago. I knew where Rube lived, and I went to see him, down on the 32nd block of Vernon Avenue. He was sitting at a big rolltop desk. He always had a rolltop desk. I said, "Well, I came to see you Jock"—all of the ballplayers called him Jock. He was such a fine guy. We talked a little and I said, "Well, the thing I came to tell you is I'm just out of the Army and I don't have any money, and

I want to go to see my mother and my sweetheart in New
Orleans. I would like to borrow $75." Same as I'd asked C.I. He
just rolled up the top of that desk and reached in the drawer:
"There it is." He gave it to me just like that. He didn't ask any
questions, he didn't say whether he wanted me to play with him
or not. Smart enough to know that that's it: I've got me a ballplayer. He didn't even talk contracts or anything. That's all, we
talked about other things. Oh God, it really broke my heart to
see an honest man. Well, you know a grateful heart. . . .

So I went on home. During the winter he wrote and said he
would like for me to come to Chicago if I wanted to come, and
offered me a contract. He offered me $150 a month. That was a
lot of money then, a big salary. I said okay.

That's the difference. Rube was just a great guy.

Through the years I got raises, and when I left I was getting
$600 a month.

This is a picture of the American Giants in 1920. We had
Jimmy Lyons, Cristobel Torrienti and Jelly Gardner in the outfield. They were all fast. We had George Dixon and Jim Brown
catching. Brown was fast, could push and bunt, and hit too. He
played first base and caught. I was on third, I'm fast. Bobby
Williams shortstop, real fast. Bingo DeMoss second, he's fast.
Leroy Grant playing first base was the only slow man on the
team. He usually hit way down by the pitcher. Tom Williams
was pitching, plus Otis Starks, a left-hander, and Dave Brown, a
great left-hander.

From 1920, when the league started, the first four years we
had a powerful team, a powerful team. Because we had gotten
together the speed, the daring, the men that could really hit, a
good pitching staff, good catching. See, Rube was smart enough,
a genius, to know how to pick men to fit into his plays, and he
used to say all the time, "If you haven't got intelligence enough
to fit into this play, you can't play here." That's all there was to
it. It isn't generally known, but Rube was so superior in his knowledge of baseball that from 1920 to 1923, the first four years of
the league, we were so far out in front of the league by July,
they had to break the season up into two halves so there would
be interest in the league the second half. Rube was so superior

in management that he got to the point that he just didn't cover up his signals a all. He just got so that he would give them openly. And of course the other ball clubs were smart enough to watch and see what was going on.

We traveled always in Pullman cars, not these buses that people go in. Whenever we were in Pittsburgh, for example, and he wanted to be in Chicago for the next day, Rube would just call up the railroad and have them put on an extra sleeping car for us. We were well rested when we got there. In the morning we'd get up and have our breakfast in a private car right from the diner. See, we were in shape to play baseball the next day. When the guys were traveling in buses, that's when I got out of baseball, when they started that stuff, riding all night. Rube was high class in every way. He really was. Now some of the players that we would meet would tell us about the hardships they had and so forth—and they did—but I never experienced that until after Robert Cole and those people got the American Giants, and that is when I quit. With Rube and C.I. everything was high class. I got my money every first and fifteenth of the month.

I became manager after Rube went to the hospital in 1926. Rube had broken up the team that spring and left only Gardner, Jim Brown and myself. Just the three of us who had been with the team from 1920. I was made captain in the spring, and when Rube became sick and went to the hospital it was about mid-season, just about the end of the first half of that season, and I was made manager. Well, I knew his system, having observed it and seen the results of all that he did. All the time I managed the American Giants I was never out of my seat on the bench, not a day, not a ball game. Every play started with me. And the ballplayers liked it. You have no trouble directing them if they know you are smarter than they are. Why? Because when that man is under direction, he doesn't have to figure, "What should I do now?" All he has to do is execute. If you know what to tell him to do, and he gets a great deal of success out of it, every time he comes up he's looking for the order. He's looking for it. Every play started with me. That's the way Rube did it, and that's the way I did it.

I was very fortunate that Jelly and Jim Brown were left on the team. With those two men as a nucleus, I made them fit into the team. They were getting on the bases, and every time they got on the bases, the other ball club was in trouble. That's why I say Gardner and Brown were very valuable to me. Very valuable.

We won the pennant in the West that year, and the Bacharach Giants won in the East. We were playing them in the World Series. Jelly Gardner was on first base, and I was at bat. I was a switch hitter, and I was hitting left-hand at this time. No one knew how I gave signals when I was at bat. Cummings was playing first for the Bacharachs, and he figured I was going to bunt with Jelly on first, a fast man, speed. So we put on the hit-and-run play, and when he charged in to get the bunt I hit a line drive by his ear! If it had been straight at him it would have knocked him out. Jelly scored all the way to the plate.

You see, the thing that makes a hitter so much more valuable when he plays a diversified game is that always the opposition is thrown off guard as to what you will do. They can't stand back on the grass and wait for you to hit a hard liner on the ground that's easy to handle. Professional ballplayers like that, you know, because, look, the ball is down there in a minute and all they have to do is field it and throw it over there. But if a man can hit the ball hard and do all of these other things too, they don't know where to stand.

You know about Turkey Stearnes? Great outfielder, fast man, good hitter. When we played against him up in Detroit, he was a trick for us. Our pitchers—Willie Foster, Willie Powell, those fellows—used to strike Turkey Stearnes out like nothing. But some of the teams in the league didn't know how to pitch to him, and naturally he did a lot of hitting. Well, he finally came to the American Giants to play with us. He was fast, I knew that. One day I said to Turkey, "Now that you're here, we are going to diversify your play." He'd been a slugger, hit a lot of home runs. But I said, "If a guy, at the wrong time, just happens to hit a fast ball to the infield, it's a double play." I said, "You have to fit into our plays." So I knew that he was fast, and I would make him bunt quite a few times. I'd tell him exactly where I wanted him to lay it down: "Let the pitcher field this one. I don't want the third baseman, I want the pitcher to come over and get it."

Well, this particular day, we had a man on first and a man on second, and we needed two runs to win the ball game, one to tie and two to win. Turkey comes to bat, and he loved the crowd. The crowd's cheering—clap, clap, clap. This is Stearnes, the great slugger, you know. And I said, "Now, Turkey, I want you to lay this right down on the third base line. I want the third baseman to field it, not the pitcher, because then he can't get the man out on third." He said, "Okay, Cap."

So Turkey comes to the plate, people cheering, you know. The man pitched him a perfect ball to bunt, right down by the knees. He acted like he was going to bunt, but he didn't. He looked up at me, I gave him the signal again: "Same thing." The man pitched him another good one to bunt, but he didn't bunt. He looked up, figured, "He's bound to tell me to hit now," because he had confidence he could knock it out of the stadium.

He looked over at me and I said, "You come on down a peg, come on out." Of course he looked worried, being taken out of the ball game. That broke his pride. He came over and sat down right by my side and I said to Powell, the pitcher, "You go up there and lay this one down." He did, the next man singled, and we scored a run.

I didn't say a word to Turkey. After a while he said, "Cap, I really was going to lay that next one down." I said, "I knew you were, Turk." And I never had to tell him again. He developed into a really great diversified player after that. Turkey could bunt, and he could pull them down to first base—and fly—and then when his time to hit came, he could really plaster them.

During those times all ballplayers developed to a high point of professionalism. I look at some of the players that are supposed to be good ballplayers today, and they are hitting balls down at their toes sometimes, over their heads, way outside. In those days the balls had to be in there for those guys. They would have to be strikes. They were really professionals. None of that swinging like amateurs. As Rube said, "The easiest way in the world to get out is to strike out." I doubt very seriously if I ever struck out in a ball game. A professional ballplayer ought to be able to hit the ball, whether it goes fair or not. You should make contact. You know, hit it someplace. And with men on the bases, Rube could depend on me to hit that ball and hit it hard somewhere, not to strike out. That pitch had to come in there. And I would hit it, because if you hit it, it may go safe. But if you just strike out, the catcher is going to get that. That's professionalism, and that's what those fellows were then.

In my case, I learned from Rube that the best thing to hit is the best ball. You know, not to hit at a bad ball. The only time I swung when it was the least bit off the plate was the third strike, so that I wouldn't get called out on strikes. I never let myself be called out. But the pitcher had to pitch until I got two strikes. He had to come in there.

I used to slide headfirst quite often. I didn't try to slide high. The easiest way to get safe is to slide as low as you can. But ballplayers get the idea that if you slide a little bit high once or twice, you are rough. Naturally I was trying to get safe all the time, but I wasn't really trying to hurt anybody at all.

Years after I had gotten out of baseball, I was walking down 61st Street here one day. I passed the barbershop and the fellow saw me going by and said, "Hey, you're Dave Malarcher, third baseman for the American Giants. Come in here." He said, "You don't know me, but I'm one of your fans. I was a real good friend of one of your pitchers, Tom Johnson. I used to see you out there, gentlemanly-looking little fellow." Yes, that's what he told me— "gentlemanly-looking little fellow"—"and I would say to Tom, 'Tom, this little fellow, sometimes I feel sorry for him out there with all of those great big guys ripping and running and jumping. I feel sorry.' So Tom said, 'What! You feel sorry for *him*? *They* better get out of *his* way. Don't you feel sorry for him any more!' "

I played third base eighteen or nineteen years, and I never paid too much attention to the other fellows sliding into me at third. I always tried to keep the runner in front of me as much as possible. If you keep him in front of you, you can see him easier. But I've been spiked several times. I broke my shoulder once to prevent a guy from getting to third on a bunted ball, but I put him out.

Two games I took part in are very significant. One was in

Detroit in 1916, which I told you about. The other was when I was managing the American Giants in 1932. Leo Durocher came down with his major league all-stars and played us in Cincinnati. We beat them 2–0. That was Leo's first acquaintance with Negro ballplayers, I'm sure. Jim Weaver, who used to pitch for the Cubs, pitched for Leo's team that day.

Remember Steve O'Neill, the catcher? Well, he was manager of the Toledo team, and I think they finished on top one season, and Steve was being heralded as a truly great manager. It was the year before he went up to manage Brooklyn. We played his team in Toledo. And when we came out that day to talk to the umpire before the game, you know, to check the ground rules, Steve just walked around like it was a common thing to be up there playing against a Negro team. So the first game we beat them 3–0, I think. The next day we beat them 2–0. We beat them three days without a run—they didn't get a run. After that Steve was friendly. But the papers didn't say too much about it. They carried it, but not much.

I have had so many white people tell me that they saw me play, that I should be in the major leagues. And if I should be in there, what about Cristobel Torrienti, Oscar Charleston and those really outstanding stars? I say that the ballplayers I'm telling you about are of the caliber in baseball of Jack Johnson and Joe Louis and Rafer Johnson in the world of athletics. They are the tops. Now those fellows proved that they were tops in all these fields. And even in science, you have some men in science who have measured up, you know. So when you talk about great Negro baseball players, you're talking about the tops.

When they admitted Roy Campanella to the Hall of Fame, he said he couldn't even carry a glove with Josh Gibson. Well, he should know that Josh Gibson wasn't the only catcher we had. He should have seen Bruce Petway! He was a great, a *great* ballplayer.

We could have had two ball clubs in the major leagues through the years that would have made it. Now, if we had picked a Negro team for the major leagues in those days, we wouldn't have had weaklings, we would have had the stars, because we would have had all the Negro stars to pick from. Just like when you picked the major league teams, you picked the best from all of the race. If we'd picked a Negro major league team, we would have been picking the best from all our teams. For example, we would have had DeMoss at second, Pop Lloyd at short, Petway catching. We would have had Dave Brown as pitcher, Frank Wickware, Bullet Rogan. We wouldn't have had a weak man on the team. All through the years we could have had a ball club that probably could have won the pennant in the major league. All Negroes. Do you see what I'm trying to say?

Well, let's look at today. In the major leagues today there are many outstanding stars. They're Negroes too, just like we were. I guarantee you, from my knowledge of baseball, I *guarantee* you, that if we had gotten in there in our times, in Rube's time, we would have had some real stars in there. Because Rube knew that if we organized a league and tried to measure up to big-league baseball standards, we would get our chance. That was his aim, to organize. And we had to have high standards. All we were waiting for was an opportunity to get in, and it finally came.

Fortunately for us, it came not too late, because Negro baseball was starting to deteriorate. The new owners that came after Rube's time did not know the value of having high-class athletes and treating them as such. They were riding them all night in those buses to break them down. It's fortunate that the major leagues let us in when they did, because under Cole and those people, they drove all night, didn't eat, didn't sleep at all. The standards were being lowered. So we were very fortunate that integration didn't come too late.

Harry Heilmann, who played with Detroit, made up an all-star team every year. I doubt that I can remember any of them other than Harry, but I think I could get records on that. Finally Judge Landis stopped him from playing against the American Giants. He said he couldn't afford to have them beaten by us, it was bad publicity.

Now I know this, that Donie Bush, who played shortstop for the Detroit Tigers, used to come home to Indianapolis every fall, and he was making all the stops between Detroit with the ABC's. The box scores and Indianapolis *Star* down there would show the players who played on each team and the results. Those records are available. There are many sources. You will be able to see who the players were and make comparisons. So there are many ways of proving it, many ways.

Certainly the big leaguers played hard. They wanted to win, of course they did.

Propaganda is a terrible thing. The propaganda of segregation and bigotry is evil. It deceives people. I used to have Negroes occasionally tell me, "Do you think Negroes can play in the major leagues?" And do you know what I would say to them? "Do you think so and so here, who is a barber, can cut hair like a white man?" I would say, "Do you think Doctor so-and-so, who is teaching in a medical school, can teach a white professor?" Well, certainly. And I would say, "What's baseball that I can't play it like a white?" And I used to say occasionally that if they say that the Negro is nearest to the savage, I think he would play better than a white, because baseball is only running and jumping and swinging a stick. He would be better. But the whole point is that the propaganda of keeping the Negro out of the major leagues made even some of the Negroes think that we didn't have the ability. It started them to thinking it too. But I said, "Just wait until we do get in there, and see what happens." And they used to ask me, "When do you think we will get in?" And I said, "When we can prove to the white man that we can bring him something, that's when we will get in there."

And that's what did it. The East-West games really did it, when the whites saw 50 to 60,000 people out there. You see, all they used to see was 10 to 12,000 at our games at the most. Well, that isn't much use. But when they saw an East-West game, that was the greatest thing in the history of Negro ball that took place after Rube Foster. Branch Rickey had more to offer those sixteen white owners than just the black boy. He had all those black fans.

Did you read the statement that Ford Frick made when they were fixing to boycott Jackie Robinson in St. Louis? I thought it was beautiful. The players were fixing to strike, you know. Frick said, "If you do, then you'll be barred from the league." I said, "What a man!" He stopped it. This was the United States of America, and every citizen had a right to play.

Occasionally when I'm in the streets I meet some of the old fans, you know, and they say, "Hello, Dave," and I don't even know them. And they say, "My goodness, you look like you could play third base right today." And do you know what I say to them? I say, "I quit in 1934 and I haven't run a step since." But I weigh 140—that's less than my playing weight. Do I look like I'm seventy-six? Every morning I touch my toes without bending my knees. I take care of myself. I don't eat any sugar. I eat three times a day, nonfattening food. I know what to eat.

I love to write, poetry in particular. After my wife died in 1946, it was such a shock that I went right into writing poetry, and from that time until now I have written innumerable poems, and this year I am going to try to publish some of them. I write about everything, everything. I'm versatile. I have many, many small short poems, and some are really long ones. A few years ago I belonged to a poetry club, and they used to come into the meetings and they would have those two-line two-verse poems, and I would come in with ten, twenty and thirty verses—long ones. Well, if you don't know much, you can't write much. Here's my longest one: *The Epic of the Second World Conflict: Man, War and the Gods. Poetic thesis on war and violent revolutions.* I was sixteen years writing that. This is the one I told you about, where I quote MacArthur shaking like a wind storm.

One I wrote after I went to a ball game in 1948 to see some of the Negro players who made the major leagues. It was written in a melancholy moment when I thought of the host of Negro players now deceased—the great ones whom the great majority of America's fans did not see. I compared them to the beautiful jungle orchids that bloom and die without ever being seen.

Dave Malarcher

Chapter 4

CRUSH HOLLOWAY

Old-time black players unanimously agree that Crush Holloway was the roughest base runner in the old Negro leagues. As little Jake Stephens—shortstop, base runner, raconteur—puts it: "By *God*! You'd be committing hara-kiri to get in the way of Crush Holloway or Jimmy Lyons. They'd cut you to death. I mean, they'd sharpen their spikes before they went out on the ball field. Like Cobb."

Pitcher Bill Foster nods: "Crush Holloway was fast. He was rough too. He'd put his spikes right here, in your mouth, if you opened it. But he was always nice. He'd hurt you, then jump up and say, 'Man, I'm sorry.' I'd say, 'Get out of here, Holloway.'"

Holloway was a fine fielder too. Against a big-league all-star team in 1928, his one-hand catch of George Maisel's fly in the ninth inning saved two runs as the Baltimore Black Sox beat Lefty Grove 9–3. That same year he raced in to make a sensational shoestring catch of a Texas leaguer in short left field with men on first and third and two out. His catch saved at least one run, as the Black Sox won again, 2–1.

The Crush Holloway I met in Baltimore in 1969 was quite different from what I had expected. Instead of an ogre, I found a disarming man in shirt sleeves standing among racks of coats and dresses in his small tailor shop in Baltimore's ghetto. Still spare and trim at the age of almost eighty, he chuckled frequently as he conjured up the memories of so many years ago, punctuating his narrative with loud hisses from his old-fashioned foot-operated pressing machine, while behind the counter his wife laughed silently with him as the stories unfolded. My last talk with Holloway came in his hospital room two months before his death from cancer in June 1972.

Crush Holloway Speaks . . .

Stealing? Oh, I was pretty good. That's what they say anyway. Yeah, I made them jump down there on second base. They were scared of me 'cause I'd say, "I'm gonna jump on you." I wouldn't really jump on them, just try to scare them; I didn't want to hurt anybody. But I filed my spikes, that's true. Most fast men used to do that. We didn't intend to hurt anybody, though, just scare them, that's all.

Naw, I wouldn't hurt anybody for anything in the world. Unless it's *necessary*. Now you see, the only place you could score was home plate. All those other bases were just temporary. But if someone gets in your way there—at home plate—when you're trying to get there [laughs], you'd jump every way—you're trying to score! Yeah, better get out of the way—you're *coming*! Coming in there. That was baseball in those days.

I see these catchers block home plate now, it's pitiful. Get in front of it and block it. If you slide, you're never going to get to home plate, you have to slide around him because he's in front of it. How you going to hook slide into home plate? You'll never get there. Never. So you go in there with two feet—rough. You run over them—you don't slide—you run over them, just keep a-running. Run all up on his arms, knock the ball out of his arms.

I remember one time the catcher for the Harrisburg Giants got the ball and came up the line, see. He shouldn't have done that. He should have stayed back there at home plate. When he

Crush Holloway

came up the line, that's when I had to do a little dirty work. No, I didn't hurt him, I didn't cut him. I just knocked his mitt and mask off, turned his chest protector around, left him sitting there on home plate. In my day those catchers learned not to block home plate on you. Those catchers respected you in those days!

Baseball's so gentlemanfied now. They don't jump at you, don't cut you, don't do anything—just slide in there and let the man put you out. The man's holding the ball down here at the base and they just slide into it. We'd go into the base with our heels up like that: kick it with our feet, knock it out of his hand. These players today slide with their hands first. We never slid with our hands. That's dangerous. A man can step on them trying to catch the ball. So there are all kinds of tricks, you know.

They don't play it now like they used to. We played with the heart. Today they play it for money. They don't hustle like they used to. We'd do everything to win.

Frank Robinson plays that same way. He'd hurt you too, yeah, he'd hurt you. But in a nice way. You don't try to cut anybody up or put him out of baseball. Some of those boys were mean. They would cut you, then get up and fight you. I wouldn't do that. I would jive, I'd say, "Oh man, I'm sorry. Go on, get up." Brush him off. See, I didn't want to hurt anybody. They were making a living like I was. But we played rough in those days— rough.

Yeah, I ran against big leaguers—Mickey Cochrane—I ran against anybody, I didn't care who they were. See, you steal on the pitcher, you don't steal on the catcher. Study the pitcher's moves. Any ordinary catcher can throw you out if the ball gets to him on time. Lefty Grove had a fair move, nothing great. Eddie Rommel had a great move though. These pitchers today don't have no kind of move. That's why Maury Wills stole so many bases off them.

My hero was Ty Cobb. Ever since I was ten years old. That's why I ran bases like I did. His picture used to come in Bull Durham tobacco. Showed the way he'd slide. That was my hero. I said, "I want to slide like Ty Cobb. I want to run bases like him." That's what made me try to run bases. I always had that image —Ty Cobb. My hitter was Home Run Baker. He didn't hit but eleven home runs in one season, but he was a good hitter. I said, "I want to hit like Home Run Baker." That was my hero too, and Ty Cobb was my man on the bases. That's what I loved. 'Cause I got all those pictures there in that Bull Durham tobacco. You don't remember that, you're too young, you don't know nothing about that.

Crush, that's my real name, that ain't no nickname. And I'll tell you how I got it. The day I was born, September 16, 1896, down in Hillsboro, Texas, my father was fixing to go see a "crash," a collision. They'd take two old locomotive engines and crash them together for excitement, sort of a fair, and my father was going to see it. Before he got on the train, somebody pulled him off and said, "Your wife is about to have a child." And when I turned out to be a boy, he named me "Crush." That's how I got my name. Oh, I've got some middle names—Crush Christopher Columbus Holloway—but I don't use those other names. I just use Crush, 'cause I like Crush better.

I was born in Hillsboro and raised in Waco. I started playing baseball on the sandlots, playing every Sunday if I could get off from home. Had to slip off early in the morning, you know, 'cause my parents wouldn't let me play Sundays. We'd play on those little lots, all the boys would get together and play all day long Sunday, two or three different games, until the sun went down. That's how I started. I just always liked baseball. I wanted to be a ballplayer.

We used to make our own balls in the country: twine and wrapping. We called them "card balls" in those days. We used to play with a nickel ball; after one game it was flat. That's why we bought a 25¢ ball, a pretty good ball. When you bought a 50¢ ball, that lasted, oh, five or six games. Then we got that $1.25 ball, that was for a whole season.

I loved baseball. Out in them cotton fields I used to take a broomstick and take a whole pile of little rocks and hit. Imagination: That was a big deal. I'd hit a home run or a pop-up. Pop said, "If you don't come in here, boy . . . out there in that dark." Just hitting those pebbles, you know? Imagination.

Don't tell me about working those cotton fields! My daddy had me out there early in the morning, getting them cows and things up. At sunrise we'd be in the field plowing. Oh that was big cotton—that was producing things down there then. Cotton and corn, wheat, all that stuff. My father owned the farm. He was a schoolteacher.

I was the oldest boy, see. Had five sisters, but they couldn't do nothing on the farm. I was the only boy he could depend on, you know what I mean? I had brothers, but they were so young, ten to twelve years younger than me. They couldn't do anything. That's why Pop would depend on me. I was his man, had to do everything. That's what I did until I got grown.

In the First World War I wanted to go in the Army so bad! I wanted to get away from that farm. The county sent thirty-one boys to the draft board, nothing but country boys. But two of us they sent back. Oh, we were physically fit. They examined me, I was 5'11½" in my stocking feet, perfect health—had to be perfect out in the country. But the quota was filled, see. Then they sent us back to the Army again. But by that time the armistice was signed, so they didn't take me again. I wanted to go in the Army so bad. That farm was *something* on me!

I didn't leave until I was twenty-one. My father said, "You're a grown man, you can do what you want to do, but I want you to stay here with me." I said, "*No!* I'm going to play baseball." I said, "That's the end of it, Pop. I got to go." He was a good father, didn't try to hold me. He knew I did my chores right. So he let me go.

I started out playing professional ball in 1919 in San Antone, Texas. It's a long story. A man named Franks from Waco—a white man, had a restaurant—he had organized us as the Waco Black Navigators. We played about three months, but every time we tried to play somewhere it rained, rained, rained. He lost all his money. A man named Moore came through looking for ball-players and Franks said, "I'll sell you the whole club. I got to get my money back." He cried when we left. So Moore bought the club out, sent us to San Antone. We were the San Antone Black Aces. The first stop he sent us to was Wichita Falls, and it was a month before we got back to San Antone. That's how the club started, 1919–20.

We had Biz Mackey catching—he was great. Highpockets Hudspeth on first base, I was second, Namon Washington in short, Henry Blackman on third—Blackman was a great third baseman too.

The Aces played in the white Texas League and Southern League parks—Dallas, Fort Worth, Houston, Beaumont, Wichita Falls. That's why those boys from Texas could play so good, they had good grounds. Not like out East, where they had to play on those little old lots. In the Texas League they had a turtle back diamond; the mound was high, and it kind of rolled down from the pitcher's box to the infield. The ball could hop off there and come down at you.

Mackey and about six other guys went up to Indianapolis in 1920. Old man Bellinger—Charlie Bellinger, he was a rich millionaire—was a politician in San Antone. He was a friend of C. I. Taylor of the Indianapolis ABC's, and he'd look out for ballplayers for him. Let me see: Mackey, Blackman, Hudspeth, Washington and about two other players—Morris Williams and

Crush Holloway, Indianapolis ABCs, 1923, back row on right

Crush Holloway stands at far right with the Indianapolis ABC's. Also in the top row are Ben Taylor, Biz Mackey, and Oscar Charleston, #2-3-4. The park is the old Federal League Park.

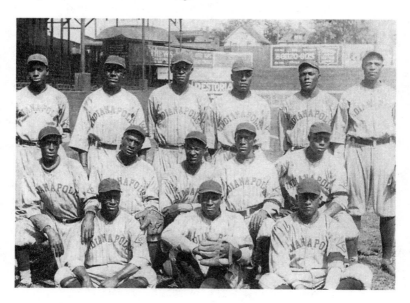

Bob McClure—went up to Indianapolis that year. It broke our club all to pieces. I didn't go that year. I didn't want to go 'cause I was mad. I was so mad I didn't know what to do.

The next year C. I. Taylor sent for me to join his team, and that was the greatest team I ever played on.

C. I. Taylor taught me how to run. I used to lead off or hit second. In my early years I was lead-off mostly. I used to hit the ball to the infield and get thrown out on first base like this: slap-slap. When I came back to the bench, C.I. said, "Young man, you ain't running." I said to myself, "I must *be* running." My fault was I'd watch the ball for a second after I hit it. That's how I lost that step. After that when I hit it I'd just shoot right on out there—*run!* Then I'd start beating them out like this: slap-slap.

C.I. converted me to an outfielder. See, we had a boy there played second base I couldn't even touch: Connie Day. One of our *great* second baseman.

I call the 1922 ABC's the best team I ever played with. They had somebody who could do everything. Six good pitchers. Mackey and Mac Eggelston were the catchers. Ben Taylor first base, Connie Day second, Morty Clark shortstop, and Blackman third. I call that the million-dollar infield. I wouldn't call the outfield a million dollars, because I was on it. But it was a great outfield too. Had some good hitters, everybody could hit that ball. I was in right, Namon Washington in left, and Oscar Charleston in center.

Charleston was the best defensive outfielder I've seen. Good judge of a ball. He'd turn his back and when he'd turn around, that ball was right there. And he was fast, oh yes, he was a fast man. But if he had time to get under a fly ball, he'd walk—he had it timed, he'd walk fast. And he'd do acrobatics. People used to come out and see him do his stunts in the outfield. And he was a great hitter too—hit lots of home runs.

In '24 we came out East here to the Baltimore Black Sox. George Rossiter had the team here. Great man, George. I don't know if he was an Irishman or what. He had a big restaurant —seafood. We were all in California that winter, and he sent all that money to get us, said, "I don't care what the price is, there's something I want." That's when we left California, the whole ball club almost, about eight of us. They paid us so much money. We were getting $170–175 out there, came out here and got 350–375. Man, you know we were going to come here!

Peter Hill got the ballplayers together. He was managing the Cleveland Tate Stars until Rossiter contacted him and got us all together. We got here the first of April, 1924. For two weeks it was the biggest snow I've ever seen in my life. All the racetracks were closed—Bowie, Laurel, all those places closed up. We stayed in Tom Smith's hotel for two weeks. It was a month before we started to train.

Pete Hill was our manager in '24 and '25. And a great manager. Played too, played left field. He was a left-handed hitter, hit to left field. Yeah, he's the man taught me how to hit to left field. I was pulling the ball. Ball on the outside, I was pulling to right. He gave me a bigger bat, see: "Now knock that third baseman down. Just step up in front of the plate, hit the ball out in front, see?" Oh, he was a great hitter.

We played the major leaguers down here in Baltimore every fall starting in 1926. We only played on Sundays, a double-header every Sunday for about three or four weeks until it got too cold to play. Then the boys would go to California or Cuba for the winter.

They'd bring Lefty Grove, Mickey Cochrane, Jimmy Foxx, Goose Goslin and Hack Wilson. Only man ever beat us was Eddie Rommel. We beat Lefty Grove twice, and he wouldn't come back any more. He says he doesn't remember? He's kidding. He can remember. He was a great pitcher though. I didn't get any hits off him. He didn't give up but a few hits. We won one game with about three hits and the next one with four. He struck out eight or nine. But he was wild, and that's the way we beat him in those days. He was with the Baltimore Orioles then, and he had a catcher named Ducky Smith from the International League. He crossed Ducky up there and threw the ball away. The man scored from third, and we beat him 1–0. Next time we beat him 2–1. Didn't come back any more. Rossiter couldn't get him back. Guaranteed him $200 every Sunday, but he wouldn't come back.

We played the Baltimore Orioles every year. They won the pennant in the International League seven years straight. Rossiter offered to play the whole team intact, winner take all, but they wouldn't play. No. Wouldn't play us. The Orioles! And we drew more people than they did. Sure! They come out there to Westport Park to see *us* play. Half the crowd was white. We had 7,000 to 8,000 in that little park. That thing was filled up every Sunday. That's how Rossiter made his money, how he could pay us all those good salaries.

In 1929 I was traded to the Hilldale Daisies. Then I went out West again in 1930 and played with Detroit. The first lights I ever played under was in 1930 in Hamtramck Stadium. The Kansas City Monarchs had those dynamos, three of them: one in right field, one in center, one in left. They were pretty good, but those high hit balls to the outfield, you couldn't hardly see 'em. You had to guess where they were coming down. The infield was good. But very seldom you hit a fast ball with those lights. I called them candle lights.

I played with the Black Sox again in '31. Joe Cambria used to scout for the Washington Senators; he bought the ball club in '32 and moved to Bugle Field—he had the Bugle Apron Company, a laundry. Then the league broke up and I went to the Black Yankees in New York, semipro. There weren't any salaries then. They played on percentage, dividing the receipts among the players. Yeah, we made some *good* money up there then.

I retired in 1937. I was playing up in Albany, New York, then. We had one colored team in the league and all the rest were white, but we won the championship. After that I came back to Baltimore and umpired the Elite Giants' games.

Satchel Paige was the toughest pitcher I ever faced. He didn't have nothing but a fast ball, but he had such great control. Yes sir, and he was so tall, when he turned it loose, it was on you. That ball looked like an aspirin tablet. You *knew* he was going to throw nothing but a fast ball, but you couldn't hit it. I tried all sizes of bats to try to hit him—big bats, short bats, light bats—but still couldn't do anything with him. Before you could swing, the ball was by you. Oh, he was a great pitcher. I would have liked to see him in the majors when he was in his prime.

Those were great players back then. But nobody knows about us anymore. If you put all these stories in the sporting pages, they could read all about it and understand how it was. But that's lost history, see? It's just past, that's all. Nobody's going to dig it up.

Chapter 5

WEBSTER McDONALD

The gentlemanly submarine-ball hurler, Webster McDonald, earned his reputation as a giant-killer against the best big-league stars of his day. His victims included Dizzy Dean, George Earnshaw, Eddie Rommel, Buck Newsom, Earl Whitehill and Jim Weaver.

"He could beat them any day of the week," says Bill Holland, who himself was one of the game's best black pitchers. "He could pitch a whole week because he didn't use much energy. He pitched underhand, and he had a good fast ball. Then he had this curve ball that comes in low, then breaks up. His curves used to rise and his fast balls would sink. Then he'd slow it up. Put McDonald on those big-league stars and they couldn't do a thing with him. He had them helpless."

McDonald's first recorded victory over the big leaguers came in Pittsburgh in 1928, when he scored a 5–1 victory over an all-star club that included Jimmy Foxx, Harry Heilmann, Bing Miller, Steve O'Neill and pitcher Jack "Picus" Quinn. Mac's best year against the big leaguers was 1930. Playing in Baltimore after the regular season, McDonald won five straight games on successive Sundays. He started with an 8–5 victory over the Yankees' Roy Sherrid, followed that with a 4–0 victory (pitcher unknown), and then a 10–0 shutout of Jim Weaver, holding Frankie Frisch of the National League champions to one hit. A week later he beat Eddie Rommel of the world champion Athletics 1–0, and finally beat Rommel again by a 5–3 score.

"When he had one of his good days, there wasn't anybody going to lick him," says ex-shortstop Paul "Jake" Stephens. "When he'd throw that fast ball, that thing jumped, and that curve ball would come in like a whip."

The curve was still crackling in 1932 when Mac beat George Earnshaw, a twenty-one game winner for the champion A's, 3–2. Jimmy Foxx smacked McDonald for a triple, but Mac himself banged out a triple to help win his own game.

That same year Mac finally lost to the big leaguers. Fred Frankhouse beat him 8–2, and Buck Newsom defeated him 9–6, although Mac won some revenge by beating Newsom in relief 9–8. The next year Mac ran up three more victories and suffered one defeat against lineups that included Moose Solters, Buzz Arlett, and two .300-plus hitters with the champion Washington Senators—Joe Kuhel and Buddy Myer.

Mac's best year may have come in 1934. During the regular season he bested Satchel Paige of the powerful Pittsburgh Crawfords 2–1 while pitching and managing the Philadelphia Stars to the Negro League pennant. In the World Series that fall against Chicago, Mac won a crucial game 5–3 against Chicago's ace, Willie Foster, and the Stars went on to win the black championship of the world, four games to three.

On top of the black baseball world, Mac sallied out against the best in the white world —Jerome "Dizzy" Dean, thirty-game winner for the world champion St. Louis Cards. Two times they faced each other, and two times McDonald came

out the winner. The scores were 7–1 and 1–0. In '35
Mac beat Diz again, 7–1 and 11–1. Philadelphia
manager Connie Mack watched the games with
envy.

Buck Leonard, the so-called "black Lou Gehrig,"
was another who respected McDonald. "He had
good control. Wherever your weakness was, he'd
throw the ball there. If you swing the bat real fast
like you were really anxious to hit, he'd slow the
ball up on you. It just would get up there. If you go
to the bat dragging around—bam—he'd throw a fast
one. The way we used to do, we used to go to bat
dragging around, looked like we weren't ready—
but we were ready. And as soon as he'd throw that
fast ball, bam, we'd hit it.

"He couldn't field his position so good," Leonard
continues. "We used to bunt on him a little. But I
don't know anyone who was a more experienced
pitcher than he, or anyone who had better control.
He was cool, never got excited, never argued with
the umpire. Well, a ballplayer who has good control
has no need to argue with the umpire."

"He was always dignified, a perfect gentleman,"
Jake Stephens says. "The only time I heard Mac
swear, we were playing in Philadelphia. I had a
strawberry on my leg, and Mac gave me the signal
to steal. I didn't go. He gave me the sign again; I
still didn't go. The batter hit into a double play. So
when Mac got in the bus after the game, I never will
forget. Rap Dixon and Chaney White had the time
of their life. Mac said, 'I ain't gonna call no names,
but next time I give a signal for a steal, there's one
certain fella in here, if he don't steal, I'm gonna sock
him right in the puss.' And everybody knew who he
was talking about. Only time I ever saw Mac get
mad."

McDonald's best game against the big leaguers—
perhaps the best of his life against anyone—would

come in 1939 By then thirty-nine years old, Mac had long since retired from full-time playing. Thus he was sitting on the bench in Baltimore as the black all-stars took the field against a white club that included Washington first baseman Mickey Vernon, Philadelphia catcher Frankie Hayes and Boston out-fielder Doc Cramer. The black·pitcher quickly got in trouble, yielding three runs and loading the bases in the second. Mac yanked him and shuffled to the mound himself. He retired the side and left the run-ners stranded, then for the next seven innings pitched perfect baseball. Not one big leaguer could get a hit. In the ninth, still losing 3–1, the blacks loaded the bases, but a double play and a great catch against the outfield screen ended the rally. Mac didn't win, but he had pitched one of the classic games of black baseball history.

McDonald was working at Philadelphia's Liberty Bell Racetrack when I interviewed him in his apart-ment in 1970. He poured a drink and spoke melli-flously, fondly of the old Philadelphia Stars and the many friends he had in baseball.

Webster McDonald Speaks . . .

Jimmy Foxx used to say all I have to do is throw my curve out there and they're beat. He used to hit the curve in the American League like nobody's business, but I'd throw him a change-up, looked like you could catch it with your bare hands, and the umpire would call a strike. The next pitch I'd push him back a little with a fast one. Biz Mackey, my catcher, would tell Foxx what was coming, and Foxx would say, "Throw me something I can hit, don't throw me that bender."

You know, Mickey Cochrane could hit that ball too. Foxx told him, "McDonald'll throw you a curve ball and you ain't gonna raise no sam with it." They had a $25 bet. Well, I didn't know anything about the bet, but the first three times Cochrane came up, I'd break one curve ball down, I'd break the other one up. Cochrane was swinging here and the ball was coming in there. I struck Cochrane out three times with my curve ball. After the game he shook my hand, says, "That's the funniest breaking thing I ever seen." So Foxx won his $25. He gave me $12.50 of it. He said, "Look, nothing made me feel happier." He got such a kick out of that bet.

I was strictly a submarine pitcher, a lot of junk. I had a good fast one, but I didn't throw it when I didn't have to. With the hard hitters, I'd time them. I'd throw mixed pitches—"Fifty-six Varieties" they used to call me. And then when I showed them a good fast ball, they weren't ready for it. I'd say, "See, you weren't ready."

I was born January 1, 1900, at 2:30 A.M. in Wilmington, Delaware. At the playground around the Y, I used to play second base. That's where I got into the habit of throwing underhand and sidearm.

Danny McClellan had the Madison Stars in Philadelphia at that time. He was a left-handed pitcher, one of the great ones. He had played on the Cuban X-Giants with Pete Hill back in 1900—I was just born then. He came to the playground and picked me, and he got Judy Johnson. We were the youngest ones on the club. We were too young to go in the Army, so we just took over.

The best colored club in the East then was Hilldale in Philadelphia. But they had so many good pitchers—Phil Cockrell, Nip Winters, Red Ryan—I couldn't break in with them. We were sort of Hilldale's farm club. Hilldale wouldn't play some of those teams around there. They wanted the big part of the meat, and we took the little end. We played percentage ball, made four or five dollars a game. Sometimes we made more, it depended. But back in those days a few dollars was a few dollars. I was a youngster in my teens, wasn't thinking of getting married, but I had to send the money home.

Back in those days there was a lot of twilight ball. We'd play in New Jersey Saturday nights, and we had a ball. If you didn't get that ten o'clock ferry back, you just stayed in Camden. We'd sit there all night waiting for the first ferry in the morning.

The next year I joined the New York Lincoln Giants, with Joe

McDonald, sitting far right, with Northfield, Minn. team.

Williams as manager. They sent me down to the Richmond Giants to help that ball club. Anyone ever mention Rats Henderson to you? He was terrific for a while until his arm went bad. His career was short, but he was great. He was with Richmond then too. We were mostly all rookies and we raised hell with the league, just like the Mets. We upset the apple cart. Here's a clipping with my won-lost record: I won fifteen and lost four.

In 1923 I went with the Philadelphia Giants. That's when I first met Dizzy Dismukes. He was another great pitcher, came here to play with the ABC's of Indianapolis. He was an underhand pitcher, and he's the man I learned it from. Who's the boy with the Yankees hit that boy and killed him? Carl Mays. Dismukes taught him how to pitch in World War I overseas. He was a very studious kind of person, he was a writer. Dizzy Dismukes used to talk to me, say, "Don't try to throw sidearm." He slung his more than I did. I went all the way down, my hand once in a while touched the ground.

When Dismukes would get to town he'd look me up, and we'd go out and have lunch and dinner together. And he'd tell me things. He worked on me about control. He taught me how to be more relaxed, to find my stride. Then you have better control and better stuff on the ball. He talked to me so much that later on I taught my young pitchers to make them hit what you want them to hit. If you have control, you don't have to have as much stuff on the ball. Or you can change the pace. Every hitter's not a good change-up hitter. I won twenty-seven and lost three that year.

We played up in New England—Jake Stephens, Bill Yancey and myself. Bill Jackman pitched for us, out of Boston. I taught him my underhand delivery. We belonged to Hilldale; when Hilldale needed somebody, they'd call us. We covered the waterfront up there, all down East, Nova Scotia, New Brunswick, Maine.

McClellan made me watch the gates. He showed me a lot of things, how to take the starting numbers on the ticket rolls, watch out they don't switch rolls on you. He showed me how to figure the money for the club's share. Later, when I became manager, I knew all this. He'd pitch me when he got ready to pitch me, but he wanted me to stay on that gate. The other fellows would walk off. He'd say, "I want somebody who'll stay there."

My last year up there was '24. In 1925 I pitched for the Wilmington Potomacs.

Next year Rube Foster of Chicago, the daddy of Negro baseball, contacted me: "I want you." See, the East was stealing Biz Mackey, Oscar Charleston and all those players from the West. So he stole me from the East. I got my best money and publicity out in the West, which I couldn't get here because there were too many pitchers ahead of me.

A lot of our boys were going south of the border, and they were barred for five years. So when the Chicago American Giants wanted me to jump my club and pitch for them, I told them that if I left my league, they'd have to give me a five-year contract, and that they did.

Rube had been an underhand pitcher too. Today those trainers, those coaches, they don't have any particular strike zone. But with Rube Foster, on the 3–2, you better break something. You better break that curve ball. And you better break it over the plate, and not over the heart of the plate either.

Rube didn't rely on the catcher. He sat in the dugout, did that [flicks his wrist] for a curve ball, or this [another motion] for a fast ball. If he did this [motion around his ankles], he meant throw that ball in low, make him "skip rope," hit him in the shins. He'd give the signals. The catcher'd get down there, waggle his fingers around, don't mean nothing. Rube just told *me* what to throw.

Remember old Jim Brown the catcher? Mean, ornery guy? He'd get down there, give you something, but I already got *my* signal from Rube. I know what I'm gonna throw. Brown come dragging up to the mound, going to give *me* hell. I said, "Jim, Rube told me what to throw."

"Damn Rube!"

I said, "Well, you tell *him* that, don't you tell me." I said, "You may as well get ready, I know what I'm going to throw." If there's a good hitter up there and the count's 3–2, he *knows* Rube's gonna call for a curve ball. Jim don't want a curve ball, Jim don't want to move. I said, "Well, you make up your mind. I'm ready."

He'd drag on back behind the plate. The hitter'd probably strike out or pop up, retire the side. Get into the dugout. Rube said, "Jim, go to the clubhouse, take my uniform off." Jim, you know, he was a big strong guy. He went to the clubhouse. Rube waited. When Jim was getting ready to go in the shower, Rube went in there and he told Jim, "Lock the door." He whipped Jim! When he told you to go in the clubhouse and "take off my uniform," that's what he meant. Rube was tough. He was tough!

People say to me, "How do you throw it over the plate in spots where you want to throw?" I say, "Every time you walk on the ball field, everything you do should have a purpose. Watch hitters go to the plate, watch how they stand and how they stride. If you get a hitter swinging low, don't pitch low. Raise the ball up on him. Watch his stride. Watch whether he's standing on the plate, whether he drags his front foot back to pull." I tried to figure hitters, their stride and their swing. I'm going to give them something bad before I give them anything good.

Many a good hitter's said to me, "How do you throw that type of pitch and get away with it?" I say in a joking way, "Well, maybe I'm throwing and praying." But I tried to figure the hitter's stride, the way he lunges in. Does he pull, or does he step straight toward the pitcher's box? A flat-footed hitter's your toughest hitter to get balls by. He slaps it. But if he's up on his toes when he bats, I mean he's my man!

Oscar Charleston could hit. And rough. Reminded me more of Ty Cobb than anyone. He hit long balls, he hit any kind. He hit to all fields. Yeah, he hit me too. Charleston hit anybody, pretty good. I tried to trick pitch him, more or less soft stuff. You couldn't get . any hard stuff by him. Now with me he always looked for something slow, a curve ball. He had a terrific eye, but I would always catch him in that big motion. He used to be always moving his bat, always moving, too energetic, I used to say I'd keep slowing it up, slowing it up on him. Throw him three balls and then try to even it up—you know he's going to look at one or two. I'd kind of dangle it around, make it a bad pitch, and then come back and nip one in there while he's waiting. Get him arguing with the umpire, he'd keep looking back at him, you'd get him upset. But if it was a close ball game, of course, then you've got to walk him.

Rube Foster had gone together with Johnny Schorling, the brother-in-law of the Comiskeys who owned the White Sox. He had a lot of power and money, and when we traveled we had a private Pullman car. They'd bring our meals back to us, the whole car was ours. Of course we stayed in colored hotels.

We had quite a team: Bingo DeMoss, second base and captain; Bobby Williams, a great little shortstop; Dave Malarcher played third, a very intelligent man; Bill Foster, Rube's younger brother, was pitching. Jelly Gardner in right field was some character. He was a big man on the team, took me around. Of course, he was a little too fast for me. He was a night-lifer. Cristobel Torrienti in center field was one of the best Cuban ballplayers, a big left-hander, a great hitter. But he liked to clown. Those were the playboys on the club—Gardner, Torrienti and Jim Brown. Always at the nightclubs. Rube used to take their money away from them. When they had a bad day, Rube said he'd take their money, suspend 'em.

But they were great guys. We won the World Series in 1926, beat the Bacharachs of Atlantic City. After the series they all came out to my house in Philadelphia and I had my wife cook chicken and biscuits for two days.

Bill Gatewood had been pitching on the ball club the first year I went to Chicago. Next year Rube released him, sent him to

Birmingham. Next spring Gatewood brought Satchel Paige up. Gatewood said to me, "Mac, that old boy can throw hard—don't know where he's throwin' the ball, though. And he got no kind of move, he can't hold nobody on first base. I told him you got a good move, I want him to watch what you're doing."

I said to Satchel, "First thing, you can't come all the way around here when you're winding up. You kind of got to watch your target. And if you do this to throw home, you got to do this—the same thing—to throw to first."

He said, "We didn't do that way in my home."

Gatewood said, "Now listen, Satchel."

"We didn't do that way."

Always what *he* wanted to do. But a guy that threw hard like that, Rube's gonna bunt him to death. Get him tired in here, in his stomach. Bend him. One over here, one over there. Drop that ball down.

From Chicago I moved up to Little Falls, Minnesota, in the Northwestern League to play with a white team. It was a semi-pro league then. It had been in organized ball, then dropped out and later came back. At first I was the only Negro there. I succeeded John Donaldson, a great left-handed pitcher. He had made quite a reputation. John was fading out then; he was much older than I was. By him talking about me, this committee came to Chicago to talk to me. His name was Donaldson, mine was McDonald. They thought we were related.

Seven hundred fifty a month, that was my top salary there. That was what lured me: from $350–$400 to $750, with expenses and transportation included. I was the highest salaried man in the league—they never paid two people that much. And after that first year I could pitch in those tournaments, make $200–$250 a game: Winnipeg, Moose Jaw and the Denver *Post* tournament.

We traveled by auto, sometimes by train: through all those big Indian reservations, Winnipeg, Saskatoon, Saskatchewan. Then we'd drop back over the border to Cheyenne, Wyoming, and back to Little Falls. We beat everybody those years. In four years up there my record was 25–3, 27–2, 26–1, and 20–2.

John Van, a Negro out of Kansas, was my catcher there for one year. But he wasn't the man they should have chosen, he shouldn't have been out there. My next catcher was Sylvester Foreman, from the Kansas City Monarchs. A very good boy, a good man.

The newsmen used to ask me, "How do you feel, playing with a white team?" I'd say, "I'm a person, a human being, an American. I've gone to school with whites, I can command respect." All my life I've had to make my way and learn to live with people. I demanded respect, nobody pushed me over.

The only time I ran into trouble was in a little place up in the oil fields on this side of the border—Plentywood, Montana. There's a lot of Southern people from Texas working in those oil fields. One night we got in late, 12:30 or one o'clock, to this little hotel. There were about twenty of us, and I was the only colored. The clerk looked over, saw me and wanted to know who I was. "Oh, he can't stay here."

"Well, if he doesn't stay here, none of us stay here."

I said, "Look, let the boys go to bed. I'll sit down in the station."

The club manager said, "If you don't sleep, they don't sleep." They got places in private homes for us—two here, two there, three or four at the Y. It was two or three o'clock before we got situated. They blackballed that hotel. The next year the hotel was begging for business, but we wouldn't stay there.

After the season was over up there, all the colored clubs back east would contact me to barnstorm with them against the major leaguers. I used to help Cum Posey out with the Homestead Grays. I stopped in Pittsburgh and barnstormed with him. I waited to hear from everybody before I decided. I made a good salary up there—in those days it was a good salary. When I came home, I wasn't hungry. I waited to see.

You know what they used to do? I'd say, "Look, I'm not going to play in the series, I'm going to take my vacation." They'd lose two or three games and they'd gang up on me, they'd make me go down and pitch.

We were playing on percentage, eighty-some bucks, you know. Jimmy Foxx, Mickey Cochrane, George Earnshaw, they said, "You should be getting the same money we're getting, boy. Don't you come back until you get your money. People come out to see *you*." So I stayed away one Sunday. Them guys, that "bleacher gang" in Baltimore, they raised so much sam, they broke chairs and everything. Frank Warfield, the Black Sox manager, called me, said, "Look, I want you down here Thursday. You're going to get your 150 bucks, all expenses. I'll get the money and put it in my pocket for you." Warfield said, "Come on out here, come out on the corner of Pennsylvania Avenue, let's walk up and down. The people will know you're here, it will be all over town by next Sunday." And I got my 150 bucks that time.

I pitched against Dizzy Dean in Shibe Park once. I threw my little nothing ball up there, had the guy set up for it. Josh Gibson was catching, caught it with his bare hand. I said, "Don't you ever humiliate me like that again, catching my ball in your meat hand." He said, "You ain't got nothing on it anyway."

Who's that man played right field for St. Louis, won the batting championship in the American League? Heinie Manush. He said, "You ever stop throwing that little nothing ball, I'll hit it out of here."

Remember Don Heffner, went up from Baltimore to the majors? A little hot-headed guy. Everybody was wrong but him. He stood on top of the plate, and I pushed him back with a pitch. He'd get right back in there. He was determined to dig in and stay on top of that plate. I said, "What you gonna do about it, ump?"

He said, "Go ahead and push him back. Push him back."

Boy, Heffner was gonna whip me! I said, "I can whip five little guys like you." He was a pain in the neck.

But Jimmy Foxx and I were very close, we were good pals. Earl Mack was their business manager, and we were good friends too. I kept our boys under control and he kept his. We made good money. We had a good thing going there. We played until the snow was on the ground.

In 1931 my wife was sick and I didn't want to go back out west. I made more money out there, did less work, but having a sick wife at home, I had to be near her. She said she couldn't go in those hotel rooms anymore. I came back east, with the Hilldale Daisies, pitched a string of twenty-seven scoreless innings.

In 1933 I helped organize the Philadelphia Stars with most of the players from the old Hilldale club. Johnny Drew, who had taken over Hilldale, didn't last long. He didn't believe in some of the systems we had in our league. See, back then most of the teams would come here to Philadelphia to play us because we had a park exclusively to ourselves in Darby, south of town. We could play three games a week at night. And we'd also play a six o'clock twilight game somewhere against one of those industrial teams. Most weekends we were playing each other in league games. But on a Sunday when some of our teams weren't booked against each other, we used to have some good spots in New York against the Bushwicks. Anyway, a booking agent booked you to play where you couldn't book yourself, to keep your team from being idle, and you had to pay him 10 percent. And that, Johnny Drew refused to do. He said he would sit down and pay his ball club for the season even if he didn't play a ball game, rather than play an exhibition game. So he finally dropped out.

In 1933 Ed Bolden (founder of the Hilldales) came to me and Dick Lundy, the shortstop—he wanted to get Lundy back into baseball—and he said, "You two can do it, you can form a new team." Lundy was supposed to be the field manager, and I was the business manager. Bolden said, "Eddie Gottlieb will be in back of us." You know who Ed Gottlieb was? He was the man who organized the SPHA's (South Philadelphia Hebrew Association) basketball team, the guy who made Wilt Chamberlain. Gottlieb was a booking man, and he and Bolden went together on the Stars. That's how we started, Bolden and Gottlieb, two partners, one colored, one white. When other clubs were hitting it rough, our ball club was playing every day.

Bolden said, "We can't pay any salaries, the boys will be on percentage." He said, "Now Gottlieb's gotta take his 10 percent off the top, after that each player takes his cut."

As the season started, we started to make some money. Gottlieb said, "I guess Chief [Bolden] has already talked to you. We got plans for you. You're handling the money, you're playing, we want you to manage the ball club too. You'll be on salary." I did all three jobs until 1937.

The ballplayers believed in me. They trusted me, they respected me. If I told them something, they could depend on it. And I made the owners live up to their agreements. So I said, "Now, I can get most any player I want," because we were out of the

league then. I could have a championship club. In '33 I organized
the club, and in '34 we won the championship. I developed some
mighty fine ballplayers.

In the pitching staff I developed Frank Holmes, Paul Carter,
and this kid Stuart Jones from Baltimore, one of the sharpest
little left-handers you ever saw—tall, lanky, like Satchel. I made
a great pitcher out of him. And I had Rocky Ellis, a little guy
who could throw hard, and a great big heart. Could beat anybody.
He's the one run Josh Gibson out the ball park. Josh couldn't hit
Rocky. He said, "You put that old wild crazy guy up there. He's
cutting the ball. I'm gonna take it out on you!"

I said, "No you're not. I'll walk you. I ain't gonna let you hit!"

Biz Mackey was our catcher, the best in baseball bar none.

Outfield was Pete Washington, Chaney White and Rap Dixon.

Dewey Creacy to Jake Stephens to Dick Seay to Jud Wilson,
that was our infield. Stephens and Seay were the best double
play combination in baseball. I called them "the acrobats."
Stephens was fast, aggressive. He could jump like a cat. But he
was controversial. The fans were 100 percent for that guy, but
sometimes he'd burn you up. Jake was temperamental. Sometimes I'd roast him because out of a clear blue sky he'd argue
with the umpires. He'd swear he was right. I'd say, "Jake, look,
all the umpires can't be wrong, some of them gotta be right."

I never used bad language. In fact, I got rid of a lot of good ballplayers because they used bad language. I'd trade them, give
them away. I didn't like that kind of language. But they burned
me up one time, Stephens and Seay. One Saturday night they
looked bad. I said, "I don't know what you boys are doing, but
it don't suit me." On the bus going back to the Y, yes, I swore at
them.

Jud Wilson was my captain. He was temperamental too—oh
boy. He'd bang you in the jaw in a minute—anybody. One of
our greatest ballplayers. But when I turned my back, he'd go into
battle, and I didn't want that. People didn't understand how I
handled him as well as I did. I made him captain to calm him,
to curb him—give him responsibility. It helped, and he appreciated it.

The Philadelphia Stars—that team did everything for two

years. We had some good base runners: Stephens, White and
Seay. When we needed a run, get one of those guys on base, you
could just bet Mackey or Wilson or one of the other guys would
hit 'em in. We had a few hitters, but when they didn't hit, we
had to run those guys Stephens and Seay to death.

Eddie Gottlieb liked to gamble. He said, "When we're playing
in Yankee Stadium, the Polo Grounds, I want Slim Jones, I
want both of you to pitch."

I said, "I'm tired. I got Rocky Ellis, I got Holmes. I want
those boys to work." No need of me managing the ball club,
pitching every other day. I would pitch every other day during
the week in twilight games, but on big days, on weekends, I
wanted Slim or Rocky, those boys, in there. I said, "Don't you
think I get tired sometimes?"

He said, "I want you to pitch the doubleheaders in New York."
No rest for the weary. And after a ball game he says, "After you
get dressed, come on back to the office." He'd keep me there
till three or four o'clock in the morning talking. Going over and
over things he wanted me to do.

Bushwick Park, Brooklyn—that was another place, every time
we went I had to pitch that first ball game. When you walked
into that park, you were playing a major league ball club; most
every fellow who played on that club had been in the majors or
was going up. Phil Rizzuto came up through those ranks. And
those gamblers: The "landlords" sit over this side, $100 bills
pinned on their lapels. The "tenants" sit over there, with $50
bills. And they used to really give me a working out. I never lost
a game in that ball park. I used to walk in Bushwick Park and
just throw my glove on the ground. That was it, the game was
over. The nearest I came to losing was when somebody dropped
a little fly ball. We went eighteen innings—I pitched the whole
eighteen innings. I beat Socks Siebold, used to pitch for Philadelphia, in Bushwick one day. I beat Stan Baumgartner, who
pitched for the Phils.

We were playing a day game once, and were going to play in
Dexter Park, the Bushwicks' park, that night. Gottlieb said,
"Look, here's $250, split it up with the boys" He said, "If you
win that second game, here's 500 bucks." We beat Bushwicks 3–2

in twelve innings! After the ball game I went to the office to get the money. He said, "You looked mighty good, *mighty* good." So I took 500 bucks, split it up among the boys.

I used to tell the boys—they already got their eatin' money for the day—"If you win this ball game today, I'll buy steak dinners for you." Out of my pocket. Those guys would rather beat me than the other team! Every time I made one of those kind of bets, they beat me. They'd eat everything! Dick Seay would sit near me, he knew I wasn't going to eat all my food. He'd finish it.

We won the Eastern division in '34, went out to Chicago for the play-off. They beat Slim the first game. Next game, Rocky Ellis—they beat Rocky. Now Mr. Bolden said, "Mac, you gotta pitch the third game."

I said, "No, Chief, wait. We gotta go back East. I want to pitch Holmes in this ball game."

He said, "No, I want you to pitch. You're the manager, but I want you to pitch." All right, I go in there and I beat Bill Foster 3–1. That made it two games to one, they're leading. We got to play one more game out there. They won that. They won three games.

We come back East. I say, "Slim, how you feel?"

He said, "Mac, I'm feeling good."

Mackey was begging me: "Pitch Slim, pitch Slim." Slim went in and pitched the first game. We were in a doubleheader because of a rain-out. We were trying to get it over with to keep from going back to Chicago. Slim pitched the first game, shut 'em out 2–0, come back, pitched a doubleheader, beat 'em 2–1. That's when Boojum Wilson got in so much trouble slugging the umpire. Ronald was our commissioner. Overnight Bolden and Gottlieb had Ronald down to the hotel, trying to let Boojum play. Ronald says, "Yes, he's going to play."

Malarcher, the Chicago manager: "Jiminy Christmas!" he says, "He knocked the man down! What's he have to do to put him out of the ball game?"

Go back the next day for the rubber game. Rocky Ellis pitched like a master. He could pitch, you know. He had heart. He won the championship for us.

Roy Campanella was a kid in Philadelphia then. On Sunday mornings when we'd go down to Baltimore to play the all-stars, he'd say, "Mac, gonna take me along?"

I'd say, "Yes, you can go along with me." Sunday morning, six o'clock, he'd be sitting there on my front steps waiting till I come out. In case somebody got a bad finger in the game, he would be there. I'd get him in the game somehow. He liked to play third base too, and boy, he was right in there. I wanted to get him on the Stars, but Bolden said, "You already got two catchers, Mac, you don't need the third boy."

At that time Mackey was managing Baltimore. He said, "Mac, I'd love to get that boy."

I said, "They won't let me have him."

He said, "Tell 'em I'll take him with me."

I was tickled to death to let Mackey get him. I said, "What a combination that will be! Mackey's gonna teach him everything he knows."

I had to manage and do my secretarial work on the road at the same time. I couldn't see every play. In 1937 I made up my mind it was too much work. They had talent, but the disposition of those players—I don't want any more headaches like that! I made my decision it was too much work, so I went into government service. But I was still available to the team until 1942. I'd manage weekends and handle personnel and pitch a few games now and then.

I retired altogether in 1942 and put in twenty-six years with the post office. Here's my certificate of service. Now I work for Liberty Bell Racetrack. I'm head of the linen department. I spend about $1,000 of my boss's money, buy all the linen for the track. This is the first year a colored man has been in this job. My boss said, "Mac, I need somebody I can trust." Oooh, I don't have any time anymore. But I love my work, I love to meet people. It keeps you alive.

I have some raggedy newspaper clippings. I sent a lot of stuff to the Hall of Fame, got a beautiful letter from the Board of Directors. They really appreciated those clippings.

I'm not bitter about missing the big leagues. What were you going to do at the time? You know what the situation was. All my life I've had to make my way and learn to live with people. How did I get along? Just like anyone else. You treat me like a man, I'll treat you the same way. I let them live their lives, I lived mine.

The year after Dizzy Dean won the pennant in 1935, I beat him 7–1 here in Shibe Park. Next Sunday, Satchel beat Paul Dean 3–1 in Yankee Stadium. Monday night Diz came back to York, Pennsylvania, and I beat him 11–1 that night. That was the day Connie Mack came in the clubhouse while I was under the showers. He wanted to congratulate me, my control, my delivery, my concept of the hitters. He said, "I'm sorry to say this, but I'd give half my ball club for a man like you."

Webster McDonald

Webster McDonald

Newt Allen (left) with fellow Monarchs. Turkey Stearnes is third from left; Eddie Dwight, father of the astronaut, is fourth, and Bullet Joe Rogan, on the right.

Kansas City Monarchs pose with House of David players. Allen is on the right in the back row. Bullet Joe Rogan is on the left in back. The first three men standing are Chet Brewer, owner J. L. Wilkinson, and George Giles.

Chapter 6

NEWT ALLEN

Little Newt Allen of Kansas City was one of the slickest-fielding second basemen the Negro leagues produced. Teaming with Monarch shortstop Dobie Moore or with Willie Wells of St. Louis, Allen sparkled on the double play. "He wouldn't even look at first base on the pivot," says Monarch pitcher Bill Drake. "He'd throw the ball to first under his left arm like the great Bingo DeMoss of Chicago."

Allen was a much better fielder than Jackie Robinson, says James Wilkinson, son of the Monarch owner, who saw both men play. Others compare the switch-hitting Allen to the Athletics' great Eddie Collins. Ted "Double Duty" Radcliffe, for one, rates Allen the best second baseman in the Negro leagues.

Allen joined the Monarchs in 1922 at the age of twenty. "We called him 'Colt,'" says outfielder George Sweatt, "because he was young. Newt was a different guy from the other players. They were mostly rough and illiterate—he was a little rough too when he was playing, though." Allen's chief partner in deviltry was his roommate, third baseman Newt Joseph. "They were characters," Sweatt grins. "But I think Allen toned down after Newt Joseph died."

Allen didn't hit too well, judging from the fragmentary averages that have been discovered. His lifetime average for six scattered Negro League seasons was only .251, though he did much better against white big leaguers, hitting them for an estimated .301 in twenty-four games.

Allen was a favorite with the fans. Five times they voted him to first place among second basemen chosen for the East-West game—1933, 1934, 1936 and 1941. In 1933 he scored more than twice as many votes as his nearest rival, and in the next year he beat out the great Sammy T. Hughes for the honor.

I met Newt Allen in the summer of 1971 in his home on a quiet street in Kansas City. He had just returned from doing some political canvassing, one of his favorite activities. For more than two hours he talked to me, leaning forward in his chair and speaking softly, with a gentle smile playing across his face.

Newt Allen Speaks . . .

I've had a wonderful career in baseball—twenty-seven years, from 1921 to 1947. I've played in almost every state in the Union, in Canada, Mexico, Puerto Rico, Cuba, Venezuela, Japan, China and the Philippines. It's been a wonderful career, and at one time I was considered a pretty good second baseman.

When the Monarchs first started back in 1920, I was only a canvas puller and ice boy out at the ball park. Baseball was my whole life. I just loved it from the beginning. I was born in 1902 right here in Kansas City. Frank Duncan and I were boys together on the Paseo at 17th Street. We were in the same school together, lived in the same neighborhood for years, and we were friends throughout our boyhood days. Another fellow with us was Rube Currie [who later pitched for the Chicago American Giants]. He and Frank Duncan lived almost next door to one another. We all used to play sandlot ball in school. We'd put in twenty cents apiece and the winner take the pot.

Newt Allen, second from right. Bullet Joe Rogan is at far right, catcher Frank Duncan second from left.

Later I used to go out and practice with the Monarchs, and when the ball game was over, I'd pull the canvas across the ball field. That's the way I would get two or three balls from the groundkeeper—that's how we got our balls to play with.

Meanwhile, Duncan had gone to the Monarchs to play. They'd been watching me, and they asked me to come try out with them. I went out twice, but at that time the manager didn't think I could make it. So I went to a semipro club in Omaha, and we had a pretty good ball club. They put us in the Nebraska State League, and when we started winning, the Monarchs began to watch me again. When they came through and played us an exhibition, I showed up good, and I left and went with them.

They used the park of the old Western League white club at 20th and Olive. There's a playground there now. It was a much smaller field than the present one. In right field they had a twenty-five- to thirty-foot screen, like you have in Boston. But in left field the bleachers went all around from the railroad track clear around to 21st Street, from left field to center field. At that time the capacity was around 25,000. It was single-deck, all wood, nothing was concrete.

Kansas City is a good baseball town, if you're a winner. You've got to win, though. That's the reason the Royals and A's had such a time. But you put a team up in first or second place, and the fans will turn up. We used to draw 14 to 15,000 people during those times, 18 to 19,000 on Sunday; and ladies' night, my goodness, we'd have lots of people. We drew quite a few people, white and colored. They're good baseball fans here, but you have to have a winner. You see how they turn out for football here, almost 60,000 people, 'cause they're winners. They don't like a loser here.

Allen, far left, with Monarchs and House of David players.

We won eight pennants in all.

I was a right-handed hitter, hit second. I was a pretty good bunter if I have to say so, a pretty good hit-and-run man. As I stayed in baseball I learned how to hit the way the ball was pitched. A ball pitched inside, pull back and hit it to left field; a pitch outside, step into it and hit it to right field; a pitch down the center, just cut and let it go where it may.

In fact, our entire ball club was like that. I'll tell you why: Between weekend series here in Kansas City against the big Negro clubs, we would go down through Oklahoma and Kansas and play those semipro clubs. Well, naturally, we could beat them, so they'd have their own town umpire. You know, in the pinches he would call a ball this far outside a strike, and strike you out. So we learned how to hit both the outside pitches and the inside pitches. It got so that the fellows in the league playing against us didn't know what to pitch. All they had to do was throw the ball down the middle to get seven out of nine of us out.

Newt Joseph was our third baseman. Joseph was a smart ballplayer. He was a great signal catcher. He'd watch everybody on the other ball club—the bench, the pitchers down in the bull pen, the coaches, the manager—and in three innings, if there was any kind of sign, he had one or two of them. He's passed now. His name was Walter Joseph, but they called him Newt. My name was Newton. After my wife and I separated, he and I lived together here in Kansas City for about five years. The two Newts.

Of course Frank Duncan was our catcher. I don't say this just because he was a friend of mine, or because I played with him, but he was a great receiver and thrower—one of the greatest. He wasn't too much of a hitter, but at that time there were only two men who were tops on him as a receiver: fellow by the name of Bruce Petway who caught for Detroit and another one named Biz Mackey, who caught for Philadelphia.

Rube Foster's Chicago American Giants were our big rivals. Foster had five or six men who didn't do anything but push and bunt, kept you moving all the time. Just kept us playing on the grass, and then they'd hit it by you. And that's for nine innings— he did that for nine innings, not just one. You had to be on your toes, and you had to have a good pitcher to try to stop them.

Now the Monarchs were just the opposite of the Giants. We had the ball team that just slammed away on the ball at all times. A fellow like myself or Newt Joseph or Hurley McNair, why, we'd upset the apple cart and bunt every once in a while and get them to looking for bunts and pull their infield in. Then we'd kind of loosen the big bats and shoot by them.

In those days every town had its own umpires, and naturally the home team was favored with them. There'd be quite a few arguments, and sometimes there was a lot of fist throwing. Oh yes, they threw fists quite often. Like the Yankees and Senators in the American League at that time. We had three or four great fights there in Chicago. We did a lot of throwing at one another, running over one another, jumping at each other. Some guy would get temperamental enough to swing at someone, and the ball-players and spectators would mix it up. It took all the 35th Street police in Chicago to stop it. Then when Chicago came here, 17 to 18,000 people would come out to see who was going to start a fight. The owners were all making money.

See that scar on my shin? Eighteen stitches in that. I got it from the third baseman of the American Giants, a fellow by the name of Dave Malarcher. I had him out by about ten feet and was going to tag him, when he came in with one foot high. I was out quite a while. It took me three years to repay him, but they say vengeance is sweet. One day we were leading by two runs, he was on first, and I took the throw at second for a double play. Well, instead of throwing to first, I threw straight at Malarcher charging into second. I hit him right in the forehead, just enough under his cap bill to keep from breaking his nose. Hurt him pretty bad. He was out of the ball game for three days. The next time he was on first and rounding second to go to third, I could have thrown the ball over his head and gotten him out, but it was just one of those "evil spirit" days. I cut down on him overhanded and hit him right in the back of the head. That hurt him pretty bad too, but that's the way they played the game then. But he never slid into me with his spikes up again.

Yes, I sure did have trouble with some of those base runners.

See this scar on my hand? Oscar Charleston jumped at me at third base, cut my glove off of my hand—as big a fellow as he was, he weighed two-something. I had him out, but he hit me, he jumped high, knocked away my glove and the ball. Years later I learned that if they jump high, watch the leg that's in the air. If he's going to try to spike with it, step aside and hook it with your arm. Sometimes your glove will catch a spike; or you want to hook your arm just past his shoes and pull. I could throw a man ten feet and break his neck almost. You do that to one or two bad sliders and you don't have any trouble out of the rest. Or hit two or three of them coming into second base in the chest with the ball —next time they'll run right out of the base path.

In my career I was a rough ballplayer, but we were all friends. You have a certain feeling toward a fellow that's nice and never had any nasty words against you. A lot of times I had a nasty feeling within myself, not against a ballplayer. I was pretty bad playing ball, yes, I was pretty bad—run over a man, throw at him. I did a lot of wrong things. But I got results out of it, because they were leery of what I was going to do, and I'd get by with it. Sometimes if we started fighting, those great big old guys would come and back me up—kept things going and livened it up!

We used every trick in the book to win a ball game. All kinds of good tricks and nasty ones. In fact, there were more nasty ones than there were good. Caused many a ballplayer to get hurt.

Catchers had a way to stop those hard sliders too. If a man was on second and he knew the runner was coming home, he'd lay his mask down right by home plate. The runner would jump and slide and hit that mask and break his hip. They don't allow that anymore.

And quite a few pitchers on every ball club would throw at batters. There's usually at least one pitcher on every ball club that you can hit good. Almost every ball he throws at you, you can hit. They seem to get to be kind of leery of you and you come up in the pinches with men on, the first thing they'll do is throw at you. I hit two home runs off a fellow named Jack Combs in Detroit, and in the next ball game, why the first pitch knocked a button off of my cap. The next one hit me right there in my side, and I had a knot in my side that big for about a week. That's the way they'd do you. They didn't mean for you to hit them. The average hitter in those days, the first thing he'd do would be get loose and get ready to duck. Sometimes your bat would go one way, your cap the other and you laying down on the ground. After Ray Chapman got killed—when Carl Mays killed Ray Chapman— that's when that beaning ball went out, but they still threw a little close to you, what they call "moving him back."

You know, in boxing there's two rules, Queensbury and the one they call "coonsbury." We played the coonsbury rules. That's just any way you think you can win, any kind of play you think you can get by with. We played pretty smart baseball in our days.

Cool Papa Bell, a great outfielder. When he hit it, you've got to throw it to the next base. The man ran so fast, we woke up to the fact that if he's on first and a man singles, he's gone. We'd have to throw it to home plate. There's a tale you've got to tell on him, though. I don't know whether anyone else will tell you, but he'd miss second base by three feet—he'd cut in a little bit behind the pitcher. I know he was fast, but how did he get to third base so quick? He wasn't going anywhere near the bag! The umpires in those days weren't quite as alert, and a lot of things passed them by. Cool Papa did that for almost a year before anybody caught on. But he was the fastest ballplayer I've seen.

Willie Wells of the St. Louis Stars was one of the greatest short-stops. It was a toss-up between him and Moore, but Wells was a smarter ballplayer than Moore. Good hitter, good base runner and a wonderful shortstop. He'd catch them with his bare hands. He and I went to California together. Wells was at short and I was at second, and we were the first Negro ballplayers whose pictures came out in the Los Angeles *Examiner*, we made so many double plays. And he was quite a guy for tagging, with that big hand and big glove. You'd go in there and he'd slap you all up side of the head.

In 1924 we played the Philadelphia Hilldales in the first colored

Newt Allen

World Series. They had some fine players. Nip Winters was a tall left-hander—oh, he was a tough man. He beat us three ball games. Scrip Lee pitched that series too. A submarine pitcher, threw from down here. I used to hear from him, he wrote Joe Rogan and me quite often. We beat him in the World Series in Chicago. It was tied 0–0, I think, in the ninth inning. He had struck me out three times with that submarine curve ball and intended to throw me a bad pitch overhand with three men on base. But I hit it down the third base line and pulled up on third. The next man, Hurley McNair, came up and singled, and we ran in about five runs and beat him.

Birmingham was another tough club back then when they had Satchel Paige and Harry Salmon, a guy they called "the black diamond." Satchel and Salmon were six-footers, they both threw sidearm and they were pretty tough. Satchel kicked his foot way up here like Dizzy Dean, then he'd throw around that foot. Half the guys were hitting at that foot coming up. We had a hard time *bunting* Satchel's throws, much less hitting them. He'd strike out eighteen or nineteen men at three o'clock in the afternoon. He didn't do that at night, he did that in the daytime before night baseball came in, back in '27, '28 and '29. Satchel was just a good hard thrower, a hard man to hit. But as far as being a smart pitcher, he never was. I still say Rogan was a better pitcher.

The circumstances under which we had to play ball were awful hard. When I first started out we used to travel by trains. Later we used buses. We used to travel all night, sleep in the bus, then three o'clock that evening get out and play the ball game. A lot of times we'd play a night game here in Kansas City and have to be in Chicago for the ball game the next night. It was a twelve- to fourteen-hour drive in the bus. By the time you got into Chicago it would be 10:30 or 11 o'clock. That's excusing trouble, stops for water and all those things. By the time you got to sleep, why it's time to get up and go play ball. Not only our club, but all the other clubs would do it, and yet they played wonderful ball.

Every ballplayer had to look out after his own paraphernalia. We had to take what they call a suit-roll. You wrapped your own uniform, your sweatshirt, your stockings, your shoes and your bats. Well now, you've got your hand bag, you've got your suit-roll with your uniform in it and you've got your bat bag. You've got to go to the train or bus and get on the thing with that. Today all the ballplayer has to do is go into the clubhouse, pull off his clothes, take a shower, put on his coat and go on out. His uniform will be wherever he's going.

The highest salary I drew was $900 a month. That was good money in those days. All the way from I'd say '29 up to around '36, the middle of the Depression. But at that time a dollar was a dollar. It takes a whole lot of dollars to make a dollar now, I mean to get the same value out of it. And we were doing something we liked.

You know, when you do something you like, you can do it real good. That was the way with myself and a lot of others. Everything I tried to do would be the best in that game.

During the Depression the league folded up. We started playing one another in different towns, but there wasn't any league schedule.

We traveled up through the Northwest with the white House of

Davids, those guys out of Michigan, where they have the colony. They had a whale of a ball club. Three of those bearded men had that pepper game, throwing the ball under their legs, behind their backs, around their necks. People would come out to see them. They'd hire ballplayers too and tell them to start growing their beards around December. The real House of David guys would put their hair up under their caps; their hair would grow pretty long. They had Frankie Salas, a boy who played with the New York Yankees organization, a good hitter and outfielder; when the Yankees sent him down to their farm team, he joined the House of Davids. They had another one named Mullins, and a pitcher named Hunter who pitched for Pittsburgh. He was quite a wild fellow, liked to drink and harass around. Well, he didn't stay in condition. Then they had two fellows named Talley and Tucker, who were major league prospects, but they wouldn't leave their colony.

Frankie Salas and another white fellow named Tapley out of Chicago, and another one named Culley were our friends. Sunday afternoons there'd be carnivals in town, and we'd all go out and we'd drink and go to these good-time houses. Well, we traveled around together so we knew each other and understood each other. We might have some misunderstanding during the ball game, but after the ball game, that was all over with and we were going out together. We stayed at the same hotels most of the time in Canada, so we got to be pretty close with one another, and it made things pretty good. A fellow who didn't want to associate with you, why, we didn't bother with him. Eventually he'd understand and we'd get talking. Used to play pool in the pool halls, used to fill up the pool halls with nothing but ballplayers.

Babe Didrikson pitched for them one year. We played against her. She was fair as a pitcher—pretty good as a pitcher—the only thing was, you couldn't treat her like a regular pitcher. Nobody would bunt on her, because she couldn't field bunts. And if somebody hit a line drive through the box, it would kill her. You just tried to place your ball away from hitting it directly at her. She had a curve ball and a fast ball, and I know players she'd strike out. That's right. But they'd only pitch her two or three innings and then take her out of there, because you had some mean and nasty ballplayers. If you struck them out once, next time they went up there, they'd cut like they were cutting for the fence. Well, they might hit a line drive and break the woman's nose or break her leg or something. But she was more novelty than anything, just a drawing card. People came out to see her pitch, and you made it look good for her. Maybe the first two innings she'd get fellows out, then in the third inning you'd run in one run on her, just one run. Then the papers would say she held the great Monarchs team to one run, the other towns would read it and come out to see her pitch. That's the way we'd do it all up through Canada, Minnesota, the Dakotas and out west as far as Wyoming and Montana. We played every day, sometimes every night.

Grover Cleveland Alexander also traveled with them one year and drew money. A lot of the Canadian people had never seen him. Satchel was with us, and he and Satchel would pitch against one another, about three innings apiece. It was just a thrill to see that duel, any way it went. Satchel was in his prime as a pitcher then, and Alexander could still throw hard, and the thing about it was, he knew how to pitch. He didn't wear whiskers, he was the only one that didn't—in fact, he said he couldn't grow any. You know, he used to be a pretty mean fellow. But he turned out to be an awfully nice guy in his late years.

A lot of players like Alexander learned that there were as good Negro ballplayers as there were white ballplayers. When they began to play in the winter leagues together they found out, hell, this is a sport for everybody, and we had good friends during those times before integration came in. We had Paul and Dizzy Dean, the Waner brothers, the DiMaggio brothers, Bob Feller, Pepper Martin, Lon Warneke, Mike Ryba. Mike Ryba used to manage a Cardinals' farm team down in Springfield, Missouri, and every time we ran across him it was just like meeting a brother or something, he was right along with the gang, whatever they did.

It was quite an experience to show a fellow man how to accept a friend regardless of what color he is. I learned that way back before integration. A man is a man. If you treat him right, you can bet your life eight out of ten times you'll get that same kind of treatment back.

Dizzy Dean was just a prince of a guy. He was a real fellow. Paul wasn't a very good mixer, but Dizzy was an everyday guy. My hits against Dizzy were pretty scarce, because he had every-thing—he was a pitcher. What year was it that he and Paul beat the Tigers in the Series? 'Thirty-four? They flew that next night to Oklahoma City and we played them. Wilkinson got up some of the white semipro ballplayers in that town to play for Dizzy and Paul against the Monarchs. We toured with them clear down to Dallas, Texas. I disremember how all the games came out. We beat 'em in Oklahoma City 4–2. We had so many people the grandstand wouldn't hold them. The ball game quit in the fifth inning—had to, people were all out in the outfield, and every inning they would press closer to try to see Dizzy. We had to stop the ball game, but the people were satisfied, they got to see Dizzy and Paul pitch. And we made $1,200 a man.

Bob Feller beat us in 1936 before he went to Cleveland, right up there in Iowa—Des Moines, I think. He beat us 3–0 that night. He could throw hard, the young man could throw hard, and the lights were kind of dim anyway, and he was setting us down one right after the other.

The winter of 1935 we made a trip to Japan, China and the Philippines. What a wonderful trip! We got $3,000 apiece before we left, and 40 percent of every game we played. That was split twelve ways, because we only had twelve ballplayers.

We left San Francisco and stayed about ten months in the Philippines, playing Philippine teams and Army teams. We were all in a league together. And we went up to sugar plantations and played clubs up there too.

After we left there we played a Chinese team over in Shanghai. Sure, they had a baseball league over there, mixed Chinese and Hawaiians, pretty well educated people. But most of those fellows were pretty small. We stayed there around a month. There were so many people, thousands of them right there in Hong Kong Bay in boats. Our boat would collect all the food left on our table, and they'd take it and spread it out on their boats and get enough out of it to make some kind of a meal. They didn't have any place to go, there was too many of them, so they lived on those boats. They'd fish from them, but they couldn't do much fishing; they just looked like automobiles in a parking lot, they were so crowded. I'm not saying there weren't decent people in China, because there are, but there was such a big mass of them it was hard for all of them to make any living. When a big boat came in, those fellows would get twenty cents a day to paint the boat. That shows how cheap wages were. It was quite amazing that something like that could ever exist. People talk about it—but when you see it, then you know it really happens.

Japan was different. The majority of them seemed to be decent, respectable, and they really had ball teams. They had some ballplayers. Sessue Hayakawa, the movie star, and a Japanese girl who was a star for Metro-Goldwyn-Mayer—I can't remember her name now—opened a movie studio in Japan and sponsored one of the best ball clubs over there. Japan was a fine country, full of fine people.

In Hawaii they had teams made up of all nationalities—Hawaiians, Japanese, two or three Negroes and quite a few Koreans. A man named Yamashiro, a superintendent down at Dole Pineapple Company, offered Rogan and me a salary and the only thing we'd have to do was check crates of pineapples and play ball two days a week, Saturdays and Sundays. At the end of the ball season, the team split all the money. The factory just furnished us the suits and the name. But we decided to come on back home and play.

Satchel came to play with us in '38, but his big career was through. His arm was sore. He had gone to Santo Domingo and pitched all winter, and that really hurts pitchers. When he came back his arm was real sore. He couldn't wipe the back of his neck. That's when the Monarchs took him.

The Monarchs had a second team then, and Wilkinson, our owner, sent Newt Joseph with Satchel out to the Northwest with the second team. Newt Joseph taught him how to throw a curve ball, and control. When he came back the second team played us out in Kansas City, Kansas, and Satchel pitched and wore us out. And he went on from there. But he was almost gone at one time— out of baseball. He was almost gone when he came to the Monarchs. He started pitching around three or four innings. Then he pitched every day, every ball game almost, and the people started coming back to see him.

You know who Satchel reminds you of when you talk with him? Remember the comedian Stepinfetchit? He talks and sounds just like him. And he can sing and dance. Oh, he's got a wonderful voice for singing, and he can dance. And he's a solid comedian, he's another Bob Hope. He can think of more funny things to say and tell you and keep you laughing all the time. Quite a character. All the ballplayers were crazy about him, because he was a showman, he was really a showman. It's not the things that he did, it's the things that he said. He was a kidder, a great kidder. He used to make some of those ballplayers so mad that they'd want to shoot him. He can really rib a fellow. And if he knew that he was getting under your skin, he'd really have your skin rolling up.

He liked to hunt. If he's got one gun, he's got a hundred, all kinds of guns. But he couldn't hit that vase right there. Can't shoot a lick, and he's always shooting.

The Monarchs developed several players who starred in the majors, especially of course Jackie Robinson. Jackie was smart, he was an awful smart ballplayer. He didn't have the ability at first, but he had the brains. We had a ballplayer here that was a much better ballplayer than he was—Willard Brown. He could hit, run, throw. But Jackie had one-third ability and two-thirds brains, and that made him a great ballplayer.

Same way with the catcher on Baltimore, Campanella. Campanella was a second-string catcher, but he had more sense than Eggie Clark, the first-string catcher. In those days there was always a clique on a ball club. Clark was in the clique, and Campanella was young. Clark would do all the catching in the big ball games, Campanella would catch the second game or catch the exhibition games. But Campanella got more out of baseball than Clark did, because he was a smarter catcher.

Larry Doby never developed into an outfielder until he went to Cleveland. At Newark he was a second baseman, one of those good-hitting second basemen. He was a fair double play man, but his weight and his size kept him from being loose like he could be in the outfield. See, there's nine innings of busy baseball in the infield, and that would kind of slow him down. If they'd catch a second baseman leaning this way, heck, they'd hit the ball over here and you can't get back to it. We had pretty smart hitters in those days. Cleveland put him out there in the outfield and my goodness, the man just didn't look back in baseball. He went on to the top. You get to be relaxed in the outfield.

I have two sons. My oldest boy's a preacher here in Kansas City. My younger boy is in Europe in the Army; he's making a career out of it.

I'm a foreman in the county courthouse now. I went into politics, and through that I got a pretty good job. I'm a Democrat, so if we win in November I'll have a good job for four more years. Satchel Paige ran for assemblyman here in 1968. They put him on the ticket as a "runner." That's to keep somebody else from running. When the voting starts, why he'll drop out. A candidate will give two men $25 and tell them to go down and file for his office. That way other candidates will say, "What's the use of me running? There's already three of them in the race. I can't win a four-way race, I wouldn't have a chance." But just before the election, the other two will drop out. Politics is dirty, it's a dirty game. You talk to anybody, it's dirty game. They'll cut one another's throat to win. I don't mean crookedness, I don't say that's crooked.

I'll talk baseball with anyone, like a little boy out there on the street. A lot of times the kids ask me, "Mr. Newt, when you were with the Monarchs, how about so-and-so and so-and-so?" Now I've got me a conversation going.

And all the old ballplayers have a get-together every year. One time in this neck of the woods, all the way down to Oklahoma City, we had some awfully good semipro ball clubs. Had some *good* semipro ball clubs. A lot of those fellows went to the Western League or the American Association. Some white players had a reunion over in Eagles Hall in Kansas City, Kansas, and one guy, Whitey Harrison, ran across me at the county courthouse and said, "We've been trying to get in touch with some of you fellows, you and Frank Duncan." He called me up later and told us to come out to the reunion. We all went over, and the last five years we've had a reunion every year, all the ballplayers, white and colored. They come from Kansas, from Oklahoma. One guy even comes down from Chicago, two or three fellows from St. Louis, and we have an all-day get-together. Some of them are old men, but they come out for that occasion. We have all the way from 150 to 200 old-timers. When you arrive at the door, they put a name tag on your jacket, and you'll see them wandering around looking at each other's tags. "Who are you?" "What about so-and-so?" "Oh, he's passed." "You remember about such-and-such a game . . . you remember that?" "Don't you remember when I did this or we did that?"

My, it's a wonderful get-together. We got a pretty good write-up about it in the papers too. You talk about hearing some baseball—everybody's talking, and among the habitual drinkers, that's when the truth comes out and there are some tall tales told. One guy says that's the only time he ever hits .300, when he remembers the old days at those parties. Some of them are retired, and a lot of them don't have too many people to talk baseball to. When they get together with some people that they knew, that they played ball with, why my goodness, they don't know when to go home. You sit there and talk and go from this fellow to that fellow and go over the things we used to do and what's happened since we met one another last time. We get quite a kick out of it. A wonderful time.

Cool Papa Bell is admitted to the Hall of Fame with Mickey Mantle, Whitey Ford, and umpire Jocko Conlan. (Photo, National Baseball Library.)

Chapter 7

COOL PAPA BELL

"Cool Papa Bell?" Satchel Paige's brown eyes dance and his mustache twitches with suppressed mirth. "That man was so fast he could turn out the light and jump in bed before the room got dark."

Bell once roomed with Paige, and while the pitcher was out galavanting, Cool Papa discovered that the light switch was defective; there was a delay of a few seconds before the lights went out. When Satch came back, Bell instructed him, "Sit down, I want to show you something." He flicked the switch, strolled over to bed, and pulled the covers up. Bing! The lights went out. "See, Satchel," he said, "You been tellin' people that story 'bout me for years, and even *you* didn't know it was true."

Like Satchel, everyone who saw Cool Papa agrees that he was probably the fastest man ever to play baseball. Faster than Ty Cobb, faster than Lou Brock—yes, probably faster even than Jesse Owens. No one will ever know how many bases Bell stole in his career, which stretched from 1922 to 1948 and covered just about the last twenty-seven years of baseball's long apartheid era. His feats are almost legends. But ex-pitcher Harry Salmon (who taught Paige to pitch in Birmingham in 1927) insists that Bell once stole two bases on the same pitch.

Bell often scored from first on a sacrifice. But perhaps his most famous feat was scoring from second on a ground ball to win the 1934 East-West (all-star) game 1–0.

In Cuba he slugged three home runs in one game against Johnny Allen, who was then on his way to the major leagues. According to Salmon, Bell chided John, "I hear you're going up to the Yankees." "Yes," Allen replied, "I have a chance to go." "Well," said Cool Papa, "I think I'll just hold you back a couple of years."

How would Cool Papa have hit in the major leagues? Over a twenty-one-year period he had ample chance to hit big-league pitching in post-season exhibitions. In 54 games against men like Bob Feller, Bucky Walters, Buck Newsom and Bob Lemon, he hit a rousing .391. Stolen base statistics were kept in only thirty-five of the games; in those thirty-five games Bell stole fifteen sacks, about one every other game.

Thus while white fans remained ignorant, white players did not. "The smoothest center fielder I've seen," said Paul Waner. Bill Veeck ranks Cool Papa right alongside Tris Speaker, Joe DiMaggio and Willie Mays. And Jackie Robinson selected Bell on his all-time all-star outfield, right between Mays and Hank Aaron.

Bell still looked as if he could play an inning or two when I met him in 1970 in his small duplex apartment in the St. Louis ghetto. While his wife entertained my sons with ice cream and cookies, Bell bounced nervously around the living room, explaining in his squeaky voice how he took his lead off first and got a jump on the pitcher almost half a century before.

Cool Papa Bell Speaks . . .

I've scored from first base on singles lots of times. Sometimes I could even score on a bunt. The last time I did that was against Bob Lemon's all-stars when I was forty-five years old. I was playing winter ball in California in 1948. Satchel Paige picked me as a reserve outfielder on his team. I had about quit playing ball, but Satchel wanted someone out there with experience. Some of those young boys just coming up, they would seem like they had a fear of those major leaguers. They'd say, "I'm not as good as the major leaguers, I don't know whether I can hit them or not."

Satchel said, "When I pitch, I want Bell to play."

I said, "Satchel, I'm not in condition, I'm just halfway in condition. I've been managing this farm team and I don't play every day." I could hit the ball, catch it, but by not being in condition, I said, "Don't let me lead off. I don't want to be coming to bat too often, get on base often."

Satchel said, "Oh, you'll be in condition. I've told all the guys what you can do and they don't believe it. And I told them you're older than me and they don't believe *that!*" I said, "I don't want to lead off, I'm not in condition." He said, "I'll pitch five innings, you play five innings, then you can come out."

So this time I was hitting eighth and I got on base, and Satchel came up and sacrificed me to second. Well, Bob Lemon came off the mound to field it and I saw that third base was open, because the third baseman had also charged in to field it. Roy Partee, the catcher, saw me going to third, so he went down the line to cover third and I just came on home past him. Partee called "Time, time!" But the umpire said, "I can't call time, the ball's still in play," so I scored.

Satchel Paige says I would have made Jesse Owens look like he was walking. Jesse Owens ran 100 yards in nine-something, and I could circle the bases—120 yards, plus—in twelve flat. So, comparing his time and mine, they said I was faster than Owens.

Jesse Owens went to spring training with us one year to draw people. They wouldn't let me run him. But he did run against horses and some ballplayers. I saw him run in San Antonio. He'd put a fellow at home, one at first, one at second and one at third. He'd circle all the bases and each guy would run one base against him, but by the time each of them got started, Jesse had built up his speed and passed them. On flat races, Jesse Owens was giving the guys fifteen yards head start. We had a guy named Speed Whatley, and Jesse Owens gave him fifteen yards in a 100-yard race; Whatley gained on him, and when he got to the finish line, Jesse Owens had just run sixty or seventy yards.

He'd run against these horses at sixty yards. He beat all the horses but one, because some of those horses were slow starters. But then they put a quarter horse in against him. I saw one of them on television the other night; he could start and stop and turn faster than the cows can. Anyway, this quarter horse got a good start on Jesse and passed him, and the people booed. That's why they wouldn't let me run. My manager said, "He can't beat you and I know you won't let Jesse Owens beat you, so I won't let you run."

I remember once Jesse Owens ran against George Case of the Washington Senators. They were going to run the 100-yard dash and Jesse Owens was going to run in his track shoes. But they said no, you have to put on baseball shoes. Jesse still beat Case.

They wanted us to run once in Cleveland, and he saw me running bases and came out on the field and praised my running and said, "I don't want to run today. I didn't bring my track shoes."

I don't know if Maury Wills ever saw me play or not. I was playing with the Washington Homestead Grays when he was a kid in Washington. I only met Wills once, here in St. Louis the year he broke Ty Cobb's record. I said, "I have noticed that you're running bases and some guy fouls the pitch off." I knew Junior Gilliam was a team man, Gilliam would probably take a strike in order to give him a chance to steal. I said, "Do you have anyone else behind Gilliam who can do that?" He said no. I said, "I'm going to tell you when I was running bases, I had about three guys behind me, and I had a signal when I was going to steal a base, on the first pitch or the second pitch. So if I'm going to steal a base, they had a chance to help me, they wouldn't hit that ball." I said, "If you had cooperation, you could steal more bases. Tell them to get back in the box, and hold the bat back. You don't have to swing as long as you hold that bat back here. If you're back here in the box, you give the catcher less room to throw. That gives you a couple of steps. And then if you don't get a good lead, he can swing at the ball."

He said, "I hadn't thought of that."

I said, "Well, that's the kind of ball we played." You don't have those kinds of players today. These players today, they don't

Cool Papa Bell

think of things like that. When we came up we played different
baseball than they do in the major leagues. We played "tricky"
baseball.

I would be alert on the bases. A lot of fellows could do the same
things I did if they were alert. A guy drops the ball and *then* they
run. I was always looking for a break. It wasn't that I was that
much faster than the other guys, it was just the way I played.
They said, "You're faster than those guys." I said, "I don't know,
they're just slow in thinking."

The best year I ever had on the bases was 1933. I stole 175 in
about 180 or 200 ball games.

They once timed me circling the bases in twelve seconds flat.
One guy said, "If you can do it in twelve, you can do it in eleven."
So he had a field day, and I was supposed to run against Tuck

Stainback, who played center field for the Yankees. The major league record was :13.3 by a guy named Swanson with Cincinnati. We were going to try to break it. Well, it rained and it was muddy and Stainback wouldn't run. He said he had a cold. But the fans kept hollering, so I ran alone in :13.1 on a wet ground.

Back then Fats Jenkins of the Lincolns was supposed to be the fastest guy out East. A white fellow had seen Fats Jenkins run, but when he saw me, he said I was the fastest man he'd ever seen. He asked me, "Bell, do you want to make some money? I can take you overseas running on tracks and nobody would beat you running." But I never did. I don't know how I would have done.

I scored from first base on singles lots of times. If the ball isn't hit straight at the outfielder, I'd score. You have to be heads up and watch those things.

I was born in Starkville, Mississippi, in 1903. My father was a farmer. He raised cotton, corn. He lived good. He wasn't a rich man, but he lived well. My grandfather was a farmer too. He was three-quarters Indian. My great-grandfather was a full-blooded Indian. I don't know what tribe—those tall, rawboned Indians with high cheekbones. He owned three trotting horses, but he couldn't put a horse on the racetrack. He had to let some white fellow do it. He never got credit for it.

When they changed the Oklahoma Territory over to a state, we had an uncle told my mother and her daddy to come down, that they could get so much land for themselves because they had the blood of Indians. He got some land in Oklahoma, but they didn't go down there.

See, my mother had about two acres of land and a house in Mississippi. My grandfather wasn't married to my mother's mother, but he reared my mother. She was with him before he had any land at all, she helped him work to get this land. When my grandfather died, he had some "outside" sons, but he had just one son from his wife.

They went to divide the land, and his son wanted all the land himself. They brought it to court, and the white people said, "Now she [my mother] was here before any of the others, she has to have a child's part." But she said, "I don't want to go into court. I'll ask my children about it." I was young then and let my older brother and sister decide. They said, "If you don't want it, don't go to court." All she had to say was, "Yes, I want my part," and she wouldn't have had to go to court. But she said, "Oh, forget about it." It was divided between the wife and the son, and we didn't get any at all.

See, they didn't know much back in those days. Some Negroes had just come from out of slavery and didn't know too much. You can't hardly fault them in a way for not knowing these things. That's why the Negro is so far behind on some things.

I started playing baseball when I was seventeen when I came to St. Louis in 1920. I played with my four brothers, who were playing with the Compton Hill Cubs in the old city league.

I used to throw the knuckle ball. If I got two strikes on you, I could throw my knuckle ball and it would just do this—dart down. I bet you I could strike anybody out with that knuckle ball. My brother couldn't catch me. But you know who could catch me with that knuckle ball? My sister.

My brother was a good pitcher, but he didn't play long. A great arm, could throw hard. For distance I don't know anyone who could throw farther. In 1923 he didn't lose a ball game; he won all his games and tied one. Then he went to Harrisburg with Oscar Charleston. Later he went to Detroit and they didn't pay him, so he quit playing ball.

My oldest brother was the best player of us at that time. He was a left-handed outfielder and catcher—could hit, run, do everything. He worked out with the St. Louis Stars, but he broke the stitches in his arm and the doctor told him not to go back. At that time, 1922, I was ready to quit baseball. I was making $35 or $40 a week at the packing house and $20 on Sunday to play ball. It was more than I could make playing ball full time, and I figured it was time to get a steady job. But the East St. Louis Cubs needed a pitcher to throw against the Stars, and they asked me to come out for just one game.

Bill Drake was pitching. My other brother, named L.Q., said Drake was the trickiest pitcher they had on the team. But he didn't throw hard. He would move the men back and forth and throw something slow. I said, "I know I can hit a home run off him"—I could hit. But I didn't hit him. I would hit the balls on my wrist, and I said, "This is a pitcher I thought I could hit." My brother always told me what a smart pitcher Drake was, but he didn't throw all that hard all the time. But he would trick you, you know. Finally, somebody else was pitching, and I hit the right field fence. That was my first hit. I was hitting the ball pretty good, but they were catching it. They beat me 8–1, but I struck out eight men. Anyway, the Stars made me such a good offer I decided to stick with baseball.

The Stars had a good team. Sam Bennett used to catch, play outfield, shortstop, any position. He had a great arm. Sam Bennett told me he gave Tris Speaker pointers in the outfield. They were both from Texas. They had a white team and a black team. The white team would go out there and work out, then the colored team would go out. When the ball was hit, Bennett would turn his back, then turn around and catch it. Tris Speaker would get with Bennett and ask him, "Would you mind showing me how you play outfield?" So Bennett told him everything he knew, and Tris Speaker had the ability to be one of the greatest outfielders there was.

For pitchers we had Deacon John Meyers, John Finner, Jimmy Oldham, Drake and Steel Arm Dickey. Dickey was a left-hander; he could throw hard. He was killed the next year. Someone stabbed him that winter and killed him. See, he was making whiskey for a guy, and the guy figured Steel Arm wasn't turning all the money in.

All those players were major-league players.

When I first joined the team, our manager, Bill Gatewood, didn't want to pitch me. The catcher said he didn't want to catch my knuckle ball. I was just a young pitcher they brought up. Gatewood told me, "Now I want you to watch everything that those pitchers do, because we've got pitchers who know *how* to pitch." In our league they threw the spitter, the screwball, emery ball, shine ball—that means Vaseline ball; there was so much Vaseline on it, it made you blink your eyes on a sunny day. Then they threw the mud ball—the mud on its seams made it sink. The emery ball would break either up or down, but if a sidearmer threw it and didn't know what he was doing, it could sail right into the hitter.

Ray Chapman [of the Cleveland Indians] got killed with an emery ball, that's why they don't throw it anymore. It was a dangerous pitch.

After I got with the Stars, we went on the road for a month, and Gatewood said, "I might pitch you and I might not."

Indianapolis was the first place we went. They really had a team. They had Biz Mackey, the best catcher ever was; first baseman was Ben Taylor; Connie Day at second; Blackman at third. In the outfield was Crush Holloway and Oscar Charleston. Well, Indianapolis beat us the first three ball games, so late in the third game Gatewood said, "Well, I'm going to try you against those guys. We're already beat anyway, you might get some experience." He thought I'd be afraid of crowds, but I said, "Don't worry about it, I've played before crowds on the sandlots"—we used to draw 10,000 or 11,000 people, more than the professional team drew. They said, "Oh that guy, he's taking it cool, isn't he?"

I had a good curve ball. And I had a knuckle ball—that was my best pitch, but he wouldn't let me throw my knuckle ball because our catcher had got hit on the finger. But I started striking out Ben Taylor and those guys—Charleston just threw his bat away. With my curve ball! I could throw sidearm, three-quarters or straight over. And I had a screw ball—I didn't know what it was; I called it an "in-drop." Ben Taylor started rubbing his eyes: "Something wrong with my eyes!" Gatewood said, "Well, you never seen a curve like that before."

I wasn't afraid. See, we all dressed in the same clubhouse with Charleston and those guys. They'd say, "Where'd you get this new boy from?" They would push me out from under the shower, spit on me, step on me. They used to do that, see, just to try to get your goat. Well, I never did pay them any attention.

So we went to Fort Wayne, a little old semipro team out there. Gatewood said, "Well, I'm going to let you pitch, get a little more experience."

We had these guys shut out at Fort Wayne. In the last of the ninth inning the outfield came in, said, "He's going to strike out everybody anyway." I didn't strike *everybody* out in the whole ball game, but I was striking out so many, the outfield came on in. So I struck out the next two men. The third man hit a little pop fly and nobody went to get it, so he went on around and made a home run off it. I struck out the next man. Only one man hit the ball.

Gatewood said, "Well, you're doing so well, we're going to Chicago, I think I'm going to pitch you against Chicago." We got to Chicago on a Saturday and he pitched Meyers, our ace pitcher. They beat Meyers, and Sunday they beat John Finner. So he said, "Well, I'm going to pitch you tomorrow," and I beat them 6–3. They had Jimmy Lyons, could drag the ball down the first base line; I'd get the ball and touch him out. He'd look around: "Now *who* touched me out?" They'd say, "The pitcher." See, they had the infield built up with high ridges on the foul line, so the ball would roll fair when they bunted it. But I stopped them from bunting. Every time they'd bunt, I'd throw them out, and beat them 6–3.

Jimmy Lyons was supposed to be the fastest man in the league. Charleston was fast too, but Jimmy Lyons was supposed to be the fastest man in the league. Rube Foster [the Chicago manager] wanted us to race. So we went out and raced, and I beat Jimmy Lyons. Maybe 75 or 100 yards, something like that. I just ran off from Jimmy Lyons. That's when I got my reputation as a fast runner.

You know that outfield in Chicago was soft, just like a carpet. I used to play in way close the way I saw Charleston play, and those hitters like Cristobel Torrienti would hit that ball way out there. I'd run and run and take that ball over my head. Rube liked that. He kept trying to get me on his team.

I was pitching against him once and the score was tied—I think it was 2–2 or 1–1, something like that. I had two strikes on me and I laid this bunt down. Frog Redus was on third base, and he scored and we beat 'em. Rube Foster kept those guys out there until nine o'clock that night talking about a ballplayer thinking. He said, "Look at this young guy, just coming into baseball, doing this."

So Rube Foster wanted me on his team. He said, "If I had you with Jimmy Lyons and all, I would have one of the best teams"—he already *had* one of the best teams. He offered seven men for me, but they wouldn't trade me. And the Kansas City

Monarchs tried to get me too. But St. Louis wouldn't let me go.

We left there and went to Detroit. We would charter a Pullman then, and I was back there asleep, and those guys came in there with a newspaper about this new pitcher, this young pitcher, going to open up the game in Detroit. They said, "Wake up, wake up. Lookee here, you're on this train sleeping and this headline says you're going to pitch in Detroit." I didn't pay it much attention.

I guess that had something to do with my name, "Cool." They said, "He's so cool he don't get excited." They started calling me Cool Bell, but Gatewood said, "We've got to add something to it. We'll call him Cool Papa."

We got into Detroit on a Saturday. I opened up the game, beat a guy name of Jack Marshall 5–4. I hit a home run off him. I could *hit* them.

I hit quite a few home runs. When I first came into baseball, I could hit that ball a long ways. I would hit twelve or fifteen home runs a year. One year I hit twenty-one. A lot of them wouldn't be over the fence, they'd be between the fielders. When I was pitching, they would say, "They think he's just another pitcher, but they ain't going to strike him out. Watch how far he's going to hit this ball." I was a right-handed hitter; I hit the ball to the opposite field too, I hit it down the right field line.

The first time I saw big leaguers was when we played the Detroit Tigers in 1922. I didn't play, I was nineteen then. Cobb and Heilmann wouldn't play us. Cobb had played a Negro team in Cuba in 1910 and got beat and said he'd never play against us again. But Howard Ehmke pitched. We beat them two out of three. After that Judge Landis, the commissioner, wouldn't let them play a Negro team under their team names. They had to call themselves all-stars. Then if they got beat, we couldn't say we beat a big-league team. Sometimes they'd play under an assumed name. Landis saw some of them out there and stopped them from playing under an assumed name.

I went to California that winter on the pitching staff to play in the winter league. We got rooms at a little hotel down by the station—a big room, had two beds. My brother Fred Bell and I slept in one. Turkey Stearnes slept in the other. He was from

Knoxville, Tennessee, hit thirty-five home runs the first year he was with the Detroit Stars. He went to Cuba and they needed an outfielder, so they put me out there. I played left field. One Saturday we were playing in Pasadena and a lot of balls were hit over the center fielder's head. I'd run over behind him and catch them. So from then on I played center field. I wasn't a pitcher anymore.

When Gatewood saw how I could run and throw, he made me an outfielder and made me change over to the left side of the plate. He said, "If you would hit the ball slow to the infield, make the third baseman or shortstop move over, you'd beat it out." At first it was a little tough on me, but they couldn't throw me out. Joe Hewitt taught me that. Joe Hewitt, Jimmy Lyons, Sam Bennett, and Jelly Gardner taught me a lot about how to hit to the infield. After those guys saw I was interested in playing ball and was trying, and I had the ability to do these things, they helped me out. I got to the point where—nobody's perfect, but they said I could do it better than the one who taught me.

I wasn't as good a hitter after I turned on my left side from my right. At first when I'd get two strikes on me, I'd turn back on my right, so I wouldn't strike out. And after I turned over on my left side, they wouldn't let me swing hard anymore. That's why I didn't hit the long ball all the time. I'd stand back from the plate and chop down on the ball. That's something I learned from the old players. By the time the ball comes down, they can't throw me out. They'd bring in their infield as if there was a man on third and no out; they couldn't get me if they played back in their normal position. I'd just hit the ball to short, and if he has to move over for it, he can't throw me out. I'd hit the ball so he'd *have* to move over. I could hit it between first and second nine times out of ten. Now take Bob Gibson or Jim Bunning: they follow through so hard, I'd hit it behind them. Those kinds of pitchers couldn't beat our team much.

Oh, it was a tough league. We had a lot of other good ballplayers that came along that were good enough to play, but we had so many ballplayers then—so many *good* ballplayers. Now, the Sculling Steel Mill in St. Louis had some of the best players you ever saw, but they wouldn't play pro ball. They couldn't make enough money at it. The same with the Post Office in

Chicago. They had some of the best players in the country. We had a lot of ballplayers better than some of those in the majors today. But some of our owners didn't think we were good enough to play in the majors. They said, "You'd have to learn a whole new system in the majors." That shows how much *they* knew about baseball!

When I came up, we didn't play baseball like they play in the major leagues. We played tricky baseball. When we played the big leaguers after the regular reason, our pitchers would curve the ball on the 3–2. They'd say, "What, are you trying to make us look bad?" We'd bunt and run and they'd say, "Why are you trying to do that in the first inning?" When we were supposed to bunt, they'd come in and we'd hit away. Oh, we played tricky baseball.

That's why we beat the major-league teams. It's not that we had the best men, but in a short series we could outguess them. Baseball is a guessing game. The major leaguers would play for one big inning. They go by "written baseball." But there's so much "unwritten baseball." When you use it, they say it's unorthodox. In our league, if a guy was on first and had a chance to go to third, he'd go just fast enough to make the outfielder throw. That way the batter could take second, see. We'd go into third standing up so the third baseman couldn't see the throw coming and it might go through him. Jackie Robinson learned that from some old players he saw in the Negro leagues. Sometimes you can teach a guy something and he can do it better than you. If the throw got by our third baseman, I'd charge in from center field, he'd flip it to me and I'd put the runner out. Or when they'd get a guy in the hot box [running him down]. Most of the time the infielders throw it back and forth and the runner just stands there in the middle. I'd run in from center and put him out. I did that numbers of times.

The Chicago American Giants had the smartest players you ever saw. They used to bat in a run on a base on balls. If they had a man on third and the batter walked, he'd just trot easy-like down to first, and the man on third would just sort of stand there looking at the stands. At the last minute, the batter would cut out for second as fast as he could go, the coach would yell, "Heh, look at that!" the pitcher would whirl around, the guy on third would light out for home, and like as not they wouldn't get anybody out.

I think we had a better system than the majors. Whatever it takes to win, we did. We were playing our style and they were playing their style. And every team had two or three good, outstanding pitchers on it. Some of them had four who could pitch in any league, anywhere. That's another reason we could beat the major leaguers in a short series, but playing a full season, with only sixteen to seventeen men, why, we couldn't last.

In '23 they told Oscar Charleston I was faster than he. They put me in the outfield to shag balls with him. We would run from right field to left field, and the one who got there first wouldn't catch the ball, he would wait for the other one, wait and see if he could catch it. They knew I was faster than Charleston, because Jimmy Lyons was faster than Charleston, and I could beat Lyons.

Oscar Charleston was a sensation ballplayer. He played right behind second base, but he could go back and get that ball. Willie Mays plays close in too, but he can't go back like Charleston could. When I first started, I played close in too; I'd run back and catch those balls over my head. But I found out that some of those balls just missed my hand. If I had been back a step, I would have caught them, so I began to play back.

Curt Flood plays back too. He catches as many balls as Mays, always did. If Mays would move back a step or two, he'd catch some of those balls that are over his head. I saw a ball hit in San Francisco, one of those high liners, hit the fence, and the guy got a triple. They said, "Mays was the only ballplayer that would have held the guy to a triple." But I say, "Uh uh. If it had been Flood, he would have caught the ball." Those things you have to learn. Mays can't go back the way Charleston did.

Oscar Charleston—if I was picking an all-star team, I don't care about those other guys, that's who I'd put in center field.

The Stars played at the park at Compton Avenue and Market Street by the old car barns. It was a wood park. At first it didn't have a top on it. I guess it could seat around 5,000 people. It had a wood fence around it, and people almost cut that fence down by cutting peepholes in it. In right field they had a house sat on a corner there, must have been about 400 feet down the line. In left was a car shed. Down the line was 269 feet, then it would slant off to center around 500 feet. By the car barn was a track running beside there. If a right-hand hitter could pull the ball he could hit it up on that shed, but they had to hit it high—about 30 feet high. The car shed was the wall. Where the car shed ended, there you had a fence. There was plenty of room out there in center field; there wasn't anybody going to hit it out of there.

Willie Wells joined the Stars in 1924. He could field—one of the greatest fielders I ever saw. And Wells was a great hitter, he *made* a great hitter out of himself. Of course he wouldn't hit fifty home runs. But in '28 we had a play-off with the American Giants—we won the first half of the season, they won the other. Wells hit two home runs off Willie Foster, their best left-hander.

By 1929 what a team we had: Quincy Trouppe catching, High-pockets Trent and Leroy Matlock pitching, George Giles first base, Newt Allen second, Willie Wells shortstop, plus Mule Suttles, Frog Redus and me in the outfield.

In 1930 we beat the major-league all-stars six out of eight games in Chicago. Pitching they had Willis Hudlin, George Uhle and Earl Whitehill. Whitehill beat us both times—he was the toughest big-league pitcher I ever faced. Down in Mexico in 1936, he beat us down there too. I ran the bases against them the same as I did any other team. If it was time to steal, I'd steal.

Now Pepper Martin of the Cardinals was a pretty good base runner. He ran kind of wild in the World Series in 1931 when he stole five bases. I played against him in 1930 on the Pacific Coast. We played in a park called White Sox Park. It had a long left field foul line, and most of our guys could get a homer on a hard grounder down the line. Pepper Martin hit one past the third baseman into the corner, and he just did make it to third base. All the people started saying, "I thought Pepper Martin could *run!*" When we played those fellows, they'd come and ask us how we did this or that, and I told Pepper how to get a lead off the pitcher. If you have a catcher with a great arm, you have to get a bigger lead. You can't steal on the catcher much. It's with the pitcher you've got to get the jump. A lot of people don't know this —you can't outrun that ball.

When you get a hit, some people are satisfied if they get a single, but if you run hard, just like you're trying to beat out a bunt, and make your turn at first, if the outfielder has to go over to get the ball, you can go to second. That's how you take your extra base, by hustling all the time. And if you're stealing second, don't be satisfied. Look up. The infielder might miss the ball, and you can get up and go to third. A lot of players expect the coaches to tell them, but the coach can't think as fast as the player can.

Well, after Martin had that good year in the Series the next year, he gave all the credit to me for stealing all those bases. They asked him if colored players could play in the majors, and he told them about playing against me and how I had helped him.

That winter in Cuba I hit three home runs in one game against Johnny Allen. I was the first man to hit three homers in one game in Cuba. Later on the major-league all-stars went down there, and Dick Sisler hit three home runs in one game, and they had a big celebration about it. José Fernandez was the manager of the Cuban Stars. He told them Dick Sisler wasn't the first fellow to hit three home runs in one game, Bell was. He said, "Wait, I'll go home to get the papers to prove it."

A lot of those white boys in Cuba had never played against colored before. Some of them didn't want to play against us down there. But the Cubans said, "We all play together here, it doesn't make any difference." We used to get a lot of them from Kentucky and around there, their first year in the majors or just out of the minors. They didn't know those Cuban boys were black. They said, "We didn't come down here to play colored." But after they got down there and started to play, it was just a changeover for them.

A lot of times you hear people talk about colored: "He's lazy, he won't work, he'll cut you, he'll steal." The colored man's no more lazy than the white. They brought them over here to help build the United States. But when they didn't pay them, of course they didn't want to work. Now they're fighting to go to school, to get a better job, get a home. How can you say they're lazy and you won't allow them to work?

The Stars broke up in 1931. The whole league broke up. In '32 we went to Detroit—Wells, Trouppe, myself and Dizzy Dismukes, the manager. At that time the Homestead Grays had two teams, the Grays and the Detroit Senators. Detroit was stronger than the

Grays. We were making money, but the Homestead Grays went broke. The Posey brothers and Charlie Walker had the Grays, but they couldn't make ends meet with two teams, so they carried us over there to Pittsburgh with the Grays. Five of us went to the Grays, but they took us off salary and we played on a percentage of the gate. When they took us off salary, some of us went back with the Kansas City Monarchs. The Pittsburgh Crawfords wanted me to play with them, but I said, "No, I promised the Monarchs." That winter the Monarchs went to Mexico, but we didn't make any money, so the next year I went on with the Crawfords.

That was 1933. When I went out East I was hitting .500. Josh Gibson was hitting more than me, but when I started gaining on him, they said, "Don't you send any clippings about what you're doing." The secretary of the Crawfords wanted to tell the truth, but they fined him. They didn't want to rate me over Josh or Satchel Paige, because I'd ask for more salary.

Sam Streeter used to keep score, but sometimes he didn't even bring the scorebook out there. I stole 175 bases that year, but they only gave me credit for 91. The last game they played I got five hits out of six, stole five bases. But they didn't take the scorebook out there that day, and I didn't get credit.

I used to let Roy Campanella and his team in the ball park when he was a little kid in Philadelphia around 1933. He probably doesn't remember that. Campanella played on a team called the Metros, and I took them to the ball park. Not the whole team; about four or five little boys. I told the man, "These are ball-players, let 'em in." I said, "They haven't got any money, but they'll grow up to be men and they'll be baseball fans."

In 1935 we played Dizzy Dean's all-stars a series. We opened in York, Pennsylvania, and in the first inning we got four runs off Diz. I hit, Jerry Benjamin hit, Buck Leonard walked and Josh Gibson hit the ball over the fence. The people started booing, and Diz went into the outfield for a while. He hated to just take himself out of a game. Satchel Paige was pitching for us, and we beat them 11–1.

At Dayton, Ohio, Dizzy's brother Paul was supposed to pitch, but he just went home. We beat them two games, and the third was tied in the ninth when the umpire called it. Otherwise we wouldn't draw when we got to New York.

In New York, I got two doubles off Diz in the first game. When Gibson came up with me on second, Diz kept telling the outfield, "Get back, get back." Jimmy Ripple was playing center field. He said, "How far do you want me to get back?" But Diz just said, "Get back, get back." It was a scoreless tie. Gibson hit a fly deep to Ripple. I rounded third and Dick Lundy, who was coaching at third, yelled stop. I stopped, but the shortstop was just getting the throw from Ripple, so I started for home again. The catcher caught the ball high, and I slid in and the umpire called me out. Well, the people came out of the stands and went after the umpire, and I like to have got cut with a knife. The umpire said, "Look, you don't do that against a big-league team—score from second on an outfield fly." So he called me out. Then Ripple tripled, and they beat us 3–0 when Ray Dandridge, our third baseman, threw the ball away. Swift won the second game 3–0. We lost the same as the first game, by a wild throw. Dean was a great pitcher.

In 1936 I played against Rogers Hornsby's all-stars in Mexico. We had taken a colored all-star team to Mexico in 1932, but we were too strong for them, so they said, "Next time just bring an ordinary team and it will be more interesting." So we went down there again in 1936, and the first thing the Mexicans said was, "Come on out tomorrow and play the big leaguers." We said, "Big leaguers! We didn't know *they* were here!" They had Jimmy Foxx and Rogers Hornsby in the infield, Heinie Manush and Doc Cramer in the outfield, Steve O'Neill catching and Whitehill pitching. It takes about a week to get used to the altitude, and they'd been down there about two weeks while we'd just arrived. But we had them beat 6–4, with two out in the ninth, when Manush was safe on first. Foxx took a 3–2 count. Then he got a ball up around his letters and hit it into the bleachers for a home run. The umpire called the game. The sun was up in the sky, but they called the game. That night we all had dinner at an American restaurant, and Foxx told us that that was a strike, the third ball the umpire called, but he said he wasn't going to argue.

Next day Hornsby hit a ball way over my head. I ran back and caught it over my head. He said, "Come here, Lefty. That was the hardest ball I ever hit. How did you catch it?"

Earl Mack, Connie Mack's son, said, "If the door was open, you'd be the first guy I'd hire. I'd pay you $75,000 a year to play ball. You'd be worth it in drawing power alone."

They beat us the last two games, so the next year we said we're going to get a good team and beat Hornsby.

In 1937 we had ten games scheduled against Hornsby in the States. He was slowing up then, but they had him advertised. Satchel Paige never could remember names. In the first game, in Davenport, Iowa, he said, "I want you to tell me when Hornsby comes to bat," so I yelled, "Here's Hornsby." Well, there was a lot of applause, but when the ball hit the catcher's glove, Hornsby would swing. Satch struck him out two times. Andrew Porter— we used to call him "Pullman Porter"—struck Hornsby out twice, but it was a night game, dark, rainy and foggy. We got five hits and they got two, but they beat us 2–1. Johnny Mize got both hits. It was tied 1–1, and Mize hit a little pop fly behind second. The outfielder ran in to get it and kind of lost the ball in the fog. It was wet and he threw it into left field, and Mize went home. That's what beat us.

Bobby Feller was just coming up then, and he pitched three innings against us in Des Moines. We got only one hit off him and no runs, but we beat them after he left, 5–2 or 5–3. We beat them a doubleheader in Denver, came back to Des Moines and beat them again, and they just canceled the last five games.

The only fight I ever got in was one year in the Denver semi-pro tournament. I slid into third base and this guy dropped the ball. When I was getting off the ground he was swinging at me. I hit him and he turned a flip. Three guys jumped from the dugout with bats. Rap Dixon on our team jumped between me and them. The umpire went behind to hold me. What was he holding *me* for? I wasn't trying to fight him—he was trying to fight *me*!

In 1937 this guy Trujillo was running the Dominican Republic, only he was having some troubles. He figured since his people liked baseball so much, if he came up with a top-notch team they wouldn't want to see him lose his job. So he imported a bunch of us from the States. There was Paige and Gibson, Samuel Bankhead, Orlando Cepeda's daddy, me and others. We didn't know we were being used for a political reason until we got there. The people told us if we didn't win the title we would be executed. Some of our boys got so nervous they couldn't play. But we won. Otherwise I probably wouldn't be here to tell about it.

After that I went down to Mexico for four years. I led the Mexican League in 1940. Led or tied for the lead in every department: hit .437, most home runs—thirteen. I hit twenty inside-the-park homers, but I didn't get credit for them. When I hit a ball between the outfielders, they wouldn't give me a home run. They said, "You're too fast." They had a short fence in Mexico. If I hit a ball on the side of that fence and made a home run off of it, they would give me a double.

I was in Cuba in the winter of 1940 and I was hitting .360. The closest man to me was forty points behind, and we had two weeks to go, about six games to play. My team couldn't win the championship even if we won those six games, so they sent all five of us American boys home, took two weeks' salary from us. I was supposed to get $500 cash for winning the batting championship, but by sending me home, I didn't get the championship. Baseball never was much for me making money.

The next year Memphis wanted me, so I went down there. They wanted me to manage if the manager got drunk. I said no. The owner was supposed to pay my transportation. He said, "Now you pay your transportation, when you get down here I'll give it back to you." After I got down there he wouldn't give it to me. And then this guy told me, "And the owner of the club is a dentist and all our players have their teeth fixed here." I didn't have a toothache and I wasn't about to pay a man to fix what didn't need fixing, so I just turned around and went home. I left and went back to the Homestead Grays.

When I went to the Grays in '43, they wanted to know, "Where did you get this young fellow out there doing all that hitting?" They thought I was young, because I was still running. Ric Roberts, the sportswriter, said, "I heard about Cool Papa Bell, played in '32. He scored from first base twice in one ball game on a single. Are you any kin to him? Are you his son?"

I said, "No, I'm the same Cool Papa Bell."

He said, "You couldn't be the same man."

I said, "I am."

Ric Roberts didn't believe that. He thought I was the son or the grandson of the man did that.

Buck Leonard was a great hitter on the Grays, but he didn't hit the curve ball as well as he did the fast ball. I said, "If you knew what was coming, could you hit the ball?" He said, "Yeah." I said, "Well, I bet I can tell you every time a curve's coming. If it's a curve and I'm on first, I'll stand with my hands on my knees. If it's a fast ball, I'll stand straight up. And if I don't know, I'll sort of swing my arms to say I didn't catch it." How did I do it? It's easy. Every time a curve is coming, what would the catcher do? He'd move his right foot over a little to be ready to catch it, wouldn't he? I remember the 1964 World Series, the Cardinals and the Yankees. I kept telling the guy next to me, "It's a curve, it's a fast ball." Heck, all I did was watch the catcher.

In '45 I was sick. I had arthritis, I was stiff, I couldn't run. I hit .308, the lowest I ever hit in my life. I couldn't throw—I could throw but it wouldn't take off. I read in this book where some guy said I had a weak arm but I could get the ball away. I had a *good* arm! But that one year, 1945, when I was sick, I don't know, I was just tight. My arm wasn't sore, but the ball wouldn't go anywhere hardly, it wouldn't take off. But before then I had an arm just as good as anybody. I didn't have the strongest arm in baseball. I had a brother had an arm twice as strong as my arm. But I could throw you out. But some of those younger fellows didn't see me until I had played twenty-two or twenty-three years.

The doctor fixed me up a remedy. He asked me if I drank, I said no, but he had this remedy made up of lemon and gin and rock candy. Next year I came back. I still was sick, but my arm loosened up, I could throw; my legs were loose, I could run. I hit .411. But that year took something from me. I never did feel right anymore. If I hit an inside-the-park home run and another double or triple, I was through. When I was young, I could hit three home runs a game and it wouldn't bother me, but I was old.

Sometimes we'd play in Philadelphia Saturday night, get in the bus and ride all night, get to Washington, go to the park— couldn't get any rooms—play a doubleheader, then go down in

Virginia someplace. I said, "You let me play Saturday night and play a doubleheader Sunday, let me rest Monday." But Vic Harris [the Grays' manager] was putting me in all those games anyway.

Jackie Robinson was with the Monarchs then, and we played them one night in Wilmington. Dizzy Dismukes, the Monarchs' road secretary, came to me and said, "Robinson will be signed in organized ball; he wants to play shortstop." But he didn't think Robinson would make it at short. He could make it at first base, second or third, but not shortstop. And if he missed his chance, I don't know how long we'd go before we'd get another chance. Because, you know, he'd tried out up there in Boston and they'd turned him down. That's what had been happening all the time. They'd have a tryout and then say, "We didn't see anybody worthwhile." Well, we wanted to show Jackie that he should try out at another position.

So Dismukes said, "I want you to hit the ball to his right, because Jackie can't go to his right too well. He can't throw you out." I was the kind of hitter, nine out of ten times I could hit the ball to any field I wanted to hit it. So the first time I hit the ball to Jackie's right. Jackie caught the ball all right, but you have to backhand it, you can't take an extra step, you have to catch it and throw. But when Jackie goes over to the right to catch the ball, he's got to take two steps before he pivots. So I beat that throw. Then I stole second base. He caught the ball and I just slid under him. Next time I came up and hit the ball the same way. He caught the ball, couldn't throw me out. I stole second base, slid by the base, reached back and tagged it. The next two times I walked both times. I stole four bases that night. He'd hold the ball down for me to slide into, I'd just step around his hands. I said, "See that? They got a lot of guys in the major leagues slide like that. You can't get those guys out like that."

There were so many people didn't want Jackie to make it. But he happened to be that guy that had that determination. He was good, but he wasn't our best player.

Monte Irvin was our best young player at that time. I gave him my batting title in 1946 in order for him to get a chance in the majors. He had been sick in the Army, but he went to Mexico, won the batting championship there, came back and hit .389. But they reversed it to read .398. I was hitting .402. We had a double-header left. The paper came out before we played and said Irvin had won the batting championship. But the fans knew better. They kept a-hollering. They said, "Irvin hasn't won, they've got these two games to play here. Bell's leading." I played in the first ball game, got two hits and two walks, and ended up with .435. The second ball game they wouldn't let me play, said I didn't have enough games for the title. The fans were mad, but they didn't know what we were doing. We were doing that to give Irvin a better chance to have a tryout in the majors. After the season they were supposed to give me $200 for giving Irvin my batting championship. But the owner, See Posey, said, "Well, look, Irvin won it"—they wouldn't give me the $200.

That's three championships I won, taken away from me.

But we would rather pass something on to help the future of the black man, because so many things were kept from us. If it did help some young fellow, I'd rather have him get the credit, because I couldn't go back. I didn't have a future, I was too old. And I wasn't the only one who kept the average down.

In 1948 Satchel Paige wanted me to manage the Kansas City Monarchs' farm team. He told me, "You never made money in baseball. This may be your chance to make some money." I was supposed to get one-third of every ballplayer that they sold to the majors that I found and developed. Satchel was on my team—he pitched to draw a crowd—when the Cleveland Indians took him.

We sold thirty-eight ballplayers; twenty of them were ballplayers that I had found, but I never got anything. I said, "Here's a boy I want, just out of high school here in St. Louis—Elston Howard." And I said, "I've got another boy I want in school in Dallas—Ernie Banks." I recommended him to Buck O'Neil, the Monarchs' manager, but he said he didn't need a shortstop. I said, "Just look at him work out," and that's how they found him. I offered Howard and Banks to the St. Louis Browns, but they didn't want them. The Cards also tried out Howard, but they didn't take him either, and I said, "If they don't want *those* two boys, who *do* they want?"

Later they sold Banks to the Chicago Cubs. I didn't get anything. They said I didn't have a contract. All I ever got was a basket of fruit when they sold Banks. A basket of fruit!

I retired after that. I figured it was time to find a steady job before I was too old. I went back to St. Louis, went to work for the city, first as a custodian and then as a night watchman. Even after I quit, people still were after me to play. The Browns in 1951 tried to get me to play. I went down there to see Satchel Paige. Bill Norman, who used to play against us before going to the major league, saw me, said, "You want to play ball?"

I said, "No."

The secretary for the Browns came over. Norman said, "Yeah, man, he plays better than anyone we got out there now in the outfield."

The secretary said, "Is that Bell you're talking about? Cool Papa Bell?"

Norman said, "Yes."

He said, "Come on over here and sign this contract, and I'll put you on the field right now."

I said, "I don't want to play."

He said, "Can you hit?"

That's all I *could* do then. My legs were bad, I had varicose veins, I couldn't run. He said, "What are you hitting?"

I said, "I'm hitting .700 there with this farm team. All I can do is hit now. I can't catch the ball the other fellow hits."

He tried to get me to play, but I couldn't play then. I mean, I couldn't run, I'd get tired. I was forty-eight years old at the time! They said, "You mean you're older than Satchel Paige is?"

I said, "Yes, I'm older than he is."

People told me I should have tried for the job just for the money, but I couldn't do it just for a paycheck. I never had any money, so I never worried about it. I just didn't want the fans to boo me, and if I had played at that age they sure would have. Sometimes pride is more important than money.

I just didn't worry about money too much.

Now when we played in California, they would bill Satchel and he would get 15 percent. When they billed me, they had those wagons all going around saying "Bell's going to be here tonight." I didn't ask for anything; I only got a cut like the rest of the ballplayers got.

Those were great times back then. We used to play a night game Saturday, get in the bus and play a doubleheader Sunday, then play another night game Sunday night. You show me a ballplayer in our old league and I'll show you a guy that can sleep standing, sitting or walking. We didn't know how bad it was until some of our guys got into organized baseball. Then we could compare things.

We didn't play in those big-league parks all the time. That was weekends when the home team was out. Other times we just played out in little playgrounds; the ground was hard and rough, and I used to slide a lot. I would get all skinned up a lot. I would get a sponge and just cut a hole out of it, put a tape around it and put it over the sore to keep my pants off it. My knee would be all skun up on both sides from sliding. It would bother me a lot of times, but I could run after I got loosened up.

Now they've got Roy Campanella on this committee to name Negro players to the Hall of Fame. But he only knows those he played against; he never saw some of the older ones. Most of those fellows were in their late years when he played against them.

If some of those fellows don't get into the Hall of Fame, it's no use putting anyone in there. I'd put in four, five, six at one time. But I'd rather put in a guy who's living first, because the dead

Cool Papa Bell and Josh Gibson in the Dominican Republic

won't know it anyhow. Then at least the guy would know he's finally being honored.

In pitching we had guys would win more games than Satchel. I'd put him in with Smoky Joe Williams, Joe Rogan, Bill Holland and some others. These guys were fast, they were smart, they knew how to pitch. But Satch made the majors, so they picked him over everybody.

Now Satchel was the fastest pitcher I ever saw. But he was in the league four or five years before he learned how to pitch. I used to say, "Look, Satchel, why don't you learn how to pitch? You don't throw the curve, you don't have control of it. And you have to have a change-up. As hard as you throw you'd really fool the batter." In 1938 his arm got sore and I told him, "See, Satchel, you've got to learn to pitch." I showed him how to throw the knuckle ball, and he was throwing it better than I was. That's what I liked about him, he didn't want anybody to beat him doing anything.

Josh Gibson I'd put in with a group of four or five catchers. Some of those others might do more than he could. The long ball was the only thing he could do better. Like Johnny Bench, I don't count him a defensive catcher. Dick Dietz of the Giants, I don't see any catcher better than he. But with the home run hitting, naturally they're going to rate Bench over everybody. Now Campanella could do everything a catcher should do, but Josh couldn't. That's how I rate them.

Our greatest all-round catcher was Biz Mackey. Or take Bruce Petway, or Larry Brown—he was a great little catcher too.

They had another boy used to catch on the team with Larry Brown named George Hamilton. He could hit the ball too. He wasn't as smart a catcher as Brown, but he could throw that ball. He was the toughest catcher for me to steal on. He wasn't even counted in baseball much—he was a second-string catcher—but that boy threw me out more than anyone. It might have been I didn't try to get the lead on him, 'cause he didn't have a name like Brown, but he had a great arm.

I used to play ball with Donn Clendenon's daddy. He used to catch with the Nashville Elite Giants, which later became the Baltimore Elite Giants. He was a good catcher and hitter.

Now I couldn't pick an all-time all-star team. It wouldn't be fair. Who would you leave off? Who would I put at third base? Oliver Marcelle was supposed to be the greatest third baseman of all time, but he couldn't hit too well. All around, Judy Johnson was better than Marcelle was.

Now Willie Wells was the greatest shortstop in the world, but the older fellows would say Pop Lloyd. And at second base who would you pick? Sammy T. Hughes or Bingo DeMoss?

I couldn't say who really was the best hitter. How can you name the best hitter? You can't name him. To tell you the truth, we had so many guys could hit: Buck Leonard, Josh Gibson, Jud Wilson, Wells, Dobie Moore, John Beckwith, Charleston, Torrienti, Chino Smith, Turkey Stearnes. Every team had four or five great hitters on it, and I don't know *who* was the best.

They can't put them all in there in the Hall of Fame. I'm one of the lucky ones, and I appreciate it. When they called me up to tell me I'd been elected, I said, "If it isn't asking too much, are any of the other boys going in?" They said, "No, they're only going to pick one." But there are a lot of old ballplayers they don't say much about. I wouldn't be satisfied if they just put in three, four or five, even if I would be in with those. I still wouldn't be satisfied, because I know some of those guys were great ballplayers. I'd like them to put Rube Foster in, because he was the father of our baseball. And Turkey Stearnes was a great boy, but I didn't even hear them call his name.

They got good players today in the major leagues, just as good as the ones back then. But I wouldn't say they were any better than those fellows. But they got the records to show; we didn't have all that.

I've got no kicks, no regrets. Of course it would have been nice to play in the majors, but I have my memories. I'm not the guy wants to be praised too much. I never wanted to be a big shot. I don't have enough money to go around to these places where an outstanding guy should go. If I know what I did, I'm satisfied.

I have a season pass from the president of the Yankees, Michael Burke. I met him here when they had this big affair for Elston Howard. Howard was a batting instructor for the Yankees, and he told Mr. Burke all about me, said I had given him a lot of tips on hitting. So Mr. Burke sent me a pass and said I would be a special guest of the club.

My greatest thrill? Well, everyone has his own favorite day. But I've got to say my biggest thrill was when they opened the door to the Negro. When they said we couldn't play and we proved that we could, that was the biggest thrill to me. There were more guys before me who didn't have a chance, and I wanted us to prove it to 'em all, black and white alike.

Cool Papa

Cool Papa Bell

JAMES "COOL PAPA" BELL

Bell

Cool Papa Bell

Cool Papa Bell

Ted Page, third from left, with Crawfords Hall of Famers Oscar Charleston, Josh Gibson, and Judy Johnson.

Chapter 8

TED PAGE

Though overlooked on a team of Pittsburgh Crawford stars alongside Satchel Paige, Josh Gibson, Oscar Charleston, Cool Papa Bell, and others, Ted was a fast, solid .300 hitter in the Negro Leagues. And he did even better against white stars after the regular season was over.

Page could hit an occasional long ball—he slammed a homer off Jim Winford of the Cardinals in 1935.

Ted was unrelated to the more famous Satchel Paige, but in their few match-ups, Ted hit Satch like a "cousin." "Don't let anyone tell you *he* couldn't hit!" Satch whistled. "Ted could hit—and bunt too. He was pretty near a .400 batter. He could hit that ball, and he could get away from the plate."

Page was also a fleet base runner. "They called me fast," said Cool Papa Bell, "but I don't know who could beat Ted Page running."

Page was courtly off the field, but he played savagely on it. "I tried to pattern my sliding after Holloway," he said.

"He was a Ty Cobb slider," winces Buck Leonard. "He was always stepping on me at first base. My toe was swelled up like two toes."

Page's slide into third baseman Tom Finley in 1933 caused hemmorhaging that took Finley's life.

Frankie Frisch, the Hall of Fame second baseman, felt Page's spikes in Baltimore just after the 1931 World Series. "He bumped into me and gave me a charley horse," Frisch said. "He rammed my right leg, and oh gosh, how that hurt." Forty-one years later Frisch and Page met again, this time at Cooperstown, for Buck Leonard's induction. "We had a lot of fun in the dining room," Frisch said with his Irish grin. "I said, 'So! I finally found the guy that bumped me and knocked me down.'"

I met Page in 1971 in his comfortable home high on a Pittsburgh hilltop. He was mild and soft-spoken, with the cultured, well-modulated diction of a radio announcer. He kept himself in excellent trim as a bowler and looked far younger than his almost seventy years.

Page's life ended violently. He was bludgeoned to death in 1984 at the age of 78, by a handy man in an argument over pay.

Ted Page Speaks . . .

Monte Irvin says the greatest team he ever saw in Negro ball was the 1934 Pittsburgh Crawfords. I'm delighted to say that I was a member of that team. And another great team, which is declared the greatest that was ever put together, was the 1931 Homestead Grays, and I'm delighted to say I was a member of *that* team. This is a picture of Josh Gibson and Satchel Paige on the Crawfords. And this is the Grays of 1931. According to our owner, Cum Posey, according to our records, that year we won 136 ball games and lost something like 17. And I'm glad to say that this picture is going into the new Sports Hall of Fame at Three Rivers Stadium.

Right on those two teams you could have picked out maybe half of them who could have been major league stars. During those years we had some good outstanding ballplayers besides Paige and Gibson. We had, just on those two teams, Oscar Charleston, Smoky Joe Williams, Jud Wilson, Cool Papa Bell, Judy Johnson, Double Duty Radcliffe, Jake Stephens, George Scales, Vic Harris, Jimmy Crutchfield, Bobby Williams, Rev Cannady, Bill Perkins, George Britt and a lot of other fellows. There are a lot of them on there that deserve a place in Cooperstown. Fine men, they deserve a spot.

Now to me, Satchel wasn't the best right-handed pitcher we had, because I killed him. Satchel told me, "I'm the worst pitcher in the world when you come up to the plate." Why did I hit Satchel so easily? I don't know. You had some ballplayers I couldn't hit with a paddle or a broom. One was Leroy Matlock. I couldn't hit him with anything; maybe it was psychological. But Satchel had nothing but a fast ball. Now why did I have to look for anything else but a fast ball? He didn't have a curve or a change-up. And it was always our contention that you cannot throw the ball by a hitter. You know, you can get one by, but you're not going to keep getting them all by. So I had no problem hitting Satchel. And I'd bunt Satchel too. We used to bunt one down the third base line, bunt the next one down first, make Satchel cover, keep him running. I knew I could beat Satchel covering the bag.

These youngsters today are of the opinion that Satchel never lost a game in the Negro leagues. They've got this in the back of their heads: He won all his ball games. Ric Roberts [the sportswriter] has the clippings of the first game we played in Greenlee Field in Pittsburgh in 1932. That was over forty years ago. We beat Satchel 1–0.* And the Crawfords had a good team—Oscar Charleston, Josh Gibson, Bill Perkins and those. One of the reasons I want that clipping is that I'd like to look at the score that shows I got two hits off Satchel and scored the winning run. I've always wanted to have this hanging on the wall somewhere.

* Page was with the New York Black Yankees then.

I went down to Pittsburgh with the New York Black Yankees—
George Scales, Clint Thomas, Fats Jenkins, Bill Riggins. Jess
Hubbard pitched a heck of a ball game against Satchel.

It was the dedication of Greenlee Field, and the ball park was
jammed. Satchel Paige was pitching; Satchel was the Attraction.
Satchel gave up only five hits, and Jess gave up only three. He
pitched a masterpiece. We only got five hits, and I got two of
them. We beat him in the eighth inning. I got a bunt single at
some point, early. Died.

The next time I got a single through the box on Satchel. This
was the eighth inning, getting awful late. So now I got to get to
second base. Can't score from first, because we ain't gonna hit the
ball that far, that often. So we had to figure, "How am I gonna
get to second base?" Josh Gibson was catching. Now Josh could
throw. I'm not going to steal on Josh, I'm going to steal on Satchel.
Tubby [Scales] says, "Now Ted, when you get on, watch Satchel.
He just raises up his leg and pitches." And I stole on Satchel.

I think Pistol—John Henry Russell—was playing second base,
and I had a reputation: "Don't get in front of him, because he
might spike you." So Russell let the ball get through him. It didn't
go any further than from here to that door. Well, you know, we
didn't just slide in there and when you get through you're all
sprawled out with your hands above your head. We slid like this
—back on your feet in a second. Shoot, I was gone! Third base.
They tried to get the ball to third base, to Harry Williams. I was
going straight at Harry, looking right at *him*. You know where
Harry went? He caught the ball, but he didn't even try to tag me.

Clint Thomas was up next. When Satchel threw that fast ball,
Clint just tapped it right over the top of Chester Williams' head
at shortstop. The only run we got.

So you got to study and find a way: How'm I gonna get home?
First I'm going to get on base. You got to get on base before you
can get home. Now you're on base, how you going to get where
somebody can single you in? But they don't do that now.

I was interviewed a while ago by KDKA, the local Pittsburgh
station, and one of the questions the interviewer asked me was,
was I bitter because I didn't have a chance to play in the big
league? I'm certainly not bitter. But one of the things that I regret

Ted Page

very much today is that I passed up a scholarship to Ohio State University. A football scholarship—I played halfback down in Youngstown. I would have had a scholarship, along with three other fellows. One of them was a white boy who grew up in my section of town, and the name should be familiar because he was an All-American end for Pitt—Joe Donches. He's a doctor in Gary, Indiana, today.

I was born in Glasgow, Kentucky, in 1903 and moved to Youngstown, Ohio, when I was just about nine. I grew up there in a neighborhood with Slavs, Polish, Italian kids. This wasn't the rich part of town, it was where the steel mill workers lived. My dad worked in the mill. My family was the only colored family. My playmates and kids that I made mud pies with were Polish kids, Italian kids. When I got around ten or eleven years old, I started to notice. I knew I was colored, but I didn't know yet that there were some things you weren't supposed to do.

We had a clubhouse, played basketball there. We called it the Booker T. Washington Settlement. Today on the same site is the

YMCA. We had a little clubhouse there, used to come from "Monkey's Nest," my neighborhood. They put us in there to keep us out of trouble. Then we started a football team of kids thirteen to fourteen years old. We had three or four white boys on the team. We became pretty good—very good. Not only we didn't lose a ball game, but nobody scored on us from 1919 to 1921.

The man who put us all together was a black man. He's an attorney now for a steel company. He had gone to school, played tackle, went to college. He started to develop these kids about 1914: Sam Robertson. And we had one fantastic football team.

Robertson used to say, "Brute strength isn't it. It's science." I was only 140 pounds, I played halfback. He'd say, "How do you get around the defensive tackle? You don't have to run over him, you can fake him out. Plan your move just before you get to him. You know what you're going to do, but he doesn't. Don't try to outrun the man. Outsmart him. All the advantage is with you when you're running open field."

Someone from Ohio State University contacted us; they wanted Joe Donches and myself. Donches had just completed his last year of high school. I was two years younger. I would have had to go to summer school and high school and then back to summer school in order to accept the scholarship. In the summer we went swimming, played ball. All these things I would have had to give up. To me, it wasn't important enough. My mother felt very bad. Sometimes I think this was the greatest mistake of my life.

Anyway, when I didn't go and finish high school, Joe didn't accept the scholarship. I used to kid people from Pitt. I'd say, "I'm the reason Joe Donches went to Pitt instead of Ohio State." Joe Donches was All-American end for Pitt in 1929. In 1929 I was very busy trying to make my name in baseball.

My first team when I left high school was Toledo in the Negro American League. This was in 1923. Rube Foster had a team in Toledo that he was just building. They played in the Mudhens' American Association park there. This is one of the reasons I didn't want to take time out to go finish high school and go to college. I had a contract to play in the Negro American League, and what would I need a college education for?

I went to Toledo—and I didn't make the team. You say, "Well, they'll farm you out." There was no such thing as being farmed out to a lower club. When you don't make the team, you try to find a way to get home. Or you get a job in that town. In my case, I went to Buffalo at the end of that season, after I'd bounced around to Meadville, Youngstown and a few of the small towns. We were playing sandlot ball, barnstorming, and we got paid. If it didn't rain, we'd get ten to fifteen dollars a game. If it rained, well, we'd just have to cross our fingers and pray that the next game we had coming up—it might be tomorrow, it might be three or four days from then—would be good weather. These were all twilight games, six o'clock. No such things as lights then. By dusk you'd have to call the game. In most cases our games were like seven innings. But we had some good ballplayers who played on just such teams.

I finished the season with a team—I think they were called the Buffalo Giants—and they were under the managership of Home Run Johnson. You may never have come across him, but he played for the [Chicago] Leland Giants back in like 1910 and '11. He was sixty years old, had been all over the world and was a famous ballplayer. Grant Johnson was a grand old man. He was sort of a rawboned fellow, dark complexion, not too big. And he loved to sing, had a beautiful baritone voice. In those days we weren't riding in buses, we were riding in cars. Jimmy Reel was there—he could sing like Billy Eckstine, a beautiful voice. Johnson always wanted to get in the same car with Jimmy.

Grant had a good ball team in Buffalo, because by him being a legend, players from all over came to play with him. And at that age he could still hit line drives. He used to say, "When you're gonna hit the ball, you can't hit it until it gets up to you. Don't go out to meet it, it's coming, it's coming." His philosophy was, if you reach out to hit the ball, you might swing at a bad ball, pop it up. And you don't have to try to slug the ball, because if you meet the ball on time over the plate, it's going to hop off your bat.

Another thing I remember Grant saying: "Don't ever take your eye off the ball." Some players turn their head when they swing. They're looking in right field. How you going to hit the ball and you're looking in right field?

I think any team in the major leagues who added a Negro

coach, or manager, would be smart. We are wasting some of this good material that is just going to rot. Now Will Stargell and I are good friends, but Stargell is popping the ball up right now. I can tell you, "Man, you're popping the ball up." But heck, you know that better than anybody. But why are you popping the ball up? Stargell is turning his head just before he meets the ball, I don't think he even sees the ball. Who am I to sit here and say something to Stargell? But I believe if they could have a slow-motion picture and let him look at that, he'd see it himself.

Anyway, Grant Johnson was the cause of me getting started. This is how I got the recognition to play winter ball in Florida. Home Run Johnson sent me. We played in Palm Beach, Florida. We left in October or November, stayed all winter down there. There were two hotels that were rivals in baseball, the Breakers and the Poinciana. I played for the Breakers.

Florida was the first time I had any chance to meet big-name ballplayers. I had never seen men like Bingo DeMoss and Bobby Williams and those guys.

Down in Florida I got $30 a month, room and board, and your laundry and all. And then you hustled for the rest of your money. And you could make money! I came home one year, I remember, with $900, clear money—that I came *home* with. That's three years' salary right there! Of course, compared to these times, $900 would have been equivalent to seven or eight thousand.

The next summer I went back to Buffalo and played with Home Run. The next winter I went back to Florida. That's where I met Smoky Joe Williams for the first time. And Nip Winters. Nip had just set down the Kansas City Monarchs in the Negro World Series. Nip and Joe were with Poinciana. Joe was a right-hander, Nip a left-hander. I was a left-hand hitter, but it didn't mean a thing to me. I hit Nip just like I hit Joe. I mean, then I didn't realize you were supposed to be weak on left-handers.

And it was through my ability to hit Joe and Nip down in Florida that I got a letter from Jim Keenan of the New York Lincoln Giants and Cum Posey of the Homestead Grays, to come up here and play. But when I got a letter from a man named Andy Harris in Newark—"We're building a team for the Negro National League"—that was the team for me. Because how was I going to play with the Homestead Grays with the guys they had? How was I going to play? So I went with a team they were just building. It may have been a mistake, I don't know.

So in 1926 I came up with Newark. It wasn't the Eagles. It was another team that Colonel Ruppert, the owner of the Yankees, I think it was, was building. The team didn't last too long, though. It folded in July, something like that. They weren't drawing, and there was no money.

So what do you do when there's no money? You wind up standing on the corner of 135th Street, playing sandlot ball with somebody. Playing baseball was an easier life than carrying bricks or cleaning windows. There were no other jobs that we could get. It was very tough. Baseball was something I had to do, really, because I didn't know how to do anything else.

Around New York there were quite a number of teams. There were the Lincoln Giants, the Brooklyn Royal Giants and some semipro teams. Baseball was good around New York. You went out to play in Brooklyn, a twilight game, why, you could come back with 25 or 30 dollars. And this was a good *week's* pay during those years, because bacon and eggs was twenty-five cents, including coffee and everything else.

Chappie Johnson had baseball teams up around Schenectady, Utica, Saratoga, Albany—up in that section—and in 1928 he came to New York and got some ballplayers to take to Montreal. He swiped ballplayers off the Lincoln Giants, off the Brooklyn Royals, anywhere he could get them from, it didn't matter. And we played in 1928 in Montreal.

Dick Seay was on that ball club, the best defensive second baseman I have ever seen, and I've seen Bill Mazeroski. I played a lot of years with Dick Seay. I was his type: no cussin', no drinkin'. Those other guys would get them a bottle of whiskey and they'd go out to the racetrack. Dick and I would get some ice cream, go back to the hotel, play pinochle.

I guess I liked Chappie better than any manager I played under. Chappie could look at a ballplayer, watch him play, be around him a little while, and discover if he had ability. I give Chappie credit for bringing me into the position where I could hold a job as a ballplayer. Everyone has slumps. I could hit the ball, sure; I could hit the ball a long ways at times. But then there are some times when you get to the place where you can't hit it, or it doesn't go safe. Then what do you do? Somehow Chappie was a good con man. He could look in your pocket, and if you had a dollar, before you knew it, you were handing it to him. And you know, Chappie conned me. He conned me into realizing that I was very fast. Chappie would say, "If I was your age"—this is where he got to me, see?—"if I was your age and could run like you can, nobody would ever stop me from getting on base." He taught me one thing for sure: If you're not hitting the ball—and who can hit every time, consistently, without running into a slump?—there is another way to get on. Bunt and push the ball if you're able to run. He taught me how to drag or push the ball, and I had a double offense, whether the ball was going down the third base line or the first base line.

I used to just take my bat like this and "carry" the ball to first base with me. When I got ready, I'd drop it down. Wouldn't drop it until I got two steps to first. By the time the ball hits the bat, they like to say, you've got two steps to first. I had five steps—I could be that far down the first base line. This is one of the things that Chappie taught me.

I don't see much bunting today. I often wonder why, but ballplayers today don't drag the ball and don't push the ball. We've got Willie Davis on the Dodgers and some good left-handed hitters on the Pirates, and I don't see why they don't push and bunt the ball, because there is not much defense for a man who can hit hard and bunt too.

If you're playing infield, I certainly would not want to play up close to Al Oliver—he can hit the ball awful hard. I wouldn't want to be in on him and have him hit the ball down my throat. But at the same time, I would have to do something if he can bunt or push the ball or drag the ball. A left-handed hitter who can drag the ball, and then can slug it with authority, he is a triple threat.

My style of hitting was to meet the ball and hit it on the line. From the same position I could bunt, I could push the ball to third. The ball is hit down the third base line and it would just die. Wouldn't go any place. Or I could turn the bat the other way, take the ball down the first base line. One of my biggest enjoyments as a baseball player was being able to bunt the ball down to Judy Johnson. He was one of our real great third basemen. I used to bunt a lot to Judy and beat him to first base. I got a big kick out of it. Or I'd give a sign that I was going to bunt and then I'd hit the ball by that third baseman, because he's charging in. All I wanted him to do was to get started with his momentum coming forward, and I'd hit it past him. I could get a double standing up.

All I wanted to do was get me on base. I felt like my job was to get on base. Long ball? I didn't hit the long ball much. I used to hit the ball on the clubhouse in Philadelphia—the clubhouse in right field was a long ways, and I hit the clubhouse. But I got more enjoyment out of just bunting the ball to third base—or first base —and beating the guy to the base.

I got to be on base. I don't mean hit the ball against the fence. I got to be on base, otherwise I can't score. Now if I don't get on base and score, I'm not going to have a job by next month. And I like this job better than I do washing those windows out there.

So I give Chappie credit for me making it to the top teams in Negro baseball: the Grays, the Crawfords, the New York Black Yankees and the Brooklyn Royals.

Dick Seay and I came from Montreal to the Royals in 1929. That's when I got my first glimpse of big-time black baseball. Dick Redding was manager of the Royals. He was one of the great ballplayers, and you don't hear much about him now. Oldtimers will tell you stories about men like Redding and Joe Williams and John Henry Lloyd. I don't think you can appreciate what these men meant to baseball, what kind of ballplayers they were.

I remember one night we were coming through the Catskill Mountains, coming from upstate New York, and we had two Pierce Arrow cars that we rode in. We had a flat tire in one. I don't know why we didn't have a spare; maybe cars didn't have spares in those days, I'm not sure. Anyhow, we had to take the other car and go find a tire. Something like one o'clock in the morning coming down the Rip Van Winkle Trail. We did finally go maybe fifteen or twenty miles, found a place open and bought a tire. Dick was the manager, road secretary and everything. So he set the tire on the running board outside, with his hand on it to hold it. I guess everybody fell asleep; I did. And when we got back and stopped, the driver got out and said, "Okay, Dick, come on, give me the tire." Dick says, "Huh? What?" He jumped up, got outside the car, there was no tire there! He had gone to sleep, and the tire had rolled away someplace. Had to go back again and buy another tire, because Dick went to sleep! Now I get a big laugh out of it, but it was no joke then. I think the tire cost us something like 25 or 30 dollars, 'cause those old Pierce Arrow cars had big tires.

Dick could do the funniest things. One time down in Cuba, he could hear a married couple in the hotel room next door. Dick tiptoed up to the wall and put a chair up next to it so he could stand on his tiptoes and look over the transom. Pretty soon he lost his balance and he came crashing right through the wall and onto the bed and everything.

Oh, yes, it was a more colorful brand of baseball in our league. First of all, today I often watch for a certain play—I think maybe I've seen it once in a while—with a man on first base who can run, and a man at bat who has good bat control. I have been involved in just such a play. Dick Seay, with the Royal Giants, hit behind me in most cases, 'cause he was a good bunter, a terrific bunter, and a good hit-and-run man. I have gone from first to third on a bunt, I have scored from second on a bunt by Dick Seay.

I could run, and I could run bases good. When I was on second and the pitcher'd go up to make his delivery to home plate, I would tear. I'm halfway to home by the time they let the ball go, because I had rounded third base, and my destination was home plate, on the bunt. The bunt would be down third base. Now the catcher's got to get it, or in most cases the pitcher. But if the catcher did come out to get it, he was a dead duck, because I would keep going.

This is one of the things that Redding did for me. He allowed us to put the play on, because Dick and I worked awful good together. Dick would give the signal, or I would give the signal: This was going to be the pitch. You've got to get your bat on that ball, and Dick was good at that. He could put his bat on the ball on waste pitches. He would save a man by getting a piece of the ball. In other words, this is the same as the hit-and-run. It *is* a hit-and-run, really. I'll tell you who I did this to: In Bushwick, I did this on Stanley Baumgartner. We used to pull it on him—and we pulled it on George Earnshaw from the Athletics. These were times you needed one run, you had to have one run. If you can get these men in the position where they can operate, this is just as important as a slugger who hits the ball out of the ball park.

Today who would be in a position to pull plays like that? Maury Wills or Willie Davis. In the major leagues they don't do it, but we did it so many times.

They don't bunt now, and I have a fit. My wife would say, "They've got coaches getting $50,000 a year, maybe they don't want them to do this." But I can't see why. You're trying to win a ball game. Why not? But everybody tries to hit the ball out of the ball park. Again, maybe I'm old fashioned. I'm trying to carry the rules of the past up to the present. I would rather see a man—two men—execute a play like Dick Seay and I did. This gives me more excitement than it would to see him hit the ball out of the ball park, because everybody's hitting the ball out of the ball park today. Maybe these plays are obsolete, I don't know.

You say, "Well, the fans like slugging." I don't know, we had some awful big crowds during those days to watch this—we called it inside baseball.

You know, the Cubans and our teams, the American teams, were always rivals. I remember one day when I was with the Brooklyn Royals, Martin Dihigo was playing shortstop. I slid into him, and you know how I slid, I undressed him. The ball went into center field; Dihigo, I don't know what way he went. Next day Dihigo pitched. He threw at me—I don't mean he threw high, I mean he threw *at* me. I said, "Okay." So I drug the ball down first base so Dihigo would have to cover first. That was the only way I could get back at him, and all of a sudden it struck him that I was after him. There was nobody but him and I there, and he had to cover with me climbing his back. You know where he went? He went into right field. He didn't go *near* the bag! Straight to right field.

When we'd play the Cubans they would always throw at me. See that spot on my temple? No hair. The guy hit me there was

Cuban, in Palm Beach. Luis Tiant, Sr. Skinny, a smart pitcher. Left-hander, threw a screwball. But when he threw me curve balls, I would just *lean* on 'em. Down in West Palm Beach I hit one off Tiant good. I was a youngster then. The next time I come up, first pitch, he got a curve ball away from me. The next one was right here—at my head. He laid me out. They poured water on me, they poured ice on me, everything. Tiant couldn't speak much English. But the guy playing third base, Arango, in his very poor English said, "You no hit *dat* one!" I'm layin' on the ground: "You no hit *dat* one." I could just hear him. My head was getting bigger and bigger. I didn't know how big it was going to get.

Stanley Baumgartner was another good left-hander. He didn't throw like most lefties, overhand. He threw sidearm. A left-handed hitter had to back up. He used to pitch every weekend on the Brooklyn Bushwicks after he came from the Phillies. One night in Bushwick Park he walked Irving Brooks, a right-handed hitter—a terrific hitter—to get to me, because I was lefty.

I hit the ball in those lights—they had lights then in Bushwick Park that went way up high, on poles—and I hit the ball into those lights in right field off of him. We talked about it years after that when Baumgartner was a sportswriter covering the Phillies. I met him at Forbes Field one time, he and a Catholic priest, Father Anthony, who played shortstop for Bushwick in his younger days. We three met at Forbes Field—Father Anthony, Baumgartner and I—just shortly before Baumgartner died.

I think I'm one of the few black players still alive who can boast playing against Babe Ruth and Lou Gehrig. I believe the year was 1928. Ruth's All-Stars, they were called. Dick Redding pitched the game. We got beat, I think, something like 4–3. Ruth got one puny double. He didn't hit the expected home run that everyone was looking for. My contribution for the day: two doubles. And the pitcher was Roy Sherrid of the Yankees. Wouldn't I like to have a picture of Ruth and I that afternoon! I got two doubles and Ruth got one.

I'm delighted to say that I played against some of our greatest major league ballplayers—pitchers included. I hit against George

Earnshaw, Ed Rommel, both Deans, Larry French, Mike Ryba. I got base hits against these guys, and they were not over the hill. Ric Roberts has my clippings of the base hits I got off them. These were just a few that I kept. I should have kept so many, but I didn't.

I was in Baltimore in 1929 and 1930 with the Baltimore Black Sox. Let's see, George Rossiter—I guess you might have come across that name—ran the Black Sox, and every fall we used to play against the major league all-stars. They would bring them into the Black Sox park there—they used to have the people hanging off the roof. Mickey Cochrane was catching, Joe Boley of the Athletics was at shortstop, Hack Wilson was an outfielder.

Center field, I think, was Jake Powell, remember the name? Jake Powell . . . created some kind of a question by some remark he made. Yeah, he made a remark over the radio regarding Negroes. It was a slip, because I used to think that Jake Powell was quite a democratic individual. I only knew him from playing against him those two years, but there was no such prejudice, to my thinking, which shows how wrong we can often be, but I had no idea Jake Powell was feeling that way. He had quite a time trying to straighten this out, but he never made it. He faded out shortly after that.

I had been up only about three years and was still getting my bearings. Rossiter had sent to New York to get Martin Dihigo from the Cubans, Biz Mackey from Philadelphia and me from the Brooklyn Royals.

I remember the 1929 World Series so well, because if memory serves me right, the Philadelphia A's scored eight runs in one inning and beat the Cubs. Then we played against most of the A's in Baltimore that October.

The last year I went to Florida was 1929, I think. I was supposed to go to Cienfuegos, Cuba, but the ball park blew down. Bruling White was in Florida. He had a smile, would have made a great public relations man today. Had been adopted by a rich white family. We bought a car, a Ford, the kind where the pedals sit here and you push this down and let it up and it's in high gear. We bought one of those things for $35 and were going to drive it back up north.

I tell people, "You didn't hear about me playing, because I got on those different ball clubs because I could drive." I would drive one car and Jess Hubbard would drive the other. They'd give you an extra $10 a month to do that. They had to have somebody, see, and I wouldn't take up the extra space.

Well, we bought this car for $35. I paid my half of it, $17.50. We drove this car all up through the South. I remember stopping in Charleston, South Carolina. We didn't stop there to put up at a hotel—at that time, forget it. We got in about eight o'clock one morning. Stopped in a restaurant to eat, and I'll always remember this: I had rice, scrambled eggs, bacon, catheads, hot biscuits. Twenty-five cents. It was too much, I couldn't eat it all. When I got through eating, I remember a kid sitting a few stools away from me, swinging around on the stool. I paid, got up, said I'm ready to go. When I got to the door, I looked back and this kid was sitting in my seat eating like hell. He was going to town eating.

I left Brooklyn and went with the Homestead Grays a short time in the beginning of the 1930 season, but I couldn't see how anybody could leave New York and come to Pittsburgh and stay. I stayed for a while—I think I stayed for about two weeks, maybe three weeks. When they got ready to leave, I sneaked off. I think they were going to Altoona, and you know, they'd wait out front for you, but I went out the back door. Dick Redding had been waiting around town, and I sneaked out the back door and got in the car with the Brooklyn Royals, and we headed into the mountains.

In 1930 the Cardinals got in the World Series and Frankie Frisch played us in Baltimore that fall. I can't remember all the guys' names, but they had a pitcher named Weaver—Jim Weaver, Big Jim Weaver. I dragged the ball down first base, and Frisch there at second had to cover. We got there the same time and I ran right up him. He had to have operations and everything. One night a few years ago I was sitting at dinner at Cooperstown and I was introduced to Frank Frisch. I said, "Well, I played against Frank Frisch in Baltimore."

He said, "You son of a gun, you're the guy broke my leg!"

I remember another game against Weaver. There used to be a

fellow who came out to the ball park and would say, "Every time you drag a base hit, you get a ten-dollar bill." I drug two base hits. I could run pretty fast. I figured: "This is an easy way to make $20."

I'd like to brag that that same year we beat Ed Rommel of the Athletics 5–3. Webster McDonald beat him. One of the reasons I kept the clipping is that I hit the top of the center field fence off Ed Rommel the first time up. Mickey Cochrane was catching and he had an idea—I don't know where he got it—that I couldn't hit a curve ball, so he had Rommel throw a curve ball. And I hit the fence with this one.

When I played the big-league all-stars, I didn't care what my batting average was. I was concerned: Am I going to hit good enough to be invited back? I idolized those ballplayers we had on our team. They were big men, they were legends. No use getting out there thinking that just because I was on the team this particular weekend that I got it made. They could do without me. If I do my job good enough, maybe I'll get a chance to go next weekend or next year.

Now the next year I came back to the Grays. George Scales had a lot to do with my coming back. They were going to Hot Springs, Arkansas. And you know, as a youngster you listened to old-timers talk about the places they'd gone and where they'd trained, and I always wanted to go to Hot Springs. They talked about hot water running out of the ground and all that business, and I thought, "This should be interesting." And this is how I got to the Grays.

Bill Perkins and Josh Gibson were our catchers. We stole Perkins out from under the sheriff's watchdogs in Dawson, Georgia. Perkins was the idol of the town; they had built a ball park for him out of old logs and broken-down doors. Everybody came to watch the ball games, and the sheriff was the ticket taker. Well, we went down in spring training and saw him and wanted to take him back north, but the sheriff said, "No, he has to stay here, we built a ball park for him." He said if we left town in the morning and his man—he didn't say "man," I'll let you guess what he said—if his man wasn't there, we better not be in Georgia. And we weren't. We hid Perkins under the bus and drove right past the sheriff sitting in front of the store.

I remember one game we played in Forbes Field, Pittsburgh. Josh played left field and he dropped a fly ball. He played it badly, really. When we were taking a shower in the shower room, George Scales was on Josh. He was ridiculing him. Josh was young and so was I. I resented the way he was talking to Josh. Now George and I had been very good friends—you might call us buddies. George and I tangled up. Buff naked, both of us were. I knocked George's tooth out. George Britt—I guess we all either feared Britt or respected him because we were afraid of him—he said, "Sit down or I'm gonna slap you down." I sat down. George sat down, his mouth all bleeding. Britt broke George and I up all by himself.

George went back under the shower, soaped up. I went on in again. You know, while we were in the shower, George charged me again under the shower. He had a knife in the shower, see, cut me in the belly. Jud Wilson and Britt both came in. Britt slammed George one way, slammed me on the floor. I think Boojum [Wilson] took me by the arm and slammed me out of the shower, out into the locker room, down on the floor. Britt finally commanded, "Sit down! You behave." And we did just that.

That night we were going to Cleveland. George and I were roommates. We slept in Cleveland in a single bed. George had his knife under the pillow, and I carried a pistol all through my baseball days. I played with this automatic in my jock strap. George slept facing this way, and I slept facing that way. He was waiting for me to jump him, and I was waiting for him to jump me. We didn't get a wink of sleep that night.

The next night George rounded up two girls, one for him, one for me, and we took them to our room. One was a waitress, the other one, I guess she was a nurse. We had a party. Forgot all about the fight. I say this to show how we lived and how we settled things.

That fall we played the major league all-stars again. I hit against Stan Covaleskie. I remember Steve O'Neill was catching, and I hit two triples off Covaleskie. They said, "You hit *him*? That's Stan Covaleskie!" You know, I didn't get a hit off him after that!

In 1932 Scales and I went back to New York with the Black

Yankees. I thought I was back to stay; I wasn't going to leave. But
by the end of May I was back in Pittsburgh with the Crawfords.
That was right after we beat Satchel 1–0. Gus Greenlee, the owner
of the Crawfords, wrote me a letter: "I want you on the Crawfords." Then he started naming the guys he had: Oscar Charleston, Josh Gibson, Jud Wilson, Double Duty Radcliffe. The year
before I had played with them on the Grays. Greenlee had raided
the Grays. He paid them a better salary than Cum Posey could
afford to pay.

Greenlee was a big man, a great big man. I remember at the end
of the season I wasn't going any place to play ball that winter. This
was a real sad time in our baseball, because I was just hanging
around the Crawford Grill. Gus said, "What you going to do all
winter?"

I said, "I don't know, man."

He said, "Okay, I got something for you to do." You know, he
had the numbers business. They had an old vacant house or the
second floor of it, in Hazelwood. They had a long space up there
where they had tables where they turned in all the numbers each
day. This was the headquarters for it. Gus gave me a chair. My
job was to sit right downstairs on the sidewalk and ring a bell.
Anybody who was coming in who wasn't supposed to be there, I
would just push a button to alert them upstairs to get rid of all
that money. That's all I did. I remember so well my pay: $15 a
week. I sat down in this chair from about one o'clock till about
3:30 when they had finished counting up all the money, sacked it
and put it in the bank. That's all I did. I never pushed the botton.
I did practically nothing all winter for $15 a week.

You say, "How did you manage?" I paid ten bucks for my
room and board—room *and* board. And I was still five bucks to
the good. I had all the rest of the day to hustle whatever I could.
I had a very fine winter.

Later I gathered why Gus did this. Right along about this time
I had developed a reputation for jumping around. Whoever
treated me the best in my opinion, that's who I was going to play
with next year. During the season I was getting $50 a week from
Gus, which was $200 a month, to play ball. And this was *big*
money in those days. And I got paid by Gus all winter. Gus treated

me like that so in 1933 I wouldn't skip away and be playing for
somebody else.

The Crawfords. Some people call that the greatest team ever
seen in Negro baseball. They'd almost have to be. They had some
awful good ballplayers. When you look at the material they had
on the team, it had to be a great one. During the 1934 team we
had Satchel and Gibson. We had Chester Williams shortstop, John
Henry Russell—Pistol Johnny Russell—was the second baseman,
Jud Wilson third baseman, and Charleston the first baseman. In
the outfield that year we had four outfielders. We had Vic Harris
—one year, the only time he ever left the Grays. Vic was playing
left field, Cool Papa Bell was playing center field, I played right
field and Jimmy Crutchfield played all the way across—left field,
center field or right field. Crutchfield was a real fine little man. All
ballplayer, give you 100 percent. He might have weighed 130 or
135 pounds. He had a lot of guts.

On the Grays I hit number one most of the time. On the Crawfords I hit from number one down to about number six. This was
my spot. In many cases I would hit in third place, and Cool Papa
Bell was the man I hit behind a lot. With Cool on base, I'd lean
back in the catcher's box. Crowd him. Now he's got to throw
around me. And I hit in front of Bell a lot. Bell was very fast. You
couldn't put a slow man in front of Bell; you had to have a man
who could run. If you had a man on first base, you had to have
a good fast man on, because if he didn't go to third base on a hit,
Bell might pass him, run over him. Bell has done this on other
occasions. When we were playing some little team that didn't
matter much, in some little town, this is another thing we did for
show. Bell hit the ball to the outfield. Whoever was on first base
would let Bell pass him, and we've gotten away with it. Nobody
would notice it. This wouldn't be done in a game that meant anything, but this is one of the things that would be amusing. I'd like
to see Cool. I haven't seen him for years and years and years.

Living conditions? Forget it. Conditions were terrible then. We
dressed in the YMCA or what-have-you. I recall playing baseball
in Zanesville, Ohio, the Middle Atlantic League team. It was
probably an AA or A team. We played in their ball park, and
there wasn't a man on their team that could have won a spot on

the Pittsburgh Crawfords. I don't remember the score, it wasn't important, but I do remember that we couldn't change clothes or take a shower in their clubhouse. Why? We were black.

We had to go to a rooming house, a place on Route 40 where they had a shotgun hall, a room here, a room over there. The most rooms were a dozen rooms. We asked the lady if she'd heat up some water before we had to drive to Columbus in our uniforms. We had to get the grime off. So she poured the water in the bath tub, half full, and all the players who had played that day took a bath in that one tub of water.

Where would we eat? We ate in Columbus, 135 miles away. Why not? There wasn't any place we could get anything to eat in Zanesville.

If we got through playing a ball game and wanted something to eat, we had to find a place that would serve us. One time going from Jackson, Mississippi, down south to New Orleans or Alexandria, Louisiana, we played a twilight game at five o'clock. It must have been nine or ten o'clock when we finished. We had to drive all the way to Alexandria, getting in there at four or five in the morning. We still hadn't anything to eat. We came across a place in the mountains, a guy selling fruit at one o'clock in the morning. Don't ask me why he was out there at that time. We stopped and got cantaloupes, melons, apples; this was our food all the way to Alexandria.

It's hard to believe, but it just wasn't human. This was the kind of life we had to live. We didn't know there was supposed to be anything different; this was the way it always was. We didn't go off and get clubs and light a fire to the restaurant. I remember when you couldn't buy a hamburger on the highway between Akron and Youngstown. And Gus Greenlee had his pockets bulging with money! Today they're *giving* the kids too much. I can remember when you couldn't *buy* it.

But we still played baseball, and I might say we played very good baseball. And we were happy, we sang, we had fun. I guess I enjoyed that life, because I stuck with it until I got a job at thirty-three years old and went to work.

We didn't clown like you may think. Baseball was a living to us. Well, how on earth could you make a living at $200 a month, or $150 a month? Josh Gibson was earning $200 a month, and I was earning the same thing. Gibson hadn't reached his height at that time. I remember when he came up to the Grays in 1930 and they picked him off a playground.

The other day I saw Manny Sanguillen in the Pirates' clubhouse after they lost a game. He had two bats, drumming with them. They just got beat, man! They should be talking about how did we lose the ball game and how we going to do tomorrow. They weren't even concerned about losing the game. When we lost a game, we'd sit up practically all night discussing it.

Why did we do that? I think I'm expressing the feelings of most ballplayers of my day. This is the way I had to keep from washing the windows in a downtown store or sweeping the floor, and these were the kinds of jobs that were out there for us. So it was better than washing the windows for $15 a week or $12 a week. That was the average salary in those days. Well, now, if I'm going to play on these teams, you got to win. And if you want to win, you got to play good. You can't play good going into the game with everything else on your mind. The ball game is the thing that's important now: how to win the ball game.

In 1934 I slid into first base in Jackson, Mississippi, and tore my knee up. This put me in a position where now I can't bunt the ball and use speed. Anybody who got me up until that year got me more or less for speed and base running. So now I had to hit. I decided that if I'm going to get on base, I've got to hit the ball and I've got to hit it safely. So this is what I did, and I learned to hit the ball then for a pretty good average. I don't know what I hit that year, but I know I hit pretty good. I *had* to hit the ball. I was just spraying the ball all over the place.

I was pitiful—according to our standards—as a base runner, except I could hit the ball. But if I hit the ball against the left-center field fence, which I could do, I was lucky if I wound up at second base. Before that time I'd have been in third base and sometimes I'd have them throwing at me at home plate.

But in 1935 I was released to Newark, to Abe Manley. They had an idea: "He's all washed up, he can't run, so he's through." They sent me to Newark and I went to spring training with them. But I didn't have it, and I was released about, oh, the middle of May. I was sort of disgusted: That was the end of it. I went to New

York, and my thought was, I'll just go look around and see if I can get a job. What kind of job I could get I had no idea, because I wasn't trained.

Webster McDonald was managing the Philadelphia Stars, and he came over to New York in a car and looked me up where we loafed around 135th Street and Lennox Avenue. He wanted me to come to Philadelphia to play with the Stars. I said, "Mac, I can't run."

Old Mac, in his soft-spoken way, spent a couple or three hours just sitting around the barbershop there. He said, "I'll tell you, Ted, I have already committed myself. I knew that you didn't have a job, and I had a feeling that I could get you to come play with the Philadelphia Stars. I have made arrangements to release two men. We know you were getting $200 to $250 a month. I don't think Chief [the Stars owner, Ed Bolden] is going to go that much for you, because you're physically not in shape. But I guarantee you right this minute $150 a month. I have made arrangements to release two men in order that we can pay you that much money." So how much were the other two getting? That's right, about $75 a month each. So I got in the car, got my bag and a few clothes, my suit-roll and all this, and hopped in the car with the baggage.

Before 1935 had ended, my knee was getting better. Jess Hubbard showed me how to tape my knee so I could run and it didn't give me pain, yet I didn't run as fast as before the accident. Jess left my kneecap open. I'd run with a stiff leg, but I could run better, without pain.

I remember one game in Bushwick Park. Mac beat the Bushwicks 1–0 in eighteen innings. You know who took him off the spot in those eighteen innings? Me. It was the eighteenth inning, there was either one man on or two men on, and Mac was struggling trying to hold this tie game. The ball was hit between the center fielder and me. My thought was, "Okay, if he don't catch it, I'm going to back him up." But somehow the ball kept staying, and when I looked, he wasn't getting to it, and I just leaped. When I quit falling and sliding, I had the ball in my hand. Yeah, my meat hand. This was one of the big thrills I had. You don't plan thrills like that, they just happen.

We played against Dizzy Dean that fall. They had Larry

French, Mike Ryba, Joe Hauser, Hack Wilson. We played nine games, and I'm sure I'm correct when I say they won two games.

I got my base hits—in fact, I got a base hit off of Dean in Philadelphia in Shibe Park, and I was real proud of it. I can remember it very well, because he had a great fast ball. I knew if he threw me the fast ball inside, I didn't know if I would be able to get around and meet it out front or not. So I was just laying and waiting for him to get it on the outside, and I just laid it down. I hit a rope, as they call it, to left field—left center, I mean. I was proud of that.

I know Josh hit the ball out of the park in York, because I hit one myself that night off Jim Winford of the Cards. Gibson got a solo home run, mine was with the bases loaded. Gibson hit his to right-center field. I hit mine to left-center, a line drive, one of those high types of line drive.

In 1936 near the end of the season, a man came up from down in the tropics. He was trying to get ballplayers to go to Santo Domingo to play. I remember we played in Wilmington this particular day. This man had so much money, he'd throw the money out on the bed, and Red Parnell, our center fielder, counted out about four or five hundred dollars. The man'd say, "Here, take it, what do you want?" Parnell up and went. Satchel went down, Josh went down.

But I just couldn't pick up that money. It was tempting, but remember, the season wasn't over yet. About in August, it was, and I remembered that Mac had really done me a favor. He picked me up when nobody had any need for me, I didn't have anything to offer anybody, there was no way for me to survive, and he picked me up and said, "Here, here's a job for you." I was grateful for that. I just couldn't see that I was going to jump up and go, and the Stars still had a month or six weeks to go in the season. I just couldn't have lived with myself.

I left baseball in 1937. I could have said, "Well, I'll retire on Social Security." Ballplayers didn't have any Social Security that they could retire on, so when you get as old as me now, what do you do? Where are you going to get a job from?

I went into the bowling game. The first Negro bowling establishment in Pennsylvania was set up here. Jack Marshall set it up. I played on the team with Jack my last two seasons in Philadelphia. So when he came here, who would he look up, naturally? He hired me as one of the workers in the place in 1941. In 1943 I bought out a quarter interest in the place, and by 1946 I had bought the entire place. Since then I've been in bowling right along.

I belong to the Greater Pittsburgh Bowling Proprietors. I'm the only Negro on the board of directors, and I write a bowling column for this paper that's printed in Philadelphia. And boy, I have made quite a contribution to the Negro in bowling, because for the last thirty years, I guess in any town you might go to, in the bowling circle they know about me.

I have had a lot to do with the development of one of the outstanding bowlers among Negroes in the country. You would probably know of her: Louise Fulton. I developed her as a bowler. I think I did a pretty good job publicizing her ability and getting her into spots where she could create interest. She was the first Negro to go into the Women's Professional Bowlers, and she had been, until we closed, a partner in my bowling establishment for about ten years.

And we have gotten integration in this town in bowling back through the years without any protest. No marching and all of this business. It has just been done, and we were accepted into all bowling circles. And we have Negroes in high offices in bowling here in this town. I feel happy that I had a part in that.

I am fortunate. I'm not really an old guy. I work for a social agency whose job is to take care of people who are down on their luck. We have quite a big operation, six offices in and around this area and in New York. We take care of unwed mothers, babies for adoption and all of this.

So I don't have any regrets. I would like to have earned some of this money—it would have been nice in my old age. But I can look back and say that at least I played with and against some of these boys. And to have been on either one of these two teams, the Crawfords and the Grays, is an honor in itself. And not just a sub, but to be a regular on these two teams was a real honor.

You look back at those days, the things that we did and how we had to live, and you have to wonder how we made it to this age. I was there when we had problems, and today I'm here when things are being changed for the good of Negroes in all walks of life. I truthfully say that I'm one of the luckiest guys in the world.

I'll say this: I'm not bitter. I think I'm very lucky to be able to say that I played with all the great ballplayers, with and against them. This is something that is unusual. I have tried to tell myself that had I played on a team that had fewer stars, I might have got more recognition. But how am I going to stand out on a team with Gibson, Satchel, Charleston, Bell? But I say, "By golly, I've got to be lucky to be on a team with men like that."

Ted "Double Duty" Radcliffe

Willie Stargell with Ted Page

Ted Page

Ted "Double Duty" Radcliffe

Tom "Pee Wee" Butts

Radcliffe catching, Josh Gibson scoring, at the East-West game in Comiskey Park.

Double Duty in his pitching mode.

Chapter 9

TED "DOUBLE DUTY" RADCLIFFE

Of all the characters who came out of the old Negro leagues, one of the more colorful was Ted "Double Duty" Radcliffe. "He could catch the first game, pitch the second—and was a terror at both of them" —that's how ex-catcher Royal "Skink" Browning of the Indianapolis Clowns puts it.

"He could go out and pitch that first ball game and shut you out, and go out and catch the second game and dare you to run—just defy you to run," adds shortstop Jake Stephens. "He had to 'cheat' you. He didn't have that good curve ball, but he could beat you 2–1, 1–0. Never got the recognition he should have received. In my book he was one of the greatest."

Everyone who knew him, however, conceded Double Duty the league lead in talking. "Radcliffe would tell some lies," chuckles Dick Seay, ex-second baseman. "He'd have us all in stitches. He talks with a lisp, you know, and down in Mexico once he told the owner his mother died twice. He wanted to go back to Chicago and wanted a little advance, so he said his mother died. The owner said, 'I thought you told me she died last month!' "

"He loved baseball, he loved to talk it," Stephens grins. "But I never heard Double Duty swear. He wanted to be where the women were, he might have been a lady's man, but he was no drinker."

When I first met Double Duty in 1970, he was overweight, playing pinochle and smoking a big cigar in a darkened social club on Chicago's South Side. We met again for a more leisurely chat on the sidewalk outside his apartment. He set up two folding picnic chairs under a tree, and as he talked, he let his eyes roam up and down the street at what the prayer book calls "all sorts and conditions of men" who passed before him. He frequently interrupted his monologue with an *obiter dictum* about this fellow who was a drug pusher or that chick who was sashaying down the sidewalk across the street. ("You got that thing shut off, don't you?" he'd ask, nodding to the tape recorder. I obediently shut it off, thus missing some of his choicest stories.)

My most recent meeting with Double Duty came at a baseball dinner in Baltimore in 1990, when, at the age of 88, he stole the show from the more famous white big leaguers there. He had been recently mugged and pistol-whipped in his Chicago apartment building, but otherwise was his bubbly, cherubic self.

Though Radcliffe has a reputation for tall tales, I have checked the stories he told me, both with other players and with newspaper files. The following story is essentially correct.

Ted "Double Duty" Radcliffe Speaks . . .

Damon Runyon gave me that nickname. He was a great fellow. He said I was the most versatile man he'd ever seen. He saw me and Satchel Paige pitch a doubleheader in Yankee Stadium in 1932. I caught Satchel in the first game and we won it 5–0, then I pitched the second game and won it 4–0. The next day when the paper came out, Runyon wrote: "It was worth the admission price of two to see Double Duty out there in action." So from that day on they called me "Double Duty."

That was 1932 with the Pittsburgh Crawfords. That was the year I won sixteen straight—and I was pitching and catching—before I lost a game.

I remember one game against the Brooklyn Bushwicks in Ebbets Field. We played before 16,000 people, more than the Dodgers could draw. Everybody was betting a lot of money 'cause Satchel was pitching the first game, but they beat Satchel 9–5. I came back the second game and shut them out 4–0. A fellow came up named Stewart—I heard he'd bet a lot of money. He used to follow us everywhere and bet on us. He gave me $200. He told me to keep $100 and buy the boys some beer with the rest. But nobody would accept anything, so I kept the whole 200.

Did I ever tell you about me and Satchel going twelve innings in Memphis when I played with the Claybrook Tigers in 1936? The Pittsburgh Crawfords and the Nashville Elite Giants were combined in a North-South game against us. We had a sellout, about 11,000 or 12,000. That was all the park would hold. They were all standing around the ropes just outside the line in left field and right field. Satchel went seven innings and Big Griffith went five innings. I pitched all twelve innings against them, and it ended up 0–0, called on account of darkness.

How did I hit Satchel? Sometimes I had bad days, and some days I didn't. Just like any other good pitcher, he was overbearing. A couple of days I had perfect days against him. No, I never hit a home run off him. The longest I hit against him was a double—two singles and a double one day in California. There wasn't anyone too tough for me to hit—the only fellow who was tough on me was Bob Feller when he was in his prime.

I played with both Satchel Paige and Josh Gibson on the Crawfords. They say Josh Gibson was the greatest catcher. Josh was not the greatest catcher; he was the greatest *hitter*. We had five or six men who could outcatch him. Josh couldn't receive with Larry Brown or Frank Duncan or Biz Mackey or Roy Campanella or any of those fellows. Of course I wouldn't include myself because that wouldn't be right, but they thought a lot of me, because I caught more East-West games than anybody. I was catching most of the West's games when I was there; the only game I'd miss was when I'd be somewhere like Mexico. I caught eight, pitched in four and hit four home runs. In 1942 Ed Bolden, the owner of Philadelphia, said I was the smartest catcher in the last several years.

My greatest thrill in baseball was in the East-West game of 1944 before 56,000 people in Comiskey Park. Barney Morris, a knuckle baller for the New York Cubans, had us beat 3–1. We put a man on base, my brother Alex doubled into right center, then I came up and hit a homer into the center field deck and won the game. You know what the people gave me that day? They gave me $700 for that home run.

I always had good success pitching against Josh Gibson. He never hit a home run off me, and I pitched against him nine years. I pitched him high and tight, and when I threw a curve ball, I made it bad and threw it away from him.

They usually called me the emery ball pitcher. I would cheat. They used to call me the Champion Cheater with that emery ball.

I played baseball for thirty-two years, from 1920 to 1951. I pitched and caught and never had a sore arm in my life. Well, I'll tell you: You cannot drink and then stay up all night and play baseball—nobody. I liked the ladies, I got my share of it. But I didn't do any drinking or dissipating much.

I was the champion pitcher in Cuba three straight years. And I was very fortunate in making good money in my day. Only one man topped me, and that was Satchel. Satchel made some money. You know, Satchel was getting 15 percent [of the gate] for seven years with the Monarchs. That's a lot of money, ain't it? Fifteen percent now in the big leagues would be something, wouldn't it?

Paige was the greatest—no comparison. I caught Satchel in his heyday, when nobody was like Satchel, nobody had the control Satchel had. You could bring Satchel or myself in with three-and-two on the batter, we'd get them out. And Satchel had something on the ball. Satchel didn't get a curve ball until 1938. He had a little wrinkle, but he didn't develop a fair curve ball until '38. He never did develop a *good* curve, but it was good enough to keep

The 1931 Homestead Grays. Radcliffe is kneeling third from right. Others: Ted Page, kneeling far right, and standing: owner Cum Posey on right, Smokey Joe Williams #5, Josh Gibson #6, and Oscar Charleston #8.

them off stride, because with that fast ball he didn't need it. I haven't seen anybody living with the speed Satchel had. I played against Bob Feller and all of them. I'm not saying this because he's colored, now, but Satchel's the greatest pitcher ever lived! You could tell Satchel was a great pitcher when he went up there and won in the big leagues in 1948.

Satchel and I were born in the same town, Mobile. Satchel didn't tell them when he was with Cleveland, but he was born in 1900. He's a few years older than me, and I was born in 1904. Yeah, I knew Satchel around Mobile, but we didn't play together until we came to the Crawfords in '32. Satchel's from Mobile; so's Hank Aaron, Billy Williams, Willie McCovey, Cleon Jones—some pretty good ballplayers come from within fifteen miles around there. In fact, I scouted Tommy Agee and Mudcat Grant down there.

I'm three years older than my brother Alex; he played third base for the Chicago American Giants. I started playing around Mobile, then I had an older brother that came here to Chicago in

1915, went into the Army and got out in 1918. Another brother and I had a chance to come up here on an excursion. This guy would take men to go to work in different places, like Akron, Ohio. We stayed over there three days working in a brick yard. We worked three days so we could draw an advance. I was a young fellow at that time, a pretty good dice shooter, so we'd shoot dice around there when we got off work. I won $18 shooting craps, so we hoboed over here where our older brother was. That was 1920, and we've been here ever since.

My people came here later, my father and all of them came up behind us. We were living at 3511 Wentworth, about four blocks from where Rube Foster's American Giants played.

I had an aunt that lived on the third floor right side of the ball park. Never had to pay. But we'd go to the park most of the time; get in before they started selling tickets and hide. Then when they started to warm up, we'd get a glove and go out in the outfield and start shagging balls. Sometimes when I was young they'd ask me to pitch batting practice, and my reward would be a Coca Cola or lemonade or something. But I enjoyed doing it, I enjoyed to get in free. They didn't know it, but I'd pitch batting practice and do anything to get in free. Now they pay a professional batting practice pitcher.

I started in to playing with a little team they called the Illinois Giants in 1920. A white guy from Spring Valley named Murphy had the team. There was a playground down there at 33rd and Wentworth where I'd go and play ball every day. Murphy came there one afternoon to bring his team in the spring, and I pitched against his team and struck out so many of them, he asked me, "How'd you like to go away and play with us? We need you." I was sixteen years old then. Well, if my daddy said I could go, I would go. When you were seventeen or eighteen years old then you still had to listen to your parents, but they don't do it anymore. My dad told me yeah, I could go. And that's the way I started out.

We'd go out every year and make $50 for every fifteen games. Murphy would pay all our expenses, which wasn't bad in those days.

We played all semipro white teams in different local towns.

We'd leave here and stay a night in Salem, Illinois. We'd leave there and go to Wisconsin, Minnesota, North Dakota, all into Canada. Traveled in a bus like those school buses. You had fourteen ballplayers, all we carried. Seven on that side, seven on this side, luggage in the back. And the owner drove the bus. Sometimes one of us would help him. They taught me how to drive because I didn't need sleep much, and so I had to drive most of the time. He would give me big money—$10 a week—to help him drive. Ten dollars was a lot of money in those days. You could get ham and eggs for a quarter.

I stayed with Murphy from 1920 to '27, then I went to Detroit with Bingo DeMoss in 1928. He came and got me over there. He had some big games with the ex-big leaguers in Flint and different places. He wanted me to pitch, so he came to my house one day. I told him, "Well, I tell you what I'll do. I don't want anything for myself, I came here to be near my mother. You give my mother and them $100 apiece, I'll go pitch." He gave it to them right away.

I stayed with Detroit in '28 and '29, and they had me pitching and catching. My first year with Detroit we played the major league all-stars. They had Charley Gehringer and Heinie Manush, and pitching they had George Uhle, Stanley Covaleskie and the Barnes brothers from the Giants, Virgil and Jess.

We had my brother Alex on third, Willie Wells at short, Jack Marshall on second and Mule Suttles on first. In the outfield we had Cool Papa Bell, center; Steel Arm Davis, left field; and Turkey Stearnes in right. Larry Brown was catching. Pitching was Willie Foster, Piggy Powell, Theodore Trent and George Harney.

We barnstormed all over southern Illinois. I started a game against them and shut them out. We didn't lose but three out of fourteen, so you know everyone must have done all right.

After that I asked Detroit for a raise. They wouldn't give it to me, so I went back with Gilkerson's Union Giants. I asked Gilkerson for more money, so in '30 he traded me to St. Louis. St. Louis traded three men to get me.

St. Louis had a great team, a hell of a team. That infield we had! George Giles was the best colored first baseman I ever saw. I'd love for you to have seen him play first base. John Henry

Russell was second, Dewey Creacy third, and Willie Wells short-stop. In the outfield we had Mule Suttles and Cool Papa Bell.

Bell was center field, a terrific base runner. The man who came closest to him as a runner was Giles. Giles could bunt on the hit-and-run, and Cool Papa would go to third base and Giles would beat it out at first before they picked the ball up. You couldn't compare Maury Wills with Bell, because they don't have catchers now that we had in our day, and we had so many great shortstops, like Wells, that Maury Wills wouldn't have made it in our league.

And we had some good pitchers—Ted Trent, Eggy Hensly, Duo Davis. Trent had a curve ball out of this world, one of the greatest curve ball pitchers ever lived. Oh, we had a ball club, I tell you, we won so many games. We won the pennant going away, by seventeen games. We came out and played the Chicago American Giants a whole season, didn't lose a game. We played them eight-een games that season and beat 'em eighteen. We beat the Home-stead Grays five out of six. And we beat Kansas City eighteen out of twenty. That's the kind of team we had. We beat Kansas City so bad, I never will forget what Newt Joseph, their third baseman, said to me: "Well, goddamn it, you won't beat us anymore, 'cause we ain't playin' you anymore."

But the man that had the Stars was so cheap. You know what top salary was in those days? Two-fifty a month was tops. I was making top money my third year in the league, 'cause I would leave. If they didn't pay me, I would go.

In fact, the next year I did leave. I went to the Homestead Grays in Pittsburgh, and that was the greatest team of all time. That was the year Josh Gibson hit the seventy-two home runs, and we won thirty-seven straight. In 1930 St. Louis had beat the Grays five out of six, but when I went to the Grays we beat St. Louis seven straight!

For pitchers we had Smoky Joe Williams, George Britt, Lefty Williams, Oscar Owens, Bill Foster and myself. We had a pitching staff! You got a team with a man like Oscar Charleston leading off at his age. That's right, he was leading off. Charleston was leading off because we had Vic Harris batting second, Jud Wilson third, Josh fourth, George Scales fifth. Oh, we had power to spare!

That was the year I hit the longest home run I ever hit. We

were playing the American Giants in Columbus, Ohio. They walked George Scales to pitch to me. I don't know how far the ball went. There was a playground for kids in back of the fence, and the left fielder didn't even bother to go get it. That was the most terrific ball I ever hit in my life.

In 1932 most of us jumped over to the Pittsburgh Crawfords. The man gave us so much more money. Gus Greenlee, you've heard of him, he was a big policy guy in the town. He wanted a team, and at that time they wouldn't let him in the league, so the first one he called was me, and I told him to get Charleston for the manager. So he took me, Charleston, Josh Gibson and Ted Page. I'll show you how bad he wanted us: He sent us to Hot Springs, Arkansas—the only time in my life I went to spring training on the eighteenth of February—went before the big leaguers would go there. He had plenty of money, he didn't care. Greenlee was one of the best.

Of course he got Satchel too. That was the year Damon Runyon saw us.

In 1934 I went out to Jamestown, North Dakota, to manage a white team, and we played the big league all-stars all the way through Canada. They had Jimmy Foxx, Luke Appling, Jimmy Dykes in the infield. Pitching was Earl Whitehill of Washington; Rube Walberg from the Athletics; George Uhle, Willis Hudlin and his boy who pitched so good with Detroit—Tommy Bridges. He won twenty-two games that year. We played them in James City, North Dakota, and Chet Brewer of the Monarchs pitched and beat 'em 6–1. I caught him that day. I pitched the next day in Bismarck against Earl Whitehill and Willis Hudlin, and I beat them 8–2. They didn't get but five hits, and we got eleven. No, Foxx didn't get any home runs. The only home runs, we hit them: I hit one, Quincy Trouppe hit one and Red Haley hit one.

Then we went to Winnipeg. Barney Brown was pitching and they beat us. Jimmy Foxx got hit on the head with a pitched ball, and they canceled the rest of the games.

The next year I played in Bismarck, North Dakota, with Satchel. He had a sore arm, and for a whole month he couldn't pitch. I said, "Just roll it up there. They're ascared of your name, they ain't going to hit it." Every game I caught four innings and pitched the last five. I remember one time we were playing out in Nebraska against all those Western League teams. I had to pitch five days in a row, relieving while he went fishing with some rich man and didn't show up till the next Sunday. You couldn't fine him cause he'd quit. That's a bitch, ain't it? I used to say, "He's bigger than the game. You can't find him and you can't fine him. What do you want with him?" I don't care if he could throw the ball so hard you couldn't see it. If he couldn't take orders, I wouldn't want him, would you?

I could give him hell, 'cause he and I were buddies. See, if he'd been a man that took baseball serious, with any kind of common sense, he might be a coach now, wouldn't he? With the reputation he had—and the Cubs need a pitching coach bad. They got a coach over there called Becker. Never played a lick of big-league ball, never pitched in his life—he was a first baseman when he did play in the minors. What does he know about pitching? I can't understand these things, can you? Baseball is mostly politics.

Churchill was the mayor at Bismarck, and boy did we have a pitching staff: Satchel Paige, Hilton Smith, Barney Morris and myself.

I never will forget when we played in that semipro tournament over there in Wichita, Kansas. Churchill wired for reservations for thirty people. The guy wired back okay. When we got there, me and Satchel walked in with the rest of them whites. He said, "Oh, I didn't know you had those colored boys. We can't take them all." Churchill said, "I got your telegram. Goddamn it, I'll sue you." So I spoke up and took him off the hook. We could have let him sue the man, but I told him, "Well, the man didn't know. Mrs. Jones got a nice rooming house up here, we'll go up there and stay." ('Course, I knew they weren't going to let me bring those girls in the hotel—I had some friends there I knew years before.) So we went up to Mrs. Jones' house, a very nice place. She even cooked for us. I'll tell you how good things were back in those days, '35. We stayed there for $3 a day, two meals a day. Churchill would come out every day and give us some money, thought we were mad and everything. Heck, we weren't mad.

Well, we won the tournament in seven straight games. Satchel pitched five games, I caught two and pitched two. In those days we got $1,000 a game, so that gave us $7,000 for the tournament. Those teams from Texas and Oklahoma and Georgia said they weren't going to come back and play anymore, because they didn't have a chance with me and Satchel. They said, "Those are big-league players—they're niggers, but they're big-league players." So they wouldn't come back and play any more in the tournament. Satchel had bought one of those cars·from Churchill. He owed him $970, I think, on it. Churchill gave Satchel the car. And gave Satchel $500 to go out to California to play winter ball.

Next year we had some young country boys from Minneapolis, Rochester, Minnesota and all up through there. I was manager. He had me drilling them young kids. They weren't known, but they could play—they were white boys, but they could play! They went to the Denver tournament in '36, and we won our first six games—I pitched until I just got tired. So we sent here and got Ted Trent to pitch, gave him $500 to pitch one game. He went out there, got drunk and throwed the game to them.

I also managed the Claybrook Tigers in '36, a little team out in Memphis. They were owned by a rich colored guy, had a town named after him down in Claybrook, Arkansas. He told me he would get me $500 a month, what I was making up in North Dakota, if I'd come down there, and twenty percent of the gate. Well, you know I couldn't turn that down.

We were playing in the white park in Memphis and we outdrew the white teams. We made so much money, the first week I made $1,200 for my part. We broke the record. We put 18,000 in there with the Cubans. Next week I made a little better than $800, so the third week he called me into his office, had the chief of police there, had the man from the Southern League Memphis Chicks, and he had two or three women secretaries dictating, and he says, "Double Duty"—these are the words he said to me—"Good morning, how are you?"

I said, "Fine. This is my wife."

He said, "How are you, Mrs. Radcliffe?" He didn't care who heard, he said, "You are a smarter nigger than I thought you was."

I said, "What do you mean?"

He says, "You making all the money, I'm paying all the bills. As soon as I pay all the ballplayers, I don't have anything left. We got to get together here and straighten that out." He said, "What we'll do, I'll just give you $750 a month."

I said, "No, the contract . . ."

He said, "I tore that son of a bitch up."

So we got together. I wouldn't take the $750 a month. I told him just like I'm telling you now: "I tell you what I'll do: You just give me $1,000 bonus at the end of the season. Write it down here, let them type it here and we'll notarize it right here in this office." So he gave me $1,000. I treated him nice. I could have taken more, 'cause I was manager and secretary and everything. But I said I'd do right by him, because he was a nice fellow. When he died, he left that boy of his about seven hundred acres of land, about fifty mules and all of those tractors, and that boy blowed that money in less than five years. I was reading the other day where he got ten years in Sing Sing for dope in New York.

I managed the Memphis Red Sox six years, 1937–1942, and that was one of the worst outfits ever been in baseball. They didn't pay their ballplayers anything. When I went down there, they had ballplayers making $75 a month, which was a disgrace to baseball. When I raised them to $150, the owner got mad with me. But your ballplayer could live off that. I don't care what kind of times it was, $75 a month was nothing for a ballplayer.

After the regular season I'd play against the big-league all-stars with Satchel Paige on the Coast. From 1941 to 1945 Satchel didn't lose a game against them. He usually pitched five innings against men like Bob Lemon, Bobo Newson, Bob Feller. Feller, there was a fine man; he'd lend me his car, anything. A swell guy. Satchel pitched nine innings against him one day and beat him 2–1. I remember one Sunday in 1943, a benefit game for infantile paralysis. George Raft, Marlene Dietrich and a lot of other movie stars were in the stands. Buck Newsom had us beat 2–0 in the ninth, and everybody said we were laying down for bets. So we scored four runs in the ninth to win 4–2. In eighteen games they won only five. We had a hell of a team. That was the year we played the Great Lakes Naval Training team. They had Feller, Johnny Mize, John Pesky, Johnny Schmitz; they beat the St. Louis Cards, who had won the pennant that year. But we knocked Schmitz out with five runs in the first inning, hit six triples that day, beat them 11–2. They wouldn't let us come back again.

Bob Feller was one of the straightest guys I ever came in contact with. We were playing Hollywood one Sunday. I was managing the team and Buck Leonard was the captain. This guy Joe Perrone out there, who was promoting the games, was going to take $2,500 off the top before we knew anything about it. Said he was going to give them their share, but he was going to take that much from ours. Bob Feller told us, "Don't take a nickel, and don't play another inning"—because we were in the fourth inning —"don't play another inning until we get it straight about the money." They had that park packed. Marlene Dietrich, Gary Cooper, William Powell—a bunch of celebrities were out there that day. But we weren't going to play another inning, give them their money back. People wanted to know what happened, but we went around and we got it straight. I think we made $227 apiece that Sunday.

In 1943 I was managing the Chicago American Giants. We won the pennant by thirteen games. We had seven .300 hitters in the starting lineup. Ducky Davenport was in the outfield. Davenport, there was another great player. He was only five feet five, weighed 147 pounds, but he could hit the ball out of any park. And field! One day, playing the big-league all-stars, Heinie Manush hit one, and that little SOB caught it with one hand going away. Manush said, "I'm glad that little SOB doesn't play in my league. He takes too many hits away from you!"

In 1944 I went down to Birmingham with Abe Saperstein, who

Double Duty Radcliffe, Brooklyn Eagles, 1935, back row on far right

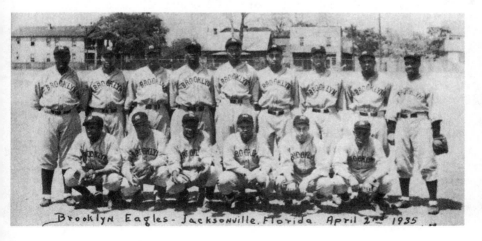

also owned the Harlem Globetrotters. Abe had a lot of different teams. He had the Cincinnati Clowns, he had the Birmingham Black Barons. He was part owner of Birmingham with Tom Hayes when the war broke out until '45.

Saperstein made his money during the war—he made the money. He'd book us where Tom Hayes couldn't get us booked. Saperstein was a smart man. He'd book us in those big four-team doubleheaders in Yankee Stadium. Every time the Yankees would leave, Birmingham would be in Yankee Stadium with twenty-five to thirty thousand people. Saperstein would get $8–9,000 on a Sunday, then every night booking you in all those good places, making all that money. He made more money than the rest of the teams. And you know, we drew more people in Birmingham than any city in the country. That's one of the best baseball towns in the world. We'd have twelve–fourteen thousand every Sunday. Every Sunday was a sellout.

Abe used to give me a new car practically every year. I'd tell Abe, "I'm having trouble with this one." He'd tell them, "Give him a car," and I'd go up there and pick it up. He just paid the note on it and never said anything about it. He just wanted me to use it, whether for baseball or anything else. It saved him a lot of money, but I wouldn't have had the car if it hadn't been for him. But wherever he wanted me to take him, I had to go. And it paid dividends. My mother always taught me, "You pray the bridge will carry you over safe, and always treat your fellow man as you want to be treated yourself."

Saperstein was my man, he was my man. He was the greatest friend to the colored athlete of anybody I know today. He's the great man in the history of Negroes, for helping Negroes. He got 'em up. I was connected with him twenty-eight years. Later on I had to take the Harlem Globetrotters out for him. I had to manage them. No matter where I'd be, I'd go.

And we won the pennant my first year in Birmingham. I got my finger broke, but they had a boy pitching for the Clowns called Peanuts Davis. I guess you've heard of Davis? He used to scratch the ball. We didn't have anyone on our team could scratch it but me, so Saperstein went to the dresser and got a plastic bag to go over my finger. He said, "We can't go to war without a gun, and Double Duty's got a gun." So I had to pitch for them with a broken finger. I had to pitch with these three fingers, and I pitched the last six innings and won the ball game 3–1. And I had to catch the last fourteen games with my finger in a cast. That's how we won the championship.

I left Birmingham in '45. When Saperstein couldn't get the team by himself, he just pulled out, and me and Tom Hayes got in a disagreement. In those days you couldn't get much gas, and I knew a fellow around here that had ration stamps, and I was the only one could get them. Hayes was paying me $750 a month for managing, but he was supposed to pay me $400 a month for my car, 'cause they couldn't use the buses. So I told him I wasn't going to play anymore, I'd play where I want.

So I went out and managed the Globetrotters the last three months. We played the House of David ball club, and did we make the money! Saperstein gave me $2500 at the end of the season. He was the greatest.

We were beating the House of David pretty bad, when we got to Seattle, Washington. They had this boy pitched for the Giants —he's a coach for them now—Larry Jansen; they had Frank McCormick, the first baseman for the Cincinnati Reds, and Frank McQuillen, an outfielder played for the Browns. They were in Fort Lewis in the Army. Abe got that team and got Larry Jansen to pitch against us.

When we got to the park in Seattle the police had to make a line for us, we couldn't get in the park, so many people. The park was a sellout. Billy Mulligan, used to play third base for the White Sox, he was president of the Seattle club. So I told him, "We've had these uniforms two months and they're dirty. I'd hate to play before a crowd like that without new uniforms." So he let me have some; he sold me sixteen uniforms for $350. They were beautiful; my ball club looked good.

We had a good little young team, but I was the only one had experience. I had announced in the paper another boy, named Lee, was going to pitch. But they all came running up to me after I went up to the office to check up on the tickets and everything. They said, "They got all them big leaguers against us today, Double Duty." I said, "Okay, they're just men like everybody else."

After we got through taking batting practice, I called a meeting in the dugout. I said, "You all don't have to worry, I'm going to pitch." And that relieved them: "You gonna pitch, Skip? We'll get 'em then, we'll get 'em then!" The big leaguers didn't know I had to cheat, you know. They didn't know I could throw that scratch ball. Anyway, God was with me. We were 0–0 in the sixth inning, I caught two men on base and hit a home run off Jansen, and we beat 'em 3–0.

I went to Mexico in 1946. Jorge Pasquel, the owner of the Mexican League, came right here and unwrapped $3,000, just like that, for me to sign. I was very fortunate. I was in the twilight innings of going out, and I was getting $750 a month and all expenses. I didn't do much catching. I was relieving and saved quite a few ball games. Then every time I hit a home run they gave me a watch and a suit of clothes. I hit seventeen home runs, batted .344 and made the all-star team at the age of forty-six! Sal Maglie and Max Lanier were playing with me, and we walked to the pennant.

In 1947 the Grays came got me from Mexico, and we won the pennant and drew fifteen–twenty thousand a game, better than the Senators. Clark Griffith was looking at me. He said if I had been white, he'd pay me so much to catch, so much to pitch and so much to pinch-hit. If Early Wynn could get $1,000 to pinch-hit, no telling how much I'd get for pinch-hitting.

Sam Bankhead got up in the bus one night—I never will forget this. Bankhead was captain. He said, "You young son of a guns better wake up. Old Man Duty getting all the glory. Duty ought to be paid all your salary, cause he's *doing* all the work."

In 1948 Saperstein signed me with the Globetrotters to play the House of David. All those players that the big teams, like the American Giants, would cut loose, why the best ones Abe would pick up for the Globetrotters. We won 105 games and lost 10. In one stretch I pitched four or five innings a day for twenty-four straight days.

In 1950 I was managing the Chicago American Giants. Ernie Banks was in our league then. You should have seen him—so skinny and little. That was my last year in colored baseball. In '51 I went up to Winnipeg managing, and we won the pennant. That was one of my greatest dreams, managing up there, because we only played three or four games a week, and they were paying me good money, and conditions were good. Stayed at the best hotels. They were great people up there, but all at once it folded up. Canada was the end of the line for me. After thirty-two years.

I played ball thirty-two years in all—managed twenty-two of them—and I never had a sore arm in my life. I never was prone to injuries. I don't understand these ballplayers now. This finger's been broke four times. This finger was split two or three times. You see that? The ball hit between the fingers and busted it clean down to here. And I wasn't out but a month. Nowadays it's a disgrace.

You see, by me being big and rugged, that's how I never was out much with injuries. I was pretty hefty, see, I weighed around 210, 215. With all that padding and stuff on, they couldn't buffalo me. You got to be ready for anything they do. When they come in, all you got to do is brace yourself, like a bull. You know if I played thirty-two years I had to take care of myself.

And the catchers nowadays, they don't know how to tag, that's the reason they get hurt so much. You've got to get the ball in this hand, the right hand. When the runner jumps, you just step aside. I used to hit them up under their chin with it. Yeah, I had a ball out there catching. Out here one day there was one player—I won't talk about him 'cause he married my niece—but I hit him on the chin, knocked him clean out. He tried to jump at me, I stepped aside and he went by and I hit him.

I'm going to tell you the truth now, I'm not going to tell you no lies: I never had any trouble guarding the plate. The roughest sliders were men like Turkey Stearnes and Newt Allen, but I never did get cut by them. Now the greatest slider there ever was in baseball was this Crush Holloway. He jumped at me once, and then when I caught him at the bat when I was pitching in Cleveland, I knocked him down twice. He said, "Are you trying to kill me?" I said, "I'm trying to make a living out there, but you tried to kill *me* when you came home." That night we went out and had some beer. That ended it. He never jumped any more, I never threw at him any more. He was a good ballplayer too.

I was secretary for the Globetrotters for two years. I went to Mexico with them, Hawaii, Honolulu—I'd like to go back to Honolulu one time. We had 33,000 in the bull arena in Mexico

City for basketball, 75,000 in Brazil. I didn't go to Brazil. I was ascared to fly, that's why I'm not still with them. I had a heart attack flying. I don't like to fly.

Saperstein got me my job scouting with Cleveland in 1962. He just called up the man, said, "I got a good man that knows as much about baseball as anybody living today and I'm going to send him out to scout for you."

They said, "Who is he?"

He said, "Double Duty Radcliffe."

They said, "Send him on."

I stayed with them from '62 to '66. Everybody I sent in, they'd get him. We got Tommy Agee, Mudcat Grant—I didn't sign them, but I'm the one scouted them and recommended them, so they signed them. They wouldn't let me sign them, 'cause they figured they'd get them a lot cheaper than me.

The Montreal Expo's wrote me a letter a while back to bird-dog scout for them. I told them I haven't got to the point where I'd lower my prestige that much to be a bird dog. If I'm good enough to be a bird dog, I want to be full-time scout or nothing. Who the hell wants to work for two or three hundred a month? If you want to get somebody, go out and pay them, ain't that right?

We had quite a few ballplayers could have made the major leagues in my day. But in the Thirties and Forties I'd have called Negro baseball about Triple-A. The big leaguers were strong in every position, where most of the colored teams had a few stars but they weren't strong in every position. But after the Grays got Josh, we didn't have any weakness. And the American Giants, with my brother, Willie Wells, Mule Suttles—they had a hell of a ball team. They had six or seven good starting pitchers; they could have held their own in the majors, I believe. I'm telling you, you take from 1932 until Jackie went into the big leagues, oh there were some powerful ballplayers.

All in the Thirties and the first part of the Forties we were drawing good crowds. Sap tried to tell the owners they should have told the big leagues to have colored farm teams. Then the Negro teams could have gone on a little longer. And if they'd done that, the majors would have more players now. It's Triple-A baseball now. Makes me sick to look at the game now.

I've had a good life. Of course, we didn't have as much luck as the people got today, 'cause we couldn't stay in the white hotels then. The only place we stayed in a white hotel was up around North Dakota or Canada. We couldn't do it around here. But then some people never had the opportunity we had. Some people come along and dig ditches all their lives.

I'm too old to move now, but you know where I'd like to live if I could? New Orleans. There's a few good ballplayers back in those woods around Mobile. The best ones come from the carney leagues. The white scouts only go to the colleges. But out in the woods the kids are tough as bricks.

Double Duty Radcliffe (left) with Chicago American Giants manager Candy Jim Taylor (right) in the Memphis Red Sox park, opening day 1939. (Photo courtesy of Phil Dixon).

Bill Foster at the American Giants' park, former home of the 1906 "Hitless Wonder" White Sox.

Chapter 10

BILL FOSTER

Willie Foster was the Cy Young of the Negro leagues. The lanky left-handed younger brother of league pioneer Rube Foster, won 138 lifetime victories, tops among all pitchers. Lefty Andy Cooper is second with 123 and Satchel Paige third at 122.

In 1927 Big Bill posted a record of 21-3 to lead the Chicago American Giants to the black world championship. Only two men, Ray Brown and Slim Jones, have ever won more in a single year. Bill leads all pitchers, including Paige, in lifetime shutouts, and ranks second to Satchel in strikeouts. And if Foster hadn't retired at the age of 33 in the midst of the Depression, he would have rung up even higher numbers.

Big Bill was a money pitcher. His 15 victories in post-season play are more than any man in blackball annals.

His manager, Dave Malarcher, says Bill was a carbon copy of his brother on the pitching mound. Pictures of the two, side-by-side, show them both with identical moves—ball held behind the head—just before they take their stride.

"Bill Foster was my star pitcher, the greatest pitcher of our time, not even barring Satchel," declares Malarcher. "Rube taught him, I didn't teach him. The art of pitching he learned from Rube."

Many a black veteran—outfielder Nat Rogers is one —insists that Foster was better than Satchel Paige, and the long pitching rivalry between these two was one of the most exciting in black ball annals.

Perhaps the most exciting rivalry in the Negro leagues was Foster against Paige, the best black left-hander against the best righty. In one double-header, Rogers remembers, Satchel was scheduled to pitch the first game against Foster but pulled out at the last minute. Bill pitched anyway and won. "When they announced Satchel to pitch the second game, Bill said, 'Shucks, give me that ball. I want to beat him.' When the game ended, Bill had 'em 6–2."

After retiring from baseball, Bill Foster moved to North Carolina as an insurance agent. He eventually settled in Lorman, Mississippi, not far from Charles Evers' Fayette, where he coached baseball and served as dean of men. That's where I met him in 1970, a tall, lean man well over six feet, with the hard stomach of a man still physically active, and sunken eye sockets and cheeks that gave him almost a death's-head look. He spoke eloquently, thoughtfully, in a deep baritone, struggling to summon back to memory a chapter in history too long neglected.

Bill Foster Speaks . . .

I think, as near as I can remember, that Satchel and I faced each other around thirteen or fourteen times. And I *think* I got the edge on Satchel when I beat him a doubleheader in Pittsburgh one Saturday, 5–0 and 1–0. I think that put me one ball game ahead of him in our careers. Terrific ballplayer! Terrific. I tell you, if you get a chance to talk to him, tell him I asked you to ask him how many times did we beat each other. But I'll tell you something: If Satchel got one run first, he would beat you; if I got one run first, he was beat. Because we didn't tire back then. I never remember being tired out there. Now that's the truth. I remember getting blasted and getting hit hard, but I never remember getting tired.

You talk about a tremendous ballplayer, one of the greatest pitchers I've ever seen, I think, was Satchel. Now, he didn't know how to throw a curve ball for a long time. I was out of baseball,

I was in the insurance business, when Satchel started throwing curve balls, so I knew him as a good fast ball pitcher. In the nighttime the ball looked like one of these "zuzu" biscuits—you know, you can go to the grocery store and buy you some of those little white biscuits. About the size of a fifty-cent piece. That's the way it looked. The ball didn't have any size on it or anything. Looked just as flat as a fifty-cent piece. Looked just like a streak or something.

My brother Rube was my first manager when I went up to Chicago to play. Rube was fifteen years older than me. He was my half-brother, but I never knew him until I was fifteen years old. He had already left home and gone to Chicago when I was born, in 1904, in Texas. Our mother brought me here to Mississippi when I was a baby. She died when I was only four, and I was raised by her folks. I went to Alcorn College—at that time it was a grade school and high school as well as a college. I knew I had a brother, and I had heard all about the great Rube Foster, but I never met thim until I went to Chicago to work in the stockyards. That was around 1918, something like that. He wouldn't let me play baseball at all. He had a ball team then and wouldn't let me play. Well, he didn't want me to play ball, that was it, he wanted me to do something else: "That's no life for you, don't play baseball." Well, I wanted to play.

I came back on down here and then when I got ready to go up again, I went to Memphis, and Bubber Lewis gave me a chance to pitch for the Memphis team. That was in 1925. Rube was manager and owner of the American Giants, and he also was president of our league. When he found out I was in Memphis, he just told Bubber Lewis to send me to Chicago, and I think that's one of the things that came between Rube and me. After Bubber had given me a chance, I didn't feel like I should have left Bubber. I just didn't want to go, but Lewis said, "I don't have any way out. He's your brother, he's president of the league and he's got a ball team. I didn't have any business, really, trying to sign you until you had talked to Rube." So he says, "You gotta go."

Naturally it was a sore spot between my brother and me for a long time. I told Rube, "Why didn't you take me before I went up to Memphis?" I never did get over that. I decided from then on I was going to do everything like *I* wanted to do it. He would try to show me the right way, and I didn't know the right way nor the wrong way. I didn't know anything. But I was just going to be obstinate, you know.

When I came to Chicago, he started me in just about every series, and I didn't stay in those ball games long enough for the water to get hot. In other words, I never did get to pitch to the eighth hitter before I was out. I wouldn't pitch for my brother. And he said he wasn't going to trade me: "I know you can pitch. I'm not going to trade you. You can just stay out there and make a fool of yourself. I'm going to send you out there, and you're going to come back in, but I'm not going to trade you." I just made up my mind, I said I'm not going to pitch. I didn't stay in a ball game as long as he was on that bench.

But Rube was a shrewd man. The more I think of it, the older I get, I can see Rube's point of view in a lot of things. And whatever he told me stuck. After he had a breakdown, after he got off the bench in '26, I went right through the same procedure that he had been teaching me. I went out there and won! That's the year they said I was one of the greatest pitchers of all time, that I had well nigh perfect control.

I could have pitched in '25, if I wasn't so stubborn, just because *Rube* wanted me to pitch!

Our big rivals were the Kansas City Monarchs, and we fought them for the pennant out here in the West in 1926. They came to Chicago for the play-off, and we had to win a doubleheader to beat them. They only had to beat us one, we had to beat them two. Bullet Rogan pitched against me in the first game. He was an *excellent* pitcher—good fast ball, good curve ball, and he could keep it down.

Well, I got out there and beat Rogan 1–0 to tie the series. When we went back into the clubhouse to rest between ball games, Cap [Dave Malarcher] says, "Who shall I pitch now in the deciding ball game? It's your all ball game"—you know how managers are, they like to get along with the ballplayers. I told him I felt all right, so they voted unanimously to let me go back if I wanted to pitch.

I went back out there to warm up. Rogan saw me warming up, said, "You going to pitch?"

I said, "Yeah, I'm going to pitch."

"Well, I'm coming back." And he came back, and I think in the first inning we made four or five runs off him. That was all. He closed the door. But I think it was 5–0 we beat 'em.

That was on Friday. We hadn't planned to leave Chicago—it wasn't in the plan that we were going to play the World Series, because everybody was expecting Kansas City. So when we beat the doubleheader, we had to get ready and go out East. Well, I had pitched a doubleheader on Friday in Chicago and then I opened up on Sunday in Philadelphia in the World Series against the Bacharach Giants.

I opened up against Rats Henderson, and I think Rats beat me 3–2. I think that's what the record will show. It seems like Chaney White drove in a run to beat me. I never did get a chance to pay Rats back, but I think I beat his team two games that series.°

Our park in Chicago was a wood structure. It was as big a playing field as any of the major-league ball parks—350 or 360 feet down the line, something like that. Four hundred, or four and a half, to left center and center. You had to hit the ball good when you hit it out of there. It seated about 18,000. Thirty-ninth and Wentworth, just across from the White Sox park—they've got a housing project out there now. I don't doubt that Rube's club would outdraw the White Sox and Cubs. When Kansas City came in there, and St. Louis, we packed them in. Yeah, quite a few white fans too. When the Cubs or Sox were playing and we were playing Kansas City, we didn't miss what the Sox and the Cubs drew. We didn't miss 'em. That place was full, packed all the time, standing room only.

° Actually the first game ended in a 3–3 tie. Foster did win two other games, including the final clincher, 1–0.

I'd just like to see the Giants and the Sox and the Cubs have a three-way play-off in the city—I'd like to have seen that. I think that would have been great, 'cause the Giants had a good ball club out there—a good ball club.

I've pitched against the Waner boys out of Pittsburgh, Paul and Lloyd. They could hit—they could hit most anything: Big Poison and Little Poison. Then they had this Heinie Manush from St. Louis, and Luke Appling. They had this boy Charlie Gehringer from Detroit—he could hit that ball too. I think they had Jumping Joe Dugan at third base. Pitching they had Earl Whitehill, who used to be with Detroit, and Jake Miller, used to be with Cleveland.

The major-league all-stars just didn't beat those teams, those Negro teams. See, we were organized as a unit, but they just came down there with one from here, one from there. They didn't have a whole lot of signals or anything like that. In other words, an all-star, picked ball club is at a disadvantage in the technical part of baseball. They just never could beat us. We beat them six or seven out of eight every time.

I don't ever remember that they beat me—no, I think they did too. They beat me a 3–2 ball game. Last year one of the big-league scouts came up to me and said, "Heh, Bill, you remember me?" I said, "No." He said, "I'm the guy that hit the ball over the right field wall off of you in Kellogg's corn flakes up at Battle Creek, Michigan." And he sure did. Somebody did hit a line drive and beat me 3–2. He hit it in right center and I don't know who it was. He told me, and I forgot his name again. He beat me, because I had 'em 2–1 and they had a man on base, and he hit that ball and beat me 3–2—in the late innings too, way late. I got the ball too high or something, I don't know what happened.

The Depression was tough. Back in the Thirties, I know, one week I lived on thirty-six cents the whole week. And out of that thirty-six cents I had to take three cents for a stamp to send back home to my foster mother to send me some money so I could come home. Now you know how long it takes a letter from Chicago to Mississippi and back—six days. Chicago had those places around there where they give you all you can eat for three cents or two cents, and I'd go down there and get one meal every day. They'd

*Bill Foster, Kansas City Monarchs, 1936, back row on left; Newt Allen,
kneeling, fifth from left*

give you a lot of mashed potatoes, spaghetti and old rank meat
balls, but you were hungry, you had to eat it. And that's what I
lived on. The team couldn't pay us, it was the Depression and
nobody was working. That was back in the WPA and PWA and
DDA and I don't know what-all A's. The people couldn't go to the
ball game, and our bosses promised us so much money, but they
didn't have it 'cause they weren't making it.

I always tell the boys about that rat I saw one day. As I was
going to the ball park one morning, I saw a rat in the alley there
sitting on a garbage can chewing on an onion. He was eating and
just crying. That was the best he could do. That was all he could
find, that onion. He was just eating and crying and kept on gnaw-
ing right on. And that shows you—any time a rat's got to eat an
onion, it's rough! But that's what happened back in '29 and '30.

So many things happened back then, I can't remember it all.
The way we ate, the way we traveled from one town to another,
play a doubleheader here, then go somewhere tomorrow—New
York—ride the bus all night. Had two or three sweatshirts in there,
they were all wet when you got to New York—honest to goodness.

I played with the Homestead Grays in '31, and we had nine starters. I pitched on a Friday, pitched my ball game and finished it. Do you know that Sunday evening it was my turn again? Everybody had pitched and everybody had stayed in the ball game! Yes sir, we played nine ball games in two days! That's a heck of a lot of baseball.

Really, I don't think there's any difference between ballplayers of that day or this day. No, I don't think there's any difference. I think that those who did it back there would have done it up here, or those who are doing it up here would have done it back there. I don't see a bit of difference in Koufax's pitching than anybody else back there, Lefty Grove and that bunch. They had the same ballplayers to pitch against. They say "the dead ball, the rabbit ball," but you had to have your control. You had to get the ball over the plate. And they had men could hit the ball. You couldn't say Babe Ruth couldn't hit the ball, you couldn't say Lou Gehrig couldn't hit the ball. You can't say Willie Mays can't hit the ball. Mays would have hit it back then just like he hits it up here. Oscar Charleston would have hit it up here just like he hit it back there.

The toughest hitter I faced, black or white? Hmmmm! That's a hard thing to say, because they had quite a number of good hitters then. In other words, you had four or five pretty good hitters on each ball club. Now no pitcher liked to see Josh Gibson come up with a man on third and that run could beat you or tie you. Nobody liked to see Charleston come up with a man on third and one out. So I don't know who I would say was the best hitter I ever met. I might could name the top ten, but yet I don't know if I could do that even.

Oscar Charleston—you're talking about a good hitter. He's a left-handed hitter and I'm a left-handed pitcher. I just didn't feel like left-handers ought to hit me; I was awful surprised when left-handers hit me. But Charlie could do that. Charleston would wait for a curve ball, because he knew a left-hander was going to throw that curve ball. I wouldn't throw him a curve ball. That's how I'd get him out. Charleston, all he got from me mostly—to hit on—were fast balls. Because he waited for curve balls and he could hit that curve ball. He could hit it a mile. To tell you the truth, he was a tremendously good hitter.

Among right-handers there was Josh Gibson. When Gibson turned that cap bill up and got in that crouch at the plate, you had your problems! He could hit it for distance. Anywhere he caught it, he could hit it. How did I pitch him? The only perfect pitch for anybody is the low outside pitch, and every time you're in doubt, that's the thing to throw. Now if he hits it, he just hits it. But it's the most effective pitch in baseball—if you can get it where you want it. Just knock all the black off the edge of that plate. I don't mean over the middle of the plate, I don't mean on the inside, I mean exactly what I say: Knock all the black off that outside corner of the plate. Right down that edge. If you can get it there, that's your best pitch. He may hit one over the fence, but just keep it there and you'll get him out.

Nobody can tell any pitcher how he feels out there on that mound when those big bats come up. And you know they're good big bats too. When you see it waving, you know that's a good bat. And you know that if you make one mistake—if you make *one* mistake—that's it! Forget it, that's all—it's over. Nice and quick. One sweep of the bat and that's all. You pitch to Josh wrong, one pitch wrong, just make *one* mistake—the ball game is over. Oscar Charleston, Buck Leonard, Torrienti, John Beckwith, Mule Suttles: I'm talking about those power hitters, one sweep of the bat and it's over.

So you've got to be scared. I don't say you stay scared, but you get scared. Now, it doesn't last long. When they announced me to pitch, and until I could throw the first pitch, I was scared to death. But when I threw that first pitch, regardless of whether it was a strike, a ball or the man hit and got on base or hit it into the stands, it didn't make any difference—I settled down just the same. But I was scared before that first pitch. What I was afraid of, I don't know. Any pitcher will tell you that: At times you just get scared. Now, he doesn't know what he's scared of. Not frightened, not afraid—he's scared. Plain down scared, that's all.

I found out one thing that you had to have was control. You had to have control of every pitch that you had. If you didn't have control of that pitch, forget it—put it over there on the side line until you can develop it. Don't bring that pitch into your ball game if you don't know how to control it. Leave it out, that's something for you to work on.

I had a pretty good fast ball, and I had a good overhanded curve ball, which was known as the "drop" ball. And then I had what they call sliders now. I had what is called a sidearm curve ball—palm down. I had a slider, an "out-shoot" and a curve ball all on the same pitch.

I didn't know anything about spitters, I didn't know anything about knuckleballs, I didn't know anything about emery balls. All I knew was the good hard fast ball, the good hard curve ball and a good sidearm curve ball. Now, if you can keep a man off balance, he can't hit the ball hard—if you can keep him off balance.

Now, how do I keep him off balance? And with what pitches? It boils down to the fact that I had to have one motion to control every pitch. You take your fast ball—an exceptional fast ball, a fast ball as hard as I could throw it. Now I take that same fast ball and with the same motion I throw it half speed, with the same motion that you threw the hardest fast ball. And then come right back and throw that same fast ball and make it almost "walk" up there—with the same motion. And have control of that pitch. That was three pitches developed out of one basic pitch. Now, go right back to the curve ball—with the same motion come right back with the medium speed, and then come right back with the same motion with the slowest speed. And control it. Then come right back with an overhand drop ball as hard as you can throw it, with the same motion medium speed, and then the same curve ball with the same motion, make it "drift." I developed nine different pitches off of three basic pitches. That kept a man off balance.

In other words, if I caught him slowing up a stride, I'd step it up. I could get him out of time by my motion. If he'd make his step and looked like he was going to time another fast ball, I'd go slow on him. The change-ups, in my estimation, were never planned before the man took a stride. I changed my pitches in the motion of pitching, after I had gotten him off balance. The catchers signaled for a curve ball, but now the catchers didn't know if it was going to be a fast curve ball or a slow curve ball or a medium curve ball, because I hadn't pitched yet. The batter hadn't committed himself yet. I'd wait until I was in my motion, until he'd committed himself.

And the next thing that I found out about pitching—this job of pitching is a little more technical than I think most ballplayers give credit for. You see, you can't forget when you're pitching out there. I can't forget what I got you out on the first time up. Because you're thinking too. And if once you catch up with me with that big bat, I'm hurt. I'm hurt, yeah, I'm hurt.

I feel that the pitcher has the advantage of the hitter—providing he stays awake and doesn't go to sleep. We have nine men to face us in a ball game. This might not be what the majors would term a method of good pitching—it might not be their method—but I had success with it: A pitcher must keep in mind what has happened, just like a computer. Everything ought to be in my head: say you're the lead-off man—how I got you out on how many pitches. Put that in [the computer]. Number-two, how'd you get him out? Put that in there. Now, for nine men, you keep that in there for each one of their first times up. When the number-one hitter comes up for the second time, as soon as you see his name: "Jackson"—I should know what I threw to Jackson the first time.

To show you how complicated it gets, I had to keep up with—I *did* keep up with—every one of those hitters as they came to bat for nine innings. If he came to bat five times, I knew his record. Now, unless somebody got me in an argument out there, I would keep up with you right straight on through. But once you get in an argument, you lose everything. They say pitchers get tired in the seventh or eighth inning. It's not that, they're not tired physically. They forgot! They forgot how they pitched to that man. He's not tired, he just forgot. He and the catcher both forgot. I've forgotten out there. I've got hurt, I've got bombed. So I stayed away from all arguments, to keep my calm or keep my cool. If I forget, I get my ears pinned back. That was my procedure. I kept up with all those fellows as they came to bat. I'd remember how I got him out, what he went for, and I knew how he was thinking then. He knew I got him out on a fast ball high inside. Now, he might be thinking that I'm not going to try that any more, and it might be a good idea for me to try the same thing again.

We didn't tire back then, and we didn't have much relief pitchers. Here's one thing I can't understand: I can't understand why

these fellows in the major leagues take two and three men to pitch
a ball game. That's one of the things I don't see. Because you
didn't get us out in our league that fast. When we started a ball
game, we finished it.

Looking at these ball teams now that are in the majors, I'd say
that you can take the Kansas City Monarchs as a whole unit and
put them in the league—any one of the major leagues you wanted
to, National or American. They were short on bench, because they
didn't have twenty-five good ballplayers, they had nineteen—but
take that team and put it in the majors. Take the American Giants,
put 'em in Chicago, right there in the majors, with a little something added to the pitching. Now I don't know about Detroit, I
don't know whether Memphis could have stood there, I don't
know whether Indianapolis could have stood it. But Kansas City,
Chicago and St. Louis. You could have taken those three ball
teams without any alteration at all, and put each one of them in
the white big league. Go right back out in the East and take the
Homestead Grays, take the Philadelphia Stars and take the
Newark Eagles—you could put them in either one of those major
leagues you wanted to. And you know what? They'd have been
playing each other in the World Series for years to come.

The majors just missed a lot of talent there, they could have
been so much further ahead if they had just stepped back a little
bit on the race question. If they had just a little more aggressive-
ness, instead of Jackie being the first one to go in there, they could
have picked up Satchel when he was twenty—he could have won
thirty ball games for them. I don't care whose team he had pitched
on, he'd have won thirty ball games. And they could have picked
up Rogan, they could have possibly picked up me.

And I don't think you'd have had anything out there to dis-
courage them. The propaganda or the insults, I don't think you
could have discouraged these fellows, because we were practically
brought up on that stuff. I mean you can't insult the man who's
been insulted all the time. The things you're going to say, he's
heard so much, he's immune to that. You might come back and
say something just the opposite and he'd say, "What'd you say?"
I don't know of anything they could do to make me madder, but
treat me very nice! If they'd treat me very nice, that might cross

me up. But I'd be expecting all that other stuff, just like Jackie did. It didn't hurt him, he didn't worry about it. He knew about it already. If I'd have gone in there to pitch, I'd have known that. It would have only given me an incentive to go in there and pitch, to be a better ballplayer.

No, no, we never had any problems barnstorming. You see, it really wasn't as bad as people might have thought. It wasn't so bad. I just thought if it was all laid in front of the major league owners as it should be put—I don't think they ever stopped to think, to consider it. It was a long time before they realized that the Negro could play baseball—actual, top-notch baseball. It was a long time before they found out that he could actually think technically. They thought we could think just generally, but they didn't think that we could think things out in detail. They didn't think we could think and remember a set of signals. But, you see, we knew. We had to do it for our bread, and we had to do it very well. We had to learn the technique of it. And it was a long time before the major leagues found out that we knew that technique. When they found out that we could, they started taking us in their league. Then we came up very fast.

Now where did it come from? It came from the old ballplayers, just like I am that's coaching here. The Negro knows how to bat, he knows the fundamentals of the game. Not only that, but he's always hungry. You give him forty or fifty thousand dollars a year to play something that he *likes* to play—and he's *hungry*— boy, you've got a *game* on your hands! He's going to *play* baseball. I'm hungry, and I like the game, and you're crazy enough to give me $50,000 to play something that I *like?* Ooh, I'm going to play *this* game!

If I could stay in the twenty-game winning bracket for ten years and not lose over four or five ball games in any one year, for $450 a month—which was top salary for three and a half months' play —what on God's green earth would I have done if they said, "All right, you've got $75,000 a year to do the same thing"? You never would have beat me out there! I mean, if I could pitch for $450 a month and win twenty ball games, I could cut that loss column down to probably one or two. Like I said, you wouldn't have beat Satchel in the majors at all hardly!

This is my tenth year coaching baseball here at Alcorn College. I stay in pretty good shape, really. At this stage of the ball game, I'm just three pounds over what I was forty years go. I played at 205, and I'm 208 now. I'm six feet two. And I feel good. I just don't have an ache or pain. I had yellow jaundice in 1926, and that's it.

I like to fish, I like to hunt. I'm either going to get killed in a car accident, fall out of a boat in a river, hit a stump and get killed, or I'm going to get killed on a deer stand, somebody shoot me for the deer. Other than that, I might live a long time. Now, I don't want to live too long. I'd like to go another ten years, but I wouldn't like to go beyond another ten years. I don't want the time to come when somebody has to lead me around. As long as I can go fishing and hunting, and own a car, I don't mind living. But once it gets to the place that I'm going to have to occupy somebody else's time to get me somewhere, I'm too independent to say that I'm going to appreciate that.

I've had a wonderful life. I don't regret anything at all that I can remember, up to this very night. Not a thing, no regrets. I don't regret being in that age, especially when you fellows come by and say, "Let me check with you on this," because that's just as much history as the history of the major leagues. It needs to be known. It just wasn't time then for Negroes in the major leagues. Oh, I could have made it all right, but it wasn't time. I feel that whatever happens, whatever it is, happens for the best. I think in terms of the affirmative and positive all the time. I never look at the negative, the bad things.

I'm not bitter that I didn't make seventy-five or eighty thousand dollars. What would I have done with it anyway? I don't know . . . I don't know. I don't know whether it would have done me any good or not. They say, "You should have waited twenty years before you were born, you would have been in good financial shape." Yeah, in that respect, but what about other respects? I might have been born with one lame leg, couldn't walk; I might have been born with a two-year-old mentality. I didn't have to be born strong and healthy like I am; I could have been born deformed some way. But no, I came in a healthy kid, so I appreciate that. I take it as it comes.

I don't think you're going to find anyone who's bitter.

Bill Foster

American Giants pitching staff. Foster is third from left, Webster McDonald far left.

Chapter 11

LARRY BROWN

When old-timers talk about the great defensive catchers of black baseball, four names predominate: Bruce Petway, Biz Mackey, Frank Duncan and a wavy-haired, light-skinned, chirpy-voiced little spark plug named Larry Brown.

Larry came out of Birmingham with pitcher Harry Salmon to join the Pittsburgh Keystones in 1921. In his first game against the great Rube Foster and the Chicago American Giants, Larry threw out so many of the Giants' speedsters that Foster's eyes popped. "Where'd you find this man at?" Foster demanded of Keystone manager Dizzy Dismukes. "One day," Foster vowed, "I'll have him catch for me." In time, he did.

Larry caught on the two great Chicago teams of 1926 and 1927, guiding them to victory in two World Series against the Bacharach Giants of Atlantic City. After a detour to Memphis and New York, he was back in Chicago for four years, 1932–35. They may have been the best years of his career. The American Giants narrowly missed another world championship in 1934. And in each of the first three East-West games, 1933–35, Brown was voted the fans' number-one choice for starting catcher. In 1934 he defeated Duncan by a two-to-one margin; in '35 he easily outdistanced Josh Gibson, who finished third.

Larry never pulled his mask off for a foul fly, and
he never staggered under them as many catchers
do; he turned, trotted back a few steps and waited
confidently for it to come down. The secret was
simple, he once told James "Joe" Greene, a youngster
coming up with the Kansas City Monarchs. A pop
foul makes a figure-eight in the air. Larry diagramed
the reason with a pencil and paper. When the bat
hits the bottom of the ball, it imparts a terrific back-
spin to the ball on the way up, but that same spin
will carry the ball forward again on the downward
flight. Many catchers overrun the ball, then stagger
back as it curves back toward home plate. "You
never knew that?" Greene smiles. "You'll find a lot
of big-league catchers catching today who don't
know that. That's what's wrong with the game
today. Some big-league catchers don't know that,
they don't go into it that deep. That's what's wrong
with the game today. Back then we weren't playing
for money."

Larry Brown seemingly had only one weakness:
alcohol. Many's the night his teammates had to
carry him home on their shoulders from a night on
the town. "But he could recuperate quick," says
Baltimore second baseman Sammy T. Hughes. "One
year we were at the East-West game and they
brought Larry in about two o'clock. He had lost all
his paraphernalia. Next day he went down to the
store and got a brand-new glove. Ordinarily with a
new glove the pitches just pop out of it. But Larry
only had one dropped ball. The night before they
were bringing him in on their shoulders. Next day
you couldn't tell he'd ever had a drink."

I met Larry Brown in Memphis on a humid summer evening in 1970. I had traced him to a local
city league game at one of the parks, and when I

arrived I asked the public address to page him. A few minutes later a shriveled little man of sixty-five with bristly white hair shuffled over to me, and I introduced myself to Larry Brown. We took a seat in the bleacher-type grandstands to watch ex-pitcher Verdell Mathis's black team get beaten pretty decisively by a white group. (Mathis, a top left-hander in the 1940's, had been Larry's special protégé.) But we barely looked at the playing field. Brown came alive when I explained my mission, and in a cheerful, piping voice began extemporaneously telling me the story of his life.

The next day we met again at Mathis's home to continue the monologue and look at the many scrapbooks Larry had brought. In them I found dozens of photos of a husky, broad-chested, beaming athlete who dominated every group picture he was in. It was hard to relate the pictures to the man before me, but the resemblance was there indeed. Yet, as the public address man had warned me the night before, Larry Brown was but a ghost of the man he once had been.

In April 1972 I read in the *Sporting News* that Larry Brown had died.

Larry Brown Speaks . . .

Did you ever hear about me being the first Negro to have a chance to enter the majors? That's right. I was catching in Havana in 1926, Ty Cobb was down there, and I threw him out five times in succession, and I wasn't nothing but a kid. I was born in 1905, so how old was I in 1926? Twenty-one.*

I could throw Cobb out because I was quicker. See, he'd get a

*This is the story as Larry told it to me. However, further research has established that Cobb played only one year in Cuba, in 1910.

jump, but I was quicker than the average guy that had been throwing at him. That's why he stole all those bases in the states. I don't know who was catching—Mickey Cochrane and all those guys up in the American League at that time. I threw him out five times in succession. Shoot, I threw that ball—slap—like that. I ain't kidding you. No, Cobb wasn't mad, but every time he came in he'd say, "That son of a bitch got me again, but I'm gonna git him. I'm gonna git that little guy." Shoot, he ain't got me yet. But every time though, that sucker'd get on. He would either hit or get on, and every time he would try to steal, I'd throw that sucker out.

Naturally, Ty Cobb was noted for his running and his sliding, but he was on the type of Cool Papa Bell, the best base runner in the Negro leagues. Now Cool Papa, his snitch was to hug the base when he's going to steal and take a lead when he wasn't. Ty did the same thing, so that's how I happened to catch him so much.

Mike Gonzales and Adolph Luque, who played in the big leagues, were down there and said, "Larry, goddamn, what in the hell are you putting on here, an exhibition or something?" I said, "No, that guy stole all those bases in the States, but he ain't running against anybody." You get what I mean? "Nobody's throwing at him." So I said, "Goddamn, he can't run."

Cobb raised hell a couple of times, but after we got in the clubhouse, he kind of cooled down a little bit. Ty Cobb asked Mike Gonzales, "Who's that kid over there?" Mike said, "He's from the States." Cobb said, "He's doing pretty good. I wonder if I can talk with him."

So Ty came in and said, "Who do you play with in the States?" I said, "The Detroit Stars." He said, "Well, how would you like to play on a *real* ball club?" I said, "Well, I'm playing on a good ball club now." I wasn't kidding him, because I think our team was as good as the Tigers. He says, "You married?" I says, "Why, yes I am." He says, "Any children?" I says, "One expecting." He said, "How would you like to stay down here and pick up on this *lingua* and come back to the States and pass as a Cuban? We'll give you $750 a month just for you and your wife to stay down here a couple of years. If you need any more money we'll pay you." I said, "To be frank with you, I don't think that will work, because I have been all over the western territory, I have been all over New York, Philadelphia, Kansas City, and naturally everybody in those states knows me and I cannot pass like that."

Besides, I had heard a rumor that he had thrown a woman downstairs in the Book-Cadillac Hotel in Detroit. That was the same year, '26. She was a maid in the hotel and she must have given him some smart talk, and he shoved her down the steps. That's the reason his teammates didn't so much approve of him after that. Whether he really did it or not, I don't know, but anyway, I decided not to do it. I said, "No, I can't accept that." I passed it up.

I played ball for twenty-two more years after that. They called me "Iron Man" Brown because I used to catch every day. I didn't miss a game. I caught 234 games one year, 1930—three in one day. Boy, was I tired! As long as I played they never called a passed ball against me, and I only missed one pop fly in my life. I got too "challantie" on it, too "olly-cott," you know what I mean? Too nonchalant—I oversported myself. I've got my fingers broken on foul tips plenty of times. This one's been broken a couple times, this one once. I can't bend this one at all. A ball went through my thumb and first finger once and cut my hand down to the palm.

I don't know who taught me to catch. I think it's a pick up. You take a tap dancer, a girl who's skating, or a girl or man in any performance. There's some things that you gotta be taught, but stars are born, they're not made.

I was born in Alabama, Pratt City, about three miles south of Birmingham. I'll tell you how I got started in baseball. My mother had passed in 1918, when I was thirteen. I was just a kid. I left home in 1919, then came back to Alabama and went to Pratt City school. At that time catchers only used a muzzle [mask], didn't have any such thing as a chest protector, shin guards or anything like that. The catcher that we had got hurt. The ball went through the muzzle and it mashed his nose. I was playing on the infield. The professor said, "Any of the rest of you boys think you can catch?" I raised my hand. I went back there and took a bat and

mashed the mask out again and put it on and started catching.
I proved satisfactory, so the professor says, "I'm gonna keep you
back there."

After that, I started working for the Tennessee Coal and Iron
Railroad Company driving the mules, taking the men to where
they worked, then picking them up to bring them back to the
barn. All I had to do was get off the wagon and turn it over to
the lady there and she'd do the rest of it. I was also playing for
the company team, and I was beginning to prove satisfactory.
There was a white boy named Larry Brown that played for the big
team of the Tennessee Coal and Iron Company, while I was playing with the little 'jive' ball club. They said, "That little kid there,
if he keeps on going like he's going, he's going to be just like Mr.
Larry Brown."

So time marched on. In 1920 Knoxville had a ball club and both
of their catchers had got their fingers busted. See how my fingers
are? So when they got into Birmingham, somebody asked, "Listen,
do you know where I can get a catcher?" A guy says, "Yes, there's
a little kid out there, he ain't no man, he ain't nothing like a man,
he's nothing but a kid." He says, "Can he catch?" The guy said,
"Yeah, he can catch." So they brought the manager of the Knoxville Giants out to where I was working. The lady said, "Red"—
they always called me Red—"two or three men's been out here
looking for you. They want you to come to the Dunbar Hotel
tonight. They want to talk to you about your baseball."

Well, I went home, got all sharp, put on the best I had. I walked
in the Dunbar Hotel and said, "Where is Mr. Brooks, can I see
him?" They said, "Yeah," and gave me his room number. I said,
"Mr. Brooks? My name's Larry Brown, Pratt City, Alabama. I
heard you were out there asking for me today." He said, "Well,
I'll be doggone. You're mighty small, you're mighty little." By that
time here comes Steel Arm Dickey. That son of a gun weighed 240
pounds, and he looked like King Kong. Mr. Brooks said, "You see
that guy there?" I said, "Yes sir." He said, "You think you can
catch him?" I said, "Yes sir, I think I can catch him." He said, "You
know we're playing tomorrow at Ruppert Ball Park in Birmingham." I said, "Yes sir, I think I can catch him. I think I can catch
anything." He said, "If you need any money for your parapher-

nalia . . ." I said, "No, I got everything I need. I got my glove, my shoes, my jock strap, my sweatshirt—I don't need nothing."

All right, the ball game gets under way. And it should be so lucky that this was the Fourth of July, 1920. All the news had reached around. You know, Birmingham is a big area, and everybody said they were going out to see Red catch. I went out there and caught a doubleheader. After the first game we went to the dugout and the manager said, "You looked good, you proved to be a man that can take care of a job. Think you can handle that position?" I said, "Well, just like I told you, I can catch." I wasn't nothing but a kid, nothing but a baby—you know I wasn't.

The manager asked me, "Do you think that you're in a position to leave with this ball club?" I said, "Yeah, my mother's passed and my sister's in Philadelphia, ain't nobody but me." He said, "Anything you want to go home and get?" I said, "No, I got my bag with me." He said, "Well, we're leaving tonight and going to Montgomery, Alabama." I said, "Well, what's the verdict on this— what's the salary?" He said, "You need any money?" I had some money coming from the Railroad. I said, "Well, I got a little money in my pocket." He said, "Well, what do you think will do you?" I didn't need too much. What the hell would I do with money? I didn't have nothing to do with it. About $20 or $25 is more than could have used. He gave me a salary, $125 a month. I accepted it. Hell, I wasn't doing anything else anyway.

It was nothing but a rough league then. We used to go in the clubhouse, a guy would be in there sharpening his spikes with a file. A catcher had to protect himself if he got the ball. If I got the ball before the runner got to me, I could get him and he can't cut me. I could lean and get him. I didn't block the plate, not unless it was necessary. Give him the plate. But if the runner and the ball connect at the same time, you have to look out for yourself to the extent of not being cut up.

Shoot, I've played against a whole lot of tough base runners. Crush Holloway wasn't too bad. He was rough, all right, but he wasn't heavy. He weighed, oh, 165 to 170 pounds. Those kind of men don't pack a lot of power. But I had one guy, Edgar Wesley in Detroit, jump up here and cut my chest protector; my mask went one way, my glove went the other way and the ball went up in the stands. I was just a kid, unexperienced, didn't know how to protect myself.

Chaney White, he was built like King Kong, but he could run like Jesse Owens. Look—one, two, three, four, five, six, seven— I've got all his scars on my leg. Hell yeah, cut my shin guards off once. His spikes went through my shin guards. I went down in a crouch to receive the ball, and he hit me above the knee with his spikes, took eight stitches up there.

You know something I did in one ball game? This was one time the umpire was wrong. The count was three-and-two, a man on first. We had a pitcher was a fireballer, good curve ball artist, good drop ball man. He threw the ball, and the ball bounced on the plate and then by me to the grandstand. I took my glove and just reached it behind me and the umpire put another ball in my glove, and I threw the runner out. They said, "L. A. (that was my nickname), you should have gone and got that ball." I said, "Hell, I *didn't* go get it, and when the umpire gave me a ball, he put the ball in play." Oh man, they had everything trying to settle it. The umpire was wrong. He didn't have any business giving me the ball. But if I'd gone and got the ball, naturally I couldn't have thrown the guy out. I pulled that off on the umpire.

Yes sir, I used to do a whole lot of trickeration. Chicago had some pretty fast runners. Well, I could throw, I could throw pretty good. The crowd used to roar to see me throw the men out. And I used to boot the ball and let it roll about eight or ten feet and go get it and then throw the guy out. Make him run. You don't see that kind of stuff anymore. You take the major leagues, they don't pull off any "trickeration" stuff. They just play. We used to do everything.

We had a play I used to pull off when I was with the Chicago American Giants in '35. A man on third and a man on second, I'd call for a pitchout and throw that to the man at third. That was just a decoy. The next pitch the second baseman is way over toward the bag as the runner is playing off. I throw the ball back to third and he takes it and shoots it to second and gets the guy off of second. You get what I mean? I mean all trickeration stuff.

I remember once we were playing in Cienfuegos, Cuba. Luque was pitching and I was catching and Oscar Charleston was playing center field. I signaled for a pitchout, and just like I tell you, every time the same man was involved—Cool Papa. I called for a pitchout but Cool Papa hit the ball between Charleston and the right fielder for a triple. One run. The inning was over and Luque came in and jumped on me. Luque said, "Brown, how come you didn't get that pitchout?" I said, "How in the hell am I going to get a pitchout and the man hit the ball against the fence in right field? Do you call that a pitchout in the National League? The ball is supposed to be far enough out for me to receive it, not the hitter to hit it."

He was fussin' and raisin' hell. "Tell you what you do. You pack up, get your stuff." I said, "All right, I've got my ticket in my pocket, got my train fare back to Havana." Oscar Charleston said, "Well, we'll all just go home." Luque says, "Oh, no, oh no, oh no."

Well, it so happened we went on to win the ball game, which knocked off the heat. We get back to the hotel. Luque came over: "Brownie, pay me no mind. In a ball game, I want to win." I said, "In a ball game, I want to win." He said, "We'll get a bottle of Bacardi and we'll drink it all down." I said, "That's as good as I want." And we forgot all about the incident.

In 1930 I went to New York and caught for the Lincoln Giants. Pop Lloyd was the manager. He was the cream of Negro ballplayers. We played our games at the Catholic Protectory reform school in the Bronx. It had about five hundred seats in the grandstand and a little small bleachers. They'd squeeze them in and get fifteen hundred to two thousand people sometimes.

Chino Smith played right field, one of the greatest hitters ever you saw. He'd hit 'em between 'em, over 'em, to the opposite field, in the trees, anywhere. What about our center fielder, Fats Jenkins? Have you seen him? He's dead? Fats Jenkins dead! He's dead too! Oh, Lord have mercy.

Pitching we had Dick Redding, Red Ryan, Neck Stanley, Connie Rector and Bill Holland.

Shoot, I can name a whole lot of top pitchers. Satchel Paige. There wasn't nothing to do to catch Satchel, you could catch him in a rocking chair, 'cause he wasn't wild. One time we were playing a game out in Los Angeles in 1931, and we were only leading 2–1 against Joe Perrone's All-Stars—Babe Herman, Walter Berger, Fred Haney—big men. Anyway, Satchel called the outfield in on the grass and struck out the next two men coming up, Frank Demaree and Walter Berger. And we only leading 2–1. He did it against the major leaguers—I know, 'cause I was catching! And the guys kept hollering, "Come on, get on there, he ain't got nothing but a fast ball." But it was so fast they couldn't hit it. The main thing about it, his ball wasn't a hard ball, but the speed was so rapid, and it would take off. I said, "Satch, you're the biggest fool ever I've seen in my life." I said, "Long as I been playing ball I never saw anybody do that but you with a one-run lead."

We go down to San Diego. A guy had come up and got me an Satchel for a battery. Now we were going to play on a high school team against one of the top white teams down there. He said, "I want you fellows to give us a good exhibition." I said, "Well, goddamn, that's all Satchel's *got* is a good exhibition." The ball game gets under way; Satchel struck out so many men until he started handing them the ball so they could hit it, to give 'em some kind of play, you know. So one guy hits the ball way past the outfielder. Satchel lobbed another one like that, the second guy hit it way out yonder out there. Then he got on the rubber and struck out the rest of them.

I was catching the ball game Josh Gibson was supposed to have hit the longest ball ever hit in Monessen, Pennsylvania—512 feet, tape measured, so they said. He hit the ball off of Sug Cornelius. Curve ball. I don't like to make alibis on pitches. If a guy gets hold of one, he gets hold of it. I went into the dugout and a guy said, "L. A., what'd you call for?" I said, "I called for a curve ball." He said, "Why didn't you throw him a fast ball?" I said, "Goddamn, if I *knew* he was going to hit the curve I *would* have called a fast ball!"

I played against Jackie Robinson the year before he went up to Montreal. You know, I've thrown him out at every base and had him turn around and score on me? I threw him out at second base, the guy dropped the ball. He went to steal third and *he* dropped the ball, and the next man hit a fly ball and he scored.

In all, I played fourteen years with the Memphis Red Sox before I quit in '47. Did you know my oldest son's a flyer with the Air Force? A lieutenant colonel. He came here to see me in his jet in 1958.

After I quit baseball I went to work as a headwaiter in a hotel and stayed there twenty-three years. The hotel closed for repairments in 1970 to put in this "drink-by-the-drink" or "drink-by-the-smell," or something like that, and they didn't hire any of the help back.

I used to know Tim McCarver when he was a boy here in Memphis. He used to come in there to the newsstand to get his papers when he played with the Christian Brothers team. After he went to the Cardinals he came in there one day with Tony Gagliano, and I had a round table discussion, greeting the fellows, saying hello. They always liked to see me, they always liked to say hello to me. That's why they came in there, mostly to say hello to me."

I was working in the dining room about six or seven years ago when Bill Dickey came in. He was scouting for somebody then, I don't remember who. Anyway, he said to me, "I understand that you were one of the great catchers of your time."

I don't like to put a medal on my chest—let somebody else do that—so I said, "I tried to do my part as a catcher. I wasn't a good hitter, or a fast man, but I did pretty good at receiving, throwing, handling the pitchers and chasing foul balls."

He said, "Well, there isn't much more that you can do." He said, "I wasn't much of a hitter myself."

I said, "Don't tell me you weren't a hitter, you could hit that ball."

In 1968 Dizzy Dean was there when the Memphis Blues opened up, and they had a big party out to the Holiday Inn. All the ex-members of the Memphis Red Sox had the privilege of coming out there as guests. When the meeting was over, I says, "Goddamn, I'm going up there and speak to Dizzy." The meeting was all over, I picked up two or three souvenir fountain pens on the table and I went up to the speaker's stand. I said, "Do you remember me?"

"You doggone right, you and that durn Satchel Paige beat me, you little . . ." I'm telling you just like it is. He had made his whole speech on Satchel. He said, "Well, I'm so glad to see you, dog-gone it, y'all sure beat me"—which we did.

We had played Dizzy in Pittsburgh in 1935 before thirty-some-thousand people. Dizzy Dean had an all-star American and National League team against an all-star Negro ball club. Satchel Paige was pitching, and I'm catching. Boojum Wilson hit a home run with two men on and beat 'em 3–0.

And now you say Boojum's dead. And Fats Jenkins and Connie Rector. Lord have mercy. You don't know how you're breaking my heart.

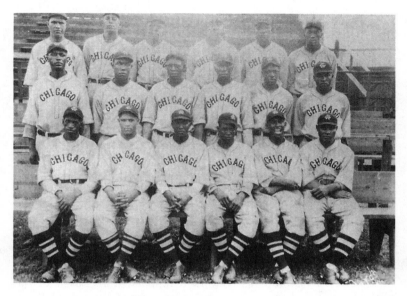

Larry Brown is second from left in front row. Manager Dave Malarcher sits to his left. Bill Foster stands behind Brown. Webster McDonald is on the right in the center row.

Chapter 12

WILLIE WELLS

Many old-timers considered Willie "Devil" Wells the finest black shortstop ever born—Mrs. Effa Manley, his owner on the Newark Eagles, would amend that to read, "the finest shortstop, black or white."

Cleveland Indians outfielder Larry Doby, who played for both Wells and Lou Boudreau, said Wells was the better of the two. Pitcher Hilton Smith rated him above Phil Rizzuto. And Double Duty Radcliffe said he was better than Jackie Robinson.

Washington Senators owner Clark Griffith said Wells and his Newark teammate, third baseman Ray Dandridge, covered the left side of the infield better than any combination in baseball. He begged sports writer Ric Roberts: "Let me know when those two bow-legged men are coming to Washington. Please don't let me miss them."

Or, as Monarchs manager Buck O'Neil put it: "This boy Ozzie Smith could field with Wells, but he couldn't hit with him."

Willie was considered a spray hitter, but in 1929 he slapped 27 out of the park in 88 games to become the black Roger Maris. No blackball player ever hit more in one year. It works out to about 50 in a modern major-league season.* It is not a fluke. Willie ranks fifth among Negro Leaguers in lifetime home runs, just 18 behind Josh Gibson, albeit with many more at bats.

---

*Wells' teammate and friend, big Mule Suttles also hit 27 the previous year to tie him. It was a short fence, to be sure, but there is some dispute whether balls pulled over the shortest part were ground-rule doubles.

His lifetime average was .331 against black big leaguers, and an astounding .638 in 25 games against whites. His highest single season mark was .404 in 1930, when Bill Terry led the white majors with .401. It's a shame they never played against each other in the same league.

Wells, incidentally, is credited with inventing the batting helmet. Black pitchers threw at him murderously. "I'd knock him down for the fun of it," Bill Drake laughed. "I'd waste two balls at him—I knew I could throw strikes when I was ready to. I liked to see him run. I'd run him across the plate and back across the plate." In defense, Wells got a coal miner's helmet, knocked the gas jet off the front, and clapped it on his head.

In the field Wells had a weak arm—"you could run alongside his ball," one old-timer smiles—"but you couldn't beat it to first." He just nipped the runner. "He'd lob you out," Buck Leonard said. To compensate, Wells played shallow—but the hitters still couldn't get the ball past him. "It looked like he had roller skates on," said third baseman Judy Johnson, shaking his head. Wells studied the batters. "If you saw me dive for a ball, you know I misjudged it," Willie said.

In Cuba one winter St. Louis Cardinal coach Mike Gonzalez watched Wells and Dandridge (then playing second base) on one double play. Wells scooped up a grounder, whipped it to Dandridge, who touched second and whipped it back to Wells to relay to first. Gonzalez gulped. "I never saw two guys play like that before," he gasped. "Well," beamed catcher Larry Brown, "that's the way they play in the States all the time."

A good example of the Wells style came in 1919 against a big-league club that included Hall of Famers Charlie Gehringer, Harry Heilmann, and Heinie Manush. In the first game, against 17-game winner Willis Hudlin, Wells went two-for-five. His ninth-inning triple knocked in the tying run; he scored the winner himself a moment later on a steal of home, kicking the ball out of catcher Wally Schang's hand. The next day he hit two triples and stole home again against Jack Miller, who won 14 games that year. Finally, against George Uhle (15-11), Wells collected three more hits, the final one knocking in the winning run in the ninth.

When I first met Wells, he was sitting alone nursing a beer in the back of a dark Harlem bar. He was too far gone with drink to talk. But I looked him up later in his small room, just around the corner from the sleazy world of Seventh Avenue, and he had a bag of stories to spill out. Still short and lithe, he sat on his unmade bed and rambled about his former days of glory.

Willie Wells Speaks . . .

What most people don't know is, baseball is such an intelligent game. You've got to be smarter than the other fellow. Everybody says I didn't have any arm, but still I threw everybody out. How did I do it? Well, you play your hitters—and your pitchers. Now this boy, Ted Trent of the St. Louis Stars, had one of those big curve balls. When he'd pitch, they'd top his ball all the time, hit them high choppers, you know? I'd be in position. If a guy couldn't pull a fast ball, I'd be in the hole behind second on him. They didn't see how I was able to get all those balls. I was always in position. I didn't have to move over two or three steps. Sometimes, when you see me dive for a ball, you know I misjudged my hitter or pitcher. That's the only way they got a ball through me. The weak arm didn't mean nothing. It was here, in the head. That's right.

The infielders are supposed to sit and watch what a pitcher throws, how a guy pulls his fast balls. See, you don't play behind every pitcher the same. Say you're pitching today, I'd play different because you're a different kind of pitcher from someone else. Maybe you don't have a fast ball like that boy has, you get him out with a change-up. The shortstop, the infielder, sits and watches the guy. I watch my pitcher warming up just like I'm going to catch, 'cause I'm the shortstop.

I managed the Newark Eagles from 1936 to 1941 and again in 1946, so Monte Irvin, Larry Doby, Don Newcombe, all those kids were my protégés. But they were three different characters, and here's where the manager comes in, here's where you've got to use a little psychology. Irvin was an easy fellow, very nice, easy to get along with. But Doby and Newcombe, there was something different. Here's a problem for me. Newcombe was kind of temperamental a little. You handled him different. You know, every ballplayer is a different character; what you say to one you can't say to another. You have to sit and watch his attitude and how he handles himself.

I left the Eagles soon after that in a row with the owner, Mr. Manley, and turned the team over to Biz Mackey. Funny thing, back in Texas, where I come from, I used to carry Mackey's glove. He came from San Marcos, a little old place down not far from my home town, Austin. I guess it's about eighteen miles from my home. Anyway, down in Austin, they had a league, and Mackey played for San Antonio—they called them the San Antonio Aces. I guess I was eleven years old, and I'd grab anybody's bat or ball to get into the park. I carried Mackey's glove, and then I came up here and played eighteen or twenty years with him. Isn't that something?

I went to college in Austin, but I was so wrapped up in baseball. I played all sports—I was wrapped up in sports, period. I guess that was my career right there. Wasn't nothing else interesting to me. Every day I had a ball in my hand, I just loved it that much.

Well, the big teams were playing down South—Kansas City, the Chicago American Giants, St. Louis—and the college picked all the best ballplayers from each school to play against those boys. They were professionals, you know; we weren't.

When Chicago saw me play they said, "We want you." Chicago wanted me and St. Louis wanted me. That was 1927 and I was only seventeen years old. So I picked the closest town. I said, "I think I want to go to St. Louis." Well, when I left Texas to go to St. Louis, my first trip, oh I cried. They said, "You're going up there but you're not going to make it." Well, I was determined to make it. If you have the desire, you'll make it. But if you give up . . .

I was the littlest thing that ever came up. They said, "I'm going to send you back." I said, "You're not going to send me nowhere." All those guys were six-footers—rough. They were rough when I came along. Rough, not educated boys like they are today. Yeah, it was rough. They'd throw at you. They'd sit on the bench and file their spikes and say, "This is for you, you son of a bitch, you." That's what they would say: "This is for you. I'm gonna send you back to Texas." I said, "You're not going to send me no place."

Well, I had a good year that year, but I couldn't hit the curve ball. Everybody in the league said, "Wells is a beautiful fielder but he cannot handle the curve ball." I could hit that fast one, number one, but I couldn't handle that curve. I think I got about three hits all season. Well, I went back to Austin to school that winter, and it was just fortunate for me that this boy, Bill Riggins, playing shortstop for Detroit, got his leg broken in California. So they said, "We want that guy, Wells. He's down there in Texas, Sam Houston College." They sent me a telegram from California, and I looked at it, and it said, "We want you to come to California to play in the winter league." My mother said, "No, you've got to finish your education first." But they were talking about four hundred dollars. Four hundred dollars! I'd never seen four hundred dollars. I said, "Mmmm-*mmmm!* Four hundred dollars!" I said, "Transportation and everything!" I said, "I want to *see* California!" I was coming into eighteen and I said, "I think I better take this chance." So I went out to California without my mother knowing it. I lived with the owner, the manager. He wouldn't give me any money. He sent all the money home, just handled me like his son.

They had three white ball clubs in California and one colored team. We were the Philadelphia Royals. They picked all the best ballplayers to compete against the major leaguers.

A boy named Hurley McNair from Kansas City, I give him a lot of credit for teaching me how to become a hitter. I still couldn't hit the curve. When they'd break that ball and I'd see it breaking, I'd just pull too much. Well, they took my left leg and tied it at home plate and threw me curve balls, curve balls, curve balls. When I came back to St. Louis the following year, they were throwing me those curve balls and I was burning them up, I was burning them up! Every time they'd break a curve ball, I'd hit

Willie Wells as manager of the Newark Eagles.

it on a line somewhere, up against the fence, or between the fielders. The manager was watching me: "What happened to this guy? He couldn't hit the curve ball, but he's handling it now." So when the season opened up, I looked over the lineup there, and the guy was going to hit me third instead of eighth. Hitting third! And you know, nobody moved me from third from that day until I retired. And I stayed for some twenty-odd years. Thirteen all-star classics in Chicago, and I was hitting third in all of them. Josh Gibson or Mule Suttles were hitting fourth—both sluggers— and I was hitting in front of them. I had to run.

I hit everybody. I didn't care what they threw. It's a fact. Didn't care who pitched. They'd pitch around Wells. "If there's anybody on base and the game is close, pitch around that guy. Forget him, just pitch to the next guy. Forget Wells. Wells is tough." See, you had to be tough. You had to have heart, desire. If you were a coward, they'd throw right here at your ear. Oh yes, there was no doubt about it. We were playing in Yankee Stadium one day against Satchel Paige. I came to bat, Satchel walked off the mound and reached in his pocket like he had sandpaper. I said, "What are you doing that for, you got such a good fast ball?" He said, "I'm gonna stick it right in your hair."

Oh, I hit everybody. Every pitcher will tell you that. That's why they threw at me so much, just like I was a rat or something. I was the first guy that bought a helmet. You see those big helmets they wear now? They'd tell me all the time they're gonna kill me: "We're gonna knock you down tomorrow." I mean they'd talk dirty to you: "Say, you little son of a bitch you, how am I gonna hit you, goddamn it, if you won't stand still?" Oh, it was rough when I came along. It wasn't easy—it *was not* easy. You'd better believe it.

See, that's the way they played. Those guys would spike. Decent slides? There were no decent slides. A guy slid at me, I'd slide right back at him. All those guys were big six-footers, bigger than me—I weighed 165 pounds. They'd say, "We gonna get you out of there." But I'd take that ball and hit them right across their noses with it.

Vic Harris of the Homestead Grays was a nasty slider. One day in Newark I took the throw and he cut my arm—just cut my uniform sleeve right off. I had to go into the clubhouse and change. So when I came up next inning, I pushed the ball between first and second 'cause I wanted him to cover first. But he didn't get it. Buck Leonard the first baseman got it, and when Harris didn't cover, I jumped at Buck. I jumped at him to cut him up. He said, "Wells, you and I are friends." I said, "Yes, but you're playing against me." That's the way they played. You didn't play easy like these guys now.

Then I lived clean, that's another thing. That's the important thing of becoming a great ballplayer. If you have that ability and treat your body right, you can make it if you have that desire. What I mean by treating yourself right is, you don't go ripping and running, you know what I mean—the girls taking it away from you, the drinks taking it away from you, late hours taking it away from you. All those things are against you. There's no doubt about it.

A lot of athletes believe that because they're popular they're supposed to be seen in all the spots. A guy would say, "That guy don't want to go out—come on, big man, give us some money." I said, "You all go ahead." I'd just go to the movies. "Oh, you're too cheap to spend any money." But it wasn't that. I was thinking about what I had to do tomorrow. I've seen many great ballplayers last four, three, two years—great ballplayers who could have been in the major leagues. But when I walked on the field, I was just as light—I was in shape. I was in shape every day. I stayed in shape.

Cool Papa Bell was my best friend on St. Louis. He was the most beautiful ballplayer and a great base runner. There's just no comparison between Bell and Maury Wills, for example. Wills did something great, stealing 100 bases, but to me the important thing is technique. You watch the pitcher's move. If an individual is smart he can pick up things. And Bell was a clean liver, he wouldn't dissipate at all. He was like me. We'd sit in the room and play cards, he and I. We were roommates. He married a girl who was my sweetheart. But he and I were just like this—friends—you know? It's been twenty-five or twenty-six years now, and it never came between us. A good relationship. A wonderful fellow. Bell, he was a beaut.

We played the major league all-stars in St. Louis in 1931. They had Bill Terry at first, Paul Waner, Lloyd Waner, Babe Herman. We had a two-game series, and we didn't win but two straight.

The first time I saw Joe DiMaggio was in Pasadena. That was 1935. They had a revolution in Cuba and we didn't go to Cuba that year, we went to California. DiMaggio came up with that wide stance. They didn't have a fence, they just had hedges out in Pasadena. A guy broke him a curve ball and Joe DiMaggio hit the ball all into the trees.

They had a heck of a ball club. They had Lefty Grove, Dizzy Dean, his brother Paul Dean. That Bob "Lefty" Grove! They told me he didn't have a curve ball. Heck, he broke a curve ball on me! If they say Bob "Lefty" Grove didn't have no curve ball, they're wrong! But we won all our games against them. We won twenty-one straight. Judge Landis stopped it after that, wouldn't let us play any more that winter. Said it was a disgrace.

But it's hard to remember all those guys. I admired all of them, 'cause they were great.

This boy Bobo Newsom was kind of prejudiced, though. He didn't mind you knowing. He'd come right out and tell you: "I'm not going to the major leagues until I can beat you niggers." He talked like that.

And I'll tell you another fellow who was like that—Early Wynn, he was like that. This boy Johnny Dunlap and I were in Cuba one year. Dunlap's a Boston boy. In Cuba, you know, after a ball game they had beer in the clubhouse because it's so hot down there, so humid, and they had the beer sitting in your locker when you came off the field. I drank the beer because I needed it. It was good. But after you left the locker room you were on your own. Well, this day Johnny Dunlap and me had just left the race-track and we said, "Let's just stop in here and have a beer," and Early Wynn made a crack at us. He's from down there in the South somewhere. He just spoke out like that. He said, "No, we don't do that. We have plantations down there." And he used that word, and he was in trouble. "Why hell," Dunlap says, "I don't sit here and hear things like that." And he popped him. A big lad, too, Early Wynn—he wasn't no midget, you know. But Dunlap messed him up so, oh he messed him up. He whipped this boy Early Wynn, and he couldn't play any more that winter.

I played in Cuba, Mexico, Puerto Rico—thirteen years in Cuba, five years in Mexico. I replaced Rogers Hornsby as manager of Vera Cruz in 1947. They called me Diablico Wells. I was a manager for so many years, and I never had a loser. And I made so much money, I can't tell you how much, but I bet it on the damn horses. I was a horse bettor.

You had to handle different ballplayers differently. Just like when I came back from Mexico to manage the Eagles in '46, they said, "We have a boy here, a big boy and he is around nineteen or twenty years old, and he is from Elizabeth, New Jersey." They said, "He can really throw the ball, and his name is Don Newcombe." So I had a talk with him. I said, "They tell me you are a pretty good pitcher." He said, "They tell me you are a pretty good shortstop." I said, "Well, it looks like I'm going to be your manager this year."

In spring training the manager is responsible for all of the sore arms and all those kinds of stuff. I handled all of the pitchers; see, this is 80 per cent of your ball club, your pitching. Well, when those kids are young and you are new to them, they're going to show you everything in spring training. They'll get out there and the first day they'll just try to fog that ball over every doggone day. So I said, "Come here, Newcombe." I took the catcher's mitt and I said, "I don't want you to throw, just lob the ball to me. Loosen up, start running, running, running." He said, "You are kind of rough, aren't you?" I said, "No, I want you to be in good shape." I built him, I brought him along in spring training, and the week before I got ready to open the season up, I said, "You are going to pitch four innings today. No more." I looked at him and said, "Are you ready?" He said, "Yes."

After four innings I asked him, "How do you feel?" He said, "I can go some more." I said, "No, you had enough." Newcombe said, "Let me pitch two more innings." I said, "No, no, no, you have showed me enough, you have showed me enough."

Well, we opened the season against the Homestead Grays. They had a *good* team—they had Josh Gibson, Buck Leonard, Cool Papa Bell—they had a terrific ball club. And do you know who my opening pitcher was going to be? Newcombe. I had built him, I had brought him along in spring training. And when I opened him against the Grays, do you know what he gave them? Six to nothing. I opened him up and he blanked those guys 6–0.

One time I heard Newcombe and my team captain kidding under the showers. We were guests at Virginia State University, and they were kidding each other about girl friends. I didn't like that, I didn't like for players to get personal with one another about their associates on the outside of the ball park. So I explained it to them. "No, sir, we don't mean a thing, we don't mean a thing, we were just kidding, just playing."

"A man isn't kidding when you are talking about his girl friend. She can be beautiful, she can be ugly, but when you start to call her names, talk about her color or how she looks, that fellow can think just as much of his little Gloria Swanson as you do about your Maureen O'Hara. I want you fellows to understand."

"Oh, no, we were just playing."

So one morning they knocked on my door at four A.M., one of them with a knife and the other with a pick. I said, "Uh huh," I said, "do you remember what I told you all at Virginia State University and you told me you were just kidding?" I said, "If you're just kidding now, you can go on and kill one another, because I am going to go back to bed."

I quit the Eagles in 1946 and turned the team over to Mackey, and he won the championship. Here's what happened:

This boy Terris McDuffie was one of my best pitchers, but he had a bad spring training. You know you can't bring a veteran along as you would a rookie. He can handle himself. I just want them to carry out my rules: "When you go into that dining room, I want you to look like a professional. I don't want you to go in there talking loud and all of that. This is your profession and I want you to treat it like that."

Well, McDuffie wasn't ready to pitch, but Manley said, "I want you to pitch him against Baltimore." So I opened him against the Baltimore Elite Giants and they hit him, so I took him out. Manley said, "Why did you take him out?" He wanted to humiliate him, see. He wanted me to pitch him again the next day.

Well, I told the captain, Pearson—all of them will tell you that these are my words—I said, "You call them all off the field," and I said, "bring Manley with you." We got in the clubhouse and I said, "Fellows, Mr. Manley says that McDuffie is going to start the ball game tomorrow. He is paying me to manage this club," I said, "but he don't have to pay me any more, because I am finished as the manager of this team. I am finished." And all of the players agreed with me.

Do you know what they did? After they won the pennant they came and got me. They said, "We want you on the bench." All of them, all of the players, said, "We want you on the bench in the World Series against Kansas City." That's right, and I stayed right on the bench with them, and all of the players will tell you, "If you see Wells, he is for the ballplayers."

You know, every ballplayer is a different character. Now there are some guys I wouldn't bother with a signal. I wouldn't give them anything to do but play. I'm not going to disturb them or come to them and say, "Look, I want you to do this or that and I want you to take this as a signal." Just let them play. Some guys don't get disturbed, but some other mechanical person, he gets upset: "What did he tell me to do?" See, he can't hit now. He can't run now because he's thinking about what I said. So I'd say, "Now, look, don't you look for a signal. You just play." But the ones that are smart, I said, "This is your signal, this is for you."

I used to give the catcher his signals from shortstop. If a batter can't handle a pitch inside, then in spring training I would never let them throw that pitch to him. Let him hit his pitch in spring training, it don't mean anything. Don't teach him how to hit in spring training. If the other manager doesn't have the experience to handle his personnel, don't you smart him up.

Now when we're at bat, I sit and look at the other pitcher—and the catcher too. Like Josh Gibson would hold his right arm like this, with the elbow sticking out. If I was coaching at third base, I'd watch, and if I saw his elbow move like that—just a little flicker—I knew it was a curve ball. If his arm didn't move, it was a fast ball. Pretty soon, they'd say, "Heh, why are they hitting everything? What's happening here?"

Some catchers are good curve ball catchers, some just love to catch that fast ball. This is where the manager comes in. When they call a lot of curves, I say "Go ahead, go ahead and run—move off that base—steal." See, this is the difference, this is the finesse in baseball. This is beautiful.

William "Devil" Wells is said

Willie Wells with St Louis Stars, 1930

NEWARK MANAGER

Willie Wells, rated as the best of the present day shortstops, is holding down that position with the Newark Eagles and at the same time is manager of Mr. and Mrs. Abe Manley's baseball team. He expects to have the team in first place in the next 15 days.

Willie Wells

Willie Wells

Willie Wells

Chapter 13

WILLIAM "SUG" CORNELIUS

"Sug Cornelius could throw a curve around a barrel," says Birmingham's Jim Canada—"and I believe he could throw it around and make it come in the barrel." That's what the hitters thought of Cornelius' curve. "He could pitch as good as any pitcher we had," adds Cool Papa Bell. "A great curve ball, fast ball; could hit, do everything." But, Bell shrugs, you never hear much about him.

Coming off the Clark University campus in Atlanta in 1933, Cornelius was so impressive that the fans gave him the third highest vote among all pitchers in the balloting for the first East-West game that year. In 1934 Cornelius rang up several memorable games. He beat Lefty Leroy Matlock and the Pittsburgh Crawfords (Gibson, Charleston, Bell et al.) 2–1 in ten innings. He lost a thriller to Satchel Paige 3–0, although each only gave five hits.

His finest performance that year came in September when he was called on again and again to play an iron-man role in a single-handed but unsuccessful attempt to stop the Philadelphia Stars in the black World Series.

Cornelius spent his career mostly with weak clubs, but still posted a 57-60 record.

He suffered a long hospitalization, during which, as his friend Double Duty Radcliffe said, "he lay there, just melting away." He died in 1989.

Cornelius was nursing a game leg when I called on him in his second-floor Chicago apartment in 1970. He hobbled around the apartment, fixing coffee and snacks for us, and told me with just a trace of bitterness of his many adventures, both pleasant and not so pleasant, in black baseball and after.

William "Sug" Cornelius Speaks . . .

Mrs. Grace Comiskey, the White Sox owner, used to look at me and shake her head and say, "Oh, if you were a white boy, what you'd be worth to my club." I told her, "I'm *not* white, I'm black." And I said, "I don't know whether I'd change to white if I could." I had nothing to do with what color I was. Had I known in the beginning what kind of world I was going to be born into, I may have, but I had nothing to do with being born, I had nothing to do with the color.

I pitched for the Chicago American Giants from 1934 to 1946, and I was told many times what I'd be worth to certain clubs if I was a white boy. They had to play somewhere every day—and night if they possibly could—in order to meet what measly salaries they were paying.

If you got $500 a month, you were tops. Back in the Depression years those salaries ran from $250 a month to $500 for really top players like this boy Josh Gibson, and I doubt whether they had another man on the ball club who was getting that kind of money. During that time I was getting $350. A little later on I was up to $400, and that was it. There just wasn't any money. The people just didn't have the money, and I think a box seat then was seventy-five cents.

I know Satchel Paige and I used to have some awful pitching duels. Yeah, I remember one particular game I think I pitched nine and two-thirds innings. I had two men out in the tenth inning, and I gave up my first hit. I walked one man in that ball game, I think it was Cool Papa Bell. I remember I walked him, 'cause I picked him off base. Turkey Stearnes was playing right field for us, and he said to me, "You couldn't see yourself pitching, but it was something to behold from where I was." I don't think over three or four balls were hit to the outfield.

They beat me in the tenth inning. Judy Johnson came up with two outs. I doubt whether Judy had five hits off me all the time I pitched against him. He hit a routine fly ball to right center field, and I rolled up my glove and started back to the dugout. But when I looked back, Stearnes was just standing there with his legs crossed. The ball could have been an easy out, but he wasn't expecting it. Jack Marshall at second base went out for it, but it fell between them.

I walked back to the mound. My arm was tightening, and I said, "If I get by this inning, I'm going to tell Dave Malarcher, our manager, to get somebody else ready." The next man up, Josh Gibson, hit me for a single. That pitch was that far outside—three feet—and he threw his bat at it and was lucky enough to make contact and get a single out of it. The next man came up and hit a little pop fly to left center field, and that fell in, so they beat me. After two outs.

A lot of white fans came from the Sox park over there to see that ball game. Back then we outdrew the Sox three-to-one. There was no question of that.

Satchel was something to behold. Show you fast balls here at your knee all day. They looked just like a white dot on a bright sunshiny day—a white dot. I imagine he'd win forty or fifty ball games a year, because his arm was just like rubber. After Paige was way up in the forties he pitched three innings every night for the entire week. And you very seldom beat him. I'll just be frank with you: If Satchel had been in the majors in his prime, Satchel would have broken all records. I'm not exaggerating. The man could throw in a cup, his control was so fine.

I've pitched against Bob Feller, Waite Hoyt, Mel Harder. I've faced Johnny Mize, Walt Dropo and this guy who used to catch for Cleveland who'd drink so much, Rollie Hemsley. When the season was over we would barnstorm with Feller and his group. Of course, when Feller was pitching we didn't get any runs back. When he and Paige hooked up, that would be a 0–0 ball game; we might score some runs after those two guys went out. We'd go to California every winter and play a month with those major leaguers. We'd play a month, we'd make more money than we'd make in two or three years playing back here in the Negro leagues. I think it was the same year when Judge Landis flew to California, and that's what broke up this barnstorming. Those guys, I think they beat Paige 1–0 in '35 and said, "We thought you guys had a ball club." Then they ended up losing seven straight. So Landis broke it up. Said they were a disgrace to organized baseball to let a bunch of sandlotters beat them. But we were a bunch of *good* sandlotters.

So we'd play the Pacific Coast clubs and the American Association. We beat those clubs. The American Association didn't win anything when they played us. The Toledo Mudhens ran away with the American Association one year and won something like four straight in the Little World Series. We played those guys Saturday night, Sunday and Monday night, and I think they got one run. We gave them one run.

They always said that Satchel put more players in the big

Sug Cornelius

leagues. If they could hit Satchel, they were big-league material.

It's no question about it. We had the same thing the whites had. We had good hitting, good fielding; they had good pitching, and we had it over here. Only thing I think: In our baseball, we had better of everything. Let's put it this way: If it wasn't better, it was as good.

We played good baseball—and as bad as we would be cheated. That happened very often. I remember Joe Hauser, who was with the Philadelphia Athletics. He hit sixty-nine home runs in the minors one year. Well, at this time he was playing for Racine, Wisconsin, and we went in there to play them, and he was walking the streets that afternoon before the game: "Joe Hauser's going to do this and Joe Hauser's going to do that." Candy Jim Taylor, my manager then, said, "Cornelius, you're pitching tonight." He said, "Joe Hauser's a pretty fair hitter. He tears up that minor-league pitching, but he can't hit when he gets up to the big leagues." Jim says to me, "You keep your fast ball on his knees, and he's not going to do too much with it." And I had a good change-up off of my fast ball.

When Joe Hauser came to bat, everybody in the stands, I think, stood up. Well, I opened up on Joe with my change, right here, a little above the knee on the inside corner—Joe was a left-handed hitter. A beautiful pitch. The umpire says, "Ball one." So I looked at the umpire. My next pitch I threw him my fast ball. This was to the outside corner, and I think it was on Joe so fast he just stopped and looked at *me*. The umpire said, "Ball two." I started down to him, and my catcher met me half-way. He said, "He's not going to call anything unless Joe thinks he can hit it, and Joe's not going to swing."

The next time I took my windup and just rolled the ball on the ground. The umpire looked at me, said, "Do you think you're being funny?" I told him, "No, you are funny." I said, "Now I'm satisfied. I *know* this is a ball." And he was going to put me out of the game. Everybody in the stands said, "Well, we want our money back then."

I don't know what happened, whether Joe talked to the manager or what, but anyway the next time I threw him a fast ball, he swung and he missed, and from then on he would take his cut at it. Anyway, I struck him out three times. On three pitches. I didn't waste anything on him. So he asked me did I ever lose any ball games. I told him, "Sure." He said, "Well, I'd like to see the guys that hit you." I said, "Well, there are guys over in my league that would hit me if I mess around with them."

My home's in Georgia—Atlanta. I was born in 1907. I got my nickname from around home. All I know is, when I was big enough to know anything, my mother told me I used to eat all the sugar I could find. And they just started calling me Sugar, and when I went to school, it wasn't Sugar anymore, it was Sug. So all down through the southern states I was known as Sug Cornelius. But when I came up this way I was Bill.

I started on the sandlot, like most kids do. Then I played in high school and a couple of years in college, Clark University. And I was a pretty good hitter, hit home runs, played up a storm. Oh yeah, I hit a lot of them, played third base, outfield, and pitched. I was an all-round athlete, because I played football, baseball, track.

Back in the summer months down home there in Georgia, we had a bunch of school kids, some of them in high school, and we used to play out to Spills Field—that was the home of the Atlanta Crackers. We outdrew the white clubs. When news got around that I was going away the next year to play baseball, the fellow who owned the ball club came out to the house and sat down and talked with me. He gave me one hundred and some dollars a month for me to stay there.

Later I went to Nasvhille, Tennessee. A fellow by the name of Tom Wilson owned the Nashville Elite Giants at the time, and I started out with him. Must have been 1929. From there I came to Memphis in '30, and I was traded to the Birmingham Black Barons in '31. You know, back in those days things were kind of lean, and figuring on going back to school, I left my money there, didn't take it out. After our last road trip, when I came back I couldn't find any of the owners. They had disappeared with my money. Strawbridge and Buck Adams, those were the two guys that owned the Black Barons at that time. And a funny thing, I've never been able to catch up with those guys.

Well, I stayed out of baseball. I didn't play in '32. I went back to

Memphis in '33, and we played the Black Barons, and I went downtown and talked to the sheriff. Anyway, I tied up the gate receipts, but I got fired for doing that, and I ended up having to pay the cost of the court too!

So in '33 I came here to Chicago, and I pitched up until '46, after I came from the Service. We started out playing at the old American Giants park at 39th and Wentworth. We played at the old park a number of years. They messed it up—they were going to have dog racing there—so then we started playing our games out at Comiskey Park.

We had a wonderful ball club here in Chicago. Most major-league clubs now, they carry something like nine pitchers. Well, maybe we'd have four, or we'd have five pitchers. And there was no word about somebody going out relieving you. Man, you'd go out and do a job; there was no relief. I guess on an average of a season I'd pitch thirty to thirty-five ball games, and very few of those ball games I got knocked out.

I sit many a day and look at those guys pitch today and say it's a disgrace the way they're messing up pitching. A man can't pitch over four or five innings now. I pitched every three days. And I've pitched many a doubleheader. I would pitch on Sunday, I'd pitch again Wednesday. I'd do that to keep razor sharp. When we'd have a couple of rain-outs or something like that, I'd have too much rest—four or five days' rest and you don't have anything on the ball. You just think you do.

I weighed about 167 or 168 pounds. And I had an exceptional good fast ball for a guy my size. I had a good drop ball, a good what they called back in those days "out-curve." And I could throw it on the corner and wake up at twelve o'clock at night and throw strikes. I never worried about that. I used to just get out and take me a paper cup and just practice for, oh maybe two hours, working my curve ball at that thing. Sometimes I'd break it in there on this corner, on that corner, on the three-and-two. A lot of guys won't throw a curve ball on the three-and-two. But it was no different to me, it was only a pitch. In pitching, to be successful, you have to master control. Once you get that, then you practice your other stuff.

I threw everything—fast ball, curve ball, and I had a screw ball which I never threw too much, because those kind of pitches would mess your arm up. In fact, I've always felt that if you had a good fast ball and were able to throw 85 percent of your pitches where you wanted to, you don't need anything else. When you lose the zip on your fast ball, then that's when your screw balls and your knuckle balls come in.

I had a quick curve ball, then I could slow it—had a wonderful change of pace. I was a right-hander, but usually I had better success with left-handers than I did with right-handers. I'd get left-handers out. I used to strike out say thirteen, fourteen, fifteen men in a ball game, and most of those were left-handers.

In one all-star game, 1936, I relieved with three men on. Jimmy Crutchfield and Chester Williams were the two men I faced. Crutchfield said he'd never seen a drop ball like the one I threw him for strike three, and he said he'd never see another one like that as long as he'd play baseball. It tickled me. I opened up on him with a fast ball, and I got two strikes on him. He said, "I know what you're going to throw me, I'll be waiting for it." And I threw it to him. And he missed that ball that far—three feet. Chester Williams came up and I threw three side-arm curve balls on the outside corner of the plate, three inches off the plate, and he swung at each one of them. When he swung at the first one, I said, "Well, if he's going for them, I'll throw him another." When he went for that, I was out in front, and I made the last one just a *little* worse than the other two. And he went for that.

Oscar Charleston was another long-ball hitter. He didn't hit me at all. I never will forget one night, we had this split season with a play-off, you know. Well, the Pittsburgh Crawfords and the American Giants had had a couple of games rained out. We ended up one game in front of Pittsburgh, and we had to play those two games off, and I pitched against Satchel. I think we beat Satchel 5–2. They had always been telling me what a good curve-ball hitter Charleston was. In the ninth inning, who did I strike out? I struck out Charlie, with a good drop ball. Like this boy Connie Johnson, used to pitch for Kansas City. I saw him pitching to Ted Williams one day, and he threw Ted a curve ball. Ted swung at that, missed, and threw his bat away, flipped the bat up in the air. I think it cost him a $20 fine by the umpire. He was talking to reporters the next day, and he said that was a picture-book curve ball. No pitcher has ever thrown a better curve ball than that. It was one of those straight overhand curves, first it was there and then it wasn't. And that's what I struck Charlie out with. After he swung and missed, he just stood at home plate and looked at me. I said, "I told you one day sooner or later I was going to throw you that curve ball." And I threw it to him.

We played the Philadelphia Stars in our World Series, it must have been in '34. We didn't beat them. Here's how it happened: We opened up in Philadelphia the first two games of the series. It rained the first day there, so we didn't play but one game, and we beat them. When we came here to Chicago, Trent beat them 3–0 on a Saturday. What we didn't want to do was to go back East. You know, riding in the bus all those years, you get tired of it. I never will forget, I begged Dave Malarcher until about eleven o'clock Saturday night to let me pitch Sunday. Up until game time Sunday, he said he didn't know. But he started Bill Foster, and I had to come in and relieve him in the first inning with the bases loaded and nobody out. I got two outs and I gave up a single, which gave Philadelphia a two-run lead, and that's the way the ball game ended, 2–0.

I came back the next day Monday and pitched nine innings and had Philadelphia shut out until the ninth inning. I gave up a run in the ninth, and we won 2–1. So it ends up we went back to Philadelphia with a two-game lead. In other words, we need one game to clinch it. They beat Trent and they beat Foster, so that tied the series. It was up to me in the last game.

The next afternoon, in Connie Mack Stadium there in Philadel-phia, I believe with Philadelphia coming to bat in the eighth in-ning, I had given up one scratch hit, a swinging bunt down the third base line with a man on third with two outs. I had Philadel-phia 3–1, and Dave Malarcher came to the mound and asked me how I was feeling. I told him fine. "Well," he said, "you've pitched wonderful, wonderful. I'm going to pitch Foster the eighth inning, if necessary I'm going to pitch Trent the ninth inning." I said, "Cap"—we all called him Cap—I said, "I feel all right, there's nothing wrong with me." But he said, "Well, I've made up my mind." So he called Foster in. They tied the score on Foster before he got anybody out. And it was just lucky that Trent came in and he got the side out. Well, you know they have a law in Philadelphia, and they stopped the ball game at 1:30 or something in the morning, still tied.

We had no pitcher for the next day, so I came back the next day. I gave up one run in the first inning, and in that ball game I doubled three straight times with nobody out, and in the eighth inning I'm still behind 1–0. So they said to me, "Hold 'em one more inning." Well, I was hot for Malarcher because I felt—well, I knew—I would have beat them that night before had he not pulled me and put in Foster. So I rolled up my glove and put it in my pocket and told him, "*You* hold 'em."

Malarcher told me, "You don't walk out of my ball game." I didn't want to say anything, so he said, "You'll never pitch any more baseball for the American Giants." I told him, "That's okay with me too." So Philadelphia went on and beat us.

Well, R. A. Cole owned the club at that time, and the next year Dave wasn't going to manage the club unless they got rid of me. They ended up getting rid of *him*. Then everybody on the club wanted to manage, and they ended up doing nothing. That was '35. And I think in '36 the ball club broke up, players went different directions. Some went to Philadelphia, some went to different clubs out East.

When we played white clubs we'd get the usual catcalls from the fans: "It's getting dark," or something like that. I remember once, I was in Dayton, Ohio. I had pitched no-hit, no-run baseball through eight innings. And I was in the batting circle, and I heard one of my players say, "Look out, Sug! Look out, Sug!" I naturally just covered up like that. And the ball hit my arm and glanced off the side of my head. You know what had happened? The pitcher had taken his windup, and took a potshot at me and called me a black son of a bitch. Well, this boy Suttles, being a big guy, got between the pitcher and his dugout, and not one of his teammates raised a hand to help him. The fans booed him, and they rushed me to the hospital. Had the ball not hit my arm, maybe I could have been dead. I know I would have had a concussion.

Well, I stayed in the hospital overnight, and it must have been about 1:30 A.M. and the sister let the manager up to see me. He sat down and talked with me, said he was sorry it happened and everything, didn't know what happened to the guy, what made him do a thing like that. I know he was under contract to one of those major league ball clubs, but they just paid him off, period, after that. Dayton didn't use him anymore.

That's just like this guy Jake Powell of the Yankees. I remember one year he was here in Chicago. Bob Elson was interviewing him and asked him what kind of work did he do in the winter. He says, "I'm a policeman, I enjoy whipping niggers' heads in the winter time." Elson cut him off the air like that, and it wasn't three weeks from then that the Yankees sold him to Detroit, and when he went over to Detroit, those fans over there threw so many balls and things at him that he was gone. Now that was a man that had been brought up, had been taught evil all through his young life. That stuff was just embedded in him.

We had problems like that. I remember we had been to New Orleans spring training this particular year, and we were on the way back North. I said to them, "You got an Illinois license on this bus," and I said, "you're going to be stopped, and God knows how much money you're going to have to pay." So we were coming through a little town, Mayersville, Mississippi, on Highway 61, I think. Foster and Powell, their home was in Mississippi. They just had to have something to eat. And they went in a restaurant. The guy wouldn't let them in the front door, but he let them in the back, with the secretary, a guy named Moore. I think Moore got about twelve or fifteen hamburgers. The guy told him, "fifteen dollars"—he don't owe but six. And you know, they had a shotgun on him, locked him up in that place back there until the police came. We had to pay that $15, and then the police fined him for disturbing the peace!

And it wasn't like that just in the South. I was up here in Marietta, Ohio, one morning. We were on our way to Dayton, and I was driving. I guess it was about 4:30 in the morning. Everybody in the bus asleep but me, and I was kinda tired. Here comes this police, just blaring his horn, pulled up beside me, asked me, "Where's the fire?"

I said, "Well, I should ask *you*, you're doing all the running."

He was the peace officer of this little small town. He said, "You ran through a red light." He had me charged with running a red light, talking back to an officer. This was Tuesday. He said the judge wouldn't be in town until Thursday, did we want to put up a bond or did we want to wait until Thursday? My secretary asked me, "You have any money?" I said, "Yeah, but I wouldn't give him a nickel." So he says, "Well, either you put up bond or you have to go to jail." I told him, "I wouldn't give you a quarter, now you can put me in jail." The secretary paid him off, but I wouldn't have given him my money, not a nickel. You ran into those things.

Every country you go into, you're going to have to pay. You take the white Mexican, he's the same way toward the black Mexican. You know some Mexicans are darker than I am. And some Cubans are darker than I am, and it's the same way.

I was in Cuba in 1939, and I won nine, lost one, and I got the best salary, $800 a month American money. I went to Mexico that summer—a lot of major leaguers went down there—and I had a pretty fair season down in the Mexican League. I was nine and two. The next year I went back, I couldn't get accommodations at the same hotel I was living in before in Mexico City. I asked the hotel manager why, and he said, "Well, you know, we have a lot of tourists that come here, and the whites say they don't live in the same hotel with you in the United States." I told him, "If that's the way you want it, that's okay." The club management got me a nice apartment.

Another year I was playing way down in Mexico somewhere. I don't know how far it was, but I'll tell you, I left Mexico City one Monday evening and didn't get there until Saturday afternoon, so you know I must have been way down there. My manager had me arrested. Well, he didn't like me, he knew what kind of money I was making. Now he claims that I borrowed 800 pesos from him on the street. I gave him no receipt, nothing, he just gave me 800 pesos for asking for it. I had to go the American consul to get out of jail.

I've faced some tough hitters, Josh Gibson was one. They've got some tape-measure home runs that Gibson hit in the old Washington ball park. Gibson's supposed to have hit one 500-and-some feet. And here at Comiskey Park, I saw him hit a line drive. You know where the bull pen is, and the wall back there where the bleachers sit? I've seen him hit a line drive all the way there. No, it didn't go in the bleachers, but it hit high up on the wall.

When I saw Oscar Charleston, he was playing first base. I've been told that he had been one of the greatest center fielders of all time. But for my center fielder, I'd have to pick that boy Bell that was with St. Louis—Cool Papa Bell. Bell was faster than Mays. If he was on second base and they bunted the ball, the pitcher could not throw to first base or he'd score. When they'd bunt the ball to me, I'd motion to first, turn around on the third base line, and Bell would bump right into me. I'd be standing there waiting for him.

At that time you could have found 250 to 500 good ballplayers. I mean players that could have made any club in the major leagues, and could have stayed there. Now Jackie Robinson and Campanella were in the Negro League. Well, I don't think Campanella had two hits off me all the while he was over here. And Jackie Robinson had one single off me, as far as I can remember. They went over there and they were .300-plus hitters. I say if a man could hit .300 in the league we were in, he'd be a .350 to .375 hitter over there. We had some pitchers that were just that tough. You take Birmingham, you take Memphis, Nashville, Kansas City—all those clubs carried five pitchers, and whenever the manager said, "You're pitching today," you pitched nine innings. You always got a good pitched ball game.

Like we used to play out East—Yankee Stadium, Detroit—we'd have 40,000 to 50,000 people. We could only get in there once on Sunday, and I think it was the drawing power of those clubs that promoted the major-league owners to thinking. They said, "Well, now those guys here are drawing 40 to 50,000 in Comiskey Park in their all-star game." The major-league all-stars would play there, maybe they'd have 34, 35,000 people. We would have standing room. Oh yes, we had whites, they would come.

But you never picked up a white paper and saw anything in there about Negro baseball. We got more publicity after Abe Saperstein was connected with the club than we had in all the years that I can remember. Then you would find something in the

Tribune. Or you'd find something in the afternoon papers. But other than that, before he came along, there was nothing.

In 1943 they had decided to make me manager of the ball club. And that's the year I went into the Army. I stayed a year and something, and then I came back here to Chicago.

Negro baseball was on the downgrade then, because, you know how rumors get around, that several major-league clubs were going to give Negroes a tryout. I know the last ball game I pitched in Brooklyn, in the old Dodgers' park, I had several guys come up and ask me how old I was. Once after I shut out a Detroit Tiger farm club, a guy walked up to me, said, "You looked pretty good." I said, "Oh it was one of those lucky days." He asked me how old I was, and I told him thirty-nine. He says, "Sorry I couldn't have found you maybe ten or twelve years earlier." He said, "I'm a scout for the Tigers. If I could have got to you twelve years ago, I'd have had a good prospect."

I came back to Chicago, I gave away everything I had—my baseball shoes, everything but my jacket. Then I read in the paper about two weeks later, out in San Diego, about eight or nine colored guys that I had played with playing with San Diego. And they all were twenty-six, twenty-eight years old. I could have kicked my own self. I think they were getting $7,500 each for six months. I could have made $7,500 a year for maybe two or three years. I said, "Well, I opened my mouth when I should have kept it closed." I should have told him I was younger. A heck of a lot of them did do it.

I thought it would have been New York, the first club to take Negroes. To tell you the truth, I thought it would have been the Yankees. But when Jackie Robinson got in there, he said the Yankees were the most prejudiced ball club he'd ever played against. I know, and the world knows, Jackie caught hell, by being the first. I know he got all the insults any man could have. They threw a cat—it would have landed in his face but I guess he threw his arms up. Down in Florida the po-lice walked out on the diamond, told him, "No niggers don't play on this diamond with no white boys."

You can say the older player is responsible for the black man even getting a chance. Had there not been a Kansas City Monarch ball club, Robinson wouldn't have been in organized baseball.

I'm going to say this: I hold the major leagues responsible, in a sense, for what happened to the Negro ballplayers. The owners didn't have the guts to come up and say, "Now, here's a good ballplayer, only he's a Negro." Branch Rickey was the only one had guts enough to attempt that. Of course now, I remember this about Dixie Walker. He said, "They'll never put a nigger on the ball club with me," when they talked about bringing Jackie up. Branch Rickey said, "Walker can go back to pick cotton."

But most all of the clubs in the major leagues began to realize the dividends the minute they put a black man on the ball club, because a lot of people that hadn't gone to the ball games, they went to see how the Negro will play. Was he as good as the white ballplayers? Jackie Robinson proved it, Campanella proved it, Don Newcombe proved it, Larry Doby, Willie Mays proved it. Durocher said Mays is the greatest he's ever seen. Now when you look at Oakland, Pittsburgh, you find more blacks than you do whites. The starting lineup has three white boys in it; the rest of them are black. And most of those clubs are drawing, and they're making money.

As poor as I was, when I left baseball, I never was one to humble myself or beg anyone. Now Abe Saperstein that owned the Harlem Globe Trotters, he and I were very close friends. When I decided to give up baseball, I guess you could call it pride, it was too much to go to him and ask for a job, although we had been very close, used to travel together. He was traveling in the bus with us, trying to book ball games. He'd get so much percentage for every ball game he booked, and that's the way we became friends. He had a little traveling basketball club, and I knew a lot of ballplayers that were begging him—every time they saw him they wanted something. Well, that wasn't my speed. If I had my health and strength, I could make it on my own.

A friend of mine I was talking to a few days back also played with the American Giants. Now, he's still traveling around with the Harlem Globe Trotters; he's been all over South America, Europe and all those old places with them. In fact, my wife always told me that I hurt my own self. It's just one of those things, it's just my makeup.

So I went to get me a job with the Pennsylvania Railroad, and

I worked with them until I took sick in 1967. I ended up having to be operated on for a circulatory condition, and so I'm on disability now, I'm not able to work and I have a pretty hard time getting up and down the steps.

If I had it all to do over again, of course I'd like to get more money out of it, because in this man's crazy world that's what counts, is money. If you've got it, you're all right. And if you don't have it, you catch it. After all these years, I end up with nothing. When you don't make it, you don't have a chance to have nothing.

The only thing I regret is that I wasn't given a chance. It was just one of those things. My skin was black and that denied me the right to play in the majors.

I have a little nephew here, sixteen years old, and he made the Chicago *Tribune* all-star team. He's hitting .487, he's fielding .960-something, and the scouts are after him. And I tell him each and every day: "You just look for yourself at all the athletes who came along in front of you, all the progress they have made. Being greedy, you could lose all that." I said, "Help somebody else."

Chapter 14

BUCK LEONARD

They called Buck Leonard "the black Lou Gehrig," and at least one authority, Monte Irvin, agrees that Buck could hit them as far and as often as the Yankee first baseman. If Leonard was the black Gehrig, then his long-time teammate on the Washington Homestead Grays, Josh Gibson, was surely the black Ruth. Together they formed baseball's most potent one-two punch between the eras of Ruth-Gehrig and Mantle-Maris, and from 1937 through 1945 brought the Grays nine straight pennants, a record probably unequaled by any other professional team in any sport.

The two were an interesting contrast in personalities. Gibson was fun-loving and liked to go out on the town. Buck was more quiet and enjoyed a good crossword puzzle.

In 1948 Leonard hit a league-leading .395 and tied teammate Luke Easter for the league home run crown. His lifetime average was .343 against black big leaguers—and .400 against whites.

I first talked to Buck Leonard in 1969 in his brick home in Rocky Mount, North Carolina, where a roadside sign proclaims that Jim Thorpe had played his first professional baseball game. Buck talked easily in a slightly high-pitched voice, punctuating his tales with a broad and gleaming smile. Some gray had crept into his sideburns, which he wore modishly long. We talked in his paneled den, filled with baseball pennants, photos, and scrapbooks.

He was such a good storyteller that I went back again and again. In 1971 I had the pleasure of listening to him talk hitting with Ted Williams—they both agreed that they were guess hitters. Ted still speaks glowingly of Buck's gleaming smile and vibrant humor.

Fifteen years later Leonard suffered a stroke that forced him to hobble slowly on a cane when he appeared at the annual Hall of Fame festivities in Cooperstown. Our most satisfying visit was back in 1972, when Leonard himself was inducted into the Hall of Fame.

Buck Leonard Speaks . . .

My best home run year, I would say, was 1948. My longest home run went out of the ball park in Newark and went behind some tanks out there beyond the right-field fence. I didn't have any way to measure it, but some fellow sitting high up in the stand said it just kept right on going. Then I hit a couple of pretty good ones in New York. I hit one in the bleachers in Yankee Stadium one Sunday, hit another in the back of the home team's bull pen.

That right-field fence in Washington was a heck of a high one, though. Then too, the ball we used just wasn't a major-league ball. It was a Wilson 150 cc, and it wasn't as lively as the big-league ball. Also we used bats off the shelf, where the major leaguers had their bats made. Then the Washington Senators started to have our bats made along with theirs. They would order 800 and order 100 for us.

I used to hit clean-up for the Grays, right behind Josh Gibson, or sometimes I'd hit ahead of him. We were drawing pretty good crowds in Washington at that time—20,000, 26,000, 28,000. Here's a picture of a game in 1942; we had 26,000 that night. That same year we played a game with Satchel Paige against Dizzy Dean and we had 29,000. Cecil Travis of the Senators was in the Service, and he played with Dizzy. And we played another game against the Kansas City Monarchs and had 30,000. At the time Griffith Stadium didn't hold but 30,000. In 1945 we drew more than the Senators, and we weren't playing as many games.

One day about 1942, Clark Griffith had come around and looked at our ball game, and when the game was over he sent word down there for Josh Gibson and me to come see him in his office. He said, "I want to talk to you fellows. You all played a good ball game today," and so on and so on. "You fellows got good size on you and you looked like you were playing to win. There's one thing I want to talk to you about. Sam Lacey [sports editor of the *Afro-American*], Ric Roberts [Pittsburgh *Courier*] and a lot of other fellows have been talking about getting you fellows on the Senators' team." He said, "Well, let me tell you something: If we get you boys, we're going to get the best ones. It's going to break up your league. Now what do you all think of that?" We said, "Well, we haven't given it much thought. We'd be happy to play in the major leagues and believe that we could make the major leagues, but so far as clamoring for it, we'll let somebody else do that." He said, "Well, I just wanted to see how you fellows felt about it." We said, "Well, if we were given the chance, we'd play all right, try to make it. And I believe we could make it." But we never heard from him again.

I always thought the Senators might be first to take a Negro, because Washington was about half Negro then. I figured if half the city boycotted the games, the other half would come. But Griffith was always looking for Cuban ballplayers. He had Joe Cambria down there scouting for him. I guess he didn't have to pay them much money—but he wouldn't have had to pay us much either.

When I started out with the Grays in 1934, I was getting $125 a month—for four and a half months. By 1941 I was making $500 a month plus 75 cents a day eating money. In 1942 they doubled my pay to $1,000 a month. I wouldn't say Josh and I pulled a double holdout like Koufax and Drysdale. See, both of us had a chance to go to foreign countries to play, and we asked for the same amount of money that we were being offered. I told them what they were going to pay me down in Mexico and asked them

would they equal it, and they said they would. My best payday was 1948; I made $10,000 that year all told, summer and winter.

I come from Rocky Mount, North Carolina. Jim Thorpe played his first professional game there in 1909 at a park over near the Parkview Hospital, where the China Tobacco Company is. I was two years old then. I lived in a place called Little Raleigh, and I started following baseball in 1921 when they moved the city park, Municipal Stadium, over near my house.

After they moved the stadium, I started going over there looking through the fence to see the fellows play. Well, then the police said you couldn't look through the fence; they made you back up five feet from the little crack you were looking through. Well, you can't look through a crack from five feet. They came out one evening and arrested everyone, and we had to go to court. The judge told us it was private property and we had to get five feet away. So we started getting boxes and looking over the fence until the police came back and told us *that* was against the law, too. Well, that pretty much handicapped us from seeing the games then. But that's how I first got interested in baseball.

Then too, minstrel shows used to go around the country—A. G. Allen, the Florida Minstrels, the Georgia Minstrels, Silas Green— and they had baseball teams too. They'd parade in Rocky Mount in the morning and then have a baseball game that afternoon.

That is, the show people would play the local team. Then that night they had the minstrel show and took *all* our money away! Well, that's what we used to say. They used to get all the money from the sporting people in the afternoon, and get all the money from the show people at night—and then they had doctors with them selling medicine to take that part of our money too!

Rocky Mount had a colored team—a semipro team—and they used to play in Tarboro, Wilson and towns like that. I used to go out there and pick up bats and things and mess around with the baseball, just like you see a mascot do now.

My favorite player when I first started going to games was Frank Walker. He managed around Rocky Mount and started baseball here. He had been to the major leagues, to the Giants and Athletics and Tigers, and he told me he roomed with Ty Cobb in 1915 and 1916. He's retired over in Bristol, Tennessee, now. He's about 70-some years old, and later he helped us form the Rocky Mount Leafs in the Carolina League in 1962.

I got out of school when I was fourteen, about 1921, and went to work at a mill that made stockings. Then I started shining shoes at the railroad station. In 1922 I went to work at the Atlantic Coast Line railroad shop for nine years and played semipro ball around Rocky Mount. We had a team called the Black Swans and another one called the Elks team. We played in Norfolk, Newport News, Wilson, all around Raleigh, Durham, Winston-Salem. Then in 1933 I went to Portsmouth, Virginia, to play with a team called the Firefighters.

I learned to play first base from a fellow named Ben Taylor, one of the greatest first basemen in colored history. His brother, C. I. Taylor, was the big baseball man who managed the Indianapolis ABC's. Ben had a team in Baltimore called the Baltimore Stars, who came down through here about 1933. We played them a game, and afterwards Ben Taylor asked me would I go with his team. I said, "What will you pay me?" He said, "I'll pay you what you're getting here and more too"—I was making $15 a week plus my board and lodging down in Portsmouth. On the way to Portsmouth, Ben had already picked up my brother Charlie to pitch for the team, and that was one thing that made me decide to go.

The fellows there at Portsmouth said, "Man, don't go there with that team. You know how much trouble a traveling team is. You get off on the road and can't get back home, and get hungry and can't eat." Well, that was true; a lot of teams were that way. I knew some fellows had gone the year before. A fellow called Pop Watkins, from out of Atlantic City somewhere, used to come down here every year with a team and get fellows to go back and play semipro ball. Anyway, I left with the Baltimore Stars, and first of all we went to Winston-Salem, Charlotte, Stateville; then we went to Richmond and Baltimore. And it was just like the people said —I just about perished to death! I'm telling you—you talk about tough, it was rough.

We were playing in Druid Hill Park in Baltimore on one of the open lots—way out, a big open field, a city park that wasn't enclosed. We would play out there at five o'clock, what they called a twilight game, and you had 3,000, 4,000 or 5,000 people sitting on the grass. You would pass around the hat, and some- times you'd get $20–$30 for the team's share. The most that *we* were getting was just board and lodging. We were staying in the manager's house. He wasn't promising us anything—he promised us, but we just weren't making it. On weekends we would go to Towson, Maryland, Pennsylvania and little towns over in West Virginia. We'd make around $50–$75. Well, he was claiming we owed him that much for board and lodging. He'd pay us $5 and $6, $3, like that.

Ben Taylor was the owner, manager and everything. He played first base, and I was playing right field. He was too old to play, but he still could hit, so he started teaching me to play first base. Eventually he quit. I don't think I was a fancy fielding first base- man—not like Showboat Thomas or Highpockets Hudspeth, for instance; I wasn't a fancy dan.

Anyway, when we decided we couldn't make any money play- ing in Baltimore, we decided to go to New York. Nat Strong was the big booking agent around New York, and we were going to let Nat Strong book us around.

We had two cars, a Buick seven-passenger and a 1929 Ford with a rumble seat. We would put nine players in the Buick and put three in the front of the Ford and two in the rumble seat. Let's see, that was about fourteen fellows. We were staying at a hotel in New York called the Dumas Hotel, and our room rent was behind. Strong had quit booking us because our team was weak, and we couldn't pay our room rent. So when they found out we couldn't pay our rent, they sold both the cars out there one morning—just had an auction sale right in front of the hotel. These fellows got some papers out and the man came over there and read the papers and they sold the two cars. That was the end of the team right there. We didn't have any way to travel, see?

Now what were we going to do? We had fourteen men sitting there with no transportation. Ben Taylor said, "Well, this is it, boys, you better go back home. I don't have any money to send you home. The manager has agreed to let you stay in the hotel until you can get some money from home." Well, we didn't have any money, period. My brother and I hated to write back home to Momma to send us some money, so we decided we would try to play with the Brooklyn Royal Giants, one of the big-league Negro teams. In the meantime Charlie wanted to come on back home because he was going to junior college. So I got a way for him to come home and I stayed out there and played with the Brooklyn Royal Giants the rest of the 1933 season.

Cannonball Dick Redding was managing the team. He was one of the greats, a burner, but he was in the evening then. Had a fellow named Huck Riles played first base. I was in right field at the time.

Country Brown played third. He was a comedian; I guess you've heard about him. We were playing semipro teams around New York, and he would go up to bat on his knees and holler, "Throw the ball up here, throw the ball up here." We had it arranged with the other team, and they knew that we were going to put on a couple of acts. The pitcher would throw the ball, the umpire would call a strike and he'd turn around and argue. Of course the fans liked that. And if he hit the ball and ran to first base, he's just call out: "I told you you couldn't pitch, I told you you couldn't pitch, I hit the ball on my knees!"

Then a little later in the game he would coach first base and take two great big dice and holler real loud. Everybody would pay attention to him, and he'd roll the dice out there and kiss the dice and roll them again and look, take them back and roll them again, then he'd rake in all the money. Then he'd point over there to the other fellow to put something down, he'd roll the dice again and win that. He'd win about two or three times. Then he'd take everything he could get—take off his cap and put it down, take off his shirt and put that down, take off his belt and put that over there. Now he's got the dice. He'd look over there see what the other fellow's got out. Now he's rolling the dice. And he'd lose. Man, he would fall down and kick, and the fans would holler.

Then about an inning later he would go to third base: "Heh, baby"—like he's telephoning—"How are you feeling? . . . What you doing? . . . You're laying down? . . . With who? . . . Oh, your sister. I thought the ice man had stopped by."

And he was a pretty good ballplayer too. I mean, he could hit and played pretty good third base.

We had a Pierce-Arrow car that we went riding around in, and we had a Cadillac. The Pierce-Arrow was a seven-passenger, had a copper body at the time.

Well I finished out the '33 season with the Brooklyn Royals and I went back to play with them in 1934. We were practicing at a place called 59th Street Park. There was a white semipro team playing there too. We were practicing there in April, and it was chilly—I mean, it was *chilly*. One night when I was in a bar, Smoky Joe Williams was working in the bar, and he said, "Look, Buck, don't you want to get with a good team?" I said, "What are you talking about?" He said, "The Homestead Grays." I said, "You think I could make that team?" He said, "Well, you can try." So he said, "I'm gonna call Cum Posey, the owner, tonight and see what he says. I've seen you play two or three times and I think you can make the team." The next day he told me, "I called Cum, he's going to send some money for you to come to Wheeling, West Virginia, for spring training. I'm supposed to buy your ticket and give you some spending money."

Sure enough, Cum sent the money and I went out with a boy named Tex Burnett, an old-time catcher. We left New York about twelve o'clock one night on the bus, and when we got to Pittsburgh snow was on the ground half a leg deep—this was in 1934, April. We went around to the hotel, saw the team, met everybody.

We practiced about a week or so and got ready to play teams around Ohio and West Virginia.

I was getting $125 a month and 60 cents a day on which to eat—60 cents! But I could get bacon, eggs and iced tea for a quarter. As the season went on, I said, "Well, I don't like it out here in this steel-mining town. I'm going to finish the season here and then I'm not coming back." But I stayed out there seventeen years.

I went to Puerto Rico in 1935 with Abe Manley's Brooklyn Eagles. We carried a good team down there. We won the first eight or nine games we played. In the spring of 1936 the Cincinnati Reds came down there to spring train. We beat them two out of three. They had Paul Derringer pitching, Ernie Lombardi catching, Sam Chapman and Kiki Cuyler in the outfield, George McQuinn in the infield. The Reds' Yannigans beat us 3–2, and we beat the Reds 5–4 and 10–3.

Josh Gibson came to the Grays in 1937. He just put new life into everybody. Our team picked up considerably when he came. We won the pennant in 1937–38–39–40–41–42–43–44–45. We won nine straight pennants.

I played with the Homestead Grays seventeen years and never missed a payday. You were always booked to play somewhere every day. There never came a day when you weren't booked to play a game somewhere. Never. Out of all that seventeen years we didn't miss but two ball games. One was during the war when they put us on a train going to Johnstown, Pennsylvania, and it didn't make connections.

Baseball was a rough life back then. We'd play 200 to 210 games a year, then go to Cuba or Puerto Rico all winter and play winter ball.

When I joined the Grays, they were a Pittsburgh team. We started playing in Washington in 1939. We would play in Washington when the Senators were on the road and in Pittsburgh when the Pirates were away.

We would leave Pittsburgh after midnight some Sunday morning to play a doubleheader in Washington. That was 263 miles over the Pennsylvania Turnpike. We would get in Washington I would say around a quarter to eleven or eleven o'clock, go out and get a sandwich, and at that time we had to be at the ball park by 11:30. They would say, "If you're not here at 11:30, we're not going to open the gates, unless we're sure you're here." With the traveling we were doing, we weren't sure whether we were going to get there or not. One time I remember our bus broke down out near Hagerstown, Maryland, and we had to call Washington and tell them to send three taxicabs out there to pick us up to get to Washington to start the game at two o'clock.

During the war we couldn't go but 700 miles a month on the bus, because of gasoline rationing. Now from Pittsburgh to Washington was 263 miles, back to Pittsburgh was 263. Well that was over 500 miles for just one trip. You could ride maybe 100 miles more, then you're through. Had to put your bus up the rest of the month and take the train. One time the conductor told us, "We don't have room on the train for you, and we're not going to let you stand up." So we stayed in the baggage car. That's right. And played that night.

We'd play a semipro team, say in Rockville, Maryland, in the afternoon and a league game in Griffith Stadium that night. Or we'd play semipro teams around Pittsburgh. We'd play the Edgar Thomas Steel Mill team, and over in Braddock they had a team. We'd start at 6:30 and play as many innings as we could get in before dark. The Grays would get $75 to $100 to play the game. For the whole team! But Sundays and weekends were the days you really expected to make enough money to pay off your players. Those were the games you played in Forbes Field, Griffith Stadium, Yankee Stadium and those parks. They were called "getting-out-of-the-hole" days.

Sometimes we'd stay in hotels that had so many bedbugs you had to put a newspaper down between the mattress and the sheets. Other times we'd rent rooms in a YMCA, or we'd go to a hotel and rent three rooms. That way you got the use of the bath, by renting three rooms. All the ballplayers would change clothes in those three rooms, go to the ball park and play a doubleheader —nine innings the first game, seven innings the second game.

The second game would be over about 6:15. We'd come back to the hotel and take a bath, then go down the street and eat and get back in the bus to go to Pittsburgh. The bus seats would recline—you'd be sitting there, and the drone of the motor would put you to sleep. We'd get back in Pittsburgh 7:30 in the morning, go to bed, get up around three o'clock, go up the river somewhere about twenty-five or thirty miles, play a night game, come back. Next evening the same thing. We logged 30,000 miles one summer. Of course you get tired around July or August. The people didn't know what we went through. They'd see us dragging around, they didn't know we'd ridden all night getting there.

You were tired, you'd ridden 200 miles to get there, rode all night last night maybe, you're going to play here today, and you got a game to play tonight somewhere. You've got to change your sweatshirt after this game, go somewhere maybe fifty miles to play tonight; you're trying to save a little from this evening's game for tonight's game. We used to play at Bushwick in New York on a Sunday evening, and go out to Freeport or out to somewhere on Long Island, and play Sunday night. Man, you're spent when you played a doubleheader at Bushwick or Yankee Stadium or the Polo Grounds. Then you go out there at night to play, you're stiff, tired and you're just forcing yourself.

We didn't have a paid trainer. We rubbed each other. If my back was hurting or my arm was sore, I'd get another player to rub it. And you'd tape yourself up the best you could. I know one time I got scratched on my leg in Washington, and we were going to Boston to play and up in New Hampshire. I needed three stitches in my leg, and they wouldn't put the three stitches in there because I was going to lose some games. I just played until it got well. Now it's got thin skin over it, and it gets inflamed every now and then. That comes from not taking care of it like it should be. Had I been in the major leagues, I would have had proper attention.

Clark Griffith said our league wasn't organized. We were organized, but we weren't recognized. If we were going to play a game in Griffith Stadium and got rained out, we're supposed to let the people know when they could come back to another game. We had a problem like this: We used to give the visiting team 30 percent of the gate receipts after expenses. Now if we got rained out with Newark on a Sunday and we were going to play the New York Cubans on a Thursday night, the Cubans didn't feel like we should use the Sunday rain checks on their game. So that's not a good organization. A good organization is where you can establish your home town and be willing and able to redeem your rain checks.

John Morrissey, the Senators' ticket manager, was the biggest help to our team, and to all Negro baseball. He's still with the Senators, and I stop by and say hello every time I'm in Washington. When we were playing at Griffith Stadium, he would ask us how many we expected for the game. We'd say, "Well, 18,000." Or if Satchel Paige was coming in to play with Kansas City, we'd say, "30,000." He'd say, "Let us use our ticket sellers and let us have your tickets printed and let us handle everything for you." He even handled the publicity for us. When they announced the Washington Senators' games for the weekend, they would announce our games for the next weekend or for that Thursday night. At that time we were playing in Washington every Sunday that the Senators were away, and Tuesday and Thursday nights.

We would charge $1 for the bleachers, $2 for the grandstand, $2.50 for box seats. During the war when the people couldn't get much gas, that's when our best crowds were. People couldn't travel, so they would have to stay in Washington on weekends. After the war our crowds started dwindling again.

Mr. Morrissey took care of police protection too. If you're expecting 18,000, 25,000 or 30,000 people, you're going to need twelve, sixteen or twenty policemen. Our crowds were unruly quite a few times. Mr. Morrissey would go along with us. He'd say, "I know how things are now, people can't travel and they're mad, drinking, but we just have to bear with it."

After the game we'd go to the office and Mr. Morrissey had our statement made out, the visiting team's statement was made out, how much went to the revenue man, how much went to the visiting team, how much our end would be. The money was baled up with the statement sheet. Everybody's sheet was separated—our sheet, the visiting team's, the revenue man's. We'd go there, look at our statement, pick up our money, leave. He would even tell the visiting team how to operate their business. Mr. Morrissey was the greatest help, not only for the Homestead Grays but for Negro baseball, period.

We used to play ball in Griffith Stadium by the football lights! Remember when they had the football lights? That's what we used to play by. Griffith Stadium had no lights then for baseball. I remember one night we were playing, it was kind of foggy, drizzling rain. And we used to go to Cleveland to play—Municipal Stadium, Cleveland, as big as that is—football lights. The ball would go up and you *just could* see it. You couldn't get a good jump on a good line drive to left center or right center. Or get a good jump on a ground ball. The lighting wasn't there. A high fly would go up by the catcher, go up higher than the lights, go up in the dark. He's standing there waiting for it to come back down.

Then during the war we had portable lights that we put in the parks. We'd install them about six o'clock or 6:30 on poles all around the field. A big dynamo out there in the outfield generated the electricity for the lights. After the game was over, we would take down the poles. We used to have trouble with outfielders running into the poles. Jerry Benjamin ran into a pole up in Niagara, New York, one night and broke his ankle. He ran into one of the guy ropes while chasing a fly ball.

Sometimes we thought the belt was slipping in the dynamo. The lights would dim and then get bright, dim and get bright. We had to stop the game about five minutes so they could pick up a little. We'd put some belt dressing on the belt that turned the wheel, to keep the belt from slipping. Some people said they were giving us about as much light as we were paying for. They said we must have owed them some money, teasing us, you know.

One speedballer had a record strike-out one night under those lights.

Down in Jacksonville they used to have a team, the Redcaps. They were redcaps in the railroad station and played ball too. Skindown Robinson, Preacher Henry, Albert Frasier and a catcher named Brown who got killed. They were riding in a car and had a flat tire one night, and he got out and was standing behind the car fixing the flat tire. Someone was standing in front of the tail-light, and a car came and ran right into the back of their car—killed three of them.

Until the late years of the league, we never kept any statistics.

Roy Campanella is on the committee to name old-time Negro stars to the Hall of Fame. He says the other members of the committee told him, "If only you could prove these things, if only you had figures." But the way it is now, it's all word of mouth.

White papers in Pittsburgh said, "If you mail the scores to us every night, we'll run them in the paper." But sometimes we weren't near a mailbox where we could mail it in every night. So that idea never really worked out.

When the Elias bureau began keeping statistics, we'd give a player the job of keeping the box score. Maybe he didn't know how to keep it. Or in the middle of the game he'd have to go in and pitch and some other player would have to finish the box score.

One Negro newspaper sent a reporter to be our official scorer and travel with the team. The paper paid his salary, but he said he couldn't live on it, so the team had to add a little something to it. But he wouldn't get to the game on time. He'd show up in the third inning and ask one of the players on the bench, "What happened in the first inning? What did this man do? What did this guy do?" Maybe the player couldn't remember. And if the guy didn't see what happened on the field, he'd put down "singled to center" or "flied out to center." Next day the newspaper story was filled with things like "he singled to center," so finally we gave him the nickname "Single-to-Center."

Or he'd come in, say, "Got a pencil?" What would *we* be doing with a pencil? The score would be about 6–0. He'd ask, "What did this man do? What did that man do?" They'd say, "So-and-so doubled to right, so-and-so walked, so-and-so flied out to center. . . ." An *none* of that was true! None of it was true!

Ballplayers back in those days were bad. They'd tell us where to go and where not to go, but you know ballplayers; you tell them not to go somewhere, and that's where they're going. Ballplayers a long time ago, their characters were low, they'd do anything to win. They're a little more refined now than they were then. Back then, when the season started a ballplayer already owed all the money that he was going to make during the summer. At that time baseball players were gamblers—they were rough. We'd be riding along the highway, I'd try to keep everybody quiet. They'd say, "What's there to be quiet for? Aw, you old-timers." It's not what's right and what's wrong, it's what you can get by with—that's the way they talked. When you talk about religion or the Bible or something like that, well shoot, that was foreign, that was foreign to them guys.

Vic Harris was our manager and he was a nasty slider. They used to get even with me for Vic Harris. Vic was playing left field and they couldn't get him, but they'd come over first base and step on *my* foot. We fellows who played infield, we didn't rough anybody, because they could pay us back. But those outfielders we had, they were rough. I don't know whether Ted Page told you or not, but he was one of them that used to cut fellows sliding into base.

We used to tell Vic, "Look, don't step on that fellow's foot, don't slide into that fellow at second base, because he's going to step on my foot trying to get even with you." The ones who were worst at it—Crush Holloway, Rap Dixon, Oscar Charleston, Ted Page, Chaney White, Vic Harris—they were all outfielders. I don't know a single infielder who would do that. That's right, Ty Cobb was in the outfield too.

Those fellows came up the hard way and they believed in playing hard. They said it wasn't dirty, it was hard baseball but clean. We said it was dirty. We said all of us are trying to make a living—our livelihood would be cut off if we were taken out of the game.

When we played semipro teams they supplied the umpires. The winner would get 60 percent of the dollar and the loser would get 40. So naturally each umpire was trying to make his team get the 60. One time we were playing in a town outside Norfolk, Virginia. Every time we got in front the umpire would fix it so they'd tie the game. In the ninth inning we were leading by a couple of runs; our owner went in there and got the 60 percent. They tied the game in the last of the ninth inning; he went back in there and they split the money. We went out there and we got in front again; he went back in there and we got the 60 percent. They tied us again, and he split the money again. We were getting ready to go back out on the field again when we said, "Wait a minute, there's no way in the world we're going to win." We said, "Let's split it and we'll play no more."

I'd say Satchel Paige was the toughest pitcher I ever faced. I couldn't do much with him. All the years I played there, I never got a hit off him. He threw *fire*, that's what he threw. Satchel had an exceptional fast ball. That was his main pitch. It would get up to the plate and just rise a little, just enough for you to miss it. If you finally did get a piece of it, it wasn't much. A little later, when his arm got sore, he developed a curve ball. I remember July 4, 1934, he pitched a no-hitter against us.

Another thing about Satchel. One time we were playing the Crawfords and Satchel an exhibition game in Monessen, Pennsylvania. The people wanted to see Satchel pitch. Well, he pitched a couple innings. Then they wanted to see him play outfield, and Satchel went into right field. Just messing around. And somebody hit a high fly up in right field, and we rushed around and looked in the outfield for Satchel to be standing under it. Satchel was standing on the sideline getting a light on a cigarette from a fellow—getting a smoke! Wasn't even in right field! Over there on the sidelines getting a cigarette. That just goes to show you how comical he was.

I remember one game in Guayama, Puerto Rico, in 1940. Satchel had only been there about a week. We had three men on base in the first inning, two outs, and Bus Clarkson, the shortstop, came to the bat. Satchel told the catcher to get out from behind the plate, he was going to walk him. The catcher said, "No, you can't walk him, three men on base, you're gonna walk a run home." Satchel said, "Well, I'd rather walk a run home than have him hit three or four home, so let's walk him." The manager came running out: "No, no, don't walk him, don't walk him." Satchel said, "I know what I'm doing." So the catcher stepped out to the side and Satchel threw four balls and the run scored. Satchel said, "Now, that's all you're gonna get today." And that's the only run we did get. He beat us about 8–1 or something. We always kidded Satchel about how he walked that run home.

I played for Mayaguez that winter, and Roy Campanella was

playing for Caguas. We were tied for the home run leadership. Here's what it says in the newspaper: "Both connected for eight home runs." Luis Olmo, used to play for the Dodgers, had four. In the play-offs Campanella hit one—we didn't get in the play-offs—and they gave him the trophy. I didn't think they should have done it. We laughed about it. It says, "Buck Leonard was also the leader in two-baggers. . . . Perucho Cepeda"—the father of the Cepeda that's with Atlanta now—"was the leader in the department of runs driven in."

Cepeda was a shortstop, and a good shortstop—big. Good hitter. Very good—exceptional. I guess it's a toss-up between him and his son. Both of them good, both of them about the same size. But we never could get him to come to the United States to play.

In 1941–42 I went to Cuba that winter. Here's some of those batting averages: Roy Partlow .441; Javier Perez .432; Pep Young .426; Orlando Cepeda .421; Frank Coimbre .401; Jud Wilson .395; Buck Leonard .389; Neil Robinson .382; Lenny Pearson .360; Johnny Hayes .358; Leon Day .338; Roy Campanella .263.

Campanella was just a kid at that time. The first time I saw him was about 1936; he was about fourteen or fifteen, catching batting practice for the Baltimore Elite Giants. They just carried him around to catch batting practice, and he learned how to catch that way. At one time Campanella couldn't hit a curve ball. But when you play winter baseball, you improve on everything. And he turned out to be a heck of a catcher, as we all know. But I wouldn't say he was as good as Josh Gibson. He could only do one thing better than Gibson, and that was stay in shape.

In 1943 I went out to the West Coast to play the big-league all-stars. They had fellows like Peanuts Lowrey, Andy Pafko, Lou Novikoff, Johnny Lindell, Junior Stephens, Buck Newsom. Satchel Paige pitched for us. We had Cool Papa Bell, Double Duty Radcliffe and me. We were playing every Sunday at Wrigley Field in Los Angeles.

Here's a clipping: PAIGE WHIFFS 14, WINS 4–3. I got two for five. The second game was tied 3–3; I got one for three. Here's one we won 11–8 against Newsom; I got two for four. The second game they won 4–3, and I got one for two. Here's another: They beat us 8–2, and we won the second game 4–1; I got one for three in the first game and one for one in the second. We were raking in about $200 a Sunday apiece.

Judge Landis ordered an end to the series after that, said they couldn't play more than ten days after the World Series ended. Pafko kept playing, and Judge Landis fined him $400.

Nineteen forty-four was my biggest payday, $1,100 a month. Josh and I told Posey we were going to Mexico, that's why he raised us to $1,100. Here's my contract: I got $4,500 a season, May first to October first. A little less than $1,000 a month. It was going to be $1,100 a month, but after they agreed to pay my board and lodging at home as well as away, that's when I agreed to $4,500. You know, we didn't have any mouthpieces like the boys got now. A ballplayer goes in the office now with his attorneys with him—attorn*eys*, not one—he's got a *firm* behind him!

In 1945 we carried an all-star team down to Caracas, Venezuela. We had Sam Jethroe, Jackie Robinson, Roy Campanella. We played against Luis Aparicio's daddy, by the way. He was a shortstop too. Here's a clipping with our batting averages. Let's see, I was hitting .425, Parnell Woods .419, Quincy Trouppe .413, Sam Jethroe .339, Jackie Robinson .281 and Campanella .211.

Robinson signed with the Dodgers the day before we left. They came to the hotel in New York where we were staying, looking for him. At that time we didn't think too much of Robinson. He had played a few games with Kansas City in 1945. He was a hustler, but other than that he wasn't a top shortstop. We said, "We don't see how he can make it." When we went down to Venezuela, we were supposed to leave New York the fifteenth of October, but some kind of revolution was going on down there and we didn't leave until about the fifteenth of November.

When we got down there, Robinson didn't look too good because he hadn't been playing as long as some of us. We didn't think he was so good—at that time. Of course now we see what he really did. You know, you can be wrong about a ballplayer. You can look at him and don't think much of him, and then he turns out to be one of the best ballplayers of all time. You can't always tell what a person's going to do in the athletic world. One thing though, a fellow with a college education is just a little better than a fellow you pick up on the sandlot. Now I see that they got the right man in Jackie Robinson, because he had the education. There were other players we thought were better players, but they got the right man after all.

They had to find the ideal ballplayer to start. They might have been looking for that one. And they finally got him. I can't think of anybody that could have been better than Robinson. A lot of things that he took, a lot of other ballplayers would not have taken.

But until then there wasn't anybody in organized ball very interested in admitting Negroes, it looked to me—Griffith or anyone else. I think they believed we could play major-league baseball, but everyone hated to be the first. There was going to be some protesting from the white guys like there was when Robinson went up there, but if you could weather that, just like he weathered it, you'd turn out all right.

Of course it was always our ambition to get into the major leagues because of the prestige and money. But all the players I talked with, even Jackie Robinson himself—well, we just weren't considering it too much.

I never thought about race prejudice much. I felt, regardless of what color you were, if you could play baseball you ought to be allowed to play, anywhere that you can play. I thought integration would come, but I didn't think it would come like it did, as quickly. I thought they were still going to keep pushing it back. Even when they took Robinson, I said, "If he doesn't make it, they're going to be through with us for the next five or ten years. But if he does make it, maybe they are going to keep him in the minors for a long time." But we were wrong.

We had discussed it. There were some people used to come around in New York, especially from the *Daily Worker* and other papers: "Don't you think Negroes should be playing in the majors? Don't you think Negroes should be doing this or that?" We said, "We're going to leave that to you all to discuss, we're going to play ball." They used to come around and say, "We're going to arrange for you to get a tryout." We said, "All right, arrange it. We'll try out any time you arrange it."

They said, "Wouldn't you agree to sign this paper?" "We're not signing anything, we're not making a statement. Any writing you want done, go ahead and do it. We're out here to play ball, we're not out here to demonstrate or anything like that." You know, they wanted us to put on some kind of exhibition, demonstrate, but we just wanted to play ball. Of course we'd like to have gone to the majors, but we were just out there to play a ball game.

We didn't think there was anything we could do. We just thought that if the change came, it was just going to have to be decided among the majors. We couldn't speed them up or anything like that. Of course, one group said if we'd demonstrate, that would speed it up, but we didn't want no part of that. All the players that I ever talked to felt, when they get ready for us, they're going to take us anyway.

There was one requirement in the major leagues that we didn't have, and that was your character. If you don't have good character, you don't stay in the major leagues long. But if you could play ball, regardless of your character, you could come in our leagues. You could be a drinker, you could be staying with another man's wife, you could be gambling, whatever you wanted to be— if you could play ball, you could stay with us. Some of our good ballplayers wouldn't have met the major-league requirements. I know one that had to straighten out his life before he could get to the major leagues. I guess you know him too. But he got it straightened out all right.

I don't know of anything that we could have done to speed it up. I don't know of anything the players could have done. Maybe our conduct might have been better. Maybe. But as a rule, your conduct can't be but so bad because you're too tired to do anything bad. When the game is over, you're too tired playing 200 ball games a season. You're too tired to do anything else. You might drink a little, but when you're drinking it's to give you an appetite or trying to rest up your nerves or something.

When Robinson went up, they talked about bringing me up, but even at that time they were looking for younger ballplayers. They were looking for players they could depend on for the next four or five years. They couldn't depend on us older guys for that many years. You take Willie Wells and Cool Papa Bell and a whole lot of others, we knew that we couldn't stand the pace for four or five years. But Larry Doby and Monte Irvin and Jackie Robinson and all those others, they could stand another five or six years. But with us, we knew we were a poor risk—any injury would stay with us longer.

Dan Bankhead was in demand then, but you know, he was just a mediocre pitcher in our league, he wasn't one of the aces. But he went up there and had a good year with Brooklyn.

I went barnstorming with Dan Bankhead the year he went to the Dodgers. We went on down south to Roanoke, Atlanta, Jacksonville, Mobile, New Orleans, to this town where they make Hadacol medicine somewhere in Louisiana, Natchez, Jackson, Mississippi, and back to Mobile.

When we got back to Mobile, I was tired of messing with the team. I was supposed to get $25 a game, but three or four times I had not gotten anything. At Jackson, the business manager was so far behind he wasn't paying anybody anything. In Mobile, we had a good crowd on Sunday and I said to myself, "Now is a good chance for me to leave." The business manager said, "Come over here to where I'm staying, we're going to settle up this evening." So I carried my suitcase over. I was going to leave that night. I set my suitcase down on the porch. He said, "All right, I'm going to take you all one at a time"—he didn't want us to see what he was paying the others.

When he came to me, he said, "Whose is that suitcase out there?" I said, "Mine." He said, "What you going to do with it?" I said, "Well, I think I'm going to leave tonight." So he said, "Well, you're not getting anything."

"What about my $25?" He said, "No, you're not getting anything. You promised to make the entire trip. We still got to go to Texarkana." Didn't pay me, not one nickel—not five cents. Well, you know, you always try to keep your railroad fare in your pocket. I had a little over $20, so I went down to the station and got my ticket and came home to Rocky Mount. Next spring I asked the other fellows, "Look here, how'd you all fare after I left?" They said, "Man, the bus broke down and we had to send off to get $200 to have the bus fixed. We didn't get no more money after you left."

We had a lot of good young players who played in the East-West game in 1948 and went to the majors: Minnie Minoso of the

New York Cubans, Junior Gilliam of Baltimore, Luis Marquez and Luke Easter of the Grays.

Easter really improved as a player in '48. Luke was big, he was strong, he was interested in the game, always played to win. We believed that if he hadn't started out too late he would have been an even better ballplayer. He was about thirty-five when he went up to the majors. He didn't even start playing ball in our league until late. He had been messing around with the Indianapolis Clowns before we got him.

We sold Easter to the Cleveland Indians for $10,000. They were going to pay another $5,000 if he went to the majors. But when he went to the majors, Luke wanted the other $5,000 himself. He had an argument with the Homestead Grays' management. At that time Rufus Jackson was dead and his wife was in charge. Luke said he wasn't going if he didn't get the $5,000, but they got together on something and Luke went on.

When you play twenty-three years, you know, you've had a lot of thrills. But I think the greatest one was when we won the Negro World Series from Birmingham in 1948. That was one of our best teams—maybe our greatest team—although Josh Gibson wasn't with us, he was dead. But we had Luke Easter, Luis Marquez and Roy Welmaker. Welmaker also went to the Cleveland Indians, and Marquez went to the Boston Braves.

Birmingham had Willie Mays with them at the time. And they really played us. Although the scores look big, the series was really close. Mays was about fifteen. He could run the fly balls and throw, but his hitting wasn't good because he couldn't hit a curve ball at that time. But a fifteen-year-old boy playing in our league was like a boy of fifteen playing in the major leagues. He could run and catch a fly ball and throw, but to think and hit, he just didn't have it yet.

That was the last Negro World Series. Griffith's prediction came true. After Negroes got in the big leagues, all the Negro fans wanted to go see the big-league teams. We'd get around 300 people to a game. We couldn't even draw flies.

I got this diamond ring in Cuba in 1948. I was on Marinao. Don Newcombe was on our team too. We had nine foreigners on each of the Cuban teams. I hit a home run one day with the bases loaded to win the ball game for my team, and they gave me this ring. It's got twenty-one diamonds in it. At that time it was worth about $500. I don't know about now.

Othello Renfroe was the cause of me going to Mexico to play a few years later. He was playing down there and called me up and wanted me to come down. They paid me $450 a month and all expenses, plus transportation. They paid us enough to stay in a second- or third-class hotel, and I paid the difference and stayed in a nice hotel. They'd pay enough for your board, but you always had to put something to it if you wanted to eat a decent meal.

In Mexico I would hit the ball, come back to the bench, say, "What do you mean giving that guy an error? Didn't you see, he couldn't handle that?" He'd erase it, put down a hit. I bought that guy a box of seegars. They would have sent me home if I couldn't hit. I couldn't afford to go home, so I bought him a box of seegars.

When Bill Veeck went out to the St. Louis Browns with Satchel Paige in 1952, I was in Mexico, and they called down there and wanted to know when I got back home would I get in touch with them. So I got in touch with them, and they wanted to know whether I would come to some town in California to spring training. But I was forty-five then. I knew I was over the hill, wasn't any use of me going out there. I knew I couldn't play ball every day. They said they wanted me to hit mostly, but I just told 'em no. Then they called again that evening about five o'clock and said they were going to send the money. I told 'em, "No, don't send any money." I didn't want to come.

I knew I couldn't play baseball every day, and I didn't even want to attempt it. I didn't want to fool myself—or try to fool myself. I could have gone out there and said I was maybe five, six, seven years younger, but I still would be through to my legs. You know, your legs will act their age. You can get glasses and you can see a little better, but what you going to do about your legs? That's what tells on you. You can wear glasses to improve your sight and build yourself up to think you're a little younger, but you can't do anything with your legs.

When age comes on you, you get tired quicker. You go out

today, get a three-base hit, slide into third base, the ball is over-
thrown, you've got to get up and go home, maybe have to slide
into the plate. When you play hard one day, the night is not
long enough for you to rest. When it's time to play tomorrow, you
haven't rested enough. It takes you longer to rest. That's what
tells on the old ballplayers. You can't get enough rest overnight
to take care of you for tomorrow. If you play a doubleheader
today, you're out for two or three days. You spend a whole lot of
energy and you don't get it back like you used to. You take an
old man my age staying up all night, hot dog, he's out—out for
two days. It's a young man's game, rather than a game for an old
man. When you realize that, stop.

I played a few games with the Portsmouth Merrimacs in the
Piedmont League in 1953. They asked me if I wanted to join their
retirement plan!

I was down in Durango, Mexico, playing ball in 1954 or '55.
Martin Dihigo was the manager at Durango. But the team wasn't
winning, and down there if you're not winning, you can just
figure on not being there long. He was fired one week and I was
fired the next. I was forty-eight years old.

I work quite a bit with kids now. I teach a Bible class on Sunday,
and I was a physical ed teacher and truant officer in the high
school. But I retired. I retired early. The children have got so you
can't discipline them at all now. It was getting on my nerves. I
just decided I would retire. Of course, when you retire at sixty-two,
your pension is way down, but when you get so you don't enjoy
your work, it's time to quit.

I'm vice-president of the Rocky Mount Leafs in the Class-A
Carolina League. In 1962 I went down and talked to Frank
Walker, the man I was telling you about who was my favorite
player as a boy. He said he was trying to get a team and won-
dered if I would help him, selling tickets and selling stock in the
team. At that time Rocky Mount would work with the Cincinnati
Reds. We stayed with Cincinnati a couple of years, then with
Washington one year, and now we're with Detroit. Cesar Tovar,
Tony Perez and Lee May all came up through Rocky Mount.
Also Ron Woods of the Yankees.

Our manager asked me to go to the ball park and tell the guys what we used to do and how we used to do it. They'd say, "You don't have to tell me, man." They don't want to know what you did, they want to know what's *going* to happen. These young people say, "Who are they? When did they play? I never knew anything about them. What book is it in? What's his record?" It would be a problem straightening that person out, telling him when Negroes played, how many teams in each league and all that.

You know, ballplayers now, they think they know it all. So you let 'em go. Baseball men say, "You don't change his style of batting if he's producing. Let him go on until he finds out he can't produce, then maybe you can tell him something."

But I could tell them how to hit the ball and the ball will go farther, and tell them how to hold the bat while you hit. You've got to learn how to hit standing away from the plate. As long as you're on that plate, close to the plate like Frank Robinson, you get hit a lot. You take Clemente for the Pirates. Now he stands away from the plate, but he still hits and wins batting championships.

I used to bat with my hands open a little, like Ty Cobb. They changed that, said I couldn't hit a breaking ball as well.

That curve ball has sent more youngsters back than any other thing. That's right—that curve ball! George Scales knew how to hit it to a T! Josh Gibson knew it to a T. They hit a curve ball farther than they hit a fast ball. I saw George Scales hit a curve ball four *miles*! Rev Cannady was the same way. They wouldn't even swing at a fast ball. Wait until you throw your curve ball. They would set it afire. The way you learn to hit a curve ball is they keep throwing it at you. You *know* you got to learn how to hit it. You get interested in it then. I'll tell you one man's been in the major leagues twenty years and still can't hit that curve—Al Kaline.

A change of pace was my weakness.

We had a boy named Red Bass on the Grays, asked me how to hit a left-hander. I said, "Bass, I can tell you from now until doomsday, but you got to *learn* how to hit a left-handed pitcher. I'm going to tell you how *I* hit them, but for you, you got to learn how to hit 'em." So I told him.

The first thing I used to do, if I was the first batter, I'd go up to the plate and look at his ball while he was warming up. Fellows don't do that now. And I guessed some. If you play ball long enough, you've got to guess. Then I opened up on left-handers, used an open stance. Face him a little. When he throws that curve ball, you can see it all the way. The main thing about hitting is watching the ball. That's the main thing: Keep your eye on the ball. They can say what they want to about batting, but you keep your eye on the ball, you're going to get a piece of it. As soon as he turns it loose, you've got to observe the spin on the ball. That's what I used to do. And I used a thirty-six-inch bat. I knew if he threw me that curve, I was going to have to bend my back to hit it.

We had to send Bass back home though, because he couldn't hit that curve. He never did come back.

I think the old players would make good coaches. Of course baseball is played a little different now. But the bat's still round and the ball is still round, the pitching distance is the same. But the thinking is a little different now. By that I mean, we used to try to teach a little more baseball, we tried to *change* them to do like we were doing. But now you don't change them so much, you let them do what they're doing so long as they get results. Well, we didn't even permit a boy to start out that way.

They say they've improved the game, and I believe it has improved. A lot of things they know how to do now that we didn't know how to do, like fundamentals. They know all the cut-offs and so on, because they're taught it. In our day they didn't have time to teach us that. We'd play ourselves into shape, we'd be playing as soon as spring training started and then played every day from then on; we didn't have any time for calisthenics or drilling on fundamentals. We had to learn by playing.

You can't compare a ballplayer now with twenty years ago. Everything's just right now. Of course twenty years from now maybe it will be just as different as it was twenty years past. But in order to compare, things got to be equal. That's why I always try to compare fellows who were playing under the same conditions at the same time.

I went down to spring training this year [1970]. Detroit didn't have any black players at Rocky Mount last year. We went down to tell them unless they give us some black players, we're going to have to find another club. The fans, black and white, said we need some Negroes.

I talked to Ted Williams, Frank Howard, Nellie Fox, all of them. That was the first time I'd ever met Williams. Williams named a few fellows that he saw play. 'Course he didn't ever barnstorm. He didn't know the old ballplayers, because he asked me about some that he had read about. He said, "Josh Gibson must have been a terror of a hitter, everybody talks about him." Then he wanted to know, "How did you fellows play ball riding around in buses?" I told him we did the best we could under the conditions.

The balls that we played with weren't major-league balls. They were Wilson balls. They didn't go as far, they didn't last as long, they didn't stay in uniform shape like the major-league balls do. And we would bat from one background in Griffith Stadium on Sunday, then Monday night we were down here in Rocky Mount batting against just any background, sometimes on an open field.

Frank Howard said, "Heh, Buck, if we find it tough to hit up here now, I can imagine how you boys found it, the conditions you were in." I told him, "Yeah."

In order to play major-league ball, you've got to play it under major-league conditions, on a major-league field. Now these fellows today, they've always played on good diamonds. The diamonds are excellent now. So there are not many bad hops. Us, we didn't have any astroturf. If you want to be a good fielder—outfielder or infielder—you've got to be playing on a good diamond. You playing on a diamond with rocks on it and you expecting a bad hop from the ball at any minute, you don't go for it with the same zip that you would on a good diamond. You'd see pebbles on the field, you'd be shaky about fielding balls.

Detroit, at Lakeland, they got four big ball fields. Rocky Mount team playing here, Toledo here, Montgomery here, Lakeland there. Now that's four teams playing, and the coach up here in this tower, right in the middle. He can stand up there and watch four teams play. All right, they got a big dormitory down there that will hold 200 ballplayers. They got a mess hall there will feed about 300 or 400. Now look, if ballplayers had had those conditions way back when Ty Cobb was playing, they'd have been better ballplayers.

So you have to figure out: What would we have done if we had come up under these conditions today? We feel like we would have done it just like they're doing it. Do just as good as they are.

One thing I believe though: What we *could* do, we were a little more able to do than they are today. We could throw the ball over the plate a little bit better than they can today. We played our games quicker. At that time no game hardly lasted over two hours and fifteen minutes. And look how many three-hour games you got now. We put a pitcher out there could throw the ball over the plate and could pitch nine innings. If you couldn't pitch nine innings, you didn't stay on the team. And we didn't have a lot of walks and we didn't have a lot of players who couldn't hit. There's a lot of players nowadays just can't hit. They go up to the bat and they wait around and step in the box, step out, step in the box, step out, the pitcher on the rubber, the manager walking out to the mound to talk to his pitcher, going back, coming back out there again. We had pitchers could go out there and stay, didn't need a lot of talking to. We had fellows at the bat could hit the ball, and they didn't need a lot of talking to. We had fellows on the bench could run, and you didn't have a lot of signals to give.

We used to lose a ball game and we'd talk about it all night the rest of the night, riding. We'd spend all night discussing it: "If I had done this, we could have scored another run, maybe won the ball game." And you didn't go to sleep until you satisfied yourself that you're going to do better tomorrow and you're going to improve on what you did tonight.

But now these ballplayers, when they leave a game, they leave it right on the field. They're talking about something else when they're together. When they leave the ball field, man, they talk about business!

We were playing for the fun of it. We got little pay. They said it wasn't too much fun, but we thought it was fun, because we were doing what we wanted to do.

I was in Cooperstown the day Satchel Paige was inducted, and I stayed awake almost all night that night thinking about it. You know, a day like that stays with you a long time. It's some-

thing you never had any dream you'd ever see. Like men walking
on the moon. I always wanted to go up there to Cooperstown.
You felt like you had a reason, because it's the home of baseball,
but you didn't have a *special* reason. We never thought we'd get
in the Hall of Fame. It was so far from us, we didn't even consider
it, we didn't even think it would someday come to reality. We
thought the way we were playing was the way it was going to
continue. I never had any dream it would come. But that night I
felt like I was part of it at last.

Buck Leonard, right, with pitcher Dave Barnhill in Cuba.

The Buck Leonard swing (Cool Papa Bell is sliding in the middle picture).
The park is Washington's Griffith Stadium.

Buck Leonard

Buck Leonard

Buck Leonard

*Yogi Berra, Lefty Gomez, Sandy Koufax, Buck Leonard,
and Early Wynn at the Hall of Fame in 1972*

*Venezuela, 1945. Front: Jackie Robinson (# 1) Back: Roy
Campanella (# 1) , Buck Leonard (# 8)*

Cool Papa Bell and Candy Jim Taylor

Larry Brown

Larry Brown

Chapter 15

HILTON SMITH

Hilton Smith was the invisible man of black base-ball. For years he toiled behind the glare of an almost blinding star known to the world as Satchel Paige, but who in reality was a hyphenated pitcher named Paige-Smith. After Satchel had pitched three innings to draw a crowd (and incidentally earn his 15 percent of the gate), Hilton Smith would trudge in from the bull pen and finish the game. And there are many black hitters who declare that of the two, when Smith appeared, the hits became even tougher to collect.

Smith's lifetime record was 73-32 with 16 saves, putting him second in the last category among Negro Leaguers. In several years going head-to-head against Paige, Smith came out on top:

	Paige	Smith
1941	7-1	10-0
1942	8-5	8-3
1943	3-9	4-4
1946	5-1	8-2

Ironically, Smith had been the star on the Monarchs before Paige arrived. Indeed, even for a while afterward Smith continued to be the ace of the staff. In 1941 Paige-Smith went barnstorming against Bob Feller and Ken Heintzelman of the white big leagues, and, wrote Bob Burnes, sports editor of the St. Louis *Globe-Democrat*, "Smith showed the best speed and sharpest curve of the quartet."

Even the New York Yankees learned to respect Smith. He beat them in Caracas, Venezuela, in the spring of 1947, and while most U.S. papers ignored the game, John Drebinger of the New York *Times* didn't. "For the first five innings," he reported, "the Bombers ran into quite a Tartar in Hilton Smith, a right-hander, who gave up only one hit, a single to Phil Rizzuto, and two passes."

I met Smith in 1969 in his handsome brick house on a terraced lot in one of Kansas City's best black neighborhoods. Although somewhat heavier than in his playing days, he did not look a bit like the grandfather he was. He talked in a high-pitched, rapid voice about the particular burden he carried for years as Satchel Paige's other half.

Hilton Smith Speaks . . .

I played twelve years with the Kansas City Monarchs, 1937–48, and I won twenty games or more every year. Not counting exhibitions, I won 161 league games and lost 22, but most people have never heard of me. They've only heard of Satchel Paige. That's because I was Satchel's relief.

Every Sunday I'd start, then Monday night come on in relief, start on Wednesday and maybe Friday, according to how Satchel was feeling. It was my turn to relieve him on all big games. He'd go two or three innings; if there was a big crowd and we had to win it, I'd go in there and save it. Then the next day I'd look in the paper and the headline would say: "Satchel and Monarchs Win Again."

I just took my baseball serious, I just went out there to do a job. But Satchel was an attraction, he could produce and he'd clown a lot. I guess it really hurt me. I tried to get away, but there wasn't anything I could do about it.

Now Satchel never did pitch much here in Kansas City. Oh no, he never did a lot of pitching here. But ooh, when he left here, my goodness, they'd eat him up all those other places, because he was an attraction, but these people here, they never did. He never was able to produce here. Some little old team would be able to hit on him, like Memphis and a lot of the teams like that. I remember '41 we opened up here against Memphis, and they got to him in about the second inning, and I relieved him. I shut them out the rest of the game, and we went on and beat them. So they never did book him in here hardly, I mean advertise him as a star pitcher. He played with us all those years but he didn't do too much pitching here. I pitched all Sunday games.

Satchel was a great pitcher, I don't take anything away from him. I'd like to have seen him in his early age, back in '29 and the early Thirties. Good God, he could throw that ball! And perfect control; he never walked anybody. He could throw it. But he hurt his arm in '37 and it didn't come back until '41. His arm was sore all those years, and he played with the Monarchs' "small team," while I was with the "big team." In '39 he came and played us over in Kansas City, and I shut him out 9–0. We just wore Satchel out. So I was the star.

But in '41 Satchel suddenly got his arm back, and that was the worst break I got. I guess in '42 Satchel was as great a pitcher as you want to see. He had a good curve ball, and he always had that good fast ball, and in '42 he just had everything on the ball. That's when he hit his peak.

I actually hit my peak, too, in '41. I was to the place then that I could just do anything, I felt that good. I thought I could go out there and get *anybody* out. I won twenty-five games and lost one that year. A semipro team in Dayton, Ohio, beat me 1–0 after I had relieved Satchel. We struck out eighteen between us; they got one hit off Satchel and none off me, but beat me on an error. It was the only game I lost that year.

In 1941 I pitched one game against Bob Feller's All-Stars. Walker Cooper was catching. Johnny Hopp was at first base—he had a good year that year, hit about .300; oooh, that guy could hit! The outfield was Ival Goodman, Stan Musial and somebody else. They hit Satchel pretty hard in the first four innings, and I came in and relieved him in the fifth. I held them, struck out six of them in five innings, didn't give but one hit, but they beat us 4–3. Bobby Feller pitched three innings, and Kenny Heintzelman of Philadelphia pitched the last six. He really broke off some jugs that day, because I doubled with nobody out and didn't score. It would have been the tying run, but the guy struck out all the rest of them.

One of my greatest thrills was beating Dizzy Dean in Wrigley Field, Chicago, in 1942. We had a turnout of 30,000 people that

1942 Monarch pitching staff that swept the Homestead Grays in four straight in the World Series. Hilton Smith is on left, Satchel Paige on right. Connie Johnson, later with the White Sox and Orioles, is next to Paige.

day. Yeah, boy, you're talking about some good baseball, there was some that day. You remember big old Zeke Bonura, used to play with the White Sox? He played first base. Buddy Lewis of Washington played third and Cecil Travis short. All of them were major league ballplayers who were in the Service, and they came up for that game. Dizzy Dean pitched the first three innings. We "carried" Dizzy, because he wasn't too good, we kind of carried him along. I beat him 3–1. Satchel pitched the first five innings for us and came out with the score 1–1. He had struck out three, walked one, gave up two hits and one run. I struck out three, didn't walk anybody, gave up one hit and no runs. Big Joe Greene, our catcher, got a hit with two men on around the seventh inning, and I held 'em. In the ninth Travis came up with one on. Barney Serrell, our shortstop, said, "Make him hit it on the ground," and that's just what it was, a double play, and the ball game was over.

Jackie Robinson used to tell me, "Hilton, you're going under the same thing with Satchel that I went under with Kenny Washington at UCLA." See, at UCLA Jackie had to play second to Kenny. Kenny was a great football player, we all heard about him, but I never heard about Jackie until I went to the Coast in 1942.

In fact, I'm the one who signed Jackie to a Monarchs' contract.

I had met him in '42 when Red Ruffing had a team in the Service out there on the Coast. Jackie asked me about getting him a job, so I wrote to Mr. Wilkinson, the owner of the Monarchs, and he wired back to keep in touch with Jackie, so I did. In 1944 he got out of the Service and joined the Monarchs.

Actually, Jackie didn't look that good. He was a little old to be a major league rookie—twenty-seven—but there weren't any good young ballplayers then. Jackie's arm was weak at shortstop; Willie Wells was better than Jackie at that position. But the Dodgers picked him on account of he'd played college baseball, he'd played with white boys before.

I was born in 1912 in Giddens, Texas, a little town between Austin and Houston. Rube Foster came from about twenty-five miles from my house, a little town right above me.

I patterned myself after my uncles. I had two uncles that my mother would let me play with. They were powerful good ballplayers. I guess I inherited my ability from them. They were good, but they played out in the country there, played for fun. I just loved it, and that was what started me off. I just made myself, didn't have a teacher. I kept picking up and looking and learning as I went up.

I started out playing with my dad, who was a schoolteacher. I played for my dad's team when I was in the tenth grade. I guess I was about fifteen. During the summertime I played with older boys—they were all grown men. I pitched against the town high school team and shut them out 2–0.

Austin had a team, the Austin Senators, a semipro team that played Houston and all the towns down there. They had a pitcher named Willie Owens who had played with Birmingham in the Negro leagues. In 1931, when I was nineteen, I went down and pitched against him one Saturday and beat 'em, I just beat 'em good. He went back to Austin and said, "My goodness, there's a little kid there, he's something else." So when the Chicago American Giants came down there to play Austin the next weekend, Austin came down and got me to pitch for them. I beat 'em 5–4 in eleven innings.

So Austin picked me up to play in Mexico. Mexico had an awful good ball club, they were good enough to play the major leaguers when they went down there that fall. Ramon Bragana was there pitching. They had Chili Gomez, who had been up there and played with Washington. I'm telling you, we had a lot of trouble beating those guys. Well, we started another boy, and they ran him out. Then I went in and relieved him and got them out. So they started me Sunday again. The manager told me just to go out there and throw hard. But my arm was so sore—I wasn't nothing but a kid and I hadn't been pitching that much baseball—I couldn't get anybody out. I don't think I got anybody out the first inning.

Next Thursday they started me again. The manager said, "Listen, I want you to go out there and try to get by the first inning." I said, "Yes sir." I asked him, "Can I throw some curve balls today?" He said, "Yeah, I guess so."

I beat 'em 5–1, and I hit in all five runs. I struck out so many of them, they didn't think I was the same pitcher.

Monroe, Louisiana, had a real good Negro team then. They were champions of the Southern Conference, had beaten everybody. They had Red Parnell out of Houston; a little old guy name of Ducky Davenport; and Barney Morris and Goose Curry out of Memphis pitching. They had a tremendous ball club. They came to Austin and played us two games. They were talking about they heard of this little schoolboy up there and said, "Well, we came up here to work him over." But we had a great big ball park and I beat 'em 2–1. They couldn't believe it. They said, "Well, this big old park, no wonder you won. When you come to Monroe"— Monroe had a small park—"we'll hit so many home runs off you. . . ." So I went to Monroe the following Sunday and beat 'em 4–2.

Monroe picked me up to play with them and carried me to Pittsburgh. That was the first time I saw Satchel Paige. I played with Monroe for the next three years. I had a great year in '32, won thirty-one games, didn't lose a ball game.

When the Pittsburgh Crawfords came down to Monroe to play us, I opened up against them. With Josh and them it was one of the best teams of all time: Oscar Charleston, Pee Wee Stephens, Ted Page, Double Duty Radcliffe. I led them 2–0 in about the sixth inning, when Boojum Wilson came up and got a hit. Then

Josh Gibson hit a home run off me to tie the game 2–2. I came out the next inning. I was only twenty years old then. I was nervous, I'd never faced those kind of ballplayers before.

I pitched against the American Giants in '33. They beat the Crawfords out that year, beat Satchel and them. Yep, they won the championship and came to New Orleans. Chicago had Mule Suttles, Willie Wells, Jack Marshall, Alex Radcliff; outfield was one of the best outfields I ever saw—major league or anybody else: Steel Arm Davis, Turkey Stearns and Nat Rogers. They were a *tremendous* ball club.

We beat them three out of five ball games. Sure did, 'cause I remember now. They beat us the first ball game, Sunday—I think it was about 5–1. They stayed over till Saturday and Bill Foster pitched against me—I'm strictly a rookie now—and I beat him 6–1. We came back and beat 'em again Sunday 3–2 in twelve innings. George Giles tripled with a man on base and beat 'em. Bill Foster came back Monday and beat us—that guy pitched three ball games in a week's time. Then I beat Cornelius. I think they got four hits, and all the hits were the infield variety, they never hit the ball out of the infield. And it was just natural stuff, I didn't know how to pitch to those guys. Curve ball and fast ball were all I threw.

I went to Bismarck, North Dakota, in 1935. The league broke up down South and Monroe went on a tour all around the Midwest. We weren't making any money, just touring around, but we were playing good ball, beating just everybody we met. I didn't know what it was to lose a ball game, I hadn't lost a ball game. We got into Bismarck the fifth of July—I never will forget that. A guy named Churchill was mayor of the city and had a ball club. Barney Morris, who played with Monroe, had gone to Bismarck earlier that spring. Satchel was pitching for them too. They were getting ready to go to this Wichita semipro tournament and they needed another pitcher. Churchill asked me about staying and I said I didn't know. He offered me $125 a month. I wasn't making a quarter, but I told him no, I didn't want to, so he said, "How about $150?" I told him okay.

I didn't lose a ball game with Bismarck the whole year, but I didn't pitch much. I played right field on that club most of the time and batted third or fourth.

When we went to Wichita, to the semipro tournament, we didn't lose a ball game. I pitched the first game and shut somebody out 2–0, I don't remember who it was. I played outfield the rest of the games and hit fourth. Satchel and Chet Brewer did all the pitching.

The next year, when I went back to Bismarck, Satchel had gone East, so I did all the pitching down there in Wichita. I won four games, and all four of them were shutouts. Last time I saw the records on that, about six years ago, my record was still holding. I had more shutouts than any pitcher who had ever been in the tournament. I don't know if anyone's broken it or not. Satchel had the strike-out record.

Actually I didn't really learn how to pitch until I came to the Monarchs that fall. I just had natural stuff before that. I learned by having such guys for teachers as Frank Duncan, Bullet Rogan and Andy Cooper.

Rogan. . . . He played with us in '38 and then he was through. He was a guy who, if you didn't know him, you'd think he was kind of a snob like, but he was a nice guy, and he used to get on you if you didn't do your job. He was umpiring, and I'd be pitching, and right after the ball game he'd come out and he'd tell me, "You've got a lot of stuff, but why'd you do such-and-such a thing?" I'd say, "Well, I don't know." He'd say, "Well, from now on, you *know*." I'd answer, "Okay, I'll do it." Next time he was umpiring and I got in the ball game, he'd say, "Un-huh, I see you're picking up."

Andy Cooper was a smart manager, and he was a great teacher—great teacher! A student of baseball. He would take me aside and just sit there and talk to me, and I'd watch how he'd pitch. And my owner, Wilkinson, would talk to me. He was a doll, that guy. He had played a little semipro ball himself and he really knew baseball. He said, "Look, you've got everything, but use your wrist a little more, see if you can't get a little more hop on your ball." I took him at his word, and sure enough it worked.

So I'd watch and observe and listen.

The first ball game I pitched in this park out here in Kansas City was a no-hitter. I beat the Chicago American Giants 4–0. Nobody got on first base—I mean a perfect game. The Giants had Sug Cornelius pitching, Larry Brown catching, Alex Radcliff. They were *hard* to beat.

I didn't lose many games that year. I probably lost three the whole season.

The Monarchs used to play Texas League teams all the time. We played Oklahoma City when they were in the Texas League in '37. They had a good team, too; they had finished way up in that league, Double-A baseball. We wanted to find out how good we were. Shoot, I pitched two ball games against them and they haven't scored yet. I beat 'em Friday night, and we played 'em two games Sunday. We beat them the first ball game, and the second game they kind of started hitting our pitching, and Cooper brought me in there. A boy named Clay Touchstone—he was a great pitcher—I had beat him. He said, "What is this, the World Series, you bring that man back in here! Doggone, let us win *something!*" But I beat them. We beat them three straight. But we wanted to prove a point, see. We didn't have a chance to play in those leagues. We wanted to prove a point that we were good enough to.

We played the major leaguers about seven games that fall, too, and I pitched three of them. I pitched eighteen innings in all, and they never got a score off me. They had Johnny Mize on first, Lonnie Fry on second. Outfield had Ivy Goodman, Vince DiMaggio and Gus Suhr. Pitchers were Mace Brown, Lou Fette—he won twenty games that year—Mike Ryba and Bob Feller.

I pitched three innings in Rock Island in relief and didn't give up any hits or runs. Bob Feller started for them, and we beat 'em, but I don't think we scored on Bob that day, he only pitched three innings. Lou Fette came on next, and we beat him. Next day I pitched six innings and didn't give up any runs. And then I beat Fette in a nine-inning game. I shut them out 10–0 in Oklahoma City.

Mize didn't get a hit off me the whole series. He was hitting everybody else, but he didn't hit me. How could that man hit that ball standing way back from the plate? I kept a-looking at him.

I guess I had a curve ball as good as anybody's in baseball at that time. My fast ball ran, it just jumped. I bet I only struck him out twice that whole series, but he would hit the ball weakly back to me. I just kept it on the outside, the curve ball would break in and the umpire would call it. He'd try to pull it and he never was able to pull it.

In 1937 I was on Martin Dihigo's team in Cuba. Josh was down there with Havana. Early Wynn was playing with Springfield in Triple-A ball, and he only won one game down there that year. And he was going to the majors the next year! He could not win down there. Boy, it was tough.

That was 1937. In '37, '38 and '39 I had tremendous years. I could pitch and hit, both. Andy Cooper'd pinch-hit me for his fourth-place hitters just as quick. Several years I hit over .400 pinch-hitting, outfield, first base and pitching.

I was pitching about four times a week, because we were playing six or seven games a week, and we only carried about four pitchers. Maybe sometimes we'd have five, that was the most. We didn't know what it was to relieve. When you went out there, you didn't look at the bull pen, you were expected to go the whole route.

They knew I wasn't wild, they knew I threw strikes. We didn't hardly walk anyone. The curve, we'd just slice it off, pfffft. And everybody threw hard. Good curve balls, and that live fast ball moved. Today you see a lot of these guys' fast balls, just straight. But our fast balls *moved*. We had to have two curve balls, a big one and a small one. Now they call it a slider, but those guys were throwing it years and years back. It kind of just darted over the corner like that. Good control.

We were tremendous rivals with the Washington Homestead Grays. Tremendous rivals. A lot of those guys could have got in the majors, they were such good ballplayers. And gentlemen— Buck Leonard and them were such nice guys. We'd set and talk and jolly one another. My goodness! I pitched against them one night in New Orleans in 1939. They had Leonard, Josh and all of them, and I struck out so many that night ol' Josh came up to me, said, "Say, fellow, look, you doctoring the ball or something?" I said, "Here it is, look at it."

Up until '42 I had more trouble with Josh than I did any other ball player. Gibson had those great big old muscle arms, weighed about 205, 6'1. He would swing flat-footed, wouldn't stride. The first time I faced him, he hit a home run off me. But in '42 I didn't have any trouble with him at all. No, from then on I really began to get him out.

I learned how to get Buck Leonard out too. I'd slow the ball up on him, screw-ball him, and slow curve balls. He'd ground out— oh, he'd get hits sometimes, but I mean I could get him out.

In 1942 I remember we played the Homestead Grays in Washington. Boston had played a day game against the Senators that day and drew 3,000; we played the Grays that night and drew 28,000. That's the year we beat the Grays four straight for the Negro world championship.

We had a tremendous ball club that year. A lot of the boys had jumped to Mexico, and they all came back in '42. We had Joe Greene catching, John O'Neil first base, Jesse Williams short, Newt Allen second. Outfield we had Ted Strong, Willard Brown and a boy named Bill Simms—he was a ballplayer never got much publicity, but he could do anything; he could hit, oooh, he could hit. Ted Strong was just as good a ballplayer as there was in baseball, but he kind of laid on the bottle. That got him in his late years.

We had a tremendous pitching staff in '42. We had Satchel, Jack Matchett, a boy named Connie Johnson who played in the majors. And Lefty LaMarque and a boy named Booker McDaniels. Nobody hardly beat us. That particular year, '42, I don't think I lost maybe one or two ball games the entire year.

This kid Connie Johnson was awful good too. He had hurt his arm when he went in the majors. I'd like to have seen *him* go in there before he hurt his arm. You talking about Satchel and me— Johnson and I would team up and beat anybody. I remember Baltimore came here with Campanella and all those good ball-players. I beat them 3–1. He came back the second game and beat them 3–1. I mean we didn't lose—he and I didn't lose. Johnson —ooh, that guy could throw that ball. He wasn't but about nineteen or twenty years old. He hurt his arm in '42. He went into the Service and came back. His arm came back to him, but nothing like it had been.

That '42 World Series. We opened up against the Grays in

Washington. I think Satchel pitched the first game, and Jack Matchett relieved him. I started the second game, Satchel relieved me. We changed around. He said, "Hilton, you've been relieving me all this year, let me relieve you, just see what we can do." I pitched five innings, he pitched four. When I left the score was 5–0. They scored four runs off Satchel, and we beat 'em 8–4. Then we went over to New York. Satchel started and Matchett relieved him, and we beat 'em 9–3. Then we went to Philadelphia and beat 'em 9–5, and I beat 'em the last ball game in Portsmouth, Virginia; I think it was 14–2. We just silenced them, just whipped em. I mean we killed their pitchers, and they didn't do anything with our pitching.

My arm went dead in 1943. I hurt it, and I played first base and outfield for two years. In '44 I began working back into shape, so I went out on the Coast that fall and played baseball against Bob Lemon, who's right down here as manager of Kansas City now. They had a good ball club. All those guys were in the Service. They had an all-star game, and I beat them that evening.

Biz Mackey caught me. Oooh, my goodness, I didn't know he was such a catcher! I think I struck out fifteen of those guys. That guy was a marvelous catcher! I just—ooh, I just was on *edge*, and it looked like all my stuff was just working. Had the hitters looking like they didn't know what to do. Mackey told me, "I don't see how in the world you *ever* lose a ball game."

My arm came back in 1945 or '46, and in 1946 we played Newark for the Negro world championship. They had Larry Doby and Monte Irvin, and I beat them two games. I beat them in Chicago 5–1, and I beat them in New York 2–1. No, that's wrong, I didn't beat them, I had them 1–0 going into the sixth inning, and Satchel came in. We had a guy from the Coast named Hamilton to replace Jackie Robinson—a good hitter, a good-looking boy. A big boy from Newark slid into second on the double play and broke his leg. Hamilton just laid there, and before we could resume play it was almost an hour. So I cooled off, got stiff and walked a man, and Satchel came in and relieved me. They tied it up, but he went on and beat them 2–1.

Monte Irvin played shortstop for Newark, and he looked awful good. Yeah, he was a *good* ballplayer. There's one guy I was really pulling for when he went to the majors.

But Doby didn't look too good. Three straight times I struck him out in Chicago, and he started jawing with the umpire. I asked him, "Doby, why do you want to jump on the umpire?" And he said, "Man, do you see my owner sitting up there in the stands? I've got to look good for her."

Roy Campanella didn't show me anything either. Campanella and I were very good friends. I used to pitch against old Campy when he was seventeen years old. I'd strike him out all the time. In the all-star game one year I struck that boy out two times.

Campanella came down to the Polo Grounds one night when we were playing Newark in the World Series, and asked me what did I think about playing with the Dodgers. He said the front office had told him to talk to me. He asked how old I was, and I told him thirty-four. Actually, they were wondering about Jackie [Robinson]. Jackie was around twenty-seven when he went up there, and they were debating whether he was too old. They knew he had to make it within one year, because if he didn't, he would be too old.

I figured I was too old at thirty-four. See, we were getting a pretty good salary, and we were afraid to go down to the minors and take a pay cut. With the Monarchs I was making $800 a month, and I felt like $400 would have been the best I could have got in Triple-A baseball. Don Newcombe went down to the minors from Newark and stayed for three years, and I don't think he was getting over $250 a month.

Had it been opened up—had there been some other team beside the Dodgers—I probably would have taken a chance. I knew the Dodgers were pretty well loaded and I'd have to sit around in the minors and they'd be slow about bringing me up, and at my age that was too much. I wouldn't have minded going down to the minors for one year, then come back up. But at that particular time I felt I was too old to have a comeback with the Monarchs if I didn't make it with the Dodgers right away. Campanella said, "Well, think it over and let me know." But I couldn't see going down there for them.

That fall I went with Satchel to play against Bob Feller's big-league all-stars. I remember they had Sam Chapman, Jeff Heath and Charlie Keller in the outfield; Mickey Vernon, who won the batting championship, was on first; Phil Rizzuto and Kenny Keltner in the infield; pitching was Feller, Bob Lemon, Johnny Sain, Dutch Leonard and Spud Chandler. I never *saw* so many good pitchers. Boy! Bob Feller said, "I wish I had this ball club all year to play with!" They had a powerhouse. Man!

We played fifteen or sixteen games, and I relieved in two and pitched two complete games. I broke even with them. They beat me 6–3, and I beat Feller 3–2. I gave up four or five hits. Vernon game me the most trouble; he got two doubles.

What messed us up was Jackie Robinson had an all-star team that fall—Monte Irvin went with him, and that left us with no outfielders. We had a pickup outfield—and Sam Jethroe had to catch when Quincy Trouppe got hurt. That really weakened our ball club defensively; we picked up a boy named Gene Benson to play center field. Artie Wilson played short, Hank Thompson played second, Buck O'Neill first. Catching, Quincy Trouppe started off, then he got his finger hurt.

We started off in Pittsburgh and went to Youngstown, played in Cleveland, Cincinnati, Chicago—just overflow crowds. We really lost a lot of money in Chicago. We had 30-some thousand there and thought we'd get ten or fifteen. They weren't expecting so many people, and Bob Feller himself had to go and try to help the ticket taker. They just rushed us. The policemen were taking up tickets and taking up money. My goodness. I don't know how much money we lost. Everywhere we went, just overflow crowds. They really poured out to see us that year. And we played some great baseball.

Hank Thompson just wore out that Bob Feller on that tour. I mean he just wore him out! He hit a home run and a double in Wichita, another home run off him somewhere else. Hit a home run in New York, because we beat Bob Feller 4–0 in New York. We had around 40,000 people, and our cut was $300 that day, each player.

Bob Feller's people made around $6,000 apiece for that trip. Ken Keltner said, "Hilton, my goodness!" I think his salary was $12,000 that year, and he cleared $6,000 for that trip.

But that was the end of it. They broke it up after that; the commissioner stopped it. Stan Musial was supposed to be on that club from the start, but that's the year St. Louis played Boston in the World Series in those little bandboxes they had for parks.

Musial got in the World Series instead of coming with us, and he must have made a little over $2,000 for winning the Series. My goodness, he raised all kind of heck about it. Some of those players said, "The heck with the World Series when we can make this kind of money here." And that was the end of it.

I guess one of my greatest thrills was pitching againt the New York Yankees in 1947—March 17—in Caracas, Venezuela. That was the first time I pitched against a whole major league ball club. And they had quite a club too, believe you me. Dr. [Bobby] Brown was about as good a hitter as I've been. Boy! He was playing third base. Rizzuto was at shortstop, Stirnweiss was playing second, first base was Tommy Henrich and Nick Etten. Outfield was Keller, big Cliff Mapes, Johnny Lindell and Yogi Berra. I think Ralph Houck was catching. Pitching they had Allie Reynolds. They had quite a ball club. I pitched six innings, didn't give up any runs and gave up one hit, to Rizzuto. We won 4–3.

So I pitched against enough major leaguers to see if I was on the level. You know, naturally if you never compete with those people, you're always in doubt in your mind whether you're good enough to play against them. But I played against them enough, and they never did hit me. So I feel that had I had a chance, I could have pitched in the big leagues.

All our source of guys being developed was through the Negro League. Yeah, they were taking them, and I don't think any of the clubs got much out of it—Doby, Irvin, Newcombe, Campanella, Ernie Banks. And they were great attractions. You could see it in '46, the first year Jackie went to Montreal. Then in '47 Negro baseball began to go back. All the people started to go Brooklynites, everybody who had never known anything about baseball. Even if we were playing here in Kansas City, everybody wanted to go over to St. Louis to see Jackie. So our league really began to go down, down, down.

It looked like it was dead, so I played in Fulda, Minnesota, in '49, and in '50 I went out to Armco-Sheffield Steel here in Kansas City. They had a ball club and they wanted me to manage it. So I said, "Well, maybe I better get on out of here." So I gave it up. I could have pitched a little more. But I'd seen so many ballplayers that just kept a-hanging around when they were over the hill, so I'd always made up my mind when I got to the place where I was going down, I'd just give it up. I'm a supervisor with Armco now. I'm lucky, I got a real good job.

A young girl asked me one day, "Did you ever play ball? I've heard my father and a lot of them talk about you. How did you get started?" and one thing and another. I told her, and she said, "Funny, there's no literature or anything. We would like to read about some of the older ballplayers, so we'd know something about them." I said, "Well, maybe eventually there will be a book or something." She said, "If you ever run across one, let us know."

It was a rough life—ride, ride, ride and ride. I remember many a day, ride a bus, get out and get you a little bit to eat, go to the ball park, go out there and pitch nine innings, play a double-header, play outfield the second game. But I enjoyed baseball, I really did. It was spoiling me. I loved it, and it was sweet. We had some great moments. I enjoyed every bit of it.

Here's the thing of it: I know we were playing better ball than some of the lower teams in the big leagues. The only difference was, they had a better bench, more people sitting on the bench. See, if we had one shortstop, we had one shortstop, and our guys just played, day in and day out. The majors had more replacements, more pitchers and reserves. Just man-for-man, we were tremendous. We'd put our ball club on the field and something's got to give; those guys could hit that ball, I don't care who was pitching. And we had pitchers could get anybody out, and could throw the ball over the plate.

I look at these eighteen- and nineteen-year-old kids today—wild, can't get the ball over to save their lives. They have good coaches who talk to 'em, tell 'em things, but one thing, I don't think they have that desire to want to play, to *want* to develop, to want to learn. They just take it for granted: "Oh, I can go out and play golf." A lot of them quit. All this opportunity they've got. But we played because we loved it. I didn't care if I never got a dime, I just loved it that well. I just used to eat and sleep baseball. And I always had a desire.

I enjoyed baseball, I really did. I tell these kids, "You wouldn't believe I made my living for thirteen or fourteen years at base-ball." They say, "You did!" I say, "Yeah, that's the only job I had. And here you all are just monkeying around here." See, I always wanted to win, and it's hard, you know—I just can't hardly take it the way these kids play ball. I always wanted to win, and I gave it my best.

I'd pick Buck Leonard as the best first baseman I ever saw. Martin Dihigo at second. Willie Wells shortstop. At third base I'd pick Kenny Keltner of Cleveland. In the outfield I'd put Sam Chapman, and Charlie Keller of the Yankees. Catcher of course is Josh Gibson. Pitching staff? I'd have to go with Lon Warneke of the Cubs. Ooh, that boy could *pitch!* And Bobby Feller, of course, and Bob Lemon, and Raymond Brown of the Homestead Grays. And yeah, oh yeah, I'd put Satchel in there too.

Hilton Smith

Hilton Smith, left, with his catchers, Frank Duncan and Joe Greene

Joe Greene at Muhlebach Field, Kansas City.

Chapter 16

JAMES "JOE" GREENE

One of the unsung stars of the "blackball" decades was James "Joe" Greene, for eight years Satchel Paige's hard-hitting catcher on the old Kansas City Monarchs.

Greene came up from Atlanta in 1936 to join the Washington Homestead Grays. "I was his roommate," Grays' first baseman Buck Leonard recalls. "He was big, strong, had a great arm. He couldn't hit a curve ball, but he could hit a fast ball four miles. So we bought him an extra-long bat, a thirty-seven-inch bat. Then he could just get a piece of that curve ball. But his hands got sore between his thumb and his first finger. Some young ballplayers, when they develop an ailment, they want to go home, they don't have that stickability. But we talked to Greene, and he stayed with us a pretty long time." Then the incomparable Josh Gibson joined the Grays as catcher, and Greene was traded to the Monarchs, which starred the one and only Paige. It was the best break of Greene's life. "We gave up on him too early," Leonard now admits. "His best years were when he was with Kansas City. He turned out to be a great ballplayer."

One of the Monarchs' star pitchers was right-hander Hilton Smith, who toiled in Satchel Paige's

shadow much as Greene was forced to play in Josh
Gibson's. "We picked Joe Greene up as catcher in
'39," Smith says, "and about the middle of the season he was really hitting that ball. In '40 he really
whipped that ball. I was telling a fellow today about
Greene when we used to play Cleveland when Sam
Jethroe was there. They told Greene, 'Well, we're
going to steal on you today. We're going to beat
you, we're going to bunt and get on, then we're
going to steal second, we're going to steal third,
we're going to bunt in runs. We gonna beat you.' I
was pitching, and only six men got on that day—I
think I gave up four hits—six of them tried to steal
and he threw out five out of six. I shut them out
6–0. They'd get on, they'd try to go down, that's as
far as they'd get. That guy could sure throw.

"In '41 that's when Greene really came into his
own, Smith continues. "That year and the next year,
'41 and '42, you can believe it or not, that guy in
my opinion was the best catcher in baseball. In '42
we played Josh's team for the world championship,
and he would woof with Josh. He'd say, "Well,
you've been talking 'bout the great Josh. I'm gonna
let you know who's the great one."* And that man
hit that ball that year. And threw out everybody.
He was a *great* catcher those two years. Then he
went into the Service and he never did come back to
his old form."

Actually Greene still had a bomb or two left in his
big bat, as he demonstrated in 1947 at the age of
thirty-five with a long home run off Bob Feller, a hit
that the Los Angeles *Times* described as "a resound-
ing homer."

Greene received me one hot summer afternoon in
1970 on the cool back porch of his frame home in
Stone Mountain, the humid Georgia town where he

---

* Greene hit .444 in the series with one homer; Josh hit .154
with no homers. The Monarchs won in four straight games.

was born and died. He greeted me in a newly starched sports shirt that showed his muscular arms, black bands of steel that he folded across his chest as we talked. He was still as lean and solid as he had been in his playing days, and he talked in a slow, deep voice, pausing frequently to search for just the right phrase to express his thoughts.

Joe Greene Speaks . . .

You've heard about the Boudreau shift. They used that on me in the colored league, and I believe some of the big leaguers saw it and did it on Ted Williams. Jim Taylor did it against me before Boudreau was even managing. They knew I was a pull hitter. If I hit the ball back through the middle, the second baseman would get the ball on the shortstop side of second base; he'd go that far to get me out. But I never thought much of it. I hit the ball too hard for them. I hit the ball right at the third baseman's foot and he couldn't touch it, one step away from him. Right by him. He didn't even have time to stoop down for it.

In Kansas City, center field was 400-something feet. Oh, my God, you've got to drive a ball almost 500 feet to get it out of center field over that wall. I hit one over the scoreboard in left-center field. I've hit lots of long home runs in Chicago's Comiskey Park way up in the stands. I hit a couple long ones in Yankee Stadium. I've popped the ball in there, reach out for a curve ball, pop it, don't hit it real good, and hit it into the left-field stands.

Josh Gibson and I were the two most powerful hitters as catchers. Josh was the toughest hitter to get out I ever saw. He was so powerful, and he was a good natural hitter. I don't think anybody exceeded him. But Satchel could get him out, Satchel never had any trouble with him. We played Josh's team, the Washington Homestead Grays, in the Negro World Series in 1942 and beat 'em in four straight games. Satchel just handcuffed Josh.

Satchel liked excitement, and created it. Satchel always wanted to be noticed, he was of these pitchers who wanted to attract the audience. Satchel would be down on a street corner with a big crowd around him talking about baseball—he's always got the conversation going—and it gets late. He calls down that he wants a police escort, and sometimes our owner would be with us and Satchel doesn't show up—and he's got to pitch the first three innings—and it's fifteen or twenty minutes to game time and Satchel hasn't showed up yet. "Where's Satchel, man?" You hear some sirens outside the park and there'd be some police on motorcycles, he'd be in a cab coming to the ball park. He did all those kind of things.

Yeah, he had a curve ball. Back in his first days, before he came to the Monarchs, they say he didn't have a curve, but when he came to the Monarchs, he'd throw a curve ball and a slider. And he had lots of pitches of his own. He had "The Four-Day Rider," "Midnight Creeper"—no, I don't know what they meant either. And his Hesitation Pitch became famous. When he went to the majors they did away with it and made him pretty mad, made him pretty mad.

I was born in 1912 right here in Stone Mountain, Georgia, just down the road a short way from where I live now. I joined the Atlanta Black Crackers in 1933 when I was twenty-one years old and stayed with them until 1935. They had fellows like Donald Reed, Red Moore Pee Eye [Pee Wee] Butts, Babe Davis, Red Hatley, James Kemp, Ping Burt and Oscar Glenn. We were in the Southern League, and I was playing first base. One night we were playing in Anniston, Alabama, and a guy by the name of Tish, who had played in the colored leagues about thirteen or fourteen years, told me, "You play all right over there on first base, you're going to make a good ballplayer. You're big, got good weight on you, but you throw like a catcher. Can you catch?"

I said, "I'm not scared to get back there, but I don't know how to catch. If you teach me how to catch, I'll catch." It didn't make any difference to me where I played as long as I played. I figured right quick if he was managing the ball club and if he was an ex-catcher, I'd have a better chance than anybody on that team of getting all the information that I wanted. So I told him, "Well, you teach me how to catch. If I don't understand something, you explain it to me." And I went up as a catcher because I always studied.

The manager of the Crackers at one time was Jones, and he was an ex-catcher. For a while Nish Williams managed the team, another catcher. He was Donn Clendenon's stepfather. Donn was a tiny little baby then, and he raised him.

When I went to the Homestead Grays in 1936, Buck Leonard and I were roommates. Buck taught me a lot. He was a great hitter too. He helped me out and I just kept going.

The toughest base runner to throw out? I don't know, I had a powerful arm. I found Sam Jethroe to be hardest. He was really fast because he'd take long steps, long steps—he could zoom! That's the truth. Jethroe had a little play he'd pull on you. If he's on first and the batter bunts the ball down the line, the third baseman's got to field the ball. If he'd catch the shortstop asleep, he'd slide into third base. He sure would do it. Yeah, he did it once or twice after he came up with the Boston Braves. Cool Papa Bell would do the same thing on you. Sure would.

I caught Jethroe several times. I went to my manager and said, "Lookee here"—they don't play it this way today, but we played to win—"suppose it's a close ball game and Jethroe is on. He's going to run, you know he's going to run. Here's my plan." When I call the first off-pitch (pitchout), the manager and everybody else sees that I've got an off-pitch. On the second pitch I do the same thing; I've got his mind on an off-pitch. Now the percentage is 95 percent he goes with two balls and no strikes because it's got to be a strike—he thinks that you won't get behind on this hitter. But the surprising thing is getting the third off-pitch. He goes and I throw him out. I got a good arm, but there's the percentage; I've got to take advantage of that too. After that you try to get the second batter. Even if you walk him, you got one man on and one out, and you stand a chance of getting a double play. That's the percentage.

I dreamed about players stealing base on me. I always believed in putting some brains in what you do. And I watched guys. The reason guys never ran bases against me is because it took me and the pitcher to get him out. Smitty [Hilton Smith] was good at it. I'd say, "If there are two outs and Jethroe is on, you know

nobody's going to hit it until he tries to steal. You know he's going
to run, you know he can't stay there. Now you forget about the
hitter, because Jethroe is your next out, not the hitter. Don't take
a big stretch. If you think he's too far away, make him get back.
You hold the ball at your chest a little longer than usual, then
step back off the mound and he's gone. You just turn around
and throw him out." Smitty could do it many times: I wouldn't
get a chance to throw him out. When you step off the mound and
turn around, he'd digging for second. You've got him out.

I built myself up as a curve ball hitter. If a pitcher's got a good
curve, he wants to rely on it as his best pitch because most hitters
can't hit the curve ball. The reason I could hit the white pitchers
was because they pitched low, and I could hit low pitches. Sometimes they'd say, "Joe Greene, you were on your knees when you
hit that." Sometime I would go almost down on my right knee.
But I'd hit it in the stands. When they tried to pitch high, I used a
36-inch bat; I had three weights in that bat. I stood back off the
plate, and I always swung fast. If I knew a pitcher would throw
high, I was ready for it. I wouldn't go up there the same way
every time. That's one thing I brand Hank Aaron for. With the
kind of wrists he's got, if he could move like Mays—Mays would
come up there all stooped down like this, or he'd come up there
standing straight up. You don't know which way he's coming up,
he's always moving, see. And he hits left-handed pitchers different
from right-handed. I've seen those pitchers get Aaron out, make
him pop that curve ball to first base. If we caught a teammate
doing these things, we'd stay on him until he'd got rid of it. Do
whatever is necessary to solve it.

We had a good bunch of fellows on the Monarchs. We had a
good team. Frank Duncan was a good manager—he was temperamental, but we all liked him. We all got along so well. We didn't
allow anything to get between us and our baseball and winning.
We liked to win. They say we had a "syndicate" there. We
admitted it too. We wanted certain guys on the ball club, and if
one man wasn't the right kind of guy, five or six of us on the ball
team had ways and means of getting him off the team. And he
knew it. The team wasn't going to join him, he's going to join the
team. He's got to weave himself into the team. We had youngsters,

we had good youngsters, but they had to have good discipline and everything else. Some guy would get a little money in his pocket, go out and stay all night. He can't play ball the next day. We could tell him the things that were coming and how he should carry himself. Today you can see an example: Mays, Aaron, Banks, Irvin, all those guys.

In 1942 we played Dizzy Dean's all-stars in Chicago, in Buffalo and in New York. We beat him in Chicago; we beat him in Buffalo too. Cecil Travis, who played third base for Washington, had gone into Service and was down in Palm Beach, Florida, and he came in on the plane to play. I beat them with a home run.

We played them in Yankee Stadium too and beat them there. I tripled. I think it was in the seventh inning. Willard Brown was hitting clean-up. Moody, who pitched for the Yankees, walked Brown to pitch to me, and I tripled and beat them 3–1.

Sure, we got a lot of white fans to our games. Our team and the Grays played in different towns in the World Series, and the white

Joe Greene

fans were coming to our games—we had our sympathizers. But the colored would stay away from white baseball. We could play in Chicago on the South Side with 30 to 35,000, and the Cubs would play on the North Side with nine to 10,000. And we could take the crowd away from the South Side if the White Sox were in. We'd have 20 to 25,000, and the White Sox would have 12 to 14,000. The same year Hank Greenberg hit fifty-eight home runs, we had 42,000 people up there in Detroit for a Negro game. But Walter Briggs, the Detroit owner, said we damaged the park and we couldn't play in it anymore.

Yes, I've had some unpleasant things happen in games. I remember the year I went up with the Grays. We were playing a game over in Pottsville, Pennsylvania, against a white team. The field was wet and the game was delayed. When we finally got the game started, some guy way back in the stands hollered, "Come on, niggers!" I looked back, and saw another white fellow had him by the collar and hit him, and he came tumbling down those steps. Later one of the white players hit the ball against the right-field fence, and when he went by, the second baseman had his back turned, and he stepped on his heel.

I said, "Well, there's nothing to do but let him get on base again and play for him if he wants to play that kind of game." So next time he came up, he hit the ball almost in the same identical place, and this time he was coming home. I got the ball way before he got there, and I moved up the line on him. He jumped in the air with those cleats in the air, and I bowled him over my head right across my back. He hit on the other side of the plate, and skinned his whole face, even his chest. Oh yeah, and he was figuring to do me in too.

But he was just a small-town player. The big leaguers didn't do anything like that. Big fellows like Dizzy Dean and all those guys wouldn't have a fellow on there that felt that way. Some fellows never played exhibition ball games against us. They felt that way, and they wouldn't play.

Yes, there was a way to speed up integration at that time. I may have played a little part in this. Fay Young was sports editor of the Chicago *Defender*, and I went down to his office. There was something that worried my mind and I had to get it off, so I said,

"Well, I'll go down there and talk to him." I told him I knew we were getting the runaround, we weren't getting a fair share or a fair chance. I told him the scheme they had. I said, "If you notice, every white team in the American or National League is scouting one or two of our ballplayers"—for example, Pittsburgh was scouting Roy Campanella and Sammy T. Hughes—"but it's nothing but a scheme." I told him the Yankees were scouting Willard Brown and me. I said, "This is something that's been going on for about three or four years." I said, "Now, I don't expect to take Bill Dickey's job"—he and I were about the same age and we were going out of baseball the same age. I said, "Brown may be a little younger then Joe DiMaggio, and both of them are center fielders, but he doesn't expect to take Joe DiMaggio's job. It's nothing but a scheme. They don't intend to sign us. They'd be afraid of a white boycott if they really signed one of us."

After I explained this to Fay Young, he said, "You know, Greene, you've probably got something there."

Well, at that time a protest wouldn't have helped, it would have slowed things down. Because we had to be intelligent enough to use the theories and the methods that the white man had used against us. We relied on the system of this country, but in a peaceful way, because we knew all the time that we had sympathizers. If it wasn't for Bob Feller, Early Wynn and Bob Lemon, the Indians probably wouldn't have signed Satchel. People came out to see Cleveland who had never been to the ball game before, especially colored people—and white too. And they couldn't have won the pennant without Paige. And those guys could see it beforehand. They said, "We need him." If there's something you want, you speak up for it. Not every player on that team spoke like that, but when the time was come, they reached down and got their share of the World Series money. That's what it meant, but some players couldn't see that far.

In 1942 I went into the Army; I was in the 92nd Division, all colored. But we were all put together with different nationalities as allies, and I found myself in company sometimes with four or five different nationalities. I was in Oran, Algiers and Italy. I was on the front line eight months and had two battle stars. I was in a 57mm antitank company.

We opened up the third front, in Italy. The 92nd Division took over between Via Reggio and Pisa, where the leaning tower is. The 370th were up near the Arno River, and we joined them just above Leghorn on the Mediterranean side.

I got some decorations and things. I was in Company B. Company L was attacking and they were going to take a pillbox. I always was a good observer, and I had my binoculars and I could see shells falling all around the pillbox on the tops of the hill. Two Germans came out with a machine gun. One had the barrel and some ammunition, the other one had the tripod. They were going to come around and get a good field of fire. They probably would have wiped out that whole company before they realized what was happening. So I called the OP [observation post]. He said, "Are you sure they're Germans?" I said, "Yes, I can tell by their hats, their uniforms. I can see 'em good." He said, "We got men right up there under them." I said, "I know it, but they can't see 'em. I can." He said, "Well, if you're sure they're Germans, you fire."

I told the guy to load, and he loaded the gun. I said, "Give me two rounds of HE [high-explosive] rapid fire." I fired two rounds and reached for my binoculars. The two Germans were pretty close together, and the first round hit right between them. Of course both of them went up in the air. By the time they came back down, the other one hit in there, and they went back in the air.

The guy said, "You get 'em?" I said, "Yeah, I got both of them. One shot was enough." Company L went on to take the mountain, and three days later when the reports came in, they said they found two dead Germans and a machine gun. Three or four weeks they called me down to headquarters. I wondered what they wanted. I went down and they gave me the combat infantry badge and wrote my mother and my wife. They knew I was overseas, but they didn't know I was in combat. I had written my wife a letter and it was raining and I folded it up like it was and sent it on to her. That's why she thought I was on the front line. I was. I stayed there eight months. That's a long time.

I went on a special mission over there. It was a church, an outpost for the Germans. There was one squad, about eight of us. We worked all night long, all night long, digging in for that gun. We had to get down low to where the shells wouldn't dig us out, you know, and get that gun up there and get it in position, 'cause once we got it up there, they could see it for God knows how far. The lieutenant and I went up there the night before, and that was the only place we could find to get a field of fire on our target. Next morning, sure enough, those shells started falling in there. We'd get in our holes, but they hit all around, busted both tires on the gun, knocked the shield off, cut a hole in it.

I had a pretty close call from a sniper—and from a shell too. I had a shell come in our hole and hit right on me, six or seven feet from me. I came up off the ground just like that from the concussion. They sent me back to the hospital, and I stayed there about three weeks.

In all, I had three guns tore up. I got another close call when we were dug in and they found out we were there. We had a tarp to keep the water off us, and I wanted to get a stick outside to hold up one corner. I went out to get the stick—I was crawling on my stomach—and brrrrt, just a line out of a burp gun right in front of my hands, about six inches in front of where my hands were stretched out. I don't know how I turned around, but they say I came sliding back in on my stomach.

We drove from Leghorn clear up to Milan, and that's way above Genoa. I had a chance to see Christopher Columbus' home. And I got a chance to see Mussolini and his girl friend. The partisans got them. They had them hanging up, but we had to take them down.

I even played against Ewell Blackwell over there in '45. We were the ETO [European Theater] champions, and he played for the MTO [Mediterranean Theater] champions, and we were playing in Nice, France. Leon Day of the Newark Eagles played for us; that's the only reason we could beat them. I hit a home run off Blackwell. I remember it so well, because the next time up I got hit.

I've been working at Sears Roebuck here in Stone Mountain ever since I quit baseball. The superintendent at Sears went to school in Kansas City. He and his wife both. He was looking for somebody who could drive a tractor there at the store. Nobody seemed to know how, so I said, "I'll go out and drive it." That Sunday morning his wife picked me up and on the way she asked me where had I worked before and I told her I hadn't worked any place, I had played baseball. She said, "You mean you played pro? What team?" I said, "Well, with about four teams, but my longest stretch was with Kansas City. She says, "Wait a minute now, that's my home. Me and Mac (that's her husband) had most of our dates looking at the Monarchs when they were in town. I know every one of the Monarchs. I know you." She did. She knew every one on the team by their names and positions. "Wait until I tell Mac this." It was a big surprise to him. He knew me too, and we went back and dug up some of those old ball games and so forth, you know.

I was just working part-time then. He came to me and asked me how did I like my job? He said, "I'm going to see if I can keep you around." And I've been there ever since. He's on the board of directors now. I see him once a year when he comes to the store.

Frank Robinson's talking about being a manager.* But they're overlooking the experience of the old players as coaches. I've played against the coaches on the Braves. Joe Sylvestri is one. All these ballplayers could help these young players, we could help 'em. And it would be good public relations, that's right. I think we deserve it. They have broken through, they have some colored scouts who can get a whole lot of colored ballplayers— and white ballplayers too. But the majors haven't done too much about coaches. If it becomes a controversy, well baseball's going to pay for it. If it reaches a point that our people stop going to ball games, baseball will pay for it. I think we ought to sit down and talk about things and iron them out and say, "Well, maybe we can do something about it." They've got white coaches, but on a lot of these teams the colored players carry the team. I think the fans would accept colored coaches, even in Mississippi.

Yeah, that's right, the colored leagues were the real major leagues. And most people don't know it. That's what would make this book very, very interesting—things that people don't know.

Most whites don't know about colored history. When I was in

* Robinson was named manager of the Cleveland Indians in 1974.

the Army in Fort Huachuca, Arizona, my officer was white. I was
reading in the Chicago *Defender* that 130,000 colored men had
been drafted, and he said, "I didn't know there were that many
in America." I said, "Well, you know it now."

Here in Atlanta a while ago they ran an article in the newspaper about how many colored millionaires there were in the
Atlanta area. It surprised many whites, because they've been
taught everything just the opposite.

Oh yeah, things have changed a lot. It takes time. I've always
lived in the South. I was raised right around this little old village
here, Stone Mountain. I was born right over there. And I try to
think about things, and I know it's as hard on white people as it is
on colored. It's something that existed before we were all born.
Today I believe it's a minority group that's pulling back and trying
to hold onto old traditions. If they could get away from all these
philosophies and just help weave this country together. All the
trouble starts from up above, guys profit off it—politicians and
people like that. North-South, North-South—everything is North-
South, North-South. I think this country would do much better if
they'd leave some of these philosophies alone. When it started, it
was a bitter thing. When this country split up, it was the South
that pulled away from the North. It seems that now the people
would be intelligent enough to get away from some of these philosophies. Because they hurt, they hurt, they really hurt.

They dedicated that Confederate memorial here at Stone
Mountain, and the man jumped on television and said, "No colored person has any business here." Now, what the heck do I care
about it? You know what I mean? If I wanted to go around there
to the dedication, I'd go. Sure, I'd go, it's none of his business,
whether he wanted me there or not.

It used to look real bad, when I thought about it, but now it
doesn't. Now it looks silly, some of the things they still do today.
That's the way it strikes me; it doesn't strike me the way they
think it strikes me, you know?

No, I don't hate anybody. Some of my people do, but all of them
don't. Most of them can understand this, because the things that
are done today, I realize come up from generations. They've been
taught these things. I see a little white child looking up at me

four years old—his parents are teaching him right there. See, he's just old enough to distinguish me and the color of my skin and his daddy's skin, and he's been told that I'm different. But there's another child don't pay me any attention because he's not taught this stuff.

There was a story in the Atlanta *Constitution* a while back about this little boy who told his mother all about his buddy and how much fun they had. So one day they ran up to her and he introduced his buddy to her. She told them, "Well, you all go on and play," and they went trotting off back to wherever they were from. That night she said, "Johnny did you know your buddy is a colored boy?" He was struck silent for a long time, then he said, "Mother, I don't know, but I tell you what I'm going to do: I'll look tomorrow when I go to school and when I come back I'll tell you."

I wouldn't waste my time teaching my child to hate. I wouldn't want him to consume up his time carrying out these things. I wouldn't want him to waste his life like that. I'd want him to live in peace. If you hate, you get all tore up. I've seen people tear themselves up, you know, and then they try to lay it on someone else because they caused it. But he's the one.

I know what segregation does from a financial standpoint. I'd be a rich man today if it wasn't for discrimination. But it isn't those guys' fault either, because all of it started before they were born. It's not their fault, it's really not their fault. It's built up so high until if you thought about doing the thing that was right, you were afraid to. You were subject to killing if you did anything different or spoke anything different. This is the first generation, I'd say, that is really trying to do something about it, to break down these philosophies, because they found out what it does to 'em. Some men still cherish those ideas, but you see children today, young men and young women coming out of the campus, and things are changing.

Like Lincoln said, "A country can't be strong and let half of its people be slaves and half free." You can't separate this country, like some people want to.

Absolutely—the fellows my age made it possible for the players today. That's right, we paved the way. A lot of people talked about how Jackie Robinson played, but he wasn't our best player.

The writers and news media didn't play this up. No, the white newspapers didn't give us much publicity, they sure didn't. They always overlooked our league. Only one time since the Braves have been in Atlanta they wrote about Hank Aaron and mentioned the Negro National League, which he came out of.

I think a benefit game for the old Negro players would be nice, because I think we made a contribution to baseball—even if some of the younger generation don't know it. I still think we did a good bit for the game.

When they inserted Red Moore and Donald Reed and me in that old-timers game in Atlanta, that was worth thousands and thousands of dollars in people going out there. I got telephone calls and cards from the people—you know, wanting to know where you're at and how you're doing and what you're doing.

We had lunch about eleven o'clock, and we were on television and radio, and then went to the ball park. We had balls autographed, picked up our uniforms and they retired Eddie Mathews' number 41 that day. We played the Braves old-timers' '57 championship team. While the Braves played, we went to dinner and looked at the ball game. After that we all met again, and that's when we really had our fun, talking, about ten or twelve of us that night. My wife really enjoyed it. She said, "I know you all out there were way over fifty years old. But you know, you looked good, you could just tell, you could just see all that baseball in you." You know, I enjoyed that.

Effa and Abe Manley, owners of the Newark Eagles

Chapter 17

MRS. EFFA MANLEY

"She was unique and effervescent and knowledge-able," says Monte Irvin of Mrs. Effa Manley, the glamour girl of black baseball in the Thirties and Forties. As co-owner of the Newark Eagles, she injected a touch of beauty and controversy into the otherwise all-male sport.

"She ran the whole business end of the team," says Irvin, who played shortstop and outfield for the Eagles. "It's too bad the other owners didn't go along with her on many of her proposals. She wanted to create a lot of innovations. She thought they had to treat the ballplayers a little better— better schedule, better travel, better salaries. And she fought about building our own ball parks The owners of the parks were independent and tough. If they saw you were doing well, they would figure out a way to take your money from you. It was tough going."

Abe Manley, the other half of the Eagles' manage-ment team, was twenty-four years older than his wife. He was born in Hertford, North Carolina, in 1876, and spent over $100,000 of his personal for-tune on the team. Much of the money was spent after the big leagues began raiding the Eagles for talent such as Don Newcombe, Monte Irvin and Larry Doby. When he finally sold, he got less than 5 percent of his investment back. But, said the

Pittsburgh *Courier*, he "spent with a smile." What did he get out of it? "I got plenty!" he once exclaimed. "I saw boys I developed enter major-league baseball. I saw Doby, Newcombe and Irvin become stars."

Mrs. Manley was active in civic work. In 1936 she took the lead in a group to save the mortgage of Edgecombe Sanitarium in New York, and she served on the Children's Day Camp Committee and the Citizens' League of Fair Play. The Citizens' League organized a boycott of Harlem stores that had refused to hire black salesclerks. She herself walked in the picket lines until the stores gave in. Wrote the Pittsburgh *Courier*: "Mrs. Manley contends that the race does not know its own strength, and when it begins to realize what really fine things the race is capable of doing, it will show rapid progress."

She was always a fighter. In 1948 when Jackie Robinson lambasted the Negro leagues and the rough life of the players in them, she replied heatedly in a magazine article that "no greater ingratitude was ever displayed." Until Robinson's Brooklyn debut began choking Negro League attendance, she said, Negro teams had an average monthly payroll of $8,000. Even afterward, the average player was still making $100 a week, "and the only reason the owners don't pay any more is that they can't afford it." In 1947, she said, the Eagles' attendance had plunged from 120,000 to 57,000. "I dropped $22,000 to keep the Eagles going. How long can any owner stand this? Compared to the small $5,000 Jackie drew last year in payment for his terrific box-office appeal, Negro League players are overpaid. Yet the papers report Jackie as haggling with Branch Rickey over an increase this year."

She rejected Robinson's charge that the black players had no contracts. "My boys have always had contracts. All owners know that the most important thing is to have a satisfied player. Otherwise you just have a man in uniform. I have had no squawks."

"The erratic scheduling," Mrs. Manley said, "is not in our hands. We do not own the parks." Her own Eagles were ousted from Newark's Ruppert Stadium to make way for the Rocky Graziano-Tony Zale fight. "Most times we have to play where we can." And rain could play further havoc with the schedule.

As for traveling, the Eagles paid $12,000 for their bus, Mrs. Manley wrote. "Many minor-league players don't get the same traveling comfort our boys get."

Hotels, she wrote, are the best the teams can provide. "Until Congress makes statutory changes about race prejudice in hotels, I'm afraid there's little we can do to better such accommodations."

I didn't discover Mrs. Manley's address until after I had left Los Angeles, so hers was the only interview that had to be conducted entirely by telephone. We had several extended transcontinental conversations, and I scribbled shorthand notes furiously while she spoke sweetly and graciously into the phone.

Eagle veterans remember her fondly. "She was a wonderful owner," said Lenny Pearson, later a successful Newark tavern owner "After I quit playing, she started me out in business. She interceded for me and spoke to people and helped me. She financed the first tavern I ever had. A beautiful, beautiful person in all ways."

Effa Manley Speaks . . .

Was I paid for Monte Irvin, Larry Doby and Don Newcombe? [Laughs.] Mr. Rickey [Branch Rickey, general manager of the Brooklyn Dodgers] didn't even answer our letters when we wrote him about Newcombe, let alone give us anything. He knew we were in no position to challenge him. The fans would never have forgiven us.

We got nothing for Newcombe, $5,000 for Monte and $15,000 for Doby. That's all.

We had others who would have developed into great stars had they been given the chance—Leon Day, Rufus Lewis, Willie Wells, Johnny Davis, Terris McDuffie, Joe Ruffin, Mule Suttles, Dick Seay. There were a dozen Newark Eagles who would have been major-league stars—not just major-league material, but stars. And the caliber of ballplayers today is not what it was when we had our Negro baseball. Dick Lundy, Oscar Charleston, Biz Mackey—they were just terrific stars.

There were so many boys. Ray Dandridge—it's a shame to pass up a fellow like him for the Hall of Fame. No question about it, an exceptional third baseman. He definitely rated right up there with Brooks Robinson. And Willie Wells, shortstop. He's the first one I feel should get consideration in the Hall of Fame. Just on the strength of Abe's evaluation, I'd put Wells on the top of the list. Abe said Wells was the greatest that ever lived, black or white. And both Wells and Dandridge were bowlegged. How they could maneuver like they did was something.

And Dick Seay—wasn't much of a hitter, but a second baseman out of this world. Lenny Pearson was a terrific first baseman. I think Lenny had a reputation for being a ladies' man; he was very, very popular with the girls. That's the only thing that kept him out of the major leagues.

That was our infield. Campanella wrote that our infield at that time was the greatest one he'd ever seen.

And Leon Day—it's a shame he was born when he was. He played every position on the field except catch, and played them all magnificently.

Those boys; my heart just aches for them that they were born too soon.

My husband and I started the Eagles in 1935. It's the darnedest thing how we met. I was born in Philadelphia in 1900. Babe Ruth made a ball fan out of me. I used to go to Yankee Stadium just to see him come to bat. I didn't know anything about the game, but little by little I caught on. My husband came from

Effa Manley

Camden, New Jersey, used to play, and he was a rabid fan. He came to New York for the World Series, and we met at the World Series. We were married in 1933, so that must have been the '32 Series. I think it was Chicago playing the Yankees, but you can look it up.

Abe had made quite a few successful investments in real estate. He just had enough money and decided there were quite a few teams barnstorming around the country—the Homestead Grays, the Pittsburgh Crawfords, Ethiopian Clowns—and Abe decided he'd like to see baseball organized. It was just a hobby. I think white major-league owners entered as a hobby too: Mr. Ruppert of the Yankees, Mr. Wrigley of the Cubs.

He named the team the Eagles—I guess he hoped they'd fly high. The first year we had the team, 1935, we played in Ebbetts Field. Mayor LaGuardia threw out the first ball on opening day. There were over 185 distinguished guests in the stands. The police commissioner had his detachment of policemen in colorful uniforms. There were four Supreme Court Justices. Every letter I sent out for this inaugural of Negro baseball in Brooklyn was answered.

And it was an awful game. We were unlucky enough to draw the Homestead Grays. I'll never forget that game. The score was

21–7. I never saw so many home runs before in my life. The mayor just had to stay for the whole game. I went home in the third inning and had my first drink of whiskey.

We drew so poorly that year that we moved the next year to Newark. We survived, but we never did draw too well. Whites? Just a few. Not enough to speak of. At that time the races just didn't mix much. So it was a losing proposition from the beginning. Fortunately Abe's money was long enough to stand it. We started doing halfway decent a couple years before Jackie Robinson went to Montreal in 1946.

Baseball really is an expensive thing to operate. The fans criticize, but especially in the case of our Negro baseball, you had the boys on the road and hotel bills. It wasn't a penny-pinching thing by any means. We paid 20 percent rent at most parks. Some of the parks were a little cheaper; I think Washington was cheaper. But that wasn't too bad, because after all, they had the stadiums all ready for us to occupy. Philadelphia played in a little neighborhood stadium, but all the rest of the teams played in big-league or minor-league parks.

In those days $500 a month wasn't a bad salary for a ballplayer, a real good player like Irvin. Money was very different then; it was equal to probably $1,000 now, or more.

The first year we had a club, I felt bad that the players didn't have a job in the winter, so I made this contact in Puerto Rico, and they agreed that if I sent the players down, they would keep them busy. I got Vic Harris of the Grays to go along with me and manage them. About half my Eagles went. On the team were thirteen men: Buck Leonard, Dick Seay, Dandridge, Sadler, a shortstop; Terris McDuffie—I think he died a couple years ago—Slim Jones. I let them have my uniforms, so they played as the Brooklyn Eagles, though some of them were from other teams. The Puerto Ricans welcomed them beautifully. I was thrilled to death. I started winter baseball for our Negro players. After that they could always find work in Puerto Rico and Cuba.

The Cincinnati Reds trained in Puerto Rico that spring, and we beat them too and won this trophy. Bacardi Rum donated it. Since I had let the players have my uniforms, they won the trophy as the Brooklyn Eagles.

Abe started right in fighting the booking agents. Abe's attitude was that baseball should have been run in a completely business-like way with the booking agents. He started an argument about promotions in Yankee Stadium. Ed Gottlieb of Philadelphia had the rights to promote the games there. Abe thought that was wrong; he thought it should be given to Sep Semler, who had the ball team in Yankee Stadium, the Black Yankees. But the fight never got anywhere. Gottlieb was able to keep the promotions.

That was one thing I did not agree on with Abe completely. I thought those other men had experience, but when I saw what his attitude was, I didn't pursue it any further. He was probably right, but I was thinking about the financial result. As a result of the fight, the Eagles couldn't get any bookings. I guess the boys told you they were idle an awful lot. We were idle half the time. We played mostly weekends, occasionally a night game in the middle of the week. We never missed a payday, but we were losing much money and Abe had to go to the bank many times. No one's happy about going to the bank every day and drawing out money, but it was his money; if he wanted to throw it away, I never complained.

Abe and I had a magnificent partnership. He got the club together and I took care of the business details. It was a perfect partnership. I never interfered in the way he ran the club, except once. Murray Watkins was a shortstop for us, and Abe wanted to trade him to Philadelphia for Pat Patterson. The word got around, and when I went to the game, the fans got all over me: "How come you're going to trade Watkins?" So I said to Abe, "Do you think you're making a mistake, Abe?" He said, "Oh, there's no comparison between the two. Patterson is sensational." So he made the trade, and the fans all liked it too.

Now I didn't like the Ethiopian Clowns. I wanted baseball to be dignified. One day when they were playing in New York, I decided to go see them, and I don't think anybody in the park laughed louder than I did. So after that I stopped complaining.

Did you ever see a picture of me in the dugout with a cap and jacket on? This boy from the New York *Post* had come over to take our pictures. I refused to pose for him. I thought it wasn't fair for me to pose. It was Abe's money and Abe's brains that got the

Eagles together. He's the one who deserves all the credit. But this boy from the *Post* just begged me. He was in tears, he said, "Oh Mrs. Manley, if I go back without a picture, I'll just be in the dog-house with my boss." So I said, "Well, what do you want me to do?" He said, "Would you put a cap and jacket on in the dug-out?" So I did, and if that picture has been in the newspaper once, I've seen it fifty times!

Were the other owners prejudiced against a woman? Oh no. In fact, Abe took me to all the meetings, of course. The first one or two meetings they felt a little bit annoyed. One day the phone rang and it was Cum Posey of the Grays apologizing for using profane words at one of the meetings. There was Posey and Sunnyman Jackson and Semler, Ed Bolden and Gottlieb, and Tom Wilson of Baltimore. Wilson was on the playboy side; he liked to have a little drink and have a little fun. Baseball wasn't that serious to him—and he was chairman of our league! Anyway, they finally opened up and were just wonderful to me. When Jackie Robinson criticized Negro ball and I sent a letter answering him, I got a letter from the other owners thanking me for the way I had answered him. So the owners ended up liking me very much.

The players? They weren't my department. All I did was pay their salaries. I didn't travel with them. Only one trip to Trenton I went along on. I would have curbed their style. They liked to sing and carry on and all, and I wouldn't have been conducive to their style.

But Abe went everywhere with them. He stayed right in the hotel with them. They always were colored hotels. In those days you didn't think too much about it, it was sort of a way of life. But they were very nice hotels.

Abe didn't go out to scout players. Usually he got tips from his friends. Monte Irvin was playing right there in the town where we played. East Orange and Newark were right next to each other, and he was the star of the East Orange high school team. So was Larry Doby the star of Paterson High School.

Monte Irvin played shortstop and outfield. There's few ball-players can do all five things—hit, field, run, throw and think. Even the great stars, many have weak arms. That was one of

Irvin's outstanding characteristics. What an arm he had! He could throw a ball from deep in the outfield straight to the catcher on a line drive. Nobody tried to take an extra base on him.

One boy Abe heard about was up in New York State, so he went up to investigate. Abe found he was on parole, he'd had some trouble. We tried to get the parole board to let us have him, but they absolutely refused. The man who had the team where he was playing didn't want to let him go, he was such a good ballplayer. So I went to the parole board in New Jersey and got them to agree to take him, and they contacted the New York board. And he was a magnificent player, and one of the nicest boys. He married a New Jersey girl and you couldn't find anybody nicer. I have a little picture of him, and I often wonder how many other boys if given the chance would turn out the same.

We had another little pitcher. The ballplayers all laughed about him, but he turned out to be a terrific pitcher—Jimmy Hill, about 5′ 5″, a sensational young pitcher. Abe had friends all through the South. He was a very well-liked man. They used to call him Honest Abe. One of his friends told him about this kid who was pitching batting practice for a white team in Lakeland, Florida. Abe went to see him and signed him. You never hear much about Jimmy. He was quite a pitcher!

Some of the boys came looking for us. I never will forget the day Don Newcombe came looking for a job. It was during the war, and I was very patriotic. We were leaving for spring training camp so short of men; Irvin and others were in Europe fighting. You know how word gets around, there was always a big crowd at the hotel when we left. Well, this man brought Newcombe, said, "Mrs. Manley, this boy wants to go to camp with the Eagles. He's a pitcher."

My first words to Newcombe were: "Well, how is it a big fine-looking boy like you isn't in the Service?"

Newcombe's first words to me were: "I've been in and out."

But we never considered him a great pitcher. It was quite a little while before he got to be a pitcher. When Rickey took him, he saw something we didn't, I guess.

The first inkling I had that Branch Rickey was interested in black players was at a press conference in New York. I received a

call from Mr. Rickey, asking me to come to a meeting. When I got
there all the black and white press was there. I was the only owner
of a black team there. Mr. Rickey announced that he was going to
start a Negro baseball league called the United States League.
This statement knocked me out. I asked him, if he was so interested in Negro baseball, why hadn't he contacted the two Negro
leagues that had been operating so long?

Mr. Rickey tried to take our parks, but he couldn't take them. I
begged the owners of the Negro leagues to try to find out what
was on his mind. I felt he was too smart to ignore. The owners
said he couldn't take the parks and they weren't concerned. Well,
they were right. He couldn't take the parks, but he did take our
ballplayers. He outmaneuvered us completely.

When Branch Rickey took Newcombe, Jackie Robinson and
Roy Campanella, the fans deserted us. That was understandable.
Some of my Newark fans used to go all the way to Baltimore to
see Robinson play in the International League.

We won the pennant in 1946. And that was the year after
Rickey had taken Newcombe from us; we didn't have Newcombe
that year. We beat the Kansas City Monarchs in the World
Series. It went the whole seven games, and we beat Satchel the
game he pitched. The boys were kind of anxious to beat Satchel.
The one who won the last game: Rufus Lewis. I think if we'd had
a chance to play the white champions that year, we'd have beaten
them too.

In 1947 my husband told me Bill Veeck's head scout at Cleveland was talking to him about Doby. Sure enough, when the
phone rang, it was Bill Veeck calling from Cleveland, and he
wanted Doby. I said, "What had you planned to give me?" He
said, "$10,000." I said, "You know very well that if he was a white
boy you'd give me $100,000." But I was in no position to bargain.
He said, "Well, I'll send you five more if he sticks." I said, "Anything you send me I'll appreciate." So he sent me $15,000.

My last words to Mr. Veeck were to make a promise never to
pay Larry less than $5,000. He made that promise. I think that's
why he put Larry right on the team. He never had to spend a
day on the farm.

But after that Negroes started going into the major leagues.

When the fans deserted us, I finally persuaded my husband to quit and sell our franchise. Several other Eastern teams quit too. The same year we quit, three other teams in our Negro National League quit. I went to the Negro American League and asked them to take in the remaining teams in our league. At the same time I got this Negro dentist, Dr. H. W. Young, to buy my team, including all the contracts, the new bus, the equipment and all the uniforms.

I had just gotten home from the meeting when I picked up a paper and saw that Branch Rickey had signed Monte Irvin for St. Paul, the Dodgers' farm. He was one of the players whose contract I had just sold to the doctor. There was a young Jewish lawyer, Jerome Kesler, who had helped finance his law school training handling publicity for the Eagles. He was now a practicing attorney, and I called him in and told him Mr. Rickey had no business taking all these people. I asked him if he would gamble with me on making an issue of it.

So he wrote to Rickey. As soon as Mr. Rickey got this letter from a lawyer, he just turned Monte Irvin loose. Wrote him a letter, said he was sorry. And did the Negro papers jump on me! They claimed I didn't have anywhere else for Irvin to work. So Kesler contacted the Yankees to take Irvin. We played in their ball park in Newark, but they weren't ready yet to take the Negro; they turned Kesler down. So we went to the Giants, and they decided to get on the bandwagon, and they paid us $5,000 for Monte. I split it with the doctor. Irvin was happy because he was right near home. The first year they brought him to the Giants, they won the pennant. I was glad to have it resolved that way. But that started the bargain basement. All the teams started grabbing the Negro players for $5,000.

So for our three men—Newcombe, Doby and Irvin—we got a total of $20,000. I thought the majors could have handled it differently. But all's well that ends well.

But Abe never felt he had been robbed of anything. He felt that by letting the boys go for such a small amount he was helping the boys, and that was enough for him. Abe died feeling he had made a great contribution to major-league baseball—and he was more interested in that than in anything else.

My husband died in 1952. Twenty years ago! I can't believe it. Where do these years go? Last month [1973] I was seventy-three years old!

When Monte was appointed to the Hall of Fame, I received this phone call from Clifford Kachline in Cooperstown about my Puerto Rico trophy. The Hall of Fame asked me if I'd send it to them. I was thrilled, because I wondered what would happen to the trophy after I die. So I shipped it to them. Air mail, express. It cost me $103.20! But now that they are at last ready to inform the public how great the Negro players were, I'm glad to cooperate, though I was unhappy about how the majors treated us before.

I've been out in Los Angeles now for fifteen years. They brought Doby by to see me. Irvin comes too. My three boys who made the majors did very well: Doby is coaching for Montreal, Monte is in the commissioner's office and Newcombe is connected with the game too.

I think the boys like us too. Abe and I were the godparents of Doby's first baby. We always did favors and tried to help when any of the boys needed us. Before Monte went to the Giants, he wanted to buy an apartment house in Orange. He was a little short of the down payment, two or three thousand dollars, I forget how much, but we were happy to lend it to him.

The thing that Abe was proudest of is the fact that most of our boys made good.

I constantly look in my scrapbook. That scrapbook is fascinating. People say, "Don't live in the past." But I guess it depends on how interesting your past is.

Chapter 18

TOM "PEE WEE" BUTTS

Those who saw Tom "Pee Wee" Butts play shortstop like to compare him to Pee Wee Reese or Phil
Rizzuto, his two contemporaries in the white majors.
"I'd compare Butts with Reese or Rizzuto or anyone
I've seen in the big leagues," says Roy Campanella,
who played with both Reese in Brooklyn and with
Butts on the old Baltimore Elite Giants. "Butts could
do everything," Roy says. "He just didn't get the
opportunity to go to the majors."

Butts is the man who made Junior Gilliam into a
big-league second baseman, the old-timers say. The
two played side by side at Baltimore, Butts at shortstop and the younger Gilliam at second. "They were
out of sight as a double-play combination," says
Lenny Pearson, who managed Baltimore in 1949, the
year they won the pennant. "Good hands, both of
them, and both of them loved the game. I always
thought Butts would make it big. He was a tremendous shortstop and a pesky hitter, sprayed the ball
everywhere. In fact, Adolph Luque in Cuba [former
Cincinnati pitching star] rated Butts even better
than Rizzuto. He had tremendous range, could go
behind second better than any man I ever saw in
my life."

"What a fielder," agrees Kansas City shortstop
Othello Renfroe. "Nothing flashy, he just made the

plays, he'd just get you at first. Everything two hands, everything cool. Down in Cuba and Puerto Rico they called him Cool Breeze."

"Gilliam went to the majors," says Monarch pitcher Hilton Smith, "but he didn't look anything like the ballplayer that Pee Wee Butts was. Butts was the type of shortstop that Jake Stephens was. In other words, he'd remind you of Phil Rizzuto. He was a good little hitter. In the majors he would probably hit around .285–275. Wouldn't hit no home runs, but he'd double on you, single and double on you all day long. And catch everything. Yeah, the majors just worked right around him. Sure did."

Gilliam joined the club in 1945, Renfroe says. "He was just a little kid they used to carry around with them. They just picked him up in Nashville and carried him around. But by the time I looked up again, he had developed into a top-notch second baseman. Butts is responsible. I don't know what kind of credit Junior Gilliam might give anybody, but Butts worked with him just like he was his own son and developed him into one of the top infielders of the Negro National League."

"It broke Butts up when Gilliam went up to the big leagues and he didn't," Pearson adds. "He wasn't too old for the majors. But he loved life, and when I say he loved life, I mean he loved life, especially women. After a game Butts had a tendency to go off on the town, while Gilliam would stay around and listen to the old-timers talk and soak up that knowledge of baseball."

When I met Butts in 1970 in his mother's Atlanta home, a neat frame house in a pleasant neighborhood, he looked as though he hadn't added an ounce of weight since his playing days. He spoke quietly, a bit nervously, in short staccato sentences and a low voice. It was our first and only meeting. Butts died in Atlanta in January 1973 at the age of fifty-three.

Tom "Pee Wee" Butts Speaks . . .

If I'd been ten years younger, I think I could have made the major leagues. My two roommates, Roy Campanella and Junior Gilliam, both went to the majors. I was glad to see them get the chance, but if the doors had opened up a little earlier, I think I'd have done pretty good. I could have been up there too.

I remember one particular night, I saw Camp leaving the hotel with his bags, so I said, "Where you going, Pooch?"—that's what I called him, Pooch. He said, "I'm going to Nashua to the Dodgers' farm." He said, "Pee Wee, come on with me." I thought he was just slipping away from the team, so I said, "No, I signed a contract with Baltimore." But he had talked to the owner and got permission to go. Camp said, "No, you can go." I said, "No, Pooch, I'm not going to go." So he left. I was twenty-seven then.

I was born in 1919, so I was nineteen when I went up to Baltimore to play with the Elite Giants in 1938. I think Campanella was sixteen. He was there the year before. He was my roomie, and he was a talker. You know, you just can't go to sleep. He'd say, "Come on, Pee Wee, let's talk about this." I'd say "Okay, go ahead," and he would talk me to sleep. He'd wake up in the morning fresh as a daisy.

I think he was a little of a "pugger" there—a fighter. We had it out one day, you know. We used to jive each other, and I think he got a little peeved off at me. I think I said something a little wrong, and I repeated it. But I wish I hadn't. He knocked me down. He was built, he was built. But I was all right. He shook my hand and said, "All over," and brushed me off.

Campanella could throw hard, but you know, he'd throw all the balls into the ground. He was quick and everything, but his arm just wasn't true. Well, I think he threw four or five balls into the dirt one day trying to get his man at second when I was a rookie.

So we had some pretty rough days. But after he got straightened out, it was all right. He had plenty of nerve, as young as he was. I think people took advantage of him when they came into home. But he would get in front of the plate and take you as you came. He wasn't a pushover, I'll tell you that.

Campanella couldn't hit that curve so good. He was a hard swinger; if he hit anything it was gone, but a curve ball he'd be off guard. If it was two feet outside, he would swing at it. George Scales, our coach, used to put two or three bats in back of him to make him stop pulling away from the curve. I think that helped him a lot.

Campanella and I were teammates on the Monterrey team in Mexico too. And it gets hot there. He was what you'd call the big gun on the team, hit the home runs. After a doubleheader, I knew he was tired, so I said, "Let's sit down and cool off." We'd sit about half an hour. He'd lose fifteen or sixteen pounds in a game. But I'll tell you where he would pick it up again—at the table. They had steaks that big—eighteen inches—and he'd eat it all.

Which was better, Campanella or Josh Gibson? Well, I've gotta be frank on this one. I really think Gibson was the better receiver, also a better hitter. But you can look at it this way: Camp was younger. And I think Camp was a little smarter than Josh was.

I was born in Atlanta, and I started playing baseball, and football too, in Washington High School here. I'm 5' 9", and I never weighed over 145 pounds, but they considered me one of the best quarterbacks in town—that's what they said anyway. That's how I got my nose broken, in a game in Nashville. I played the whole game with it. I knew it was broke, but I didn't know how bad until I looked in a mirror afterwards. I just felt disgusted when I saw it. The doctor wanted to break it again and fix it right, but I told him it hurt enough the first time I broke it, so he told me to just keeping pulling it down and straighten it out a little more. So that's why I still have a little crooked nose today.

I started playing baseball with the Atlanta Black Crackers in 1936 when I was seventeen. But the one thing I regret was, I shouldn't have quit high school.

John "Red" Moore was our first baseman, and he was one of the

Pee Wee Butts

greatest fielders I saw in a long time. He really was. I think the Atlanta (white) Crackers were thinking of getting him at one time. Another fellow was a catcher, Big Greene. He had a good arm, could throw, could get the ball to you on time so the runner wouldn't have a chance to go through his act and spike you or something like that.

You know how they'd do. They would sharpen their spikes. They used to carry files in their uniform bags. I saw those fellows sharpen their spikes, and that sort of scared me too. So I got me a file too. I said, "If they can do it, I can do it too." Gabby Kemp, at second, said he'd take all the throws, but I knew he couldn't take them all the time, because of the hit-and-run, he had to be on the ball to cover his area. So I said, "No, you better let me take it."

Let's take one night we were playing Jacksonville, and Philip Holmes—you've probably heard of him, he was one of the dirty players, I called 'em—he came into second and slid pretty hard and knocked me down. That started a rhubarb because they all wanted to protect me. I was sort of the prize star, and I was younger too. So he roughed me up that night and I couldn't sleep. Next day Gabby Kemp asked me if I wanted to play. I said, "Yeah, I won't get my money if I don't play." He said, "You can sit it out."

So I did sit it out because it did shake me up a little. But I said, "I'm not going to let him stop me like that." So next night I told

Gabby I was ready. I've been ready ever since. I went in and started playing—hard. You just have to hang in there.

I stayed with the Black Crackers for three years, and then the Baltimore team came down and played us and they gave me a tryout. I didn't want to leave home, but when the Black Crackers started to break up, I said, "Well, I guess I better." They picked up me and Red Moore. We got on the train to Baltimore that night, and that was one of the biggest thrills I ever had. Big town, big buildings—at that time Atlanta didn't have anything like that. I wanted to leave town as soon as I got there, but after I stayed there awhile I was all right. I finally stayed there and enjoyed every minute of it. Got to meet Campanella and Gilliam and everyone else. Yep, I enjoyed it all.

But the first game I played, you know what happened? Three balls in the grandstand. You know, when you first start, you get shaky. I mean I *threw* them in, I didn't *hit* them in. I only hit ten home runs in my whole career. I wasn't strong enough, I guess.

That night the manager, Felton Snow, asked me, "What's wrong?" I said, "Well, you know how it is when you first start, you're a little scared." He said, "Aw, come on, "Cool Breeze,"— that's where I got the name of Cool Breeze, right there—"don't be nervous, you can do it." He gave me a big lift there.

That's the way it had to be, so I stuck with 'em. Had a good stab at it too.

When I first got to Baltimore we were playing in Oriole Park, where the Triple-A club played. They kept that park in pretty good shape. But when they tore that park down, we had to get Bugle Field. They didn't have but two groundkeepers, so it was pretty hard to keep the grounds up. I used to go out myself and sort of look around for bad spots before I'd start playing. The ground was pretty bad, just a little too sandy, but there wasn't anybody who got his eyes put out or anything like that; I guess we were pretty lucky.

I always did like to go to Yankee Stadium, a good park, good grounds. Bad hops, you'd very seldom get one. For one thing, it looked like a hotel from the outside, it didn't look like a baseball park. Boy, the first time I saw it! You know, you want to act like you've seen things, but I sort of cut my eye up at the building and said, "What kind of park is this?" When I got inside, Snow said, "Come on, Pee Wee, this is the first time you've been in here, I'll show you around." I went out and looked at the field and said, "Snow, I thought this was a hotel!" That was another time I was a little shaky. Just seeing New York got me a little shaky. And after I got to the stadium—boy. But after all those bad fields, that was a good one. After that, every time they said New York, I was ready.

George Scales [traveling secretary] was a great teacher at Baltimore. He was a "hot boiler." Scales was a little hard on you, but if you'd listen you could learn a lot. I used to have trouble coming in on slow balls. I'd have to come up to throw. He said, "No, Pee Wee, that's not the way a good shortstop does." He drilled me hard until I finally caught on to it. He hollered, "There, now you got it." And it came to me just like that.

I got most of my hits off fast balls. If you can keep your eye on the fast ball, you'll be able to hit it. I never was a curve ball hitter, but if someone would try to sneak a fast ball, I'd get a little hit. They always said I hit high balls, they said I hit them off my cap bill. But I thought they were strikes. That's where I got my home runs. I think I only hit ten in my whole life.

You know the first home run I hit? I think it was in Altoona. Anyway, I could hardly make it around third, I was so weak in the knees. I just couldn't make it. When it went over the fence, I almost fell, I got weak in the knees. I just didn't have any idea it would be gone. But that was my worst enemy. I started swinging too hard. Scales told me: "You forget about the home run. The more you swing, the less you hit the ball. You just get on base, walk, anything. Don't you try to hit home runs." Sure enough, he stopped me right there. He cooled me on that. I choked up on my bat, cut down on my swing and started to get those hits. That's the type joker Scales was, he was watching everything.

I never could gain any weight. They thought I couldn't play every day, but I could. They were going to give me some kind of shot. My mother told me, "Well, you're not meant to be fat. Don't worry about your weight, nothing wrong with your weight." But Scales said, "Don't you run none, you might run all your weight off."

Scales could get what he needed out of you. Some of the fellows were temperamental, but they couldn't do it to him. I played against him once down in Puerto Rico, where he was managing. He didn't have too good a team, just a little old team there, but he could get everything out of them. They could run. We had the big bomb, Willard Brown of the Monarchs—*"Esse hombre"*—that means "that man" in Spanish. Every time he'd come to bat they'd say *"Esse hombre."* They just knew he was going to hit a home run. The pitchers that Scales had, they were young, a new team, and Brown was taking advantage of them. But the next year, Scales got us. They won the championship. He had made them into a team. That shows you how good he is. He can do a lot for a team.

My first year in Puerto Rico, I think I made forty-some errors. My manager, Vic Harris said, "What's the matter, you been drinking?" I said, "No, I don't know what's wrong." I think I was staying up too late. That shows you, when you don't take your rest, especially in sports, you can't do so good. After that I did pretty good.

I only played against Satchel Paige one game. He pitched four innings, and I was leading off. I used to be quite a lead-off hitter, but when they said "Satchel Paige," I kind of got a little shaky. They said he didn't have a curve, but if I'm not mistaken he threw me one on the last strike. I went up there looking for a fast ball, so I came back to the bench and said, "I thought you said Paige didn't have a curve ball." They said, "He don't." I said "Yeah? But he just threw me one." He had developed a curve ball. After the game he said to me, "They told you I didn't have a curve ball, didn't they?" I said, "Yes, Snow told me. I see you've got one now." He said, "Yeah, I was just saving it for all you young ones who come up there and think I don't have a curve ball."

But I don't think he was the toughest pitcher I faced. Dave Barnhill was. I always said he was throwing a spitball. You know, when you can't hit you've got to say something.

Joe Black. Boy, you mentioned a pretty hard thrower there. He joined us in 1943. At first he wanted to be a shortstop, but Scales said, "My land, we got too many shortstops now." Joe didn't have too good a curve, but he had a slider. He was big and strong; I think that's what kept him up so long in the big leagues. If he'd been puny and skinny, I don't think he'd have made it. I think there was something wrong with his finger, that's why he couldn't throw a curve. Scales drilled him, but he never could get that finger bent right to throw the curve ball. But that's what gave him a better slider. But a fast-ball pitcher, they're going to catch up with him sometime. You've got to have something else, a curve, to go with it. Fast balls, you get them in batting practice, you don't get them in the game. If Joe had had a curve ball, I think he'd have lasted a couple more years in the big leagues.

Junior Gilliam joined us in 1945. He had everything. He could think quick. Gilliam was a quiet guy, but when he got on the field he had more pep than you'd think he had. He could make a team go. We were roomies too, and he was another little talker. We'd talk about baseball for about an hour, then I'd roll over and go to sleep. He was really a baseball nut. I had to watch him, keep my eye on him, because he was a little younger than I was, and the fellows told me to keep my eye on him, don't let him go running around. I'm fifty-one now, so I guess I've got about fifteen years on him.

Just like me, Gilliam didn't want to stay in Baltimore when he first came up. I think he got a little lonely, had a little girl back home. We told him, "You can get that later."

George Scales is the guy who taught Gilliam what he knew. Gilliam was a right-handed batter, but Scales turned him over to be a switch hitter. That's how Gilliam evened up his hits. I really think he was a better left-handed batter than he was right. Right-handed he was stronger, but he wouldn't get as many hits. When Scales switched him over, that's when he started hitting.

They said he had a weak arm, but he really could get rid of the ball and make those double plays. He wouldn't stumble over the bag. Sometimes I'd say he wouldn't even touch it. He really liked third, but George Scales said, "No, you'd make a better second baseman." And I think he did. Snow was the manager and he was a third baseman. Sammy T. Hughes was on second—he'd gotten a little older, slowed up, so they tried Gilliam on second. It really helped me too. We got to be pretty good together. I think

Gilliam was better than Hughes. Sam was tall, and a taller man playing with a short one don't go together. Hughes would throw a little high to you, but Gilliam would keep it down. That's the way you make double plays. We got to know each other pretty well, and that made it a lot better. They called us the $4,000 combination.

I see Junior most every time he comes through Atlanta with the Dodgers. When I see him at the game, I wave my hand at him: "Hi, Junior." Last year the last game he played here he said, "I think I'll be coming down to see you this winter." I said, "Do that." Because he's one of my best friends.

Baseball's a good game, I like to play it, I like to see it. Especially Hank Aaron. He's one of my prize players. You know he was in our league too. He was a shortstop. The first time I played him, he hit one between third and short. I came to find out Aaron was a dead pull hitter. Finally the third baseman would get close to the bag and I would get even closer to third—the only way we could round him up.

First time I played Willie Mays, he was in Birmingham. One of our players hit the ball back to the fence, he went back and caught it. Threw it all the way back to home plate. That's the first time I knew he had an arm. Everybody started hooray-ing about that arm. When he was in the big leagues and we had a day off, we used to go where he was playing and cheer for him.

Monte Irvin of Newark was an all-round athlete, he could play most anything. Until he got to the big leagues, he was sort of a spray hitter; where the ball was pitched, that's the way it would go. I think after they got him in the big league they had him pull it a little more. I think he hit more home runs.

Baltimore won the pennant in 1949. After that the club fell apart money-wise, so a fellow from Nashville bought the team.

Gilliam went up to Springfield, Massachusetts, for a tryout in the minor leagues. Next morning I looked up and saw Gilliam and I said, "I thought you went to Springfield." He said, "I did. We went up there, but nothing happened."

I sure was glad for Gilliam when he finally did make it. I was glad. But I hated to see him go. We had to get another second baseman and start in all over again. I don't think Gilliam wanted to leave, himself. I had to coax him, "Get up there, Gilliam, you gotta go. You'll be making more money and everything." We used to lay in bed talking about that. He was wishing he could go, but after he got the chance he didn't want to go. I pushed him on. I said, "You better go." George Scales said, "Here's your chance, you better go. Here's your chance to make money." That was the main thing.

Well, I wish they'd started ten years sooner, I think I could have been there too. The only thing, I'd have to prove I could hit the curve ball, but I think I could have done that too.

After Gilliam left, I just sort of vanished away. I went to Canada, played there about a year. Willie Wells was my manager, and we won the pennant. But I didn't want to go back, it was too cold up there. Judy Johnson, the old-time third baseman—he's a scout for the Phillies—asked me if I wanted to try Class A baseball. I told him I did, so I went to Lincoln, Nebraska. And that's when I found out I was slipping, sure enough. You know, when you start missing balls that far—three inches—its time you were thinking about hanging it up. Lincoln wanted to send me down to Class B baseball. I said, "Whoops, this is all, right here." I said, "I'm gonna rack it up." I didn't think it would be fair to some other youngster coming up if I went back just because my name was Butts. My job was all finished. But for one year I didn't do anything. I just moped around.

I was up to New York a few years ago to see Campanella. That auto accident he had in 1957, that was a hurt moment for me. Sure was. It shook up a lot of people. My mother and I talked about it. It could have happened to anybody, but why Pooch? Just coming into his years in baseball, a man who was happy about his job. When I saw him in New York, I said, "You look real fat, rolling in that chair." He said, "Well, Pee Wee, I'm going to get as fat as I can." He didn't have the smile he used to have, I could tell that right off the bat. We talked for a while, and I kept looking at his neck. You could tell it just wasn't right, you know, but you hate to stare at a person.

By that time Harry Williams, who was running Camp's liquor store, came by. He used to play ball too, he was one of the good second basemen with the Black Yankees. I told Harry I didn't want to talk about the accident, but he said, "Yeah, go ahead and talk about it, he wants you to talk about it."

Camp had a little place in the back where he could go and have his beer, so we went back there, and sure enough, he told me all about how it happened. He said, "Well, Pee Wee, I guess I'll be in this wheelchair the rest of my life." And that was another hurt part. I could feel the wetness in my eyes. I said, "Aw, Pooch, you'll walk again." He said, "No, Pee Wee, I don't think I will."

The Atlanta old-timers game in 1969, that was a big thrill. One of the best thrills that I had, meeting the players, talking to them. It was a good feeling. I was shaking hands with great ballplayers. Johnny Logan and I played in Puerto Rico together, he was there, and we talked about most everything. Logan said, "It looks like you're in shape now." I said, "Yeah, I'm in shape, but I can't do anything now." We had lots of fun.

Those really were the good old days, huh? You know, I'd like to do it all over again.

Chapter 19

OTHELLO RENFROE

Othello "Chico" Renfroe loves to talk. Old-timers laugh at the photo of him, Satchel Paige, and other veterans found on p. 343. "You *know* he's going to be in front," says Buck Leonard. Even Paige had to concede him the first row.

Renfroe was also a scrapper. "He could fight left-handed, right-handed, uppercut, kick," says Monarch catcher Sammy Haynes. "If there was a fight, it would be either Renfroe fighting or two girls fighting about him."

In 1971 Renfroe met me in his suburban split-level Atlanta home, got out his scrap books, propped his feet on the coffee table, and summed up his impressions of a chapter of American history that will never return.

Othello Renfroe Speaks . . .

Baseball lost something when Jackie Robinson went into organized ball. Something died then—the Negro leagues. There was always so much *color* in the Negro League games. Now they would call it showboating, but I thought Negro baseball was so *colorful.*

Oh we've had some great guys. The owner of the New York Black Yankees, Sep Semler. It would be nothing to see Semler when the game gets close—you'd be playing on percentage 60–40, winner gets 60—and the man would be sliding home with the winning run, and Semler would be out there at home plate sliding with him. I mean we had some color! In these days people call them showboats and clowns, but there was always so much color in the game.

At first base it was just indescribable how Showboat Thomas could field. Or this guy Red Moore. Those guys could play first base. You know, people used to come into the ball park early to see colored teams take infield practice. They took a real lot of pride in throwing that ball around. On that double play, you know, Artie Wilson of Birmingham and Piper Davis could just make that double play look unreal. And a good fungo hitter like Winfield Welsh of the Black Barons or Frank Duncan of Kansas City could hit that sharp ground ball—oh, it was just like a show within itself. A little showboating as they call it now, but it was colorful. I enjoyed it just as much as the fans. We had some ballplayers, a lot of class about them. We used to call them "shadow men," you know, looking down at their shadow and all.

Take Satchel Paige. He was the most comical man you ever saw in your life. When we were warming up, he'd take infield practice at third. Just *throw* it over that diamond, man, *flip* it to second. Oh, what an attraction, what a colorful man!

In Washington, D.C., people packed Griffith Stadium to see Satchel. He never traveled by bus, he traveled by his own car. One night we were waiting for Satchel to come and start a game, and he had gotten into an altercation with a traffic policeman because of speeding or running a red light or something. He got there late with a police escort and siren and everything! Satchel liked the fast life. He always had fast cars, Lincoln Continentals, tailor-made suits and plenty of women. But he married this girl in Kansas City and started raising a family, and he settled down. There's not a Negro baseball player will say anything against Satchel, because he kept our league going. Anytime a team got in trouble, it sent for Satchel to pitch. So you're talking about your bread and butter when you talk about Satchel.

Goose Tatum was a showman all the way too. Played first base for the Indianapolis Clowns.° Tatum was a fair player, not major-league timber but he got the job done. Tremendous fielder around first base. Long, long arms hanging down to his knees. You ought to see him catch a baseball with that great big first-base pad and flip it up and fling the ball home. People just went crazy over him. They loved him.

The Clowns had an act, Goose Tatum and King Tut. He's dead

° And later played basketball with the Harlem Globetrotters.

now. They'd go through a tooth-pulling act where Goose was the dentist and Tut was the patient. Tut would fill his mouth up with corn, and Goose kept pulling his teeth and pulling his teeth and it never seemed to do any good. So he'd go get a firecracker and light it, and as soon as the firecracker would go off, King Tut would jump up and go hollering and spitting out all the corn, like all his teeth were coming out.

When you played ball against them and they did the same thing every night, they still kept you in stitches laughing every night. They were a show within themselves, plus they had a good ball team. Hank Aaron, I guess, was their best ballplayer. They paid the salary for the league, because any team able to barnstorm with the Clowns made money. They packed them in—small towns or large towns, they packed them in.

I always was a nut for baseball. I was born in Jacksonville, Florida, in 1923. Did anybody ever tell you about the great colored team in Jacksonville, called the Jacksonville Redcaps? Well, let me tell you just how great they were. These big-league teams would come to Jacksonville to train—Elite Giants and New York Cubans, Chicago American Giants and Newark Eagles—and they would play this team made up of redcaps. The guy that owned the team gave them jobs working at Terminal Station as redcaps.

At shortstop they had Philip Holmes, who's here in Atlanta now scouting for the Braves; second base a guy named Skindown Robinson; a great first baseman who's dead now named Mint Jones—oh, he could stretch, he was beautiful. And they had a pitcher by the name of Preacher Henry. Preacher Henry had the premier drop ball. And they could win ball games. You had a lot of 1–0 games in those days because the ball wasn't alive. And gosh, Preacher Henry shut out many a team down there. Preacher Henry, what a great one.

This was during the Thirties, anywhere from 1935–36 up until around World War II. They went up and took the franchise in Cleveland one year and played under the name Cleveland Buckeyes. They had a tragic automobile accident: parked on the side of the road fixing a flat tire and two of the players were killed— Buster Brown a catcher and Smoky Owens a pitcher—and that just about ended the team.

In 1936 when I was thirteen, the great colored teams came down to Jacksonville to train—the Newark Eagles, the New York Cubans, the Elite Giants, the Chicago American Giants. I was bat boy for all of them. After going to high school and being a bat boy for all those guys, I tell you what I did: I ran away from home in '38 to be bat boy for the Chicago American Giants. I was fifteen. My mother had remarried, I had a stepfather, so I used that as an excuse. She said, "Well, you've got to be a man someday. When you need me, call me."

When we got to Nashville, the manager, Candy Jim Taylor, said this was about as far as he could carry me, because the owners of the team were getting on him for spending too much money. One guy was particularly kind to me. I talked to Alex Radcliff, Double Duty's brother, and told him that I was going to hitch-hike, do anything, to get to Chicago. He told me when I got there to go to see an old-timer named Bingo DeMoss. So I hoboed my way, and when the team got there, I was already there ahead of them. Bingo DeMoss took me in just like his own son all during the baseball season. His son had gotten killed riding on the back of a truck. You know how Chicago is, he used to run with a gang. Well, DeMoss kind of took me as his boy. I also worked for Louie the groundkeeper—the old-timers will remember him—a big black old fellow, lazy, just drug around. He also took care of me just like I was his own boy.

I lived with DeMoss, and I bet he kept me up until two or three o'clock in the morning talking baseball. He'd talk to me about a great center fielder, Jelly Gardner. He'd tell me stories about the great pitcher Smoky Joe Williams, and of course Dizzy Dismukes. Cristobel Torrienti—aha, some of the tales they tell on that guy. He must have been something! They say Torrienti hit the ball farther than anybody.

And DeMoss was always talking about the great Indianapolis ABC team which was managed by C. I. Taylor. And the great Kansas City Monarch team—the old Monarch team of 1922–23 —Bullet Rogan, José Mendez, John Donaldson, Frank Duncan, Dobey Moore.

The Monarchs had another great team in '38. Buck O'Neil played first; they had a great second baseman by the name of

Barney Serrell who's in Mexico now; shortstop was Jewbaby Johnson, a kid out of Little Rock; Duncan catching. And here's another
great one: Willard "Home Run" Brown. Another outfielder was
Ted Strong, a basketball player, one of the original Globetrotters.
And Hilton Smith—what a pitcher, one of the great ones.

Well, when the season was over, I hitchhiked back down South,
and my folks took me back in just like nothing had happened.
But as I say, I always was a nut for baseball. And it paid off,
because I played ten years of professional baseball—all the islands,
Venezuela, Puerto Rico, Mexico.

I played a little football in high school—that's where I got my
nickname "Gangster," because I was a pretty hard player. I grad-
uated from high school in 1942, went to Carr College for a year,
and then I went to Honolulu and worked at Pearl Harbor. I got a
chance to play there, and it gave me a few indications that I
had a chance to stay in baseball. I decided to go out and play a
little professional baseball myself, went out to Los Angeles and
Texas and ended up with the Kansas City Monarchs in '45. Of
course this was a wartime team, but we did have Jackie Robinson.

He had a different baseball background from most of us in the
Negro American League, because he had played under white
coaches. He never was the shortstop that Pee Eye Butts was or
Willie Wells. But he had the fundamentals, made all the plays

Othello Renfroe, left, at reunion of old ballplayers

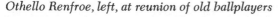

and a terrific base runner. He ran the catchers crazy in our league. Ran 'em crazy.

Our salaries ranged from $250 a month to 500. I don't think we had anybody making much more than $500 on our ball club. I know Jackie Robinson raised Sam about his salary. Boy, you talk about a negotiator, it was that Robinson. I tell you, he'd give our general manager, Dizzy Dismukes, gray hairs.

I can recall as if it was yesterday the night Jackie Robinson was picked out for organized baseball—the night *he* knew he was picked out. We were playing in Chicago and Jackie had a bad shoulder, couldn't play short. He talked them into playing first base. He told us before the game that scouts were there watching us and for everybody to hustle. But Jackie always talked organized baseball, so we didn't pay him any attention. I think he had had a shot with the Chicago White Sox back when he was in college—he and a pitcher named Nate Moreland out on the West Coast. And in '45 the Red Sox called him, Marvin Williams and Sam Jethroe up to Boston for a tryout, but they didn't keep any of them. So anyway, Jackie told us to hustle and we all laughed. We always laughed at him because he was so *serious*, you know.

So the game was over and we got ready to leave for Kansas City and we waited on Jackie for an hour. Dismukes decided he wouldn't wait on Jackie, and we took off. Next day Jackie showed up at the ball park for practice. Dismukes wanted to fine Jackie for missing the bus. Jackie was a terrific curser, the guy could curse. Jackie told them they could have the ball team. He left and went back to California.

We went to the West Coast that winter to play with Satchel Paige, and Jackie played a couple games with us. They signed him that winter of 1945.

We never had any doubt about Jackie's ability, but we wondered whether or not he could take the stuff that he took in the majors. We never thought he could take it. We have pulled up in service stations in Mississippi where drinking fountains said Black and White, and a couple of times we had to leave without our change he'd get so mad.

He had intelligence, but if Mr. Rickey had known about Jackie's temperament, I don't think he would have signed him. A highly intelligent guy, didn't drink, didn't smoke, didn't run after any women, very much in love with the girl he's married to now, Rachel. He didn't like ballplayers carousing at night—not Jackie. He liked to play pinochle, a little cards, but no night life.

They picked him for his intelligence. But we had a lot of ballplayers we thought were better ballplayers. Jackie had only played in our league one year. Willard Brown, who played for us, could hit the ball and outrun anybody in any league. But he'd only play hard on Sunday; he'd loaf the rest of the time.

We always thought that Ted Strong was about the most ideal ballplayer. Had all the tools. A switch hitter and could play just about anywhere. Anywhere you put Ted, Ted was at home—first base, shortstop, outfield. From outfield he could really throw; you couldn't take a turn from first to third on him. He wound up in the Texas League as Brown did. Getting old, fat, out of shape, but he was up around the home run leaders in the Texas League.

Hank Thompson of the Monarchs was another one who was a real fine ballplayer, but Hank always had trouble drinking, plus he was mean as hell, a mean, mean guy. Kept some kind of weapon on him all the time. Thompson and Brown both left us in '47 to go to the St. Louis Browns. They were among the first Negroes in the American League.

They could tell some tall tales about ballplayers they picked up in these little country towns who would come out and pitch with football shoes on or tennis shoes, and they could throw a ball so hard. The Kansas City Monarchs were very good at that, picking up guys in little small towns in Texas and Arkansas and taking them to town and buying them clothes—you know, guys who didn't even know what a suit of clothes was. But I tell you, those guys could step out of those clubhouses Sunday sharp as a tack, good dressers, good-timers, no curfew. If you had a guy on the team who drank, he drank.

We got $2 a day to eat on, and we had some guys so stingy they'd save some of the eating money. When we traveled through the South, a lot of places we couldn't get a decent meal. We ate out of grocery stores, sardines and cheese and cinnamon buns. A lot of towns we went in we couldn't shower in the dressing room, but it didn't matter. When we hit the field, we played ball. I mean we had some heated ball games.

We had a good, tough league, man. Any ballplayer who left

the Negro leagues went either directly to the majors or to Triple-A. Of course, Branch Rickey had the audacity to send Campanella and Newcombe to Nashua. You know, that was a joke.

The Washington Homestead Grays had a great team. The best hitter I ever saw was on that club—Buck Leonard. Yes, he was better than Josh Gibson, average-wise. I always get an argument on that, because a lot of people think Josh was a better hitter.

The longest home run I ever saw Josh Gibson hit was in Shibe Park. He hit it over everything. Didn't even bounce. Left-center. Over the roof—clear over.

In the outfield Cool Papa Bell. What a gentleman. What a lead-off man. Oh this guy, he went to the West Coast to play with me and Satchel in 1947, and the people out there just fell in love with him. Very neat dresser, quiet, a fine fellow. He slapped the ball when he hit it, slapped it and could outrun it. Run? You're telling me. I saw him score from first on a sacrifice against the big leaguers. Yeah, let me tell you about that. They got him in a chase. How did that thing happen? Anyway, when they got finished throwing at him, he ended up scoring. That was in California. I was on that ball club. That had to be 1947 or '48. I was there.

Jud Wilson played third for the Grays. Ooh, he'd fight you too. Jud was an old man too, he was bald-headed, built like a wrestler.

I tell you, just about everybody would fight. Very seldom you played a ball game—a really close ball game, two teams fighting for a pennant or for second place or something—you didn't have a fight. The game was just that heated. The manager didn't want you out there if you didn't have some fight in you. You'd fight your own teammates if they were loafing.

In Baltimore, Roy Campanella was fifteen in 1938—great big —biggest fifteen-year-old boy I ever saw in my life. But at fifteen he could throw that ball to second base! They talk about Bench throwing now. You should talk to Pee Eye Butts. When Butts and those guys would take infield practice, they'd get mad at Campanella for throwing the ball so hard. And he was strong. He struck out a lot in his younger days. The old-timers were tough. I mean, they weren't college boys and they weren't too stuck on youngsters going out and taking their jobs. But everybody took Campanella as if he was their own son when he first came up. He was always a likeable guy.

Barney Serrell of Kansas City or Piper Davis of Birmingham, I guess those were the premier second basemen. Davis could make all the plays, he was tall, *smooth*. Oh yeah, better than Gilliam. Gilliam didn't blossom until later, and he didn't play in our league long.

Shortstop's where you get your biggest argument—Wells or Butts. Also Sam Bankhead and a guy from Cuba—Garcia. Wells could hit. Butts was a .275–.280 hitter, a tremendous ballplayer. He was good—I think better than Reese, but I wouldn't say better than Rizzuto. The year I barnstormed against Rizzuto, the plays he made, I'd just have to put him in a class by himself.

We played the 1946 Series against the Newark Eagles. Went seven games. Let me give you a little idea about the World Series. First game: We got 30,000 people in the Polo Grounds and beat Newark 3–1. A guy named Hamilton beat me out at shortstop, a tall guy. I'm on the bench. On a double play Bob Henrey, the big right fielder for the Eagles, slid into second to break up a double play and broke Hamilton's leg almost in two. So I got an opportunity to play. And of all the hitters in the '46 World Series, I outhit everybody including Larry Doby and Monte Irvin.

Next game, Kansas City, then back to Newark, and we split those two ball games. And we came to the seventh and deciding game, Hilton Smith against Rufus Lewis. Lewis gave up three hits and they beat us 3–2. That ball park in Newark was nothing but a bandbox; oh man, for a guy to pitch a three-hitter in that old Newark ball park was really something. Pat Patterson at third for Newark had to go back to his high-school coaching job in Texas and a little boy took over and helped beat us—Half a Pint Israel, that was his name. Lives in Bowie, Maryland.

I made the mistake in '46, when I had my best year, of accepting a job in the off-season as a bartender in Kansas City. I started drinking that beer, and when I went to spring training next season, I was roly-poly.

In '47 the Monarchs picked up this shortstop in Davenport, Iowa. A young kid came out to take infield practice along with me. I saw greatness in this guy, and I was slowing up. This kid was Gene

Baker, who went on to the Chicago Cubs. I was slowing down, and the next year I was traded to the Cleveland Buckeyes. But not before I had the pleasure and privilege of catching Satchel. Even after I got fat, I always could throw, and I was a pretty good hitter. So the manager said, "Well, look, you just can't move anymore, so we'll put you behind the plate."

The amazing thing about Satchel was his control. Satchel would warm up before a ball game and put down a little piece of paper and throw over that paper. Then he'd have two guys stand up and put their bats down and throw between the bats on each side of the plate. We'd go out on the West Coast every fall to play and he packed them in.

In 1945 Satchel had taken a team to the West Coast and toured with Bob Feller. Bob Feller and Satchel always got along good. Bob was an ideal businessman. He knew how to make the money.

I tell you what, I'll be honest with you: The colored barnstorming teams I have been on played against the cream of the crop of the big leaguers—and we weren't the best of our league. The team Satchel Paige was supposed to get together in 1946, a lot of them left and went to Puerto Rico. If he had put that team together, Bob Feller and them would have caught hell. In fact, I never would have been able to go. They got me after a few of the others wiped out.

In 1946 I tell you who we played against. Bob Feller had at third base Kenny Keltner, shortstop Phil Rizzuto, second base Johnny Berardino, first base Mickey Vernon who won the batting championship, catching Frank Hayes and Rollie Hemsley. Outfield was King Kong Keller, Sam Chapman and Jeff Heath. Pitchers Spud Chandler, Gordon Maltzberger of the Chicago White Sox, Ed Lopat, knuckleballer Dutch Leonard and Feller. I guess we made between $5,000 and $6,000. Our cut was better than the Red Sox and Cardinals. That's why the commissioner after that year wouldn't let you barnstorm until the World Series was over. We had a plane and Feller had a plane. We played about eleven games; I believe they won six, we won five.

We beat them in Yankee Stadium. Let me tell you a story about that game. We were running short on pitchers, so when we got to Yankee Stadium we had an old left-hander, Neck Stanley, a spitballer. When he'd take the ball up to his mouth he'd also cut it, make it do tricks. I was in the bull pen warming Stanley up. After Satchel pitched his three innings, Stanley came in to pitch the other six. He struck out, oh I guess five or six with that cut ball, and he made Feller's team look so bad that we were going to play that night in Baltimore, and when we got ready to fly over to Baltimore, Feller said, "Not with that guy." Wouldn't let him go any farther. I mean Stanley humiliated them in Yankee Stadium!

But Bob Feller, what a curve ball this guy had, besides a motion. Oh, man, he'd blind you. He'd take that left foot and raise it up and twist that body around and man when he'd throw that ball —can you imagine him having that delivery when he first came up and he was *wild*? That's a great gentleman, though, a great ballplayer.

How did I hit against Feller? Not too well, not too well. Two other guys I never could get a hit off of—one guy in Mexico threw nothing but fast balls with a little slider and kept the ball down all the time and I bet I grounded out twenty times without getting a hit. His name was Ramon Bragana. And Dutch Leonard—if anybody else had a knuckle ball in comparison with Dutch Leonard, I'd like to see it. I broke bats—he broke bats off in my hand and everything.

October 1947, here's a clipping: Satchel pitched against players like Ferris Fain, Kenny Keltner, Andy Pafko, Ralph Kiner, Jeff Heath, Bob Feller. That's a good lineup. Then Ewell Blackwell brought in a team. Remember Bob Dillinger, Peanuts Lowrey, Johnny Lindell, Al Zarilla and Johnny Berardino (who's a movie and television star now)? And we beat them 4–3. I played third in that ball game. Let's see, I got one hit against Blackwell. And Satchel beat the major leaguers again in Los Angeles, 5–1: Pete Coscarart, Max West, and 6,000 fans.

We also made big money in Latin America. We monopolized the leagues down there until organized ball came along. They'd pay a guy $1,000 a month, all expenses, no income tax. A guy could go down there and save $3–4,000. Plus every home run was a gift. Oh man, before Castro you couldn't beat Cuban baseball, couldn't beat it. That was the best, the strongest league you ever want to see.

I was in Mexico from '50 to '51. Martin Dihigo was manager of Vera Cruz then.

I was Peck's bad boy in Mexico. I played like Eddie Stanky, sliding hard, breaking up double plays, fighting umpires. That's the only way you could exist. You had to fight. Especially in the Latin American countries. If you went down there and they found out you were a coward, that was all.

While Jorge Pasquel was in Africa, an umpire and I had a few words on a close call at first base and I slugged him. The President of the league suspended me, and the Immigration Department deported me. They kept me there all day, and when nighttime came they put me in a car and rode and rode and rode. I said, "Oh, oh, I guess this is it." But they put me on a plane to San Antonio, Texas. But I returned, and the umpires said they didn't want to umpire if I played. And this is what the *Sporting News* wrote: "Pasquel Back in Mexico, Unlimbers Six-shooter." He fired the umpires. Then he called on high government officials and had the deportation order revoked. When the umpires refused to work, he fired them all.

My last year in baseball, 1951, I was playing in Minot, North Dakota, and I got a letter from Campanella asking me if I wanted to go barnstorming with him: "Would you like to go and help me catch?" "Gosh," I said, "would I!" He had me come up to New York and we barnstormed against a major-league team. I was the only minor leaguer on the team. His team consisted of Bob Boyd on first, Junior Gilliam at second, I believe Larry Doby played third. Outfield was Bill Bruton. Joe Black and Don Newcombe pitched. We played all the big parks, made tremendous money. But this is when Campanella proved that he was a champ. He got $1,000 a man guarantee to go to Honolulu to play three games against an all-star team that had Nellie Fox at second, Harvey Kuenn at short and Enos Slaughter in right. He said, "I'm going to take this guy with me, and he's going to get the same cut we get." He made everybody on the team take enough money out of their cut to make me make the same. Yeah, Campanella's a great guy, great guy. You can't imagine how great he is, how much he's respected among ballplayers. His going to the major leagues never changed his attitude.

After that I left baseball and came here to Atlanta and went into the postal service. Now I'm a sportscaster, sports director of WIGO, Atlanta. They call me "Chico Enriquo on Sports."

And let me tell you this about the Atlanta Braves, the most wonderful thing. The Atlanta Braves are one of the only teams in the major leagues that have had old-timers' games and let the players from the Negro leagues play.

Dick Young of the New York *Daily News* called me the other day [1970], said there was a plan to get all of us to go to New York to pick a black player for the Hall of Fame. He said they might pick two, but that would be the limit. There would be too much squawking if there were more than that. But there's no way in the world you can leave out Martin Dihigo, Pop Lloyd, Oscar Charleston, José Mendez, Josh, Satchel, Buck Leonard and all that crowd.

I have six sons now, two boys in college—one boy pitching and one boy catching at Florida A&M—and I've got two in high school playing. I'm real proud of them all, don't give me any disciplinary problems. Baseball has really been good to me. I've got no squawks. I can really say baseball's the great American game, although it did discriminate against us for many years.

But when Robinson went into organized baseball it took something away from Negro baseball. It died with Robinson. Let me tell you, we played the World Series in '46 against the Newark Eagles and we just had tremendous crowds everywhere we went. Washington, D.C., whenever the Monarchs went in to play the Homestead Grays, Satchel pitching and Josh Gibson catching, just fantastic crowds.

The promoters made the money. But we made enough money to buy nice clothes and live good during the baseball season. We all had to go to work during the off-season, but we always looked forward to playing. Everything was major league. Oh, we traveled in buses, had to ride 400–500 miles, get out and play ball. But the Sunday doubleheaders were always something. We were always in a big park on Sundays—New York, Chicago, some big town in the South on Sundays. The East-West game we played in Chicago always had anywhere from 30,000 to 50,000. And everybody looked forward to it.

We had thrills, we had everything. It was the greatest experience of my life.

Sunset Before Dawn

BY DAVID MALARCHER

Thou wert among the best
   Who wrought upon this earth,
O dead! Thine *endless* rest
   Is merit of thy worth. . . .

O, minds of fleetful thought!
   O dead who lived too soon!
What pity thou wert brought
   To twilight ere the noon!

But sleep thou on in peace,
   As orchids which did bloom,
Like pure unspotted fleece
   Within the forest's gloom.

APPENDIX

Lifetime Statistics

I want to thank Dick Clark, Paul Doherty, Jorge Figueredo, Merl Kleinknecht, and Jim Riley for their special help in compiling the statistics.

The following persons also contributed to the immense task:

Luis Alvelo, Terry Baxter, Dick Cramer, Debbie Crawford, Bob Gill, Bob Hoie, Jim Holway, John Holway Jr, Tim Joyce, Neil Lanctot, Larry Lester, Jerry Malloy, Joe McGillen, Joe Overfield, Bill Plott, Mona Peach, Mark Presswood, Rob Ruck, Mike Sampson, Arthur Schott, Michael Stahl, A. D. Suehsdorf, Gerald Vaughn, Diane Walker, Edie Williams, and Charles Zarelli.

Appendix

BIG BILL DRAKE
(PLUNK)

b 6/8/95 Sedalia MO, d 10/30/77 St Louis, BL   TR   6'   210

		g	w	l	ip	r	tra	h	so	bb	sv
1914 Tennessee Rats											
1915 Brinswade SD		semipro									
1919 STL Giants		-	0	1							
1920	STL Stars	27	9	16	163	60	3.32	102	45	27	0
1921	s	36	22*	11	251	114	3.22	236	132*	74	0
1922	STL,KC	11	6	5	56	32	5.16	42	14	17	0
1923	KC Monarchs	31	17	9	137	65	4.27	96	30	34	
1924		19	12	10	125	42	2.52*	-	-	-	0
1925		-	10	3	73	62	4.92	96	49	-	0
1926 IND ABCs		-	7	6	86	55	6.40	55	20	20	0
1927	DET Stars	-	11	8	136	85	5.62	141	39	46	0
1928-9 Did not play											
1930 SL		1	1	0	8	3	3.25	12	2	3	0
		-	85	69	1035	518	4.50	960	331	221	0

Playoff

	g	w	l	ip	r	tra
1925 KC	1	0	1	9	4	4.00

World Series

	g	w	l	ip	r	tra	h	so	bb	sv
1924 KC	4	0	1	14	8	5.26	14	5	5	0
1925	2	0	2	11	10	8.18	16	6	3	0
	6	0	3	25	18	6.48	30	11	8	0

Vs white big leaguers

	g	w	l	ip	r	tra	h
1920 Cardinals	1	0	0	-	-	-	
1921	2	0	2	20	14	6.30	26
	3	0	2				

California

	g	w	l	ip	r	tra	h	so	bb
1924-5	20	11*	5	155*	-	-	-	70	54*

				Combined						
Negro League	-	85	69	1035	518	4.50	960	331	221	0
Post-season	7	0	4	36	22	5.50	30	11	8	0
Vs white big league	3	0	2	20	14	6.97	2			
	-	85	75	1091	554	4.48	992	342	229	0

Appendix

Dave MALARCHER
GENTLEMEN DAVE

B 10/18/94 Whitehall LA, D 5/11/82 Chicago, BB TR 5'7 150

	g	ab	h	2b	3b	hr	hr%	ba	sb	psn
1916 IND ABCs	12	40	13	1	2	0	0	.325	1	2b
1917	60	201	52	9	0	0	0	.259	3	rf,3b
1918 US Army	14	53	12	1	1	0	0	.227	0	
1919 DET,CAG	5	18	6	0	0	0	0	.333	0	3b
1920 CHI Am G	-	110	28	2	0	0	0	.255	5	
1921	67	250	49	6	0	0	0	.196	0	
1922	-	83	15	0	0	0	0	.181	2	
1923	90	316	90	19	3	1	3	.285	12*	
1924	-	302	90	-	-	-	-	.298	20*	
1925	80	304	99	9	0	2	4	.326	11	
1926	71	251	65	8	1	1	2	.259	8	M
1927 M	73	271	69	7	3	1	2	.255	-	
1928 M	17	57	14	0	0	0	0	.246	2	
1929-30 Did not play										
1931 M	15	44	14	0	0	0	0	.318	0	
1932 M	1	4	0	0	0	0	0	.000	0	
1933 IND Amer G M		Did not play								
1934 CHI M	1	4	0	0	0	0	0	.000	0	
	-	2308	616	62	10	5	1	.267	64	

			Playoff						
1916 IND	1	1	0	0	0	0	0	1.000	0
1926 CHI	8	26	8	8	1	0	0	.308	1
1928	7	18	3	0	0	0	0	.167	0
	16	45	11	0	1	0	0	.244	1

			World Series						
1921 CHI	–	13	0	0	0	0	0	.000	0
1926	11	35	9	0	0	0	0	.257	4
1927	9	28	6	1	0	0	0	.214	3
	–	76	15	1	0	0	0	.197	7

			Vs white big leaguers						
17 Fred Schupp	1	4	1	0	0	0	0	.250	0
22 Dick Kerr	1	4	0	0	0	0	0	.000	0
23 DET Tigers	3	11	4	0	0	0	0	.364	0
	5	19	5	0	0	0	0	.263	0

			Combined						
Negro League	–	2308	616	62	10	5	1	.267	64
Post season	–	121	26	1	0	0	0	.215	8
Vs white majors	5	19	5	0	0	0	0	.263	0
	–	2448	647	63	0	5	1	.264	72

Appendix

CRUSH CHRISTOPHER COLUMBUS HOLLOWAY
(CRUSH)

b 9/16/96 Hillsboro TX, d 6/72 Baltimore, BB TR, 6' 180

	g	ab	h	2b	3b	hr	hr%	ba	sb
1921 IND ABCs	92	330	95	-	-	-	-	.288	-
1922	81	275	67	14	6	0	0	.244	9
1923	67	257	80	12	7	8	17	.311	14
1924 BAL Bl Sox	68	340	104	-	-	-	-	.306	11*
1925	73	306	86	4	5	1	1	.281	7
1926	65	252	66	6	2	3	7	.262	3
1927	69	294	71	4	5	4	8	.235	7
1928	39	166	47	6	2	1	3	.283	5
1929 PHI Hilldale *p*	-	*304*	*90*	*19*	*3*	*4*	*7*	*.296*	*29**
1930 DET Stars	72	298	70	9	9	0	0	.265	11
1931 BAL	54	200	60	5	4	0	0	.300	3
1932 PHI,NY	48	208	63	0	0	0	0	.303	3
1933 BAL	-	172	52	5	6	6	17	.302	6
1934 AC Bach G	-	220	28	0	0	0	0	.140	1
1935 BRK Royal G	14	51	9	-	-	-	-	.176	
1936-8 No record									
1939 BAL Elite G	3	4	0	0	0	0	0	.000	
	-	3681	988	84	49	27	4	.268	109[3]

p as published

					Playoff				
1930 DET	7	29	11	0	0	0	0	.379	1

					Cuba				
1924-5 HAV Reds	-	135	42	5	3	0	0	.311	0
1928-9 ALM Blues	-	117	31	5	3	1	5	.265	3
	-	252	73	10	6	1	2	.290	4

			California						
1922-3	8	37	10	2	0	0	0	.270	
1923-4	12	48	12	2	1	0	0	.250	
1925-6	41*	159*	59	7	1	4	14	.371	
1926-7	33	122	30	4	1	1	4	.246	
1927-8	14	56	14	0	0	2	10	.250	
1929-30	15	54	20	6	2*	0	0	.383	
	123	476	144	21	5	7	8	.303	

© 2007 William McNeil

			Vs white big leaguers						
1925	1	4	1	0	0	0	0	.250	1
1926-7 California	4	19	5	0	0	0	1	.263	0
1927-8	1	4	3	0	0	0	0	.750	1
1928	1	4	0	0	0	0	0	.000	1
1931	1	4	1	0	0	0	0	.250	
	8	35	10	0	0	0	0	.256	3

			Combined						
Negro League	-	3681	988	89	44	27	4	.268	109[3]
Playoff	7	29	11	0	0	0	0	.379	1
Cuba	-	252	73	10	6	1	2	.290	4
vs big leagues	8	35	10	0	0	0	0	.256	1
	-	3997	1082	99	50	28	4	.271	115[6]

Appendix

WEBSTER McDONALD

b 1/1/00 Wilmington DE, d 6/12/82 Philadelphia, BR TR 6' 189

	g	w	l	ip	r	tra	h	so	bb	sv	
1918 PHI Madison Stars											
1919 Richmond Giants		15	4								
1920 PHI Giants											
1924 PHI Hilldales	-	1	0								
1925 WIL/WAS,CHI	-	9	11	84	26	2.78	61	27	14		
1926 CHI Amer G	15	11	4	113	33	2.92	100	72	22	1	
1927	18	10	5	136	43	2.85	111	64	26	0	
1928 Minnesota											
1929 CHI a	4	2	2								
1930 BAL a	2	1	1	16	3	1.69	12	9	1	0	
1931 PHI a	5	5	0	49	8	1.47*	8	4	3	0	
1932 WAS/WILM	12	3	9	34	49	12.97					
1933 PHI,CHI	10	6	3	61	21	3.10	69	1	14	0	
1934 PHI	21	13	3	152	42	2.49	66	17	3	0	
1935 PHI	26	10	7	129	42	2.94	98	8	9	0	
1936	41	12	16	105	72	4.32	72	25	20	1	
1937	14	5	5	69	34	4.43	23	9	2	0	
1938	16	5	6	63	18	2.57	39	5	0	0	
1939	25	6	10	68	34	4.50	20	0	0	0	M
1940	-	1	1								M
	-	100	83	1051	408	3.84	659	241	114	2	

a Spent most of the years in Minnesota. They might have cost him an extra 30 league wins.

				Playoffs			
1925 CHI	2	2	0	18	3	1.50	
1934 PHI	2	1	0	16	6	3.13	
	4	3	0	34	9	2.38	

World Series									
1926 CHI	2	0	1	11	10	9.35	15	2	5	0
1927	2	1	1	13	6	4.15	14	8	2	0
1929	2	2	0	-	0	0.00				
	6	3	2	24	16	6.00	29	10	7	0

Vs white big leaguers						
1925 Foxx, Heilmann 1	1	0	9	1	1.00	
1930	7	6	0	54	13	2.17
1931	4	3	1	27	11	3.67
1932	3	1	2			
1933	4	3	1	36	17	4.25
1935	2	2	0	18	2	1.00
1939 a 1	0	0	8	0	0.00	
	22	16	4	152	44	2.61

a Pitched 8.1 hitless innings of relief

Semipro		
1928 Little Falls MN	25	3
1919	27	2
1930	26	1
1931	20	2
	98	8

Combined									
Negro League	-	100	83	1051	408	3.84	659	291	114
Post-season	10	6	2	58	25	3.88			
Vs white big league	122	16	4	152	44	2.61			
	-	122	89	1261	477	3.78			

NEWT ALLEN
(COLT)

b, 5/19/01 Austen TX   d 6/11/88 KC, BR   TRUE   5'8"   160

Year		g	ab	h	2b	3b	hr	hr%	ba	sb	psn
1921 Omaha Federals											
1922 KC Monarchs		1	4	3	0	0	0	0	.750	0	2b
1923 KC Monarchs		28	102	22	1	3	0	0	.216	0	3,s
1924		89	368	101	11	3	2	3	.274	0	2
1925		94	378	116	9	10	6	8	.307	16	
1926		89	354	82	14	3	1	12	.232	0	
1927		77	293	98	16	3	2	7	.334	-	ss
1928		27	112	32	8	1	1	5	.286	3	s,2
1929		80	316	101	24	6	3	5	.330	23	2
1930		73	299	99	16	4	2	4	.331	12	
1931 KC,STL Stars		-	213	61	-	-	-	-	.286	-	s,2
1932 KC,HOM,DET		66	254	77	10	0	1	2	.303	4	2b
1933 KC		33	112	31	4	1	1	5	.277		
1934		8	34	7	2	1	0	0	.206		
1935		4	15	4	2	0	0	0	.267		
1936 KC		-	126	34	3	1	0	0	.270	1	
1937		47	198	77	6	2	0	0	.389	7	
1938		-	103	30	3	0	0	0	.291	2	
1939		-	126	34	-	-	-	-	.270		
1940		22	97	31	4	1	0	5	.320	0	of,2,s
1941		27	102	25	2	1	0	0	.245	1	2b
1942		25	93	29	-	-	0	0	.312	0	3b
1943		-	98	18	0	0	0	0	.213	0	2b
1944	p	-	103	33	7	1	0	0	.202	4	1b,of
1945	p	10	35	17	2	1	0	0	.485	0	2b
1946 no record											
1947 IND Clowns	p	2	4	2	-	-	0	0	.500		
		-	3939[5]	1164	144	42	19	3	.296	73	

Playoff

1925 KC	7	27	11	-	-	1	20	.407
1926	8	28	5	0	0	0	0	.179
	15	55	16	1	0	0	0	.291

World Series

1924 KC	-	39	11	7	0	0	0	.282	1
1925	6	27	7	1	0	0	0	.259	1
1931	8	28	7	3	0	0	0	.250	1
1937	2	8	2	0	0	1	68	.250	0
1942	4	14	4	1	0	0	0	.267	0
	-	116	31	12	0	1	5	.267	3

East-West games

1936-41	4	15	0	0	0	0	0	.000

Cuba

1924-5 Almendares	-	48	15	1	2	1	11	. 313
1936-7	-	234	66	-	-	-	-	.282
1937-8 HAV,ALM	-	175	47	4	1	0	0	.269
	-	457	128	5	3	1	1	.280

California

1924-5	29	118	51	4	1	0	0	.254
1926-7	23	78	12	1	0	0	0	.282
1927-8	13	56	14	1	1	0	0	.250
1928-9	29	126	46	14*	2	2	5	.365
1929-30	28	111	47*	13*	2*	0	0	.423
1930-1	15	63*	19	2	0	2	18	.301
	137	552	189	35	6	4	4	.342

Appendix

Vs Big Leaguers

1925-6 California	1	4	0	0	0	0	0	.000	
1926-7	4	19	5	0	0	1	28	.263	
1927-8	9	39	12	1	1	0	0	.308	
1927 Thurston	1	4	1	1	0	0	0	.250	
1928-9	2	11	3	-	-	-	-	.273	
1930 Grove,Newsom	1	4	1	-	-	-	-	.250	
1931	2	6	3	-	-	-	-	.500	
1932	1	2	2	-	-	-	-	1.000	
1933 Dean	1	4	0	0	0	0	0	.000	
1935	3	12	4	-	-	-	-	.333	
1936 Bowman	1	4	0	0	0	0	0	.000	
1937	4	17	5	-	-	-	-	.294	
	30	126	36	-	-	-	-	.286	

Combined

Negro League	-	3939	1164	144	42	19	3	.296	73
Post season	65	171	47	12	0	2	6	.275	3
East-West	4	15	0	0	0	0	0	.000	
Cuba	-	457	128	5	3	1	1	.280	
Vs whites	30	126	36	-	-	-	-	.302	
	-	4708	1375	161	45	22	3	.292	76

JAMES BELL
(COOL PAPA)

b 5/17/03 Starkville MS,   d 3/7/91 St Louis,   BB   TL   6'   165
Hall of Fame 1974

	g	ab	h	2b	3b	hr	hr%	ba	sb	psn
1920 Compton Cubs										
1922 SL Stars	22	60	26	3	1	3	28	.433	0	p,of
1923	35	93	18	4	1	1	6	.204	2	
1924	62	231	73	15	1	0	9	.316	9	
1925	95	414	144	32*	5	11	15	.348	23*	
1926	91	394	140	23	7	17	23	.355	8*	
1927	-	457	144	15	5	13	16	.315	1	
1928	72	310	103	16	6	4	7	.332	7	
1929	89	359	112	25	6	4	6	.312	28	
1930	66	279	101	17	6	7	14	.362	15	
1931	27	103	32	1	1	0	0	.311	1	
1932 *	84	337	118	22	8	2	3	.350	14	
1933 PIT Craws	90	364	122	14	9	4	6	.335	7	
1934	-	291	106	3	1	0	0	.364	5*	
1935	61	258	84	12	8	1	2	.326	9*	
1936	31	119	37	4	1	0	0	.311	0	
1937	8	34	8	1	0	2	32	.235	0	
1938-41 Mexico										
1942 CHI Amer Gia	-	86	32	3	0	0	0	.372	0	
1943 WAS Hom Gray	63	252	94	7	6	0	0	.373	9	
1944	68	272	78	11	4	4	8	.274	0	
1945	26	99	25	5	0	1	6	.253	2	
1946	-	87	38	1	1	0	0	.435	0	of,ph
	-	4899^2	1635^2	235^2	77^3	74	8	.334	136^2	

* Detroit, Pittsburgh, Homestead, Kansas City

Appendix

Playoff

1925 SL	7	27	11	0	1	0	0	.407	0
1926	8	33	10	1	0	0	0	.303	
1930	6	25	7	2	0	1	22	.280	0
1933 PIT	1	6	2	0	0	1	92	.333	0
1935	7	24	3	0	1	0	0	.125	0
	29	115	33	3	2	2	10	.287	0

World Series

1929 CHI	4	17	3	0	0	0	0	.176	0
1943 WAS	6	27	8	1	1	0	0	.296	0
1944	5	23	6	0	1	0	0	.273	2
1945	4	14	3	1	0	0	0	.214	0
	19	81	20	1	1	0	0	.247	2

East-West

1933-44	7	28	5	1	0	0	0	.179	2

Cuba

1928-9 Cienfuegos	-	157	51	10	7	5*	18	.325	17*
1929-30	a -	220*	57	14*	4	3	8	.285	-
1930	-	54	17	1	2	0	0	.315	-
1940-41 Almendares	-	138	41	5	3	2	8	.297	11
	-	569	166	30	16	10	10	.329	28

A Hit three homers in one game January 1 1929

Mexico

1938 Tampico	40	160	57	7	6	6	21	.356	9
1939	58	226	80	16	2	5	11	.354	12
1940 Torreon,VCr	89	382	167	29	15*	12*	18	.437*	28
1941 Monterrey	100	421	132	21	15*	4	5	.314	14
	287	1189	436	73	38	27	12	.367	63

Dominican Republic

1937	16	66	21	4	3	0	0	.318

California

1922-3	3	6	4	0	0	1	92	.667
1923-4	7	17	3	0	0	3	97	.176
1924-5	30	120	48	2	0	1	5	.400*
1930-1	11	31	8	0	0	1	18	.258
1931-2	9	41	17	1	0	0	0	.415
1933-4	43*	163*	59*	15	4*	6	20	.362* 22
1934-5	24	98	30	6	5*	1	6	.306
1936-7	5	19	9	3	1	3	87	.474
1937-8	10	41	1	0	2*	1	13	.341
1940-1	2	9	6	0	0	0	0	.667
1943-4	12	38	12	3	0	0	0	.323
1944-5	3	13	8	1	0	0	0	.615
	159	596	219	31	12	16	15	.368

(c) William McNeil

Vs white big leaguers

1923-4 California		3	13	4	0	0	1	42	.308	
1929		5	22	6	0	0	0	0	.273	0
1930 Meine,Bayne		2	5	1	0	0	0	0	.200	-
1931 French,etc		6	16	8	2	0	1	34	.500	1
1932		1	3	0	0	0	0	0	.000	0
1933-4 California		22	75	24	5	0	1	7	.320	
1934-5		4	19	8	0	3	0	0	.421	
1935 Dean etc	x	4	15	5	0	0	0	0	.333	0
1936		7	30	12	1	0	0	0	.400	0
1937-8 California		1	4	1	0	1	0	0	.250	
1943 Hughes		1	4	0	0	0	0	0	.000	0
1943-4		5	19	8	2	0	0	0	.421	2
1943-4 California		1	5	3	0	0	0	0	.600	
1944-5		1	4	2	0	0	0	0	.500	
1946 Vander Meer		1	4	1	1	0	0	0	.250	-
1948 Lemon etc	y	5	12	6	1	0	0	0	.500	0
		62	230	89	12	4	3	7	.387	3

Appendix

		Combined							
Negro Leagues	-	4899	1635	235	77	74	8	.334	136
Post Season	48	196	52	4	3	2	6	.268	2
East-West	7	28	5	1	0	0	0	.179	2
Cuba	-	569	166	30	16	4	4	.329	28
Mexico 1940-41	189	803	299	50	30	16	11	.372	42
Vs white big leaguers	62	230	89	12	4	3	7	.387	3
	-	6495	2246	332	130	99	8	.346	210

TED PAGE
B 4/22/03 Glasgow KY, D 12/1/84 Pittsburgh, BR TR 5'11 175

	g	ab	h	2b	3b	hr	hr%	ba	sub
1923 -4 Buffalo Giants									
1926 Newark									
1927-8 Mohawk Giants									
1929 BRK Royal G	1	4	0	0	0	0	0	.000	0
1930 BRK	–	39	15	–	–	–	–	.384	
1931 HOM Grays	37	150	56	5	9	0	0	.346	0
1932 NY,PIT	63	318	70	–	–	–	–	.220	
1933 PIT Crawfords	52	190	61	7	7	3	9	.321	4
1934 PIT a	6	20	4	0	0	0	0	.200	0
1935 PHI Stars	45	177	59	3	3	3	9	.333	
1936 PHI	25	104	25	2	0	4	21	.240	0
1937	28	130	31	2	1	3	2	.238	0
	260	1025	265	17	20	13	6	.259	4

a Injured leg

Playoff
1933 PIT	1	5	3	0	0	0	0	.600	2

World Series
1931 HOM	7	26	5	0	1	0	0	.333	0

Vs white big leaguers
1930 Sherid,Weaver	–	17	7	0	2	0	0	.412	0
1932 Stengels	–	30	12	0	0	0	0	.400	0
1934 Deans	–	7	1	0	0	0	0	.143	0
1935	11	2	0	0	0	0	0	.182	0
	–	65	22	0	2	0	0	.338	0

Combined
Negro League	260	1025	265	17	20	13	6	.259	4
Post season	8	31	8	0	1	0	0	.258	2
Vs white majors	–	65	22	0	2	0	0	.338	0
	–	1121	295	17	23	13	6	.263	6

Appendix

TED RADCLIFFE
(DOUBLE DUTY)

b 7/7/02 Mobile AL, d 5/17/05 Chicago   BR   TR   5'10 190

	g	ab	h	2b	3b	hr	hr%	ba	sb	p:
1920-27 Illinois Gi										
1928 DET Stars	66	253	67	12	4	8	17	.268	1	
1929	32	125	39	7	2	3	13	.310	4	
1930 SL Stars	57	184	54	12	2	6	18	.293	4	
1931 HOM,DET Wolves	10	33	3	0	0	0	0	.091	0	
1932 CHI Amer Giant	46	152	41	10	0	5	18	.270	2	
1933 HOME,COL Buck	27	98	33	3	2	0	0	.337	1	
1934 CHI	* 4	10	6	0	0	1	55	.600	0	
1935 BRK Eagles	14	39	10	0	0	0	0	.258	0	
1936 South Dakota										
1937 CIN,CHI	-	185	51	1	6	1	3	.276		
1938 CHI,MEM	-	102	23	5	3*	1	5	.225	7	*·'
1939 MEM Red Sox	-	24	4	0	0	0	0	.167	0	
1940 Mexico										
1941	4	10	5	2	0	0	0	.500	0	
1942 BIR Bl Barons	-	37	11	-	-	1	15	.297	0	
1943 CHI	-	72	17	1	0	2	20	.236	0	
1944 BIR	p 26	93	20	4	0	0	0	.215	1	
1945 Did not play										
1946 WAS Hom Grays	4	3	1	1	0	0	0	.333	0	
	-	1430	385	58	19	28	11	.269	20	

* played most of year in South Dakota
** c,p,lf

		Playoff								
1930 SL	6	14	5	1	0	0	0	.357	0
1934 CHI	-	5	1	0	0	0	0	.200	0
1943 CHI	2	5	0	0	0	0	0	.000	0
	-	24	6	1	0	0	0	.333	0

		World Series								
1929 CHI	1	2	1	0	0	0	0	.500	0
1931 HOM	3	15	5	1	1	0	0	.333	0
	4	17	6	1	1	0	0	.353	0

	East-West game									
1936-44	6	13	4	0	0	1	42	.308	0	c,p

	Cuba							
1938-9	-	33	6	-	-	-	-	.182

	Mexico							
1940 Vera Cruz 1	33	77	19	4	1	0	0	.247

	California							
1937-8	4	18	6	0	0	1	31	.333
1943-4	7	22	4	0	0	0	0	.282
	11	40	10	0	0	0	14	.250

© 2005 William F McNeil

	Vs white big leaguers								
1929-30	1	3	1	0	0	0	0	.333	0
1934	2	9	5	0	0	0	0	.556	0
1943 California	4	16	6	0	0	0	0	.375	
1946 Mexico	1	4	3	-	-	-	-	.750	
	8	32	15	0	0	0	0	.469	

	Semipro							
1935 Wichita Tourney	-	27	8	3	0	0	0	.296
1936	-	8	3	-	-	-	-	.375
	-	35	11	3	-	-	-	.314

	Combined								
Negro Leagues	-	1423	384	58	19	27	11	.270	20
Post-season		41	12	2	1	0	0	.293	0
East-West	6	13	4	0	0		42	.308	0
Cuba	-	33	6	-	-	-	-	.182	-
Mexico	33	77	19	4	1	0	0	.247	1
Vs white majors	8	32	15	0	0	0	0	.469	
	1619	438	64	21	28	10	.271	21	

Appendix

PITCHING

	G	w	l	ip	r	tra	h	so	bb	sv	
1930 SL Stars	19	9	3	93	29	2.80*	86	39	19	3	
1931 DET,HOM	-	2	6	171	97	4.59	125	58	20		
1932 Homestead Grays	23	13	8	138	63	4,11	60	14	12	1	
1933 Bismarck ND											
1934 CHI Amer G a	3	1	1	1	6	3.60	3	6	6		
1935 BRK Eagles a	14	4	7	65	37	5.12	59	19	9	0	
1936 CIN Tigers	-	0	0	12	0						M
1937 MEM Red Sox	1	0	0								M
1938 MEMPHIS	10	4	6	57	24	2.31*	48	26	9	0	M
1939 MEM,CHI	-	3	10								
1940 Mexico											
1941 MEM Red Sox	-	4	1	15	6	3.60	9	0	1	0	
1942 BIR Bl Barons	1	0	0	3	1	3.00		4			
1943 CHI Amer G	-	0	1								M
1944 Did not pitch											M
1945											M
1946 WAS Hom Gray	20	4	3	45	23	4.60	26	12	3	2	
	-	44	47	647	286	3.98	360	160	67	5	

a Spent part of year in Bismarck ND

Playoff

	G	w	l	ip	r	tra	h	so	bb
1930 SL	3	0	1	7	6	7.71	12	5	3

World Series

	G	w	l	ip	r	tra
1929 CHI	2	2	0	15	0	0.00

East-West game

	G	w	l	ip	r	tra	so	bb
1938-41	3	1	0	-	-	-	2	3

Mexico

	G	w	l	ip	r	tra	h	so
1940 V Cruz Blues	21	5	6	81	60	5.93	121	54	29

	North Dakota									
1934 Jamestown		22	17	3	151	45	2.68	103	157	17 3
1935 Bismarck	e	5	4	0	41	8	2.00			
		27	21	3	192	53	2.48			

Courtesy of Kyle McNary

	Vs white big leaguers								
1930	1	1	0	5	0	0.00	2	8	1

	Combined									
Negro League	-	31	37	290	126	3.91	235	102	47	5
Post-season	5	2	1							
East-West	3	1	0	-	-	-	2	3		
Vs white big league	1	1	0	5	0	0.00	2	8	1	
	-	36	38	295	126	3.84	239	113	48	

Appendix

WILLIE FOSTER
BIG BILL

b 6/12/04 Calvert TX, d 9/16.78 Lorman MS BB TL 6'1 195
Hall of Fame 1996

		g	w	l	ip	r	tra	h	so	bb	sv
1923 MEM Red Sox		8	6	3	70	20	2.57	37	30	11	
1924		1	1	0	9	1	1.00	1	14	3	0
1925 BIR,CHI		14	7	0	67	16	2.15	49	39	20	0
1926 CHI Amer G		20	11	5	137	31	2.03*	86	77*	37	
1927	s	29	21*	3	199	59	2.67	164	118*	50	2
1928		30	14	10	208	85	3.68	168	118	55	0
1929		26	11	7	152	67	3.96	130	75	39	3
1930		34	16	10	199	82	3.71	173	134*	51	3
1931 CHI,KC		9	4	2	51	6	1.06	16	43	6	1
1932 CHI	s	21	13	7	158	42	2.39	100	48	18	1
1933		-	11	7	149	51	3.08	55	52	8	1
1934 CHI,KC		15	7	5	74	24	2.92	9	-	1	0
1935 CHI		7	4	2	36	8	2.00	28	10	11	0
1936 CHI,PIT		6	3	2	33	19	5.18	22	9	9	0
		220	129	63	1543	511	2.98	1035	767	342	11

31 shutouts

		g	w	l	ip	r	tra	h	so	bb	sv
Playoff											
1926		3	2	1	22	7	2.86	9	-	0	
1927		3	2	0	18	4	2.00	9	-	-	0
1932		3	3	0	27	10	3.33	17	-	0	0
		9	7	1	67	21	2.82	35	-	1	0

		g	w	l	ip	r	tra	h	so	bb	sv
World Series											
1926 CHI		4	2	0	28	8	2.54	26	19	13	1
1927		4	2	2	24	9	3.38	28	13	10	0
1929		1	1	0	9	3	3.00	3	-	-	0
1931 HOM		3	3	1	36	16	4.00				
		12	8	3	97	36	3.34	57	32	23	1

		g	w	l	ip	r	tra	h	so	bb	sv
East-West game											
1933-4		2	1	1	-	-	-	6	4		

				Denver Post					
1934	1	1	0						

				Cuba					
1927-8	16	6	8						

				Vs white big leaguers			
1929 AL Stars	3	2	1	18	3	1.50	18
1930	1	1	0	9	1	1.00	9
1931	1	1	0	9	3	3.00	9
	5	4	1	36	7	1.75	36

				California					
1926-7	7	6	0	55	-	-	-	49*	!7
1930-1	11	9	0	68	-	-	-	53	20
1931-2	10	9	1						
	28	24	1						

© 2002 William F McNeil

				Complete						
Negro League	220	128	62	1543	511	2.98	1121	425	342	11
Post Season	21	15	4	153	49	2.88	110	32	24	0
East-West	2	1	1	-	-	-	-	6	4	
Cuba	16	6	8	-	-	-	-	-	-	
Vs white majors	5	4	1	36	7	1.75	36			
	264	154	76	1732	567	2.75	1267	463	370	12

Appendix

LARRY BROWN

b 9/5/05 Pratt City AL, d 4/7/72 Memphis, BR TR, 5'8 190

	g	ab	h	2b	3b	hr		hr%	ba	sb
1921 Indianapolis ABCs	9	29	6	0	1	0	0	.207	1	
1922	No data									
1923 Memphis Red Sox	12	32	5	0	0	0	0	.156	0	
1924	53	163	34	4	6	1	3	.209	3	
1925	40	117	29	6	1	0	0	.248	0	
1926 Detroit Stars	47	135	33	3	4	2	8	.244	1	
1927 Chicago,Memphis	-	254	70	11	5	0	0	.276	4	
1928 MEM	86	286	87	16	3	1	2	.304	1	
1929	65	215	63	8	2	5	13	.293	0	
1930 NY Lincoln Giants	-	74	19	1	1	0	0	.257	1	
1931 NY,MEM,CHI	-	124	35	2	2	4	18	.282	1	
1932 NY BlackYankees	18	67	4	0	0	0	0	.060	0	
1933 CHI American Giants	40	138	29	-	-	-	-	.210		
1934	37	120	46	7	0	0	0	.383		
1935 CHI,PHI	30	114	27	1	5	0	0	.237	0	
1936 Philadelphia Stars	33	103	16	1	0	0	0	.155	0	
1937 PHI,MEM	26	95	11	-	-	-	-	.116		
1938 MEM	-	47	8	1	1	1	12	.167	0	
1939 -	57	15	1	0	0	0	0	.263	1	
1940 MEM,CHI	-	77	20	1	1	0	0	.260	0	
1941 MEM	-	31	6	1	0	0	0	.194	0	
1942	15	47	10	3	0	0	0	.213	0	M
1943	10	41	9	2	0	0	0	.220	0	
1944 *p*	*36*	*82*	*16*	*2*	*1*	*0*	*0*	*.194*	*1*	
1945 *t*	*16*	*28*	*8*	*2*	-	-	-	*.286*	*0*	
1946	1	3	2	1	0	0	0	.667	0	
	-	2479	607	74	32	14	3	.244	14	

Playoff

1930 NY	8	26	10	0	0	0	0	.385	1	
1934 CHI	-	13	3	0	0	0	0	.231	0	
	-	39	13	0	0	0	0	.333	1	

		World Series								
1927 CHI	8	21	4	1	0	1	26	.190	0
1929	4	13	3	3	1	0	0	.231	0
	12	34	7	4	1	1	14	.206	0

		East-West game								
1933-41	7	14	4	0	1	0	0	.286	0

		Cuba								
1924-5 Santa Clara	-	32	8	0	1	0	0	.250	-
1926-7 Cienfuegos	-	65	16	2	2	0	0	.246	0
1927-8 Cuba	-	114	29	3	3	0	0	.254	0
1928-9	-	100	35	4	2	0	0	.350	0
1929-30 Almendares	-	161	45	5	0	0	0	.280	0
	-	472	133	14	10	0	0	.282	0

		Mexico								
1941 Tampico	29	96	21	2	0	0	0	.219	0

		California								
1931-2	6	23	8	0	0	2	44	.348	
1934-5	24	77	28	4	0	1	7	,364	
	30	100	36	4	0	3	16	.360	

© 2002 William For McNeil

		Vs white majors								
1934-5 California	4	14	4	2	0	0	0	.286	

		Combined								
Negro League	-	2479	609	74	32	14	3	.244	14
Post season	-	73	20	4	1	1	8	.278	0
East-West	7	14	4	0	1	0	0	.286	0
Mexico	29	96	21	2	0	0	0	.219	0
Vs white majors	4	14	4	2	0	0	0	.286	
		2676	658	82	34	15	3	.245	14

Appendix

WILLIE WELLS
(THE DEVIL)

b 8/10/08 Austin Texas, d 1/22/89 Austin BR TR 5'9" 167
Hall of Fame 1997

		g	ab	h	2b	3b	hr	hr%	ba	sb
1924	SL Stars	55	213	56	16	3	1	3	.263	2
1925		94	375	100	15	8	10	15	.267	14
1926		85	280	104	14	3	12	24	.371	8
1927		111	403	146	20	6	23*	32	.363	5
1928		72	289	102	22	4	17	32	.353	2
1929	w	88	334	123	21	6	27**	44	.368	21
1930	w	77	288	116	32*	3	15*	29	.403	17
1931		25	101	28	3	0	5	27*	.263	0
1932	DET,HOM,KC	-	244	69	12	2	1	2	.283	9
1933	IND Am Giants	53	170	45	18	4	2	6	.265	8
1934	CHI Am Giants	40	159	42	10	8*	2	9	.264	3
1935		45	159	43	9	3	2	7	.270	7
1936		38	182	44	8	1	4	12	.242	0
1937	NWK Eagles c	38	103	33	4	1	1	10	.320	0
1938		26	92	37	4	2	6	35	.402*	1
1939		54	179	57	4	1	3	9	.318	3
1940-1 Mexico										
1942	NWK	44	164	58	9	0	7	23	.354	6
1943 Mexico										
1944	NY Bl Yanks a	2	8	4	0	0	0	0	.500	0
1945	NWK	12	37	8	1	0	0	0	.216	0
1946	NY,BAL	36	130	30	7	2	1	4	.231	0

$$3910^6 \quad 1245^7 \quad 229^4 \quad 57^8 \quad 139^5 \quad 20^9 \quad .318 \quad 106^3$$

** Tied Negro League record
a Spent most of the year in Mexico

		Playoff							
1925 SL	–	17	2	0	0	1	32	.118	
1926 SL	7	27	4	1	0	0	0	.148	0
1928	7	25	8	1	1	3	66	.325	0
1930	7	30	12	2	0	1	18	.400	0
1934 CHI	–	15	3	0	0	0	0	.200	
1939 NWK	4	14	1	0	0	0	0	.071	0
	–	128	30	4	1	5	21	.234	0

		World Series							
1929 CHI	4	16	8	2	1	0	0	.500	1

		East–West							
1933–45	9	36	10	3	1	0	0	.281	1

		Cuba							
1928–9 Cienfuegos	–	152	51	7	3	1	4	.336	5
1929–30	–	177	57	9	6	2	6	.322	–
1935–6 Santa Clara	–	177	63*	8	4	5*	16	.356	–
1936–7 Almendares	–	88	30	3	0	3	19	.349	1
1937–8 ALM Blues	–	126	36	4	1	4̲	17	.286	–
1938–9	–	187	52	7	2	0	0	.278	3
1939 Hom Grays	5	20	6	0	0	0	0	.300	0
	–	927	295	38	16	15	9	.318	9

		Mexico							
1940 Vera Cruz	84	339	117	30*	2	3	5	.345	17
1941	100	403	140	29	6	9	12	.347	14
1943 Tampico	87	319	94	15	4	4	7	.295	10
1944 V Cruz,Mex C	83	293	86	13	3	10	19	.294	9
	354	1354	437	87	15	26	11	.328	50

		Puerto Rico							
1941–42 Mayaguez	–	–	–	17	–	–	–	.378	–

Appendix

```
                        California
1924-5              9     32   10    1    0    1   17  .313
1926-7             33    105   19    6    1    0    0  .181
1927-8             14     48   15    3    0    0    0  .313

1930-1             13     57   17    2   2*    2   19  .275
1931-2              6     24   10    0    0    0    0  .417
1933-4             41    158   56   19*   1    6   21  .355  16
1934-5             27     94   28    9*   2    2   12  .319

1944-5              3      9    2    0    0    0    0  .222
                  ───    ───  ───   ──    ─   ──   ──  ────
                  146    528  159   40    9   11   11  .301
```
© 2002 William F McNeil

```
                   Vs white big leaguers
1925-6 California    2     6    1    0    0    0    0  .167
1926-7              7     24    9    4    0    0    0  .375
1927-8             1      4    1    1    0    0    0  .250

1929 Whitehill,Uhle 5    22    9    2    3    0    0  .409   1
1930 Whitehill     2      7    1    0    0    0    0  .143
1930-1 California   3     12    3    1    0    1   46  .250

1931-2             1      4    3    0    0    0    0  .750
1932 Winegarner    1      3    2    0    0    1  183  .667
1933-4 California  18     61   23    8    0    3   27  .377
1934-5             5     22   10    2    1    0    0  .455
1935 Bridges,Rowe  1      4    2    0    0    0    0  .500

1939 Feller        1      4    0    0    0    0    0  .000

1945 Barrett,Branca 4    10    4    1    0    0    0  .400
                  ───   ───   ──   ──    ─    ─   ──  ────
                   51   183   68   19    4    5   15  .372
```

```
                       Combined
Negro League      3910[6] 1175[7] 223[4] 58[8] 139[5] 20[9] .301 104[3]
Post Season        144     38    6    2    5   19  .264   1
East-West           36     10    3    1    0    0  .263   1
Cuba               927    295   38   16   15    9  .318   9
Mexico             742    257   59    8   12    9  .346  31
Vs white majors    183     68   19    4    5   15  .372   1
                  ────   ────  ────  ──  ───   ──  ────  ───
                  5942   1843  348*  89  176   16  .311  147
```
Wells ranks third in at bats, third in hits, first in doubles,
fifth in homers, and fourth in stolen bases

WILLIAM CORNELIUS
(SUG)

b. Atlanta 9/4/06 d Chicago 10/30/89   BR   TR   5'10   168

		g	w	l	ip	r	tra	h	so	bb
1928 NAS Elite Gia		1	0	1						
1929 MEM Red Sox		8	3	5	49	30	2.52	49	30	11
1930 MEM/BIR		27	7	10	133	86	5.82	124	55	60
1931 MEM		15	1	0	15	8	4.80	14	7	3
1932 No record										
1933 IND American G		15	7	5	66	40	5.45			
1934 CHI American G		19	5	11	70	39	5.01	52	16	8
1935		10	4	3	60	57	8.56	28	12	9
1936 No record										
1937		16	9	4	107	52	4.37	56		
1938		20	8	4	99	65	5.91	43	68	15
1939		14	5	7	72	27	3.38	33		
1940 Mexico										
1941 Chicago		-	4	6	37	11	2.68			
1942		-	0	7						
1943-4 US Army										
1945 Chicago	*p*	*17*	*5*	*4*	*91*	*65*	*6.43*	*107*	*36*	*119*
			58	67	799	477	5.37	506	224	128

			Playoff						
1937	5	0	1	9	2	2.000	7		

			East-West						
1935-8	3	1	1	5	-	-	10	2	1

			Mexico			
1940	-	7	9	-	-	5.04

		Combined	
Negro League	-	54	64
Post Season	1	0	1
East-West	3	1	1
Mexico	-	7	9
	-	62	75

Appendix

WALTER LEONARD
(BUCK)

b 9/8/07 Rocky Mount NICE   d 11/27/97 Rocky Mount   BL   TL   5'11   185
Hall of Fame 1972

	G	ab	h	2b	3b	hr	hr%	ba	sb
1933 AC Bach Gia	No record								
1934 HOM Grays	-	106	35	0	0	5	26	.330	0
1935	64	233	77	9	1	3	25	.300	0
1936	31	118	34	1	1	5	26	.288	0
1937	-	167	59	7	3	10	33	.353	0
1938	26	99	42	0	0	6	33	.424	0
1939 WAS Hom Grays	37	101	36	3	1	6	45	.356	0
1940	65	217	82	1	5	11*	28	.378	1
1941	40	106	35	4	9*	5	26	.330	0
1942	29	111	17	5	0	0	0	.153	2
1943	71	259	92	15	12	3	6	.355	0
1944	85	295	105	25*	8	7	13	.356	1
1945	26	85	31	4	2	4	26	.365	0
1946	47	113	30	2	3	4	19	.265	0
1947	31	105	43	11	-	7	37	.410	1
1948 p	47	157	62	-	-	13*	46	.395*	1
	-	2272	780	87	45	89[7]	22[9]	.343[8]	6

		Playoff							
1939 WAS	5	18	8	1	0	2	61	.444	0
1941	2	7	3	0	0	1	79	.429	0
	7	25	11	1	0	3	66	.440	0

		World Series							
1937 WAS	3	11	5	2	0	0	0	.455	0
1942	4	18	3	0	0	0	0	.166	0
1943	6	22	6	1	1	0	0	.272	1
1944	5	16	8	1	0	1	33	.500	1
1945	4	15	3	0	0	0	0	.200	0
1948	No data								
	22	82	25	4	1	1	7	.305	2

East-West game									
1935-48	13*	48	15	1	1	3	34	.313	2
Cuba									
1936-7 Marianao	-	171	52	3	1	1	32	.304	4
1939 Hom Grays	6	22	6	0	0	0	0	.273	0
1948-9 Marianao	-	65	15	4	0	2	17	.231	0
	-	258	73	7	1	3	6	.283	4
Puerto Rico									
1940-1	-	119	46	17*	-	8*	37	.389	
Venezuela									
1945-6	-	47	20	-	-	-	-	.425	
California									
1943-4	10	31	11	0	2	0	0	.355	
Vs white big leaguers									
1936 CIN Reds	1	6	1	0	0	0	0	.167	0
1943 California	1	4	3	0	1	0	0	.750	0
	2	10	4	0	1	0	0	.400	0
Combined									
Negro League	-	2272	780	87	45	89[7]	22[9]	.343[8]	6
Post-season	29	113	36	5	1	4	19	.319	0
East-West	13	48	15	1	1	3	34	.313	0
Cuba	-	195	58	3	1	1	3	.297	4
Vs white big league	2	10	6	0	1	0	0.	.400	0
	-	2638	895	120	45	98[7]	20[6]	.339.	10

Appendix

HILTON SMITH

b 2/27/12 Giddings TX   d 11/18/83 Kansas City   BR   TR
5'11   185, Hall of Fame 2001

		g	w	l	ip	r	tra	h			
1932 Monroe LA		1	0	0	6	2	3.00				
1933		2	2	0	18	1	0.50				
1934											
1935-6 Bismarck ND											
1937 KC Mon	n,r	15	9	4	84	16	1.85	42	43	7	0
1938 Monarchs	s	18	13*	2	112	41	3.30*	82	59	6	0
1939		17	8	4	89	22	2.20*	49	60	12	5*
1940	a	13	6	4	37	13	3.16	20	36	11	0
1941	s,a	14	10*	1	83	20	2.17	34	35	3	1
1942		7	4	3	51	33	5.82	54	24	13	0
1943		14	5	5	85	32	3.40	47	23	2	0
1944	b	8	1	2	3	0	0.00	5	0	0	
1945		8	6	2	59	22	3.36	23	12	0	0
1946		14	6	2	64	21	2.94	31	15	7	3
1947		7	6	0	34	11	2.91*	28	4	2	0
1948		11	1	2	46	-	-	68	27	23	
		152	77	31	747	234	2.83	488	338	88	9

n No-hitter May 15
a Pitched part of year in Mexico
b Sore arm

	World Series									
1942 KC	1	1	0	5	0	0.00	7	1	1	0
1946	2	1	0	14	2	1.29	15	12	3	0
	3	2	0	19	2	0.95	22	13	4	0

	East-West Game								
1938-41	4	1	1	10	3	2.70	5	10	5	0

	Cuba		
1937-8 Marianao	14	6	3
1939-40	9	4	2
	23	10	5

				Mexico						
1940 Nuevo Laredo	14	5	3	87	49	5.09	95	60	27	
1941	12	3	5	63	27	3.88	49	35	23	
	26	8	8	150	76	4.56	144	95	50	

				California			
1944-5	3	1	1	12	4	3.00

				Vs white big leaguers						
1937 Stars	2	1	0	12	0	0.00	5	11	1	0
1941 Cards	1	0	0	5	0	0.00	4	6	2	
1942 Deans	1	1	0	3	0	0.00	1			
1944 Lemons	1	1	0	9	1	1.00	3			
1946 Fellers	1	1	0	9	2	2.00	10	3	1	
1947 Yankees	1	0	0	5	0	0.00	1	2		
	6	4	0	43	3	0.63	24	22	4	

				Semipro		
1935 Bismarck	9	6	1	72		
Wichita Tourney	1	1	0	9	0	0.00
1936 Wichita Tourney	4	4	0	36	0	0.00
	14	11	1	117		

Courtesy of Kyle McNary

				Combined						
Negro League	149	77	31	747	231	2.82	488	338	88	9
Post-Season	4	1	1	19	2	0.95	22	13	4	0
East-West	4	1	1	10	3	2.90	5	10	5	
Cuba	23	10	5							
Mexico	26	8	8	150	76	4.56	144	95	50	
Vs white majors	6	4	0	34	2	0.53	21	20	6	0
	212	101	46	960	314	2.94	680	476	153	9

Appendix

JAMES GREENE
(JOE)

b 10/17/11 Stone Mountain GA   d 7/19/89 Decatur GA   BR TR   5'11   195

		g	ab	h	2b	3b	hr	hr%	ba	sb
1932-7 ATL Bl Crackers		no record								
1937 Atlanta		1	4	2	0	0	0	0	.500	
1938 WAS Hom Grays		No record								
1939		69	15	2	1	2	0	0	.217	1
1940 KC Monarchs		20	75	19	-	-	-	-	.253	
1941		-	67	21	-	-	-	-	.313	
1942		41	97	35	-	-	-	-	361	1
1943		-	8	1	0	1	0	0	.125	
1944-5 U.S. Army										
1946 KC	*p*	*49*	*140*	*42*	-	-	*4*	*16*	*.300*	
1947	*p*	*-*	*-*	*-*	*-*	*-*	*-*	*-*	*.324*	
1948 CLE Buckeyes		53	144	37	2	2	6	23	.257	2
		-	550	159	3	5	10	10	.289	4

p As published

World Series

1942 KC	4	18	8	1	0	1	31	.444	

East-West game

1940-42	2	6	0	0	0	0	0	.000	0

Mexico

1941	101	389	139	23	12	4	17	.357

Vs white big leaguers

1942 Fellers	3	4	2	0	1	1	0	.500
1946 Feller Stars	2	8	1	0	0	1	69	.125
	3	12	3	0	1	1	8	.250

Combined

Negro League	-	550	159	3	5	12	10	.282	4
World Series	4	18	8	1	0	1	69	.250	
East-West	2	6	0	0	0	0	0	.000	0
Mexico	101	389	139	23	12	4	17	.357	
Vs white big leaguers	3	12	3	1	1	1	48	.250	
	-	975	309	28	18	18	10	.317	4

TOM BUTTS
(PEE WEE)

b 8/17/19 Sparta GA   d 1/73 Atlanta   BR TR 5'7 145

		g	ab	h	2b	3b	hr	hr%	ba	sb
1938 ATL Black Crackers		-	44	15	-	-	-	-	.341	
1939 IND,BAL		-	86	42	-	-	-	-	.488	
1940 BAL Elite Giants		62	234	73	13	0	1	2	.312	1
1941		65	243	39	4	0	1	2	.160	0
1942		40	151	34	3	2	0	0	.225	4
1943 Mexico										
1944 Baltimore	p	*41*	*143*	*44*	*4*	*4*	*0*	*0*	*.308*	*1*
1945		35	123	37	7	2	0	0	.301	2
1946		46	164	55	6	4	2	7	.342	6
1947	p	*44*	*296*	*97*	*7*	-	*1*	*2*	*.321*	*6*
1948 No record										
1949 BAL	p	*86*	*333*	*29*	*4*	-	*0*	*0*	*.265*	*4*
		-	1817	465	48	12	5	2	,256	24

Played four more years in the Negro League, 1950-1953

		Playoff								
1939 BAL		-	25	7	1	0	0	0	.280	0

		East-West game								
1944-48		4	6	0	0	0	0	0	.000	0

		Cuba								
1947-48 Almendares		-	285	7	8	3	0	0	.246	13

		Mexico								
1943 Monterrey		80	286	71	13	1	1	2	.248	9

	Combined								
Negro League*	-	1484	436	44	12	5	2	.294	20
Playoff	-	25	7	1	0	0	0	.280	0
East-West	4	6	0	0	0	0	0	.000	0
Cuba	-	285	71	8	3	0	0	.246	13
	-	1800	514	53	15	5	2	.286	33

*Through 1947

Appendix

OTHELLO RENFROE
(CHICO)

b 3/1/23 Newark NJ d 9/3/91 Atlanta   BR TR 5'11 175

	g	ab	h	2b	3b	hr	hr%	ba	
1944 KC Monarchs	1	3	1	0	0	0	0	.333	
1945	15	36	12	3	0	0	0	.333	2b,lf,ss,c
1946	10	32	5	0	1	0	0	.157	
1947	No record								
1948 Cleveland Buckeyes	No record								
1949-50 IND Clowns	No record								
	26	71	18	3	1	0	0	.254	

			World Series						
1946 KC	4	17	7	0	1	0	0	..412	

			East-West						
1946	1	1							

			Mexico						
1950 Torreon	79	276	73	19	4	4	8	.264	6
1951	33	126	33	5	1	4	17	,266	3
1952	16	47	10	1	0	2	23	,213	0
	128	447	116	25	5	10	12	..260	9

			Minor League						
1954 Minot ND	64	219	45	-	-	-	-	.274	

			Combined						
Negro Leagues	26	71	18	3	1	0	0	.254	
World Series	4	17	7	0	1	0	0	..412	
East-West	1	1							
	31	89	25	3	2	0	0	.281	

INDEX

Aaron, Hank, xvii, xviii, 108, 173, 304–305, 313, 336, 341
Adams, Buck, 239
Agee, Tommy, 173, 186
Alexander, Grover Cleveland, 4, 100
All Nations, 27–28
Allen, A. G., 253
Allen, Johnny, 108, 122, 135, 230
Allen, Newt, xiv, 90–106, 121, 185, 195, 290
American Expeditionary Forces League, 48
Anson, Adrian "Cap," 2
Anthony, Father (ballplayer priest), 154
Appling, Luke, 177, 194
Apracicio, Luis, 267
Arango (ballplayer), 154
Arlett, Buzz, 26, 71, 87
Atlanta Black Crackers, 330–32
Atlantic City Bacharachs, 6, 17, 18, 50, 78
Austin Senators, 284–85
Austin, Fred, 20, 127

Babich, Johnny, 230
Baker, Gene, 347–48
Baker, Home Run, 62
Baltimore Black Sox, 6, 7, 18, 66–68, 155
Baltimore Elite Giants, 329, 332, 334–36
Baltimore Stars, 254–56
Bankhead, Sammy, 10, 125, 184, 270, 347
Banks, Ernie, 129–30, 184, 219, 220, 294, 305
Barnes, Jess, 175

Barnes, Virgil, 175
Barhill, Dave, 334
Barr (umpire), 36
Barrett, D., 231
Barrow, Ed, 10
Bass, Red, 274–75
Baumgartner, Stan, 84, 153, 154
Bayne, Bill, 133, 230
Bearden, Gene, 15, 136
Becker (coach), 178
Beckwith, John, 133, 197
Bejerano, Abernathy, 20
Bell, Cool Papa, xiv, xv, xvii, 9, 15–16, 19, 23, 33, 96, 107–40, 141, 143, 160, 166, 175, 176, 208, 213, 225, 227, 234, 236, 246, 266, 269, 303, 346
Bell, Fred, 117
Bell, L. Q., 112–14
Bellinger, Charlie, 64
Bench, Johnny, 132, 346
Benjamin, Jerry, 123, 262
Bennett, Sam, 29, 114, 118
Benson, Gene, 293
Benswanger, Bill, 12
Berardino, Johnny, 348, 349
Berger, Walter, 214
Berra, Yogi, 294
Birmingham Black Barons, 97, 169, 182, 239, 271
Bishop (ballplayer), 87
Black, Joe, 334–35, 350
Blackman, Henry, 64, 66, 115
Blackwell, Ewell, 307, 349
Bodie, Ping, 26
Bolden, Ed, 6–7, 82, 85, 86, 163, 172, 322

Boley, Joe, 155
Bonura, Zeke, 11, 283
Boudreau, Lou, 218, 301
Bowman (pitcher), 106
Boyd, Bill, 21
Boyd, Bob, 350
Bragana, Ramon, 285, 349
Branca, Ralph, 231
Brewer, Chet, 177, 287
Bridges, Tommy, 177, 217, 231
Briggs, Walter, 306
Britt, George, 143, 158, 176
Brock, Ed, 28
Brock, Johnny, 28–29
Brock, Lou, 107
Brooklyn Royal Giants, 6, 17, 149, 151, 256–57
Brooks, Irving, 154
Brown, Barney, 10, 177
Brown, Bobby, 294
Brown, Buster, 341
Brown, Dave, 49, 55, 189
Brown, Jim, 49, 50, 77, 78
Brown, Larry, 132, 171, 175, 205–17, 218, 256–57, 288
Brown, Mace, 288
Brown, Mordecai, 3
Brown, Ray, 10, 296
Brown, Willard, 21, 103, 106, 290, 305, 307, 333, 343, 345
Browning, Royal "Skink," 169
Bruton, Bill, 350
Buffalo Giants, 147–48
Bunning, Jim, 118
Burke, Michael, 133–34
Burnes, Bob, 280
Burnett, Tex, 257
Burt, Ping, 302
Butts, Pee Wee, 20, 302, 327–38, 343, 346

Cambria, Joe, 68
Camnitz, Howie, 3
Campanella, Roy, xviii, 6, 12, 15, 54, 86, 103, 123, 131, 132, 171, 246, 248, 263, 265–67, 290, 292, 294, 307, 318, 324, 327, 329–30, 332, 337–38, 346–47, 350
Canada, Jim, 234
Cannady, Rev, 143, 274
Caplinger (pitcher), 136
Carresquel, A., 187
Carter, Paul, 83
Case, George, 110
Cepeda, Orlando, 21

Cepeda, Perucho, 21, 125, 266
Chacon, Pelayo, 33
Chamberlain, Wilt, 82
Chambers (pitcher), 87
Chandler, A. B. "Happy," 14
Chandler, Spud, 15, 293, 348
Chapman, Ray, 96, 115
Chapman, Sam, 258, 292, 296, 348
Charleston, Oscar, xvii, 6, 19, 20, 54, 66, 76, 78, 95, 113, 115, 116, 120, 133, 143, 160, 166, 173, 176, 177, 196, 197, 213, 241, 246, 264, 285, 318, 351
Chicago American Giants, 5, 6, 18, 40, 49–55, 76–78, 94, 119–20, 121, 189, 191–94, 200, 203–4, 205, 232, 233, 235, 240–42
Chicago Cardinals, 8, 18
Chicago Leland Giants, 3
Churchill (mayor, Bismarck, N.D.), 178–79, 286
Clark, Eggie, 103
Clark, Monty, 66
Clarkson, Bus, 265
Clemens, Verne, 30
Clemente, Roberto, 21, 274
Clendenon, Donn, 36, 132, 303
Coates, John, xvii, 16
Cobb, Ty, xvi, 3, 7, 59, 62, 78, 107, 110, 117, 207–8, 254, 264, 274, 277
Cochrane, Mickey, 62, 67, 73–74, 80, 87, 155, 157, 208
Cockrell, Phil, 74
Coimbre, Francisco, 21, 266
Cole, Robert, 50, 55, 217, 243
Coley, Sam, 28
Collins, Eddie, 90
Combs, Jack, 96
Cominsky, Charles, 2, 78
Cominsky, Grace, 235
Cooper, Andy, 287, 289
Cooper, M., 106, 166
Cooper, Walker, 282, 288
Cornelius, William "Sug," 215, 234–49, 286, 288
Coscarat, Peter, 349
Covaleskie, Stan, 158, 175
Cramer, Doc, 73, 87, 124
Crawford, Sam, 3
Creacy, Dewey, 83, 176
Crowe, George, 21
Crutchfield, Jimmy, 143, 160, 241
Cuban Giants, 2, 17
Cuban X-Giants, 2, 17
Culley (ballplayer), 99

Cummings (pitcher), 51
Currie, Rube, 26, 91
Curry, Goose, 285

Dandridge, Ray, 10, 124, 218, 318, 320
Danning, Harry, 10
Dauss (pitcher), 217
Davenport, Ducky, 181, 285
Davis, Babe, 302
Davis, Duo, 176
Davis, Johnny, 318
Davis, Peanuts, 182
Davis, Piper, 340, 347
Davis, Steel Arm, 175, 286
Davis, Willie, 150, 153
Day, Connie, 66, 115
Day, Leon, 266, 318
Dean, Jerome "Dizzy," 11, 70–72, 81, 87, 97, 100–1, 106, 123–24, 135, 155, 163, 166, 216, 225, 251–52, 282–83, 305, 306
Dean, Paul, 87, 100–101, 106, 123, 155, 166, 225
Demaree, Frank, 214
DeMoss, Bingo, 36, 45, 49, 55, 78, 90, 133, 148, 175, 342
Derringer, Paul, 258
Detroit Senators, 122–23, 169
Detroit Stars, 7
Dickenson, Murray, 15, 136
Dickey, Bill, 215–16, 307
Dickey, Steel Arm, 114, 210
Didrikson, Babe, 99–100
Dietz, Dick, 132
Dihigo, Martin, 153, 155, 273, 289, 296, 350, 351
Dillinger, Bob, 349
DiMaggio, Joe, 100, 108, 225, 307
DiMaggio, Vince, 100, 288
Dismukes, Dizzy, 75, 122, 128, 342, 344
Dixon, George, 49
Dixon, Rap, 8, 72, 83, 125, 264
Doby, Larry, xviii, 15, 101, 219, 221, 248, 269, 291, 292, 294, 315–18, 322, 324, 326, 347, 350
Doherty, Paul, xvii, 16
Donaldson, John, 28, 79, 189, 342
Donches, Joe, 145, 146
Downs, Bunny, 29
Drake, Bill "Plunk," 22–38, 90, 113–14
Drebinger, John, 280
Dreke, Valintin, 20
Drew, Johnny, 81–82
Dropo, Walt, 236

Drysdale, Don, 252
Duffy, Hugh, 13
Dugan, Jumping Joe, 194
Duncan, Frank, 91–93, 104, 171, 205, 287, 304, 340, 342, 343
Dunlap, Johnny, 226
Durham, Bull, 62
Durocher, Leo, 11, 54
Dykes, Jimmy, 12, 177

Earnshaw, George, 70, 71, 80, 87, 153–55
Easter, Luke, 21, 250, 271
Edelman (pitcher), 106
Eggelson, Mac, 66
Ehmke, Howard, 117
Eller, Hod, 30
Ellis, Rocky, 83–85
Elson, Bob, 244
Ethiopian Clowns, 319, 321–22
Etten, Nick, 294

Fagan, Bob, 31
Fain, Ferris, 349
Farrell, Luther, 20
Feller, Bob, 15, 33, 100, 101, 108, 125, 135, 173, 180, 181, 231, 236–37, 280, 282, 288, 292, 296, 300, 307, 348–49
Fernandez, José, 122
Ferrick (pitcher), 189
Fette, Lou, 106, 288
Finley, Charlie, 38
Finner, John, 114, 116
Fitzsimmons (pitcher), 106, 230
Flood, Curt, 120
Flores (pitcher), 279
Forbes, Frank "Strangler," 4
Foreman, Sylvester, 80
Foster, Andrew "Rube," xvii, 2–3, 5–8, 15, 16, 31, 39, 41, 48–50, 52–53, 55, 56, 76–78, 94, 116, 133, 146, 174, 189, 191–92, 205, 284
Foster, Bill "Willie," 51, 59, 71, 78, 85, 121, 175, 176, 189–204, 242–44, 286
Fournier, Jacques, 30
Fowler, Bud, 1
Fox, Nellie, 276, 350
Foxx, Jimmy, 67, 70, 73–74, 80, 81, 87, 124, 177
Frankhouse, Fred, 71, 87, 166
Frasier, Albert, 262
Frasier, Vic, 135, 231
Freeman, Buck, 35
Freese, George, 21

Freitas (pitcher), 279
French, Larry, 135, 155, 163–64, 166, 217, 230, 231
Frick, Ford, 10, 12, 56
Frisch, Frankie, 71, 87, 142, 156
Fry, Lonnie, 288
Fullis (ballplayer), 87
Fulton, Louise, 165

Gagliano, Tony, 215
Gaines, Joe, 21
Gall, J. E., 28
Galloway, Chick, xviii
Garcia, Mike, 136
Gardner, Jelly, 49, 50, 78, 118, 342
Gatewood, Bill, 29, 78–79, 114–15, 117, 118
Gehrig, Lou, 154, 196, 250
Gehringer, Charley, 87, 175, 194, 219
Geisel, Harry, 36
Gelbert (ballplayer), 87
Gibson, Bob, 34, 118
Gibson, Josh, xiii-xv, 8–10, 12, 15, 16, 19–21, 54, 81, 83, 123–25, 131–33, 142–44, 157–60, 162, 164, 166, 171–73, 176, 177, 186, 196–97, 205, 214, 223, 227, 229, 235, 236, 245, 250–52, 258, 266–67, 271, 274, 276, 285–86, 289–90, 296, 299–301, 330, 346, 351
Gibson, Sam, 136
Giles, George, 121, 175, 286
Gilkerson (team owner), 175
Gilliam, Junior, 110, 271, 327–29, 332, 335–37, 347, 350
Glenn, Oscar, 302
Globetrotters, 183–85
Gomez, Chili, 285
Gonzales, Mike, 208, 218
Goodman, Ival "Ivy," 282, 288
Goodwin, Lonnie, 26
Gordon, Ed, 8
Goslin, Goose, 67
Gottlieb, Ed, 82, 84–85, 321, 322
Gould (pitcher), 106
Grant, Charley "Chief Tokahoma," 2
Grant, Mudcat, 173, 186
Gregg (pitcher), 231
Green, Silas, 253
Greenberg, Hank, 306
Greene, Guy, 27
Greene, James "Joe," xviii, 206, 283, 290, 299–314, 331
Greenlee, Gus, 9, 159, 161, 177
Griffith, Clark, 8, 14, 171, 184, 218, 252, 260, 268, 271

Grove, Bob "Lefty," 59, 62, 67, 106, 196, 225, 230

Haines, Bib, 24
Haines, Jess, 30
Haley, Red, 177
Hall of Fame (Cooperstown, N.Y.), xvii, 131, 142, 263, 277–78, 326, 351
Hamilton, George, 132, 291, 347
Haney, Fred, 214
Harder, Mel, 236
Harney, George, 175
Harrell, Bill, 21
Harridge, Will, 11
Harris, Andy, 148
Harris, Vic, 128, 143, 160, 176, 224, 264, 320, 334
Harrison, Whitey, 104
Hatley, Red, 302
Hauser, Joe, 164, 238
Hawkins, Lemuel, 22–23, 31
Hayakawa, Sessue, 102
Hayes, Frankie, 73, 87, 348
Hayes, Johnny, 266
Hayes, Tom, 182
Heath, Jeff, 15, 292, 348, 349
Heffner, Don, 81, 87
Heilmann, Harry, 55, 70, 87, 117, 219
Heimach (pitcher), 87
Heintzelman, Ken, 280, 282
Hensley, Rollie, 236, 348
Henderson, Rats, 75, 193, 279
Henrey, Bob, 347
Henrich, Tommy, 294
Henry, Preacher, 166, 262, 341
Hensly, Eggy, 176
Herman, Babe, 214, 225
Herrmann (pitcher), 279
Hewitt, Joe, 118
Hickey (American Association president), 33
Hilcher (pitcher), 279
Hill, Jimmy, 323
Hill, Peter, 67, 74
Holland, Bill, 70, 132, 214
Holloway, Crush, 59–69, 115, 185, 212, 264
Holmes, Frank, 83–85
Holmes, Philip, 331, 341
Homestead Grays (Pittsburgh and Washington), xiii, 7, 18, 80, 110, 122–23, 126–28, 142, 156, 157, 159, 165, 169, 173, 176, 196, 251, 257–65, 271, 289–91, 303, 306, 319–30, 346

Hopp, Johnny, 282
Hornsby, Rogers, 30, 124–25, 226
Houck, Ralph, 294
House of Davids (Michigan), 98–99, 183
Howard, Elston, 129, 133
Howard, Frank, 276
Hoyt, Waite, 236
Hoz, Miguel de la, 21
Hubbard, Jess, 144, 156, 163
Hubbell, Carl, 10
Hudlin, Willis, 121, 135, 177, 219, 230
Hudspeth, Highpockets, 64, 255
Hughes, Sammy T., 91, 133, 136, 206, 279, 307, 335–36
Hunter (pitcher), 99

Indianapolis ABC's, 4–6, 45–47, 66, 115, 342
Indianapolis Clowns, xvii, 340–41
Irvin, Monte, 15, 20, 128–29, 142, 219–21, 250, 269, 291, 293, 294, 305, 315–18, 320, 322, 325, 326, 336, 347
Israel, Half a Pint, 347

Jackman, Bill, 76
Jackson, Rufus, 271
Jackson, Sunnyman, 322
James, Bill, 4
Jansen, Larry, 183
Jenkins, Fats, 112, 144, 214, 216
Jethroe, Sam, 13, 19, 267, 293, 300, 303, 344
Jimenez, Hooks, 33
Johnson, Chappie, 149–51
Johnson, Cornelius, 8, 241, 290
Johnson, Grant "Home Run," 3, 147–48
Johnson, Heavy, 31
Johnson, Jack, 54
Johnson, Jewbaby, 343
Johnson, Judy, 74, 133, 143, 151, 236, 337
Johnson, Lou, 21
Johnson, Rafer, 54
Johnson, Tom, 53
Johnson, Walter, xvi, 4
Jones, Cleon, 173
Jones, Mint, 341
Jones, Stuart "Slim," 83–85, 189, 320
Joseph, Newt, 90, 93, 94, 102, 176

Kachline, Clifford, xvii, 326
Kaline, Al, 274
Kansas City Monarchs, xiii, xiv, 6, 7, 18, 24, 37, 90, 92–103, 129, 192, 200, 204, 233, 247, 281, 283, 287–91, 296, 301, 304–5, 342–43, 345, 347–48
Keenan, Jim, 148
Keller, Charlie "King Kong," xiv, 15, 292, 294, 296, 348
Keltner, Ken, 15, 292–93, 296, 348, 349
Kemp, James Gabby, 302, 331–32
Kennedy, Vern, 135
Kesler, Jerome, 325
Kimball (pitcher), 136, 188–89, 279
Kiner, Ralph, 349
Kleinknecht, Merl, xvii
Kline (pitcher), 166
Koufax, Sandy, 196, 252
Kress, Red, 135, 189, 279
Kuenn, Harvey, 350
Kuhel, Joe, 71, 87

Lacey, Sam, 252
La Guardia, Fiorello, 13, 319
La Marque, Lefty, 290
Landis, Kennesaw Mountain, Judge, xviii, 7, 10–13, 55, 117, 225, 237, 267
Lanier, Max, 184
Lavan, Doc, 30
Lee, Scrip, 97
Lemon, Bob, 15, 108–9, 136, 180, 291, 293, 296, 297
Leonard, Buck, xiv–xvi, 9, 10, 12, 15, 20, 72, 123, 133, 142, 181, 197, 219, 224, 227, 250–79, 289–90, 296, 299, 303, 320, 346, 351
Leonard, Charlie, 254, 256
Leonard, Dutch, 15, 293, 348, 349
Lewis, Bubber, 36, 191
Lewis, Buddy, 283
Lewis, Rufus, 318, 324, 347
Lillard, Joe, 8
Lindell, Johnny, 266, 294, 349
Lloyd, John Henry "Pop," xvi, xvii, 3, 6, 20, 55, 133, 151, 213, 351
Logan, Johnny, 338
Lombardi, Ernie, 258
Lopat, Ed, 348
Louis, Joe, 13, 54
Lowrey, Peanuts, 266, 349
Lugue, Adolph, 208, 213, 327
Lundy, Dick, xvi, 82, 124, 318
Lyons, Jimmy, 29, 49, 59, 116, 118, 120

McCarver, Tim, 215
McClellan, Danny, 74, 76

McClure, Bob, 66
McCormick, Frank, 183
McCovey, Willie, 173
McDaniels, Booker, 290
McDonald, Webster, 39, 70–89, 135,
    157, 163–64, 217, 230
McDuffie, Terris, 228, 318, 320
McGraw, John "Muggsy," 2
McHenry, Austin, 30
MacIntosh (ballplayer), 37
McNair, Hurley, 94, 97, 222
McPhail, Larry, 11, 13–14
McQuillen, Frank, 183
McQuinn, George, 258
Mack, Connie, 4, 72, 87
Mack, Earl, 81, 125
Mackey, Raleigh "Biz," xvi, 6, 20, 64,
    66, 73, 76, 83, 86, 94, 115, 132, 155,
    171, 205, 221, 228, 291, 318
Maddox, Lefty, 24
Maglie, Sal, 184, 188
Maisel, George, 59
Majerkurth (umpire), 36
Malarcher, David "Cap," 39–58, 78, 85,
    94, 189, 193, 236, 242–43, 353
Maltzberger, Gordon, 348
Manley, Abe, 162, 221, 228, 258, 315–
    16, 318–26
Manley, Mrs. Effa, 218, 315–26
Manush, Heinie, 81, 124, 175, 181, 194,
    219
Mapes, Cliff, 294
Mapp (pitcher), 87
Maranville, Rabbit, 4
Marcelle, Oliver, 20, 133
Marquard, Rube, 4, 36
Marquez, Luis, 20, 21, 261
Marshall, Jack, 117, 164–65, 175, 236,
    286
Martin, J. B., 11
Martin, Pepper, 100, 121–22
Matchett, Jack, 290–91
Mathews, Eddie, 313
Mathewson, Christy, 4
Mathis, Verdell, 207
Matlock, Leroy, 121, 143, 189, 234
May, Lee, 273
Mays, Carl, 75, 96
Mays, Willie, xviii, 21, 108, 120, 196,
    246, 271, 304–5, 336
Mazeroski, Bill, 149
Meine, Heinie, 106, 135, 230
Melton (pitcher), 279
Memphis Red Sox, 216
Mendez, José, 3, 4, 28, 342, 351

Mesa, Pablo, 20
Metcalfe, Ralph, 8
Meusel, Bob, 25, 36
Meyers, Deacon John, 87, 114, 116
Millán, Félix, 21
Miller, Bing, 70
Miller, Dempsey, 31
Miller, Jake, 194, 219, 230
Miller, Walter, 135
Mills, Charles, 29
Minoso, Minnie, 270
Mize, Johnny, 125, 180, 236, 288
Moody (pitcher), 305
Moore (team owner), 64
Moore, Dobie, 31, 90, 96, 133, 342
Moore, Joe "Red," 10, 302, 313, 330–
    32, 339
Moreland, Nate, 12, 344
Morris, Barney, 172, 178, 285, 286
Morrissey, John, 261
Mulligan, Billy, 183
Mullins (ballplayer), 99
Murphy (team owner), 174–75
Musial, Stan, 107, 282, 293
Myer, Buddy, 71

Narleski (ballplayer), 87
Nashville Elite Giants, 239
"Nation, Carrie," 28
National Baseball Library, xviii
Neun (ballplayer), 87
New York Black Yankees, 144
New York Lincoln Giants, 4, 6, 17, 18,
    74, 149, 213–24
Newark Eagles, 200, 221, 226–28, 291,
    315–16, 318–24, 347
Newcombe, Don, 15, 219, 221, 226–
    27, 248, 271, 292, 294, 315–18, 323,
    324, 326, 346, 350
Newsom, Buck, 70, 71, 87, 108, 135,
    136, 180, 188, 226, 266, 279
Norman, Bill, 130
Northrup, Jim, 21
Novikoff, Lou, 266
Nugent, Gerry, 12

O'Doul (ballplayer), 67
Old-Timers' Association, 46
Oldham, Jimmy, 114
Oliva, Tony, 21
Oliver, Al, 150
Olmo, Luis, 266
Olson (pitcher), 189
Oms, Alejandro, 20
O'Neil, John "Buck," 19, 20, 129, 342

O'Neil, Steve, 54, 70, 87, 124, 158
Ott, Mel, 10
Owens, Jesse, 9, 13, 107, 109–10, 212
Owens, Oscar, 176
Owens, Smokey, 341
Owens, Willie, 284

Pafko, Andy, 266, 267, 349
Page, Ted, 141–68, 173, 177, 264, 285
Paige, Leroy "Satchel," xiii–xiv, 7–9,
    11, 13, 15, 23–24, 33, 68, 71, 79, 87,
    97, 100, 102–4, 107–9, 123, 125, 129,
    130, 132, 141–44, 159, 160, 164, 166,
    170–72, 177–78, 180, 189–91, 200,
    214, 216, 223, 235–37, 241, 251, 261,
    265, 266, 272, 277, 280–81, 283,
    285–87, 290–92, 296, 301–2, 307,
    324, 334, 340, 344, 346, 348–49, 351
Parmelee (pitcher), 166
Parnell, Red, 34, 164, 285
Partee, Roy, 15–16, 108
Partlow, Roy, 21, 266
Pasquel, Jorge, 11, 184, 350
Patterson, Pat, 10, 321, 347
Pearson, Lenny, 220, 228, 266, 317, 318
Pedroso, Eusaquio, 3, 4
Pedroso, Fernando Díaz, 21
Pegler, Westbrook, 8
Pellot, Victor, 21
Perez, Javier, 266
Pérez, Tony, 21, 273
Perkins, Bill, 143, 157
Perrone, Joe, 181, 214
Pertica, Bill, 26
Pesky, John, 180
Petway, Bruce, 3, 46, 54, 55, 94, 132,
    205
Phelps (ballplayer), 87
Philadelphia Giants, 17, 75
Philadelphia Hillsdales, 6, 7, 18, 74, 76,
    81, 96–97
Philadelphia Stars, 71, 81–85, 88, 163–
    64, 200, 242–43
Phillips (pitcher), 87
Pittsburgh Crawfords, 88, 123, 142,
    143, 159–60, 165, 171, 177, 241, 285
Pittsburgh Homestead Grays, see Home-
    stead Grays
Plaskett, Elmo, 21
Pillette, Howard, 106, 230
Porter, Anderson "Pullman," 125
Posey, Cum, 9, 80, 123, 142, 148, 159,
    257, 267, 322
Posey, See, 123, 129
Powell, Jake, 10, 155, 244

Powell, Piggie, 87, 175
Powell, Willie, 51
Powers, Jimmy, 10

Quinn, Jack "Picus," 70, 87

Radcliff, Alex, 40, 172, 173, 175, 286,
    288, 342
Radcliffe, Ted "Double Duty," 90, 143,
    159, 169–88, 266, 285
Reardon, Beans, 36
Rector, Connie, 214, 216
Redding, Cannonball Dick, 4, 151–52,
    154, 156, 214, 256
Redus, Frog, 116, 121
Reed, Donald, 302, 313
Reel, Jimmy, 147
Reese, Pee Wee, 327, 347
Renfroe, Othello, 272, 327, 328, 339–51
Reynolds, Allie, 294
Rickey, Branch, 13, 14, 56, 248, 316,
    317, 323–25, 344, 346
Riggins, Bill, 144, 222
Riles, Huck, 256
Ripple, Jimmy, 87, 124
Rizzuto, Phil, 15, 84, 281, 292, 294,
    327–28, 347, 348
Roberts, Ric, xvii, 13, 14, 16, 126, 143,
    155, 218, 252
Robertson, Sam, 146
Robeson, Paul, 13
Robinson, Brooks, 318
Robinson, Frank, 61, 274, 310
Robinson, Jackie, xiv, xvi, xviii, 6, 12–
    14, 22, 56, 90, 103, 108, 119, 128,
    186, 200, 215, 246–48, 267–69, 283–
    84, 291–94, 312, 316, 324, 339, 343–
    45, 351
Robinson, Neil, 266
Robinson, Skindown, 262, 341
Rodriquez (ballplayer), 47
Rogan, Bullet Joe, xvi, 31, 55, 97, 102,
    132, 192, 193, 200, 287, 342
Rogers, Nat, 189–90, 286
Rommell, Eddie, 62, 70, 71, 76, 87,
    155, 157, 166
Ronald (baseball commissioner), 85
Roosevelt, Franklin D., 14
Rossiter, George, 67–68, 155
Rowe, Schoolboy, 106, 217, 231
Rucker, Nap, 3
Rudolph, Dick, 4
Ruffin, Joe, 318
Ruffing, Red, 284
Runyon, Damon, 170–71, 177

Ruppert (team owner), 319
Russell, Branch, 31
Russell, John Henry "Pistol Johnny,"
    87, 144, 160, 175–76
Ruth, Babe, xvi, 25, 107, 154, 196, 250,
    318
Ryan, Red, 74, 214
Ryba, Mike, 100, 106, 135, 155, 164,
    288

Sadler (pitcher), 320
Sain, Johnny, 15, 293
St. Louis Giants, 6, 18, 28–30, 32, 38
St. Louis Stars, 113–17, 120–21, 175–
    76, 200, 225
Sales, Frankie, 99
Salmon, Harry, 97, 107, 108, 205
Sanguillen, Manny, 162
San Antone Black Acres, 64–66
Saperstein, Abe, 181–84, 185, 246, 248
Scales, George "Tubby," 15, 143, 144,
    158, 176, 177, 274, 333–35, 337
Schang, Wally, 219
Schlichter, Walter, 3
Schmidt (pitcher), 188
Schmitz, Johnny, 180
Schott (pitcher), 279
Schupp, Freddie, 30, 106, 230
Seaver, Tom, 34
Seay, Dick, 83–85, 149, 151–53, 170,
    318, 320
Seinsoth (pitcher), 279
Semler, Sap, 166, 321, 322, 339
Serrell, Barney, 283, 343, 347
Sherman, Johnny, 78
Sherrid, Roy, 70, 87, 154, 166
Siebold, Socks, 84
Simms, Bill, 290
Sisler, Dick, 122
Slaughter, Enos, 350
Smith, Chino, 20, 133, 214
Smith, Ducky, 67
Smith, Hilton, xiv, xv, 11, 178, 280–
    98, 299, 303–4, 328, 343, 347
Smith, Ken, xvi
Smith, Wendell, 13
Snider, Pancho, 28
Snow, Felton, 332–33, 335
Society of American Baseball Research,
    xvii
Sothers, Buzz, 71, 87
Southern (ballplayer), 87
Speaker, Tris, 108, 114
Stainback, Tuck, 111–12
Stanky, Eddie, 350

Stanley, Neck, 214, 348–49
Stargell, Will, 148
Starks, Otis, 49
Stearnes, Tuckey, 51–52, 117–18, 133,
    175, 185, 236, 286
Stengel, Casey, 6, 31
Stephens, Paul "Jake," xviii, 59, 71, 72,
    76, 83, 84, 143, 169, 170, 266, 285,
    328
Stine, Lee, 135, 217, 230
Stirnweiss (ballplayer), 294
Stovey, George, 2
Strawbridge (team owner), 239
Streeter, Sam, 123
Streuss (pitcher), 87
Strong, Nat, 255–56
Strong, Ted, 290, 343, 345
Styne (pitcher), 279
Suhr, Gus, 288
Suttles, Mule, xvi, 8, 15, 121, 175, 176,
    186, 197, 222, 286, 318
Swanson (ballplayer), 112
Sweatt, George, 22, 39, 90
Swift, Bob, 87, 124, 133, 166, 187
Sylvestri, Joe, 310

Tapley (ballplayer), 99
Tatum, Goose, 340–41
Taylor, Ben, 30, 66, 115, 254–56
Taylor, C. I., 30, 41, 45, 48, 50, 64,
    66, 254, 342
Taylor, Candy Jim, 238, 301, 342
Taylor, Glenn, 218
Taylor, Tony, 21
Terry, Bill, 10, 225
Thevenow (pitcher), 135, 166
Thomas, Clint, 144, 188
Thomas, Showboat, 255, 279, 339
Thompson, Hank, 15, 19, 293, 345
Thompson, Sandy, 19
Thorpe, Jim, 253
Thurston, Hollis, 106, 135, 217, 230,
    231
Tiant, Luis "Sr. Sinny," 154
Tobin, Jim, 136
Tolan, Eddie, 8
Torres (pitcher), 188
Torrienti, Cristobel, 49, 54, 78, 116,
    133, 197, 342
Touchstone, Clay, 288
Tovar, Cesar, 273
Travis, Cecil, 11, 251, 283, 305
Traynor, Pie, 218
Trent, Theodore "Highpockets," 121,
    175, 176, 179, 220, 242

Trouppe, Quincy, 121, 122, 177, 267, 293
Trucks, Virgil, 231
Tut, King, 340–41
Tyler, Steel Arm, 33

Uhle, George, 121, 135, 166, 175, 177, 187, 219, 230
Urbansky (ballplayer), 87

Van, John, 79
Vander Meer (ballplayer), 136
Vargas, Esteban, 21
Vaughn, Jim, 217, 231
Veeck, Bill, 9, 12, 108, 272, 324
Vernon, Mickey, 15, 72, 87, 292–93, 348

Waddell, "Rube," 2
Walberg, Rube, 177
Walker, Bill, 230
Walker, Charlie, 123
Walker, Dixie, 248
Walker, Frank, 254, 273
Walker, Moses Fleetwood, 1
Walker, Welday, 1
Wallace, Bobby, 29
Wallace, Dick, 29
Walters, Bucky, 108, 135, 230
Waner, Lloyd, 100, 194, 225
Waner, Paul, 100, 108, 194, 225
Warfield, Frank, 80
Warneke, Lon, 100, 106, 296
Washington, Kenny, 283
Washington, Namon, 64, 66
Washington, Pete, 83
Washington Homestead Grays, see Homestead Grays
Watkins, Murray "Pop," 255, 321
Weaver, Big Jim, 54, 70, 71, 87, 106, 156, 166, 217, 230
Well, Rogan, 31–32
Wells, Willie, 15, 19, 90, 96, 121, 122, 133, 175, 176, 186, 218–33, 269, 284, 286, 296, 318, 343, 347
Welmaker, Roy, 271
Welsh, Winfield, 340
Wesley, Edgar, 212
West, Max, 349
Whatley, Speed, 109

White, Bruling, 155
White, Chaney, 72, 83, 94, 193, 212, 264
White, Sol, 3, 16
Whitehill, Earl, 70, 87, 121 124, 135, 177, 187, 194, 230
Wickware, Frank, 55
Williams, Billy, 173
Williams, Chester, 144, 160, 241
Williams, Harry, 144, 337
Williams, Jesse, 290
Williams, Joe "Cyclone" or "Smokey," xvii, 4, 5, 7, 74–75, 132, 143, 148, 151, 173, 176, 257, 342
Williams, Lefty, 176
Williams, Marvin, 13, 344
Williams, Morris, 64
Williams, Nish, 36, 303
Williams, Robert "Bobby," 45, 49, 78, 143, 148
Williams, Ted, xiii, 241, 276, 301
Williams, Tom, 49
Wills, Maury, 62, 110, 153, 176
Wilkinson, James, 90
Wilkinson, W. L., 8, 11, 28, 31, 101, 102, 284
Wilson, Artie, 19, 293, 340
Wilson, Hack, 67, 155, 164
Wilson, Jud "Boojum," xvi, 20, 83, 84, 85, 87, 133, 143, 158–60, 176, 216, 266, 285, 346
Wilson, Tom, 239, 322
Winegarner, Ralph, 106, 135, 230
Winford, Jim, 87, 135, 141, 164, 166
Winters, Nip, 74, 97, 148, 189
Woods, Parnell, 267
Woods, Ron, 273
Wright, Bill, 20
Wrigley (team owner), 319
Wynn, Early, 184, 226, 289, 307

Yancey, Bill, 1, 76
Yokely, Laymon, 7
Young, Big T. J., 46
Young, Dick, 351
Young, Fay, 306
Young, H. W., 325
Young, Pep, 266

Zarilla, Al, 15, 349

A CATALOG OF SELECTED DOVER
BOOKS IN ALL FIELDS OF INTEREST

CONCERNING THE SPIRITUAL IN ART, Wassily Kandinsky. Pioneering work by father of abstract art. Thoughts on color theory, nature of art. Analysis of earlier masters. 12 illustrations. 80pp. of text. 5⅜ x 8½. 0-486-23411-8

CELTIC ART: The Methods of Construction, George Bain. Simple geometric techniques for making Celtic interlacements, spirals, Kells-type initials, animals, humans, etc. Over 500 illustrations. 160pp. 9 x 12. (Available in U.S. only.) 0-486-22923-8

AN ATLAS OF ANATOMY FOR ARTISTS, Fritz Schider. Most thorough reference work on art anatomy in the world. Hundreds of illustrations, including selections from works by Vesalius, Leonardo, Goya, Ingres, Michelangelo, others. 593 illustrations. 192pp. 7⅛ x 10¼. 0-486-20241-0

CELTIC HAND STROKE-BY-STROKE (Irish Half-Uncial from "The Book of Kells"): An Arthur Baker Calligraphy Manual, Arthur Baker. Complete guide to creating each letter of the alphabet in distinctive Celtic manner. Covers hand position, strokes, pens, inks, paper, more. Illustrated. 48pp. 8¼ x 11. 0-486-24336-2

EASY ORIGAMI, John Montroll. Charming collection of 32 projects (hat, cup, pelican, piano, swan, many more) specially designed for the novice origami hobbyist. Clearly illustrated easy-to-follow instructions insure that even beginning papercrafters will achieve successful results. 48pp. 8¼ x 11. 0-486-27298-2

BLOOMINGDALE'S ILLUSTRATED 1886 CATALOG: Fashions, Dry Goods and Housewares, Bloomingdale Brothers. Famed merchants' extremely rare catalog depicting about 1,700 products: clothing, housewares, firearms, dry goods, jewelry, more. Invaluable for dating, identifying vintage items. Also, copyright-free graphics for artists, designers. Co-published with Henry Ford Museum & Greenfield Village. 160pp. 8¼ x 11. 0-486-25780-0

THE ART OF WORLDLY WISDOM, Baltasar Gracian. "Think with the few and speak with the many," "Friends are a second existence," and "Be able to forget" are among this 1637 volume's 300 pithy maxims. A perfect source of mental and spiritual refreshment, it can be opened at random and appreciated either in brief or at length. 128pp. 5⅜ x 8½. 0-486-44034-6

JOHNSON'S DICTIONARY: A Modern Selection, Samuel Johnson (E. L. McAdam and George Milne, eds.). This modern version reduces the original 1755 edition's 2,300 pages of definitions and literary examples to a more manageable length, retaining the verbal pleasure and historical curiosity of the original. 480pp. 5³⁄₁₆ x 8¼. 0-486-44089-3

ADVENTURES OF HUCKLEBERRY FINN, Mark Twain, Illustrated by E. W. Kemble. A work of eternal richness and complexity, a source of ongoing critical debate, and a literary landmark, Twain's 1885 masterpiece about a barefoot boy's journey of self-discovery has enthralled readers around the world. This handsome clothbound reproduction of the first edition features all 174 of the original black-and-white illustrations. 368pp. 5⅜ x 8½. 0-486-44322-1

STICKLEY CRAFTSMAN FURNITURE CATALOGS, Gustav Stickley and L. & J. G. Stickley. Beautiful, functional furniture in two authentic catalogs from 1910. 594 illustrations, including 277 photos, show settles, rockers, armchairs, reclining chairs, bookcases, desks, tables. 183pp. 6½ x 9¼. 0-486-23838-5

AMERICAN LOCOMOTIVES IN HISTORIC PHOTOGRAPHS: 1858 to 1949, Ron Ziel (ed.). A rare collection of 126 meticulously detailed official photographs, called "builder portraits," of American locomotives that majestically chronicle the rise of steam locomotive power in America. Introduction. Detailed captions. xi+129pp. 9 x 12. 0-486-27393-8

AMERICA'S LIGHTHOUSES: An Illustrated History, Francis Ross Holland, Jr. Delightfully written, profusely illustrated fact-filled survey of over 200 American lighthouses since 1716. History, anecdotes, technological advances, more. 240pp. 8 x 10¾. 0-486-25576-X

TOWARDS A NEW ARCHITECTURE, Le Corbusier. Pioneering manifesto by founder of "International School." Technical and aesthetic theories, views of industry, economics, relation of form to function, "mass-production split" and much more. Profusely illustrated. 320pp. 6⅛ x 9¼. (Available in U.S. only.) 0-486-25023-7

HOW THE OTHER HALF LIVES, Jacob Riis. Famous journalistic record, exposing poverty and degradation of New York slums around 1900, by major social reformer. 100 striking and influential photographs. 233pp. 10 x 7⅞. 0-486-22012-5

FRUIT KEY AND TWIG KEY TO TREES AND SHRUBS, William M. Harlow. One of the handiest and most widely used identification aids. Fruit key covers 120 deciduous and evergreen species; twig key 160 deciduous species. Easily used. Over 300 photographs. 126pp. 5⅜ x 8½. 0-486-20511-8

COMMON BIRD SONGS, Dr. Donald J. Borror. Songs of 60 most common U.S. birds: robins, sparrows, cardinals, bluejays, finches, more–arranged in order of increasing complexity. Up to 9 variations of songs of each species. Cassette and manual 0-486-99911-4

ORCHIDS AS HOUSE PLANTS, Rebecca Tyson Northen. Grow cattleyas and many other kinds of orchids–in a window, in a case, or under artificial light. 63 illustrations. 148pp. 5⅜ x 8½. 0-486-23261-1

MONSTER MAZES, Dave Phillips. Masterful mazes at four levels of difficulty. Avoid deadly perils and evil creatures to find magical treasures. Solutions for all 32 exciting illustrated puzzles. 48pp. 8¼ x 11. 0-486-26005-4

MOZART'S DON GIOVANNI (DOVER OPERA LIBRETTO SERIES), Wolfgang Amadeus Mozart. Introduced and translated by Ellen H. Bleiler. Standard Italian libretto, with complete English translation. Convenient and thoroughly portable–an ideal companion for reading along with a recording or the performance itself. Introduction. List of characters. Plot summary. 121pp. 5¼ x 8½. 0-486-24944-1

FRANK LLOYD WRIGHT'S DANA HOUSE, Donald Hoffmann. Pictorial essay of residential masterpiece with over 160 interior and exterior photos, plans, elevations, sketches and studies. 128pp. 9¼ x 10¾. 0-486-29120-0

CATALOG OF DOVER BOOKS

THE CLARINET AND CLARINET PLAYING, David Pino. Lively, comprehensive work features suggestions about technique, musicianship, and musical interpretation, as well as guidelines for teaching, making your own reeds, and preparing for public performance. Includes an intriguing look at clarinet history. "A godsend," *The Clarinet,* Journal of the International Clarinet Society. Appendixes. 7 illus. 320pp. 5⅜ x 8½.   0-486-40270-3

HOLLYWOOD GLAMOR PORTRAITS, John Kobal (ed.). 145 photos from 1926-49. Harlow, Gable, Bogart, Bacall; 94 stars in all. Full background on photographers, technical aspects. 160pp. 8⅜ x 11¼.   0-486-23352-9

THE RAVEN AND OTHER FAVORITE POEMS, Edgar Allan Poe. Over 40 of the author's most memorable poems: "The Bells," "Ulalume," "Israfel," "To Helen," "The Conqueror Worm," "Eldorado," "Annabel Lee," many more. Alphabetic lists of titles and first lines. 64pp. 5³⁄₁₆ x 8¼.   0-486-26685-0

PERSONAL MEMOIRS OF U. S. GRANT, Ulysses Simpson Grant. Intelligent, deeply moving firsthand account of Civil War campaigns, considered by many the finest military memoirs ever written. Includes letters, historic photographs, maps and more. 528pp. 6⅛ x 9¼.   0-486-28587-1

POE ILLUSTRATED: Art by Doré, Dulac, Rackham and Others, selected and edited by Jeff A. Menges. More than 100 compelling illustrations, in brilliant color and crisp black-and-white, include scenes from "The Raven," "The Pit and the Pendulum," "The Gold-Bug," and other stories and poems. 96pp. 8⅜ x 11.
0-486-45746-X

RUSSIAN STORIES/RUSSKIE RASSKAZY: A Dual-Language Book, edited by Gleb Struve. Twelve tales by such masters as Chekhov, Tolstoy, Dostoevsky, Pushkin, others. Excellent word-for-word English translations on facing pages, plus teaching and study aids, Russian/English vocabulary, biographical/critical introductions, more. 416pp. 5⅜ x 8½.   0-486-26244-8

PHILADELPHIA THEN AND NOW: 60 Sites Photographed in the Past and Present, Kenneth Finkel and Susan Oyama. Rare photographs of City Hall, Logan Square, Independence Hall, Betsy Ross House, other landmarks juxtaposed with contemporary views. Captures changing face of historic city. Introduction. Captions. 128pp. 8¼ x 11.   0-486-25790-8

NORTH AMERICAN INDIAN LIFE: Customs and Traditions of 23 Tribes, Elsie Clews Parsons (ed.). 27 fictionalized essays by noted anthropologists examine religion, customs, government, additional facets of life among the Winnebago, Crow, Zuni, Eskimo, other tribes. 480pp. 6⅛ x 9¼.   0-486-27377-6

TECHNICAL MANUAL AND DICTIONARY OF CLASSICAL BALLET, Gail Grant. Defines, explains, comments on steps, movements, poses and concepts. 15-page pictorial section. Basic book for student, viewer. 127pp. 5⅜ x 8½.
0-486-21843-0

THE MALE AND FEMALE FIGURE IN MOTION: 60 Classic Photographic Sequences, Eadweard Muybridge. 60 true-action photographs of men and women walking, running, climbing, bending, turning, etc., reproduced from a rare 19th-century masterpiece. vi + 121pp. 9 x 12.   0-486-24745-7

CATALOG OF DOVER BOOKS

ANIMALS: 1,419 Copyright-Free Illustrations of Mammals, Birds, Fish, Insects, etc., Jim Harter (ed.). Clear wood engravings present, in extremely lifelike poses, over 1,000 species of animals. One of the most extensive pictorial sourcebooks of its kind. Captions. Index. 284pp. 9 x 12. 0-486-23766-4

1001 QUESTIONS ANSWERED ABOUT THE SEASHORE, N. J. Berrill and Jacquelyn Berrill. Queries answered about dolphins, sea snails, sponges, starfish, fishes, shore birds, many others. Covers appearance, breeding, growth, feeding, much more. 305pp. 5¼ x 8¼. 0-486-23366-9

ATTRACTING BIRDS TO YOUR YARD, William J. Weber. Easy-to-follow guide offers advice on how to attract the greatest diversity of birds: birdhouses, feeders, water and waterers, much more. 96pp. 5³⁄₁₆ x 8¼. 0-486-28927-3

MEDICINAL AND OTHER USES OF NORTH AMERICAN PLANTS: A Historical Survey with Special Reference to the Eastern Indian Tribes, Charlotte Erichsen-Brown. Chronological historical citations document 500 years of usage of plants, trees, shrubs native to eastern Canada, northeastern U.S. Also complete identifying information. 343 illustrations. 544pp. 6½ x 9¼. 0-486-25951-X

STORYBOOK MAZES, Dave Phillips. 23 stories and mazes on two-page spreads: Wizard of Oz, Treasure Island, Robin Hood, etc. Solutions. 64pp. 8¼ x 11.
0-486-23628-5

AMERICAN NEGRO SONGS: 230 Folk Songs and Spirituals, Religious and Secular, John W. Work. This authoritative study traces the African influences of songs sung and played by black Americans at work, in church, and as entertainment. The author discusses the lyric significance of such songs as "Swing Low, Sweet Chariot," "John Henry," and others and offers the words and music for 230 songs. Bibliography. Index of Song Titles. 272pp. 6½ x 9¼. 0-486-40271-1

MOVIE-STAR PORTRAITS OF THE FORTIES, John Kobal (ed.). 163 glamor, studio photos of 106 stars of the 1940s: Rita Hayworth, Ava Gardner, Marlon Brando, Clark Gable, many more. 176pp. 8⅜ x 11¼. 0-486-23546-7

YEKL and THE IMPORTED BRIDEGROOM AND OTHER STORIES OF YIDDISH NEW YORK, Abraham Cahan. Film Hester Street based on *Yekl* (1896). Novel, other stories among first about Jewish immigrants on N.Y.'s East Side. 240pp. 5⅜ x 8½. 0-486-22427-9

SELECTED POEMS, Walt Whitman. Generous sampling from *Leaves of Grass*. Twenty-four poems include "I Hear America Singing," "Song of the Open Road," "I Sing the Body Electric," "When Lilacs Last in the Dooryard Bloom'd," "O Captain! My Captain!"–all reprinted from an authoritative edition. Lists of titles and first lines. 128pp. 5³⁄₁₆ x 8¼. 0-486-26878-0

SONGS OF EXPERIENCE: Facsimile Reproduction with 26 Plates in Full Color, William Blake. 26 full-color plates from a rare 1826 edition. Includes "The Tyger," "London," "Holy Thursday," and other poems. Printed text of poems. 48pp. 5¼ x 7.
0-486-24636-1

THE BEST TALES OF HOFFMANN, E. T. A. Hoffmann. 10 of Hoffmann's most important stories: "Nutcracker and the King of Mice," "The Golden Flowerpot," etc. 458pp. 5⅜ x 8½. 0-486-21793-0

THE BOOK OF TEA, Kakuzo Okakura. Minor classic of the Orient: entertaining, charming explanation, interpretation of traditional Japanese culture in terms of tea ceremony. 94pp. 5⅜ x 8½. 0-486-20070-1

MAKING FURNITURE MASTERPIECES: 30 Projects with Measured Drawings, Franklin H. Gottshall. Step-by-step instructions, illustrations for constructing handsome, useful pieces, among them a Sheraton desk, Chippendale chair, Spanish desk, Queen Anne table and a William and Mary dressing mirror. 224pp. 8⅛ x 11¼.
0-486-29338-6

NORTH AMERICAN INDIAN DESIGNS FOR ARTISTS AND CRAFTSPEOPLE, Eva Wilson. Over 360 authentic copyright-free designs adapted from Navajo blankets, Hopi pottery, Sioux buffalo hides, more. Geometrics, symbolic figures, plant and animal motifs, etc. 128pp. 8⅜ x 11. (Not for sale in the United Kingdom.)   0-486-25341-4

THE FOSSIL BOOK: A Record of Prehistoric Life, Patricia V. Rich et al. Profusely illustrated definitive guide covers everything from single-celled organisms and dinosaurs to birds and mammals and the interplay between climate and man. Over 1,500 illustrations. 760pp. 7½ x 10⅛.   0-486-29371-8

VICTORIAN ARCHITECTURAL DETAILS: Designs for Over 700 Stairs, Mantels, Doors, Windows, Cornices, Porches, and Other Decorative Elements, A. J. Bicknell & Company. Everything from dormer windows and piazzas to balconies and gable ornaments. Also includes elevations and floor plans for handsome, private residences and commercial structures. 80pp. 9⅜ x 12¼.   0-486-44015-X

WESTERN ISLAMIC ARCHITECTURE: A Concise Introduction, John D. Hoag. Profusely illustrated critical appraisal compares and contrasts Islamic mosques and palaces–from Spain and Egypt to other areas in the Middle East. 139 illustrations. 128pp. 6 x 9.   0-486-43760-4

CHINESE ARCHITECTURE: A Pictorial History, Liang Ssu-ch'eng. More than 240 rare photographs and drawings depict temples, pagodas, tombs, bridges, and imperial palaces comprising much of China's architectural heritage. 152 halftones, 94 diagrams. 232pp. 10¾ x 9⅞.   0-486-43999-2

THE RENAISSANCE: Studies in Art and Poetry, Walter Pater. One of the most talked-about books of the 19th century, *The Renaissance* combines scholarship and philosophy in an innovative work of cultural criticism that examines the achievements of Botticelli, Leonardo, Michelangelo, and other artists. "The holy writ of beauty."–Oscar Wilde. 160pp. 5⅜ x 8½.   0-486-44025-7

A TREATISE ON PAINTING, Leonardo da Vinci. The great Renaissance artist's practical advice on drawing and painting techniques covers anatomy, perspective, composition, light and shadow, and color. A classic of art instruction, it features 48 drawings by Nicholas Poussin and Leon Battista Alberti. 192pp. 5⅜ x 8½.
0-486-44155-5

THE ESSENTIAL JEFFERSON, Thomas Jefferson, edited by John Dewey. This extraordinary primer offers a superb survey of Jeffersonian thought. It features writings on political and economic philosophy, morals and religion, intellectual freedom and progress, education, secession, slavery, and more. 176pp. 5⅜ x 8½.
0-486-46599-3

WASHINGTON IRVING'S RIP VAN WINKLE, Illustrated by Arthur Rackham. Lovely prints that established artist as a leading illustrator of the time and forever etched into the popular imagination a classic of Catskill lore. 51 full-color plates. 80pp. 8⅜ x 11.   0-486-44242-X

HENSCHE ON PAINTING, John W. Robichaux. Basic painting philosophy and methodology of a great teacher, as expounded in his famous classes and workshops on Cape Cod. 7 illustrations in color on covers. 80pp. 5⅜ x 8½.   0-486-43728-0

CATALOG OF DOVER BOOKS

LIGHT AND SHADE: A Classic Approach to Three-Dimensional Drawing, Mrs. Mary P. Merrifield. Handy reference clearly demonstrates principles of light and shade by revealing effects of common daylight, sunshine, and candle or artificial light on geometrical solids. 13 plates. 64pp. $5\frac{3}{8}$ x $8\frac{1}{2}$. 0-486-44143-1

ASTROLOGY AND ASTRONOMY: A Pictorial Archive of Signs and Symbols, Ernst and Johanna Lehner. Treasure trove of stories, lore, and myth, accompanied by more than 300 rare illustrations of planets, the Milky Way, signs of the zodiac, comets, meteors, and other astronomical phenomena. 192pp. $8\frac{3}{8}$ x 11. 0-486-43981-X

JEWELRY MAKING: Techniques for Metal, Tim McCreight. Easy-to-follow instructions and carefully executed illustrations describe tools and techniques, use of gems and enamels, wire inlay, casting, and other topics. 72 line illustrations and diagrams. 176pp. $8\frac{1}{4}$ x $10\frac{7}{8}$. 0-486-44043-5

MAKING BIRDHOUSES: Easy and Advanced Projects, Gladstone Califf. Easy-to-follow instructions include diagrams for everything from a one-room house for bluebirds to a forty-two-room structure for purple martins. 56 plates; 4 figures. 80pp. $8\frac{3}{4}$ x $6\frac{3}{8}$. 0-486-44183-0

LITTLE BOOK OF LOG CABINS: How to Build and Furnish Them, William S. Wicks. Handy how-to manual, with instructions and illustrations for building cabins in the Adirondack style, fireplaces, stairways, furniture, beamed ceilings, and more. 102 line drawings. 96pp. $8\frac{3}{4}$ x $6\frac{3}{8}$. 0-486-44259-4

THE SEASONS OF AMERICA PAST, Eric Sloane. From "sugaring time" and strawberry picking to Indian summer and fall harvest, a whole year's activities described in charming prose and enhanced with 79 of the author's own illustrations. 160pp. $8\frac{1}{4}$ x 11. 0-486-44220-9

THE METROPOLIS OF TOMORROW, Hugh Ferriss. Generous, prophetic vision of the metropolis of the future, as perceived in 1929. Powerful illustrations of towering structures, wide avenues, and rooftop parks–all features in many of today's modern cities. 59 illustrations. 144pp. $8\frac{1}{4}$ x 11. 0-486-43727-2

THE PATH TO ROME, Hilaire Belloc. This 1902 memoir abounds in lively vignettes from a vanished time, recounting a pilgrimage on foot across the Alps and Apennines in order to "see all Europe which the Christian Faith has saved." 77 of the author's original line drawings complement his sparkling prose. 272pp. $5\frac{3}{8}$ x $8\frac{1}{2}$. 0-486-44001-X

THE HISTORY OF RASSELAS: Prince of Abissinia, Samuel Johnson. Distinguished English writer attacks eighteenth-century optimism and man's unrealistic estimates of what life has to offer. 112pp. $5\frac{3}{8}$ x $8\frac{1}{2}$. 0-486-44094-X

A VOYAGE TO ARCTURUS, David Lindsay. A brilliant flight of pure fancy, where wild creatures crowd the fantastic landscape and demented torturers dominate victims with their bizarre mental powers. 272pp. $5\frac{3}{8}$ x $8\frac{1}{2}$. 0-486-44198-9

Paperbound unless otherwise indicated. Available at your book dealer, online at **www.doverpublications.com**, or by writing to Dept. GI, Dover Publications, Inc., 31 East 2nd Street, Mineola, NY 11501. For current price information or for free catalogs (please indicate field of interest), write to Dover Publications or log on to **www.doverpublications.com** and see every Dover book in print. Dover publishes more than 400 books each year on science, elementary and advanced mathematics, biology, music, art, literary history, social sciences, and other areas.